I0889644

WISDOM'S PASSING

The decline of American public education in the post-World War II era and what we can *really* do about it

Dr. Steven Porter

BARCLAY HOUSE • New York, N.Y.

WISDOM'S PASSING

©1989 by Barclay House. All rights reserved. No portion of this book may be reproduced or utilized in any form or by any means, electronic or mechanical, including electrostatic or photo copying, recording, information storage or retrieval systems, or computers, without prior permission in writing from the publishers.

Published by:
Barclay House
15 West 44th St., New York, N.Y. 10036

Typesetting, music engraving and layouts by:
Excelsior Typographers and Engravers, Unltd.

First Edition

Cover illustration by: Del Bouree Bach

International Copyright Secured
Printed in U.S.A.

Library of Congress Cataloging-in-Publication Data

Porter, Steven, 1943-
Wisdom's passing.

Bibliography: p.
Includes index.
1. Education--United States--History--20th century.
2. Public schools--United States--History--20th century.
I. Title.
LA209.2.P56 1989 370'.973 89-14964
ISBN 0-935016-71-6

Acknowledgements

I would like to express my thanks to four people whose dedicated work helped make this book possible. To Dr. Marya Porter in California and Ms. Judith Stein in New York, my deep appreciation for editing the manuscript. To Mr. Allen Thompson, my gratitude for reading the manuscript with a teacher's eye and for offering pungent and relevant suggestions. Finally, to Rita Porter, for endless hours of discussion, encouragement, typing, and editing, and most of all, sharing my dream for a better public school system.

WISDOM'S PASSING

Outline of Contents

Preface

WHEN THE EDUCATION Commission appointed by President Ronald Reagan published its findings in the now famous document entitled "A Nation at Risk," it may have raised a few eyebrows, but it didn't tell us in the teaching business anything we didn't already know. In fact, it left out so much of what we had long suspected and long experienced that it became something of a joke in the faculty rooms of our schools—at least the faculty rooms of which I was a part.

What the President's Commission Report did do, however—and in all fairness, the only thing it was designed to do—was to publicly expose the surface of an American dilemma which threatened then and threatens now the survival of our way of life. That, in turn, sparked a bevy of responses from one end of the country to another, some foolish, some well-intentioned—but all lacking a coordinated national focus.

At present, nearly a decade after the report, we are just as much at risk, in fact, in my view, even more so because we seem hellishly intent on stumbling from one moronic set of solutions to another.

I believe that our problem lies in two important areas: first, that many of us do not acknowledge the severity of our dilemma, and second, that we seem doggedly reluctant to honestly face the causes which have created it.

As to the first, let me tell you a little story by way of example. About the time the commission report came out, I was preparing a book for publication. As it happens it was a college text on the training of secondary school music teachers which in one chapter discusses the changing character of American students, a topic with which we shall deal later on in some detail.

"Oh, you shouldn't write anything like that," the publisher's editor said to me.

"Anything like what?" I asked.

"That stuff about declining SAT scores and drug use in the schools."

"Really?" I answered. "Don't you think it's something of a problem?"

"Sure, it's a problem," he countered, "but you're overdramatizing it. Every generation has its problems. Every generation has always seemed to be on the wrong track according to its parents and teachers."

Let us for the moment concede the editor's point that things are no worse now than in any other generation. I don't believe that, and in some of the pages ahead, I'll try to show you that the sexual behavior, substance abuse, family decay, and learning declines of current day students are far worse than they ever were in previous generations. But for the sake of argument, let us concede the point.

Even if the quality of today's crop of kids is equivalent to the quality of past crops, there is a significant difference between them, and it is this: today's child, the post-World War II child, inhabits a world which for the first time in the life of this planet is capable of destroying itself.

The progress of mankind has always hinged on a tenuous thread. We are, after all, not a species which passes on the mechanisms of survival genetically. We require each generation to learn anew the arts of loving, of building, of improving, of nurturing life itself. If in past generations those arts went unlearned—and even the most casual reading of history will confirm that all too often in man's tenure on earth they did—the occasional lapse merely bludgeoned a decade here, a century there. High prices for educational failure, yes, but prices which could nevertheless be paid because life was capable of going on.

Not so today. Today the tenuous thread of survival from generation to generation has lost its margin of error. In the madness of a single day, a single week, and not much more, the thread could be broken forever.

That my editor did not see the abiding urgency of today's situation was to his personal discredit. That we fail to see it as a people may, I fear, mean the end of our species.

As to the second barrier to our education reclamation—our insistence on avoiding the root causes of our problems—we are the trapped victims of our own social and educational structures.

Let me spell that out in less esoteric terms.

It seems that no matter what lofty purpose a social institution may have at its inception, it quickly adopts as its major goal nothing so much as its own survival. In doing so, it seeks to maintain a facade of perfection and power. Admissions of error or weakness will thus not come easily, if indeed they come at all.

In times of obvious crisis, then, most reports as to the causes of the crisis will tend to absolve the reporter of any wrong-doing and blame the other guy for the current state of affairs. The commission which includes members of a teaching union, an administrator's organization, a board of education, a government agency, will rarely, if ever, tell you that the union, the organization, the board, or the agency is to blame for the dilemmas of the moment.

The "cover your ass" credo has become axiomatic in our society from the stonewalling of the Watergate White House to the investigation of America's schools. It is thus difficult, if not impossible, to rectify problems in education when many of the real facts go unspoken or are soft-soaped to the point of meaninglessness.

All of which brings us to this book. It is not written by an agency, a committee, or someone who is shilling for a power bloc lurking in the wings. Rather, it is the product of the research and experience of a twenty-year veteran of the educational wars. That doesn't mean it's "the ultimate word." Far from it. But it does mean that no one is pulling my strings as I write it. No matter how it may be biased by personal opinion or colored by personal experience, it is an honest attempt to discuss a serious problem.

And what does that mean to you, the reader? It means exactly what I tell my own students in class: that you should read it, check out its facts and ideas in other sources, and form as reasoned and honest a judgment as you can without falling victim to your own prejudices or the temptation to "cover your own ass."

It means that you should investigate my credentials as an educator to make sure I have some reasonable connection to the topic. It means that you should try to confirm or counter my research with research of your own as honest and unbiased as you can make it.

But most of all, it means that you should think and think hard about the ideas you will encounter, and if you find them worthy of implementation that, in concert with your fellow citizens, you work constructively to institute them for the benefit of education.

Toward those ends, this book is dedicated.

Chapter One

The Sociopolitical Context of American Education after World War II

Chapter One

The Sociopolitical Context of American Education after World War II

ALTHOUGH THERE ARE some basic principles of education (like the student/teacher relationship or the fundamental need to read) which remain fairly constant from one era to another, a great deal of the education of any given time is shaped by the characteristics of that time. Thus, if we are to assess in any meaningful way the state of American education in the years following the Second World War, it would be wise to begin with a general assessment of the environment in which that education took place.

In the pages of this chapter, we will look briefly at some of the more important aspects of the world as it emerged after 1945 and try to relate them to what is going on in our schools.

The end of white Western Colonialism

If not by the conclusion of World War II itself, then certainly in the decades which followed it, a nearly five-hundred year trend of European domination drew steadily to a close. What had begun with the tentative explorations of Marco Polo; what had continued with the navigations of Columbus and Drake, Magellan, Balboa, and Cortez; what had shaped the world through the Open Door Policy in China and forged for England an empire on which the sun never set was no longer a dynamic, global force.

"Old landmarks are worn down," writes historian R.R. Palmer. "The British Empire and gold standard pass away. The ascendancy of Europe, of the West, of the white races nears its close; all these must learn to negotiate with others, not to rule them."[1] Against this changing tide occurred the great political struggles of the post-war era: Korea, the Chinese Revolution, the Cuban Revolution, Viet Nam, the Middle East conflicts, the emergence of the so-called Third World nations of Asia and Africa, to name just a few.

The influence of such events on the internal American scene was profound. For example, as non-white nations outside the United States sought an end to white domination, so the non-whites within the American border joined the new wave of egalitarian democratization. Led by heroic figures like Dr. Martin Luther King, Jr., millions upon millions of Americans reawakened to the promise of America's founding dreams.

The effects of this global and national transfiguration on American education were enormous. Immigrants from Korea, Taiwan, Viet Nam, Cuba, and many other nations, for example, poured into the coastal metropolitan areas of the country and gradually spread into the interior. As they gained ascendancy in both numbers and power, new educational elements arose to accommodate them and the ideological trends of which they were a part. Changes of curricula to include Asian and African studies, bilingual education programs, courses teaching English as a second language, the advent of busing to achieve racial balances in formerly homogeneous schools—all these and more in part owed their emergence to the end of white Western colonialism.

However one feels about these trends, and we shall return to view them again in the chapters below, no evaluation of current educational realities should fail to account for them or fail to see them as part of a process of global change.

East/West schism

The United States emerged from the Second World War with an economic and military position of unrivaled supremacy. It was, however, not an unchallenged supremacy. Clearly, if America was to be the champion of a Western bloc whose credo was essentially tied to a capitalist economy and representative democracy, the Soviet Union would champion an Eastern bloc whose economy was decidedly socialist and whose political organization was decidedly totalitarian.

The rivalry was quick to emerge and quick to be recognized by both sides. In Russia, Stalin moved to establish the Communist domination of Eastern Europe. He brought both Poland and Czechoslovakia under Soviet military influence, pressed Turkey for a share of the control of the Dardanelles, and embarked upon a systematic campaign to divide Germany permanently between a reborn Western and an emaciated Eastern zone.

In an effort to counter Russian policy, American President Harry Truman took decisive action of his own. With the aid of America's war allies, he withstood the Soviet blockade of Berlin through a miraculous airlift of supplies and appointed Secretary of State George Marshall to administer a plan by which Russian aggression in Europe might be checked through the economic revitalization of war-torn nations.

"The seeds of totalitarianism," Truman explained, "are nurtured by misery and want. They reach their full growth when the hope of a people for a better life has died. We must keep that hope alive."[2]

This jockeying between America and Russia in the immediate post-war period was anything but a temporary condition. On the contrary, it was the paradigm on which the next decades would be fashioned. The atmosphere of hysteria which characterized the investigations of U.S. Senator Joseph McCarthy into Communist influences in America, the Cuban missile crisis, Soviet incursions into Afghanistan—to name just three of countless examples—were all played out in a drama whose central theme was the titanic schism between East and West.

The effect of this schism on American education was profound. It manifested itself primarily in the application of learning to defense-related purposes. Remember, as the bulwark of Western democracy, it fell chiefly upon the shoulders of America to provide the scientists and technicians, soldiers and weaponry which would guard the free world against Communist or Socialist aggression. Whatever England or France or Italy or Japan would contribute, it was up to the U.S. to supply the overwhelming portion of the West's protective umbrella. All of which meant that American schools would have to out-produce Russian schools in the decades following World War II.

Perhaps the most dramatic example of this educational dynamic was the reaction of the United States to the U.S.S.R.'s launching of their Sputnik I satellite. The fact that Russia had beaten America to a new technology, one with clear and sinister military overtones, was enough to spread panic through the governmental community. It quickly became apparent both to the Pentagon and to Congress that if the U.S. was to overtake Russia in space, the battle would have to be fought first in the American classroom. So an alliance was struck between defense and education, an alliance of which educational historian Diane Ravitch writes the following:

> Well before Sputnik, there were clear signs of discontent with the quality of American schools...After Sputnik, however, the broad popular demand for a federal response to meet the Russian challenge prompted Congress to pass the National Defense Education Act in 1958 (NDEA). This act provided fellowships, grants and loans to encourage the study of science, mathematics, and foreign language and funded school construction and equipment...Sputnik came to be a symbol of the consequences of indifference to high standards. In popular parlance, Sputnik had happened not because of what the Russians had done but because of what American schools had failed to do.[3]

The significance of education to the military and economic health of the free world continues to be inescapable today. U.S. competitiveness in foreign markets; the development of space technology; American industrial productivity; the training of American scientists and technicians; the ability to upgrade and service sophisticated weaponry; the development of skilled leaders in both government and industry are all issues which continue to occupy us long after the Sputnik era.

Assessments of where American education is at present, how it got there, and where it needs to go must take into account current geopolitical realities, particularly as they effect the position of international leadership held by the United States.

Changing economic patterns

It seems almost simplistic to say it, but one can neither rationally trace the post-war course of American education nor reasonably chart its future without taking into account the local, national, and global economies which affect it.

From the most general view, educational economics tends to parallel broad trends in national and international economics. Booms tend to loosen dollars for our schools; busts tend to tighten them; general trends in labor/management relations are generally echoed in the schools; wars and military excursions which impact on the total economy generally impact on the teaching economy; demographic realities which affect the general dynamics behind the distribution of goods and services are pretty much found in academia.

Broadly speaking, following the Great Depression and Second World War (the two major economic forces between 1930 and 1945), America enjoyed a post-war boom which lasted until about 1970. It was the national manifestation of an international condition which saw the industrialized nations of the Northern Hemisphere dominate world economies to an enormous extent. A.G. Frank notes in his analysis of global economics in the post-war era that only eight nations (the United States, West Germany, Japan, the Soviet Union, Italy, France, Great Britain, and Canada) account for 80% of the world's non-military exports and about 50% of its food consumption while containing only about 25% of world population.[4]

Frank goes on to state that from 1950 to 1970, while world population rose by

46%, industrial production rose 180%. In the U.S. alone exports increased from $61 billion to $312 billion, a 285% rise as measured in constant prices.[5]

The picture begins to change, however, after about 1970. Annual growth begins to slow, and in some years (such as 1970 in the U.S.) it is negative. The total GNP of the seven leading industrial nations of the West is negative in 1974 and 1975. Much of the world's economy experiences cyclical periods of recession, declines of industrial productivity, increased periods of inflation, higher rates of unemployment, and periods of crisis due to short-range phenomena like oil price fluctuations and long-range phenomena like increasing national debts and negative trade balances.[6]

In the U.S., rising unemployment (from 3.8% in 1968 to 8.5% in 1975), double-digit inflation, a deficit balance of payments (over $30 billion per year by 1977), and an increase in the national debt to over $2 trillion have all characterized the post-1970 era. By the 1980's, American economic degeneration is an acknowledged reality even by the government itself.[7]

To these broad economic facts, one must add considerations specific to education in gaining a comprehensive view of the fiscal context in which our schools function. Those specifics include the nature of public school funding, school enrollments, the spending habits of the young, and the influences of industries which service education.

Since the Constitution of the United States places the burden of primary and secondary education in the hands of the separate states (a condition of which we will speak in subsequent pages), it should not surprise us that only a small percentage of the per pupil cost of education comes from the federal government. In 1971 the average yearly per pupil cost was $911 of which $112 (or 12.3%) came from federal aid. By 1981 the per pupil cost had risen to $2,724 of which $234 (or 8.5%) came from federal sources. In 1971 state aid accounted for about 38% of per pupil costs, the remainder coming from local property taxes. By 1981 states were picking up an average of 47% of the costs, the remainder still coming from property taxes at the local level.[8]

It is important in assessing the rise of education costs to take into account the effects of the inflation which gripped the national economy in the decade of the 1970's. Figures from the National Center for Educational Statistics comparing 1971 expenditures with 1981 expenditures, for example, show that even though the 1971 dollar figures are much lower than the 1981 figures, they nonetheless amount to 27.7% of total state/local outlays, while the 1981 figures amount to only 24.5%—a decline in the percentage of state and local budgets allocated to schooling.[9]

Similar things can be seen in statistics covering teacher income. Average teacher salaries rose from $9,269 in 1971 to $19,157 in 1981. When adjusted for inflation, however, this dollar gain represented a 13% *decline* in real purchasing power.[10]

Important in assessing current educational realities are the data on student enrollment and teacher supply and demand. The enormous baby boom of the 1950's and 1960's was followed by a period of unprecedented decline. From a high of 46 million public school students in 1970, enrollments dropped to under 39 million in 1985. They are expected to rise slowly to around 41 million by 1992.

> In the 1970's, initial enrollment declines were not followed immediately by declines in the number of teachers employed. Not until the late 1970's did the number of classroom teachers begin to decline in the public schools...In the late 1970's severe budgetary constraints...slowed further improvement of teacher-pupil ratios...The number of public school teachers began to decline after 1977, decreasing from 2.21 million in that year to 2.11 million in 1982.[11]

The number of teachers needed during the 1983-87 period to replace outgoing ones and provide necessary services was projected by the NCES as 777,000. Between 1988 and 1992, when student population is expected to rise, the figure changes to 924,000. On an annual basis, that means that America's schools will need an average of 185,000 new teachers each year from 1988 to 1992. Whether or not they will be forthcoming is another matter.[12]

Along with specific factors relating to educational funding, pupil enrollments, and the availability of teachers, there are more subtle factors to consider in the economic equations of education. Increased wealth in the post-war boom created an enlarged middle class with a large population of children who had money to spend. A new consumer group therefore arose capable of supporting a panoply of industries designed to cater to it. Fashions, motion pictures, music, automobiles, drugs, alcohol, literature—all these and more began to constitute a "youth market." As they did so, they had profound effects upon how young people behaved and upon what they did and did not respond to in school. On this subject, educator Paul Copperman writes the following:

> The unfortunate lessons the post-war generation learned in infancy and early childhood were reinforced in late childhood and adolescence as a result of American economic, technological, and demographic expansion. Poverty prevents a society from pandering to the whims of its spoiled children. Affluence does not. A pioneer family needed the help of its children in order to survive. The post-World War II family did not. They wanted to protect their children from all possible suffering. Their affluence permitted them to do so far too successfully.[13]

Finally, there is the economics of the "education business" to consider. Publishers and computer companies, manufacturers of basketballs and snare drums, colleges and cap-and-gown salesmen may all wish to strive toward superior educational results, but the bottom line for each is that they must continue to make a buck in order to survive. The temptation is thus present for each of them to provide the educational marketplace not with what it needs to achieve excellence, but with what it may be cajoled into buying. In this regard, the condition of a lot of modern textbooks has become something of a problem to many educators, so much so that the Association for Supervision and Curriculum Development devoted the whole of its April 1985 issue of the trade journal *Educational Leadership* to the topic. The following comes from that issue.

> If school districts continue to believe there is no problem with textbook selection and do not provide both time and training for textbook evaluation, then selection committees will continue to focus evaluation on pretty pictures, favorite topics, amusing agents, and seducing sales presentations.[14]

We will devote more time to the issue of educational economics in the chapters to follow. For now it is important that we are cognizant of economics as a significant factor in the sociopolitical context of American education after World War II.

Technological impact

If one reads the history of the human species in modern philosophical terms, human behavior is not a static thing but rather one which changes as man interacts with new events and new discoveries. Whatever remains constant in man's "nature" from era to era (and one presumes that his fundamental physical and social needs vary little or so slowly as to be "almost" constant), many of man's actions—his thoughts and deeds—are shaped by more immediate forces, forces which he then uses to reshape his world in turn. Perhaps that is what J. Bronowski meant when he observed that "history is not events, but people."[15]

In the years since World War II mankind has forged a staggering number of new technologies, staggering both in quantity and quality. They have profoundly changed his world and his behavior, and as we are about the business of defining a social and political context for current education, we ought to take notice of the impact of some of them. For the sake of this discussion, we will look at a few of the more startling technological additions to contemporary society: the technology of self-destruction, medical technology, the technology of travel and communication, the technology of data dissemination, and the technology of space.

Where before the advent of nuclear weaponry the chief aim of modern nations was the establishment of a secure and expanding economy, the atomic age now presents, as John Kenneth Galbraith puts it, a "higher task,"[16] the task of collective survival. Try to think of that concept not in the context of the half-century which has elapsed since World War II, but rather in the context of cosmic history.

Accepting current theories of the origins of our solar system, it has taken some 10 to 14 billion years to produce the world we know today. Ten to 14 billion years—and in all that time, nothing on the earth save the laws of nature herself had the power to destroy the progress of life. But now, chiefly through the technologies of the post-war era, we have at hand a civilization capable of planetary annihilation. Nuclear warfare, ecological manipulation—these are the playthings of contemporary man, and they contain the potential for miscalculations which are total and irrevocable. Astronomer/philosopher Carl Sagan speculates that self-destructive technologies may be the crucible in which the survivability of a given life form is tested. The civilization which reaches the ability to destroy itself and does not, emerges into a kind of cosmic brotherhood, joining all the other life forms which have survived by learning to live with their technologies rather than dying as a result of them.

Just how many life forms have made it into the cosmic brotherhood is a matter for either statistical or philosophical speculation. But the answer is really beside the point for us here and now. Whether there are millions or only us, we are, as Sagan writes, "at an epochal, transitional moment in the history of life on earth. There is no other time as risky, but no other time as promising for the future of life on our planet."[17]

The implications of nuclear and ecological self-destruction on education are at once inescapable and profound. From the point of view of curriculum, they have triggered a call not only for courses in advanced technology, but also for courses in the development of values which can better enable us to apply technology for survival.

In a paper prepared by Edward Cornish for the World Future Society, "preventing World War III" led the list of critical issues for the remainder of our century.[18] For Cornish and many of his contemporaries, the study of self-destruction is, in fact, the only viable vehicle we have for surviving our technology. Just think for a moment: who is not touched by this issue? What scientist can invent any longer without thinking of the consequences of his work? What diplomat or legislator can function without being mindful of our tenuous future? What judge can assess law, what voter can fail to be unaffected by man's new ability to end the world?

Beyond a curricular impact, the technology of self-destruction can breed attitudes which shape behavior and have a real influence on what students and teachers do in the classroom. The urgency behind John Kennedy's statement that we are "the last, best hope of mankind;" the anxiety we felt during the Cuban missile crisis; the nihilism expressed by the youngster who says, "why should I care—we're only going to blow ourselves up anyway;" these are all attitudes spawned by the technology of self-destruction. They affect the movies we make, the treaties we sign, the way in which we learn in school. As educator Glen Heathers writes, the influences of self-destructive technology go beyond the changes they impose on the individual. Such technology "profoundly influences his view of the world and of himself and leads to various types of effort to find meaning, emotional security, and self-expression."[19]

If nuclear and ecological technology reshape our behavior as it relates to the future, twentieth century medical technology reshapes it as it relates to the present. Let us consider just three of many possible examples: the advent of psychology, modern contraceptive technology, and our new ability to sustain life through drugs and surgery.

It would be difficult to underestimate the impact of Sigmund Freud upon the modern world, not so much because his every theory is accepted but because he unleashed an era of self-investigation in man which has touched every corner of man's existence. Psychology is a governing force in endeavors which range from advertising to criminology. In education, however, it has taken on the dimensions of a primal force. In the works of dozens of noted educators from Piaget to Dewey to Bruner and beyond, the act of learning for a child is seen as a function of psychological condition as much as physical or environmental condition. Psychologist Winfred Hill, for example, writes that learning for a child is not merely the simple process of data transfer from teacher to pupil.

> He also learns from his books, from his fellow students, and from the physical arrangements of the school. Part of what he learns is measurable...while another part involves changes...in attitudes, emotions, social behavior and a variety of other reactions.[20]

Nor is psychology solely a determinant in the training of the student. Arthur Jersild points out that it is a fundamental force behind the proper training of the teacher. The developmental and psychoanalytic theories of Horney, Sullivan,

Fromm, Freud, Adler, and Jung all combine for Jersild in a unified theory of self-investigation which he considers essential for an educator. "A teacher cannot make much headway in understanding others or in helping others to understand themselves unless he is endeavoring to understand himself," Jersild writes.[21]

Finally, psychology has in recent years become the underlying force in the training of educational administrators and in the analysis and understanding of the organizations and people who comprise the educational community. From the theories of self-actualization by Abraham Maslow to the techniques of motivation developed by Thomas Sergiovanni, psychological awareness has become the sine qua non of educational management. In fact, the best educational leaders seem to be those capable of discerning the underlying psychology of the individuals and institutions with whom they deal. Having assessed them in this way, educational leaders are able to, as Robert Owens puts it, differentiate their management style by using "contingency" theories which are "closely linked to...the motivational level and...the skill level of followers."[22]

In the area of contraceptive technology, there have been monumental changes of behavior which have followed the widespread use of items like the birth control pill. On the obvious side, the removal of the fear of pregnancy has made the post-1945 world considerably more sexually active, particularly in the secondary school population. As a result, the entire overt morality of our present school-age culture has undergone quite a metamorphosis.

It is difficult to say with certainty *exactly* what effect contraceptive technology has had on the sexual behavior of people simply because one does not ask each generation (and if one *does* ask, the answers are really unverifiable), "what are your sexual habits?" We therefore rely on circumstantial evidence to tell us what is probably going on. For example, in 1960 the number of babies born to unwed American girls between 15 and 19 years of age was 87,000. By 1978, the number had increased nearly 300% to 240,000.[23] Increases in venereal disease and abortions among the youth of America contain similar circumstantial evidence. Researchers in the field like Dr. Theodore Lidz of Yale University published findings that recent changes in adolescent mores have permitted sexual intercourse to become an accepted part of adolescent experimentation;[24] and in answer to a question on the spread of venereal disease in modern society, Dr. David Reuben writes the following:

> The recipe goes something like this: take a sexually vigorous young lady...add birth control pills and maybe a little marijuana...stir in some false confidence in penicillin, a dash of hippie philosophy, and a lot of immaturity...put all the ingredients into a snappy new car that goes into some swinging neighborhoods, and mix thoroughly...incubate for ten days and the infection that results will be astounding.[25]

Beyond the changes of overt sexual behavior wrought by modern contraceptive technology, however, is an even more profound change: a change in the role of women in modern society. Freed from the burdens of pregnancy, today's women now have a much greater choice than ever before between motherhood and other careers. Spurred, no doubt, by changing economic and social conditions, millions of women have relied upon contraceptive technology to avert the traditional role of childbearer, opting instead for careers which in former generations were all but unavailable.[26] The results of this phenomenon have been far-reaching indeed. More and more women have joined the workforce; more women have opted to have babies later in life; more women have opted for the status of single (as opposed to married) motherhood; and many more women have chosen to go to school. In 1970, for example, women represented only 41% of total college enrollment. By 1982, they represented 52%, a majority.[27]

To the rest of modern medical technology, we must consider the entire phenomenon of life expectancy itself. In 1920 the average American male lived to 53.6, the average American female 54.6. By 1980 the averages had risen to 69.8 and 77.5, respectively.[28] The fact is that new drugs and surgical techniques are keeping us alive much longer with the consequence that America is growing older. The implications of this condition on education are clear. People find themselves more and more frequently with second careers, and this has increased the enrollment of older citizens in our schools, spurring an entirely new phenomenon, the "adult education" program. Retraining older workers for new technologies and training adults for second careers has, in some institutions, become the primary focus of attention. The overall increase of adult populations on American college campuses since only 1970 is startling. In that year, 72% of the students enrolled in college were under the age of 25. By 1982 the figure had dropped to 61% per year, and the trend seems to be continuing.[29]

What this means for America's school children is that grade school, high school, and college may be only the first round of their educational lives. Their ability to be educationally and vocationally flexible in middle age and beyond may become one of the most important aspects of the learning process.

As if the technologies of which we have already spoken were not enough, the world since 1945 has changed in yet two more profound dimensions: it has been shrunk in size and expanded in knowledge. There was a time, and it was not so long ago, when the separate communities of mankind, scattered as they were to the four corners of the globe, were isolated unto themselves. The Sherpa in Nepal had no idea of the tribesman of Kenya, and he had no interaction with the rancher in Western Alberta. Then came the car, the plane, and with them a new meaning to geopolitical relationships. There was a time, and it was not so long ago, when the dissemination of ideas took years. Then came the printing press, the technologies of mass production and mass distribution, and finally the electronics revolution and the computer. Now the business of everyone is everyone's business. There was a time, and it was not so long ago, when nations saw themselves in the single terms of national chauvinism. England was for England, Germany for Germany, Spain for Spain. Then came the technologies of space exploration, and all the world could see planet Earth from the perspective of the moon where national boundaries don't show up and petty chauvinism loses its meaning.

The manifestations of these technological trends on education can be seen in the microcosmic world of classroom behavior and the macrocosmic world of general educational attitudes. Consider, in relationship to the first, things like television, computers, microchip calculators, the pursuit of foreign languages; consider, in relationship to the second, growing feelings of dehumanization and a growing need for values clarification in the curriculum.

In 1950, for example, only 9% of American homes had TV sets. By 1983 it was 98%, with an average of 1.8 sets in each home and an average of 6.8 hours watched daily by each person.[30] It is estimated that by the time an American youngster has been graduated from high school, he will have spent 15,000 hours watching TV as compared with 13,000 hours in the classroom.[31] We will return to view the impact of the television age on learning in the pages to follow. For now, being aware of the pervasiveness of TV in the modern world will help us assess the context in which education occurs. The same may be said for the computer.

Virtually unknown in the 1960's and found only sparingly in the 1970's, computers used as tools of secondary school instruction numbered 38,000 in 1980. By 1982 it was 90,000. In 1975 there were only 5,000 bachelor's degrees granted by American colleges in the field of computer sciences. By 1981 it was over 300% more,[32] and the trend toward greater computer use has continued through the mid-1980's. From 1982 to 1983 alone the use of computers doubled at the junior high level and increased 50% at the senior high level.[33]

The implications of such technology are not at all clear. On the one hand, students and teachers are under increasing pressure to develop computer literacy at earlier and earlier ages. On the other, many educators wonder why we need routine math drills when an inexpensive pocket calculator will compute square roots and percentages with the push of a button. As educator Harold Shane puts it, "(We) have a lot to learn about the learning process and individual learning styles. Lacking such knowledge, we could end up merely cloning inadequacy more rapidly by means of the computer."[34]

Again, what we do about the impact of technology on education will be the subject of many of the pages to follow. For now, in defining the general context of post-1945 education, we note its many facets and ubiquitous presence.

Changes in the quality of life

There is a feeling which has been expressed by many post-World War II people that along with the great advances made since 1945 (and perhaps in some ways *because* of them), society has become a harsher, more unsettling place. Often these feelings are vague, difficult to define, difficult to substantiate. They seem to express a growing discontent with what we have come to call "the quality of life." They seem to bespeak an attitude which says, "Yes, I now live longer and have a microwave oven to cook my dinner in three minutes, but somehow I was happier before."

I remember, by way of illustration, seeing a cartoon not so long ago in one of the educational trade journals. Frame one was labeled "1920." It showed little Johnny about to leave home for school. Johnny's mom hands him his lunch bag and says, "Now you be a good boy today." Frame two was labeled "1980" and in all respects was exactly like frame one except that mommy is saying, "Now don't you take any crap from your teacher today."

To the extent that art mirrors society, one can often find these attitudes reflected in pre- and post-war works. A marked increase in sexual explicitness and overt violence, for example, characterizes post-war films, and in American popular music one clearly sees a harshness of rhythm, melody, volume, and lyric where once expression was considerably more poetic. There is a world of difference between the culture which sings, "You are the promised breath of springtime," and the one which sings, "Why don't we do it in the road."[35]

Diane Ravitch comments on this metamorphosis of spirit as it was reflected in American schools. She writes the following:

> Although some few big-city high schools were vast educational factories in 1945, most...were small compared with what was to come...Even where teachers led independent lives, they were expected to spend after-school hours as supervisors of extracurricular activities and to know their students; they, in turn, could count on parents to support and reinforce the demands made by the school...Alcohol was seldom permitted...drugs were unheard of, and even the social lives of students were regulated...
>
> Much had changed by 1980. The drive to consolidate small schools and small districts had largely succeeded...the number of school districts shrank dramatically from 100,000 at war's end to 16,000 in 1980. While total enrollment in elementary and secondary schools nearly doubled during that thirty-five year span (from 23 million to 40 million), the number of schools dropped from 185,000 to 86,000...
>
> The trade-off, of course, was that bigness meant impersonality, bureaucratization, diminished contact between faculty and students, formalization of relationships among colleagues, a weakening of the bonds of community...No longer part of a community of values shared with students and parents, teachers and administrators found it difficult to administer discipline or even to establish rules that everyone found acceptable...
>
> The invasion of drugs...in the 1960's...dulled students' senses and insulated a portion of the student body from adult standards. The lingering influence of the counter-culture...left many adults wondering whether there were any standards of learning or effort or behavior worth defending.[36]

What Ravitch reports of the educational community is, of course, merely an echo of the general social macrocosm. Research conducted by Hadley Cantril shows a marked change in attitudes toward the quality of life from 1959 to 1979.

Cantril asked people to rate the country on a scale of 1 to 10. He then asked them to project what they thought the ratings would be in five years time. In 1959, the nation was rated a 6.7 with projections that it would be 7.4 in five years. By 1979 the rating had dropped to 4.7 with a projection of a further decline to 4.6 within five years.[37]

While it is difficult to identify the actual causes of attitudes like these, one can surmise that the economic declines, political unrest, wars, assassinations, and cultural changes which characterized American life from 1960 to 1980 played a significant part. Such suppositions are supported by the data which attend many indicators of societal behavior. Let us consider a few examples.

In 1960 there were 8,464 homicide victims in the U.S. The national population at the time was 179.3 million. By 1980 the number of homicide victims had risen to 24,278—almost a 300% increase. The population during that time, however, rose only 26% to 226.5 million.[38] Similar increases are found in other categories of crime.

From 1970 to 1980, for example, rape increased by 98.9%, robbery by 42%, assault by 78.9%, burglary by 56.2% , and auto theft by 9.1%.[39]

In 1961 there were 19,000 suicides in America. In 1981 there were 26,010, an increase of 18.5% even when adjusted for population differences.[40] Much of this increase was due to a sharp rise in the suicide rate of young people. For example, in 1970 the rate among white males between 15 and 24 years of age was 13.9 per 100,000. By 1980 it was 21.4.[41]

The institution of marriage became increasingly more unstable as the decades of the century moved on. In 1920, for example, there were only 1.6 divorces per 1,000 population. In 1930, it was still 1.6. By 1940, it was 2.0; in 1950, 2.6; in 1970, 3.5; and in 1980, an alarming 5.2. To say this in another way, by 1980, for every 1,000 American marriages, there were 490 divorces—a ratio of nearly 50%.[42]

The use of drugs in America reached epidemic proportions in the years following World War II. Jonathan Harris in his book on organized crime in the United States calls it a "tidal wave." He quotes U.S. Attorney General William French Smith as saying that the amount of money spent by U.S. citizens on drugs is "about equal to the combined profits of America's five hundred largest corporations," an estimated 120 billion dollars a year.[43] James Mills writes that internationally people spend more on drugs than food, housing, clothing, or education. Not only have "Mafia" bosses taken leading roles in the supply chain, but the Yakuza crime syndicate of Japan, Latin American criminal networks (particularly those in Colombia, Bolivia, and Cuba), and more recently, terrorist networks based in the Middle East have all become major dealers for the insatiable narcotics appetite.[44] James Comer of Yale University writes that the involvement of youth with narcotics not only draws them into a vortex of physical degeneration, but leads them more and more frequently into crime—often crime of a violent nature.[45] The 1979 National Survey on Drug Abuse conducted by the U.S. Department of Health and Human Services' Alcohol, Drug Abuse, and Mental Health Administration gives us the alarming statistics on American high school seniors. By graduation from high school, 93% have used alcohol, 71% tobacco, 60% marijuana, 57% stimulants or tranquilizers, 13% psychedelic hallucinogens, 16% cocaine, 12% inhalants, and 1% heroin. Recent government estimates have placed the use of cocaine alone to over 20 million Americans or about 10% of our total population.[46]

The statistics surrounding other social indicators do not offer much more sanguine pictures of the quality of life in the forty or so years since the end of the Second World War. The increase in overt sexuality, for example, has created a Frankenstein monster in the area of venereal disease and public health. From 264,158 reported cases of gonorrhea in 1961, there were 984,330 in 1981, a population-adjusted increase of 195%. Incidents of syphilis rose 23.8% from a reported 21,982 cases in 1970 to 27,204 cases in 1980, and most recently, the outburst of AIDS in America has reached epidemic levels which present what Surgeon General C. Everett Coop has called the most serious public health menace of the century.[47]

The figures are also grim in the area of environmental quality. Increases in water pollution discharges, air pollutant emissions, hazardous waste sites, pesticide contamination, and endangered animal species have all been reported since the end of World War II.[48] There have been growing concerns about industrial pollution as well, and it is now common for geographical locations to be rated as to quality of life in part for the quality of the physical environment. Dr. Thomas Bowman, for example, has ranked the major metropolitan areas of America both by air pollution ratings and water pollution statistics in an effort to help Americans define where it is best to live.[49]

Warnings have come from many quarters that if post-1945 societies do not begin to treat the biosphere of the planet with greater care and intelligence, future generations will face disasters of unimaginable dimensions ranging from global diseases to the destruction of life as we know it. From the pioneering work of Rachel Carson in the 1950's to current efforts by organizations like the Sierra Club, the care of the environment has been permanently wedded to American concepts of life quality.[50]

Closely allied to concerns about the physical environment have been reactions to the demographics of post-war America which have shifted major segments of the population from rural to urban and suburban areas. Once regarded as an escape from urban blight and overcrowding, American suburbs in the 1980's have become more and more like the cities they were designed to avoid. A recent report published by *Congressional Quarterly* says this of the subject:

> The gap between the reality and myth of suburbia often makes it difficult to come to grips with the changes occurring there...In recent years many suburban communities have become heterogeneous, urbanized areas...struggling with cities over a broad range of issues: integration, declining employment, transportation, and housing for the poor.[51]

Ironically, the same society which gave us nuclear power, contraceptive protection, a home outside the city, and a two-car family at the very same instant provided the problems of ecological pollution, venereal disease, an overcrowded suburbia, and clogged transit arteries which now erode the quality of our lives.

To all of the statistics above, we can add things which appear from time to time in our newspapers yet do not fall conveniently into the figures kept by government census divisions or public opinion pollsters: the innocent housewife killed by ingestion of arsenic-laced aspirin, the college girl crushed to death when pushed by an unknown assailant in front of a moving subway train, the high school principal shot-gunned by a failing math student, the sexual and physical abuse of a young baby at the hands of its drug-crazed parent.

It is indeed a different world for the child going to school now than it ever was before the Austrian Anschluss or the bombing of Pearl Harbor.

Domestic political instability

It would be difficult to imagine a period of greater political turbulence than the decades which followed World War II. With perhaps only the Civil War era as the exception, no succession of years saw as continuous an onslaught on American domestic tranquility as did the period from 1945 to 1987. Consider what occurred: the Korean War; the assassination of President Kennedy; the Viet Nam War; the assassinations of Martin Luther King, Robert Kennedy, and Malcolm X; the Watergate scandal and subsequent resignation of President Nixon; the proliferation of terrorism against Americans abroad; and most recently, the attempted assassination of President Reagan and the Iran/Nicaragua controversy which rocked his administration.

It is probably impossible to calculate with precision the full effect of these events on American life. The one inescapable conclusion of political and social researchers who have studied them, however, is that they have profoundly changed the way in which Americans perceive their government. In particular, they have contributed to a cynicism and distrust of authority which has pervaded not only the adult population but the school population as well. Consider the following findings by way of example.

On June 1, 1973, as the nation struggled through the agonies of the Watergate investigation, the Gallup Organization asked a sampling of American people, "Do you believe there are senators and representatives now serving in Congress who won election by using unethical and illegal methods in their campaigns?" 67% responded "yes," only 33% "no" or "no opinion." A follow-up poll two years later (May 30, 1975) asked, "How much confidence have you in Congress?" While 40% responded "a great deal" or "a lot," 57% answered "little" or "none." (3% said "no opinion.")[52]

Twenty years after the assassination of John Kennedy, on November 20, 1983, the Washington Post published a survey which asked how people felt about the various Congressional investigations into the event. Four out of five Americans stated that they did not believe the government version of things. "Implicit in this skepticism," writes researcher Henry Hurt, "is a feeling that the public has been deceived by those vested with the special trust to conduct national affairs..."[53]

By the 1980's, as the *Congressional Quarterly Report* puts it, "a number of important changes were drastically altering the nation's social and political atmosphere. The civil rights and anti-war movements, together with the coming of age of the baby boom generation, led to widespread questioning of authority of all kinds."[54] How these trends are revealed in the classrooms of America will be a topic to which we will return in the pages below, but no serious evaluation of current educational realities should fail to take them into account both as part of school life and the fabric of life in general.

The pace of change itself

To every aspect of the socioeconomic environment we have thus far viewed, we finally add the speed at which the environment itself is changing.

Consider how stable your life would probably have been in centuries past. Perhaps your ancestors had a small farm in south-central Ireland, sheltered in medieval times by a feudal castle, dominated perhaps by the invasions of England from time to time. What would really have changed for you from one generation to another? Given an economic upheaval here, a political upheaval there, you would have worked your land, cut your peat, borne your children in ways far more similar than different. Perhaps you would have travelled to the New World to start afresh in a more promising economic and social environment. Yet still, in your colonial village or as you braved the American prairie, your daily routines would not have been so strikingly different from 1700 to 1750 to 1800 to 1850 to 1900.

Enter the twentieth century, however, and the rate of change for you begins to accelerate. Technology sweeps you into new social and personal roles. Traditions become more and more challenged and thus less and less pervasive. Soon, sociological impermanence becomes a way of life, and with it you are forced to cope with the dissociative reactions which occur when the human psyche is asked to adjust too often and too quickly.

"If future shock were a matter of physical illness alone, it might be easier to prevent and to treat," writes Alvin Toffler. "Psychophysiologists studying the impact of change on various organisms have shown that successful adaptation can occur only when the level of stimulation—the amount of change and novelty in the environment—is neither too low nor too high."[55]

The pace of modern life, the dissemination of modern information, the rate at which modern invention occurs often renders things out-of-fashion or obsolete before they have a chance to see a first application. What Toffler calls "the bombardment of the senses," "the information overload," eventually leads to levels of physical and spiritual stress which can destroy the individual and the processes in which the individual is involved.[56]

Consider the plight of the science teacher and student whose textbook becomes outmoded even before the curriculum can be unfolded in the space of an academic year. Consider the physician whose initial training is but the opening round of annual updates which must be absorbed through trade journal articles or mandated refresher seminars. How do they continue to cope semester after semester, patient after patient, and what are the repercussions of their plight on the next generation of students and teachers?

Easy questions? Hardly. But questions with which modern educators must deal if they are to assess current realities and plan future strategies.

Further implications of post-1945 life for education

From time to time in the pages above we have noted some of the ways in which the major trends of post-1945 society may have affected American public education. Now that our brief survey of those trends is concluded, we again turn to the implications of our data for the current state of our schools. In doing so, it is important that we do not claim to present definitive or complete listings of cause-and-effect phenomena. To begin with, that is probably an impossible task on the face of it, and in any event, the chapters which follow this one have as their aim in part to flesh out the relationships between modern life and modern schools topic by topic. What the pages immediately below can do, however, is to give us a general sense of how post-World War II society invades the pedagogical process. Indeed, that is important enough, for if we are to succeed in repairing our educational classroom, it is incumbent upon us to be aware that some of our work—perhaps much of our work—will have to be done not inside but outside that room.

Consider, for example, the very makeup of the child who enters the classroom today. The student of the 1980's is the product of the parents who cut their social teeth on the counterculture of the 1960's. Remember, those were the Americans who in huge numbers embraced the use of drugs, disdained the institution of marriage, presided over an era of social anomie unprecedented in American culture. One assumes that many of the behavioral patterns exhibited by the adolescents of the 1960's did not entirely disappear when those adolescents became the childbearers of the 1980's.

From a physiological viewpoint alone, consider what that means. The marijuana, the tobacco, the alcohol, the pills, the hallucinogens, etc. ingested by mom and dad are the potential genetic legacy of the child who now inhabits the classroom. The venereal disease which spreads apace in the cultures of casual sexuality may find its way not only into the bodies of the initial sexual practitioners, but all too tragically into the bodies of their offspring—the very offspring who now comprise our school population. Nor is the legacy merely one which manifests itself at birth. If the parent has continued to use the marijuana or cocaine, then the influence upon the child may linger long after birth. It may become a part of the growth process of the new generation and can, indeed, be the foundation of the statistics of current teenage drug abuse cited earlier. If the lifestyle of mom and dad continues to be that of casual sexuality, it may be absorbed as an object lesson in the child and, indeed, become the foundation of the teenage pregnancy and venereal disease rates cited earlier.

Consider now the potential effects of the divorce rates, the economic declines, and the changing role of women on our current crop of kids. In any given school at any given time it is now likely that between 25% and 50% of the children will come from broken homes. Many more will live in families where both parents work. Still more will live with mothers who have opted to raise their children outside the institution of marriage. The emotional and psychological scars of family instability are very real, and they visit themselves with greater and greater frequency in the school environment. The tender and touching scenes of films like "Kramer vs. Kramer" are played out by the hundreds of thousands in contemporary American life, and we cannot expect a latch-key child with little or no home supervision or a child who has just weathered a Family Court custody battle to come to school with normal behavior patterns or a bright outlook. It is thus not surprising that we see the hyperactivity, learning disabilities, emotional disorders, or levels of hostility toward authority that we do in the students of today. For some teachers it is as if the special education classes of yesterday have become the regular classes of today, and the stress of coping with so much aberrant behavior is more than many modern educators can bear.

Exactly how deep teacher discontentment runs is not entirely clear. The latest data from the Center for Educational Statistics are somewhat contradictory. A 1985 survey of American teachers conducted for the Metropolitan Life Insurance Company by Louis Harris and Associates found that 44% of the educators were "very satisfied" with their teaching careers. Another 35% declared themselves "somewhat satisfied" while only 21% claimed to be "somewhat or very *dissatisfied*." On the other hand, 53% advised young people *against* becoming teachers and only 47% claimed that they felt respected as a teacher in today's society.[57]

What seems fairly clear is that at this point in time education is not attracting as many teachers as it is projected to need, and the candidates it *is* attracting tend to be the least academically astute of our college crop. Consider the following findings which support these sad conclusions. For every year from 1987 to 1993 the projected demand for teachers exceeds the projected supply. In the 1992-93 school year the teacher shortage will be particularly acute with a projected demand of 215,000 and a projected supply which ranges from 190,000 at its most optimistic to only 90,000 at its most pessimistic. Thus, as it stands now, it appears that we will be 25,000 teachers short in 1992-93 given the *best* of circumstances. We in fact may be as much as 125,000 short.[58]

As to the quality of those who actually do go into education, the news is even more dismal. Researchers for the U.S. Department of Education write the following:

> Teacher quality is very difficult to assess. One of the few teacher characteristics that appears to correlate with student performance is the teacher's academic ability. Historically, recruits to teaching have been drawn from among the least able college graduates, and the academic ability of teacher candidates declined through the 1970's according to standardized test scores.[59]

In fact, the SAT scores of teachers currently in our schools is almost 100 points below the average of other college graduates (921.57 as compared with 1011.80).[60]

In education, when one hires in an era of labor shortage and when one knows that the labor pool is yielding the least attractive candidates, it is an inescapable conclusion that poor education is going to continue for years into the future. The mediocre teacher who squeaks by his or her period of probation to achieve tenure will likely visit that mediocrity on the next twenty years of clientele. That is an implication of the educational decline of the past decades which is perhaps the most irksome of all. The same society which has produced the least capable students has also produced the teachers least capable of turning the tide.

All of which is not to say that the job education has done has been entirely dismal, or that the fault of educational decline lies entirely at the foot of the teacher. We have already seen that the teacher—less academically astute than others though he may be—is dealing with impossibly complex phenomena. He is also dealing with students who in recent times have eschewed the traditional American work ethic in favor of a philosophy of selfishness. This change in work ethic is seen by many to be a direct result of the affluence and pampering of the post-war family.

"Many social observers view the changing attitudes toward work as an outgrowth of the 'psychology of entitlement'," writes researcher William Thomas.

> ...Workers have an expanding sense of what is due them as rights of employment or citizenship...From pensions to health care to long vacations to a high standard of living, the perception by workers of what constitutes their rights is inexorably being enlarged.
>
> Such attitudes usually are attributed to the so-called "permissive generation" of the late 1940's and 1950's...the "instant gratification," self-indulgent "Me Decade" with a taste for high-priced living and little interest in self-denial.

Thomas goes on to point out that all the post-war generations are plagued by the "curse of affluence" where many youths—while perfectly content to enjoy the fruits of their parents' labors—see themselves as either incapable of matching the accomplishments of their parents or unwilling to pay the often high physical and emotional prices of "success."[61] Thomas's observations are in large measure supported by the most recent statistical surveys. The studies of Bachman, Johnson and O'Malley, for example, reveal that although today's youth enjoy considerable spending power (often amounts exceeding fifty dollars per week), their vision of the future is rather gloomy, clouded by concerns about declining job markets, crime, and the threat of nuclear war.[62]

Many of our current high school students, especially those with low socioeconomic status, particularly those from American Indian, Hispanic, and black populations, "cope" with education by dropping out of it. In 1985, for example, over 25% of American 18 year-olds failed to complete high school; and a 1980 study of dropouts among sophomores shows rates of 29.2% for American Indians, 18% for Hispanics, and 17% for blacks as opposed to only 12.2% for whites and 3.1% for Asians.[63] Alarming as these figures are, however, they should be placed in historical context. In 1940, a little more than 75% of American adults over the age of 25 were *not* high school graduates. By 1982, the figure had dropped to about 14%.[64] So while we do have a large dropout problem, we are still educating more of our people for longer periods of time. The question is how *well* are we educating them and what are we to conclude from all of these facts and figures?

I urge you not to be hasty in rushing to answer these questions. I urge you not to shoot from the hip in an effort to wound your favorite enemy or vindicate your favorite hero. Yes, many of the statistics are alarming, but the causes are many, the problems complex, and the solutions not readily apparent. Besides, there is blame for everyone here. For the incompetent teacher and the union which protects him, there is blame. For the cowardly administrator and the system which produces him, there is blame. For the over-indulgent parent who has failed to provide either stability or a sense of values, there is blame. For the board of education who uses the school as a means of attaining personal power, there is blame. For the social institutions which glorify violence, provide drugs, and confuse morality with pleasure, there is blame. For the students who allow themselves to accept mediocrity, there is blame.

Before we make any rash judgments or foolish promises to ourselves, let us agree simply to apply the observations of this chapter to the various facets of education with which we will deal in the pages ahead. If we do that we will stand a better chance to accurately assess where we are and to suggest meaningful courses of action which may take us where we wish to go.

References for Chapter One

1. ***A History of the Modern World,*** R.R. Palmer (rev. ed. Joel Colton). New York: Knopf, 1960. p. 876.
2. ***A Short History of the United States,*** Allan Nevins and Henry Steele Commager. New York: Knopf, 1966. p. 546.
3. ***The Troubled Crusade: American education 1945-1980,*** Diane Ravitch. New York: Basic Books, 1983. p. 229.
4. ***Crisis: in the world economy,*** Andre Gunder Frank. New York: Holmes and Meier, 1980. pp. 1-19.
5. ***Crisis,*** A.G. Frank. p. 3.
6. ***Crisis,*** A.G. Frank. pp. 20-102.
7. ***World Economy: changes and challenges,*** Hoyt Gimlin, ed., Editorial Research Reports. Washington, D.C.: Congressional Quarterly, 1983. Forward.
8. ***The Condition of Education,*** 1984 ed., Statistical report prepared by the National Center for Educational Statistics; Valena White Plisko in charge of preparation. Washington, D.C.: U.S. Government Printing Office, 1984. pp. 3-12 ff.
9. ***Condition of Education,*** 1984 ed., NCES. p. 42.
10. ***Condition of Education,*** 1984 ed., NCES. p. 12.
11. ***Condition of Education,*** 1984 ed., NCES. p. 7.
12. ***Condition of Education,*** 1984 ed., NCES. p. 8.
13. ***The Literacy Hoax: the decline of reading, writing and learning in the public schools and what we can do about it,*** Paul Copperman. New York: Morrow, 1978. p. 165.
14. "What Every Textbook Evaluator Should Know," Connie Muther. In ***Educational Leadership,*** April 1985 (Vol. 42, #7). p. 8.
15. ***The Ascent of Man,*** Jacob Bronowski. Boston: Little, Brown and Co.,1973. p. 438.
16. ***The Affluent Society,*** 4th ed. John Kenneth Galbraith. Boston: Houghton Mifflin, 1984. p. 270.
17. ***The Cosmic Connection,*** Carl Sagan. Garden City, N.Y.: Anchor, 1980. p. 39.
18. ***Curriculum Planning: a new approach,*** 4th ed. Glen Hass. Boston: Allyn and Bacon, 1983. p. 87.
19. "Education to Meet the Psychological Requirements for Living in the Future," Glen Heathers. In ***Journal of Teacher Education.*** Summer 1974 (Vol. 25, #2). pp. 108-12.
20. ***Learning: a survey of psychological interpretation,*** Winfred F. Hill. San Francisco: Chandler, 1963. pp. 2-3.
21. ***When Teachers Face Themselves,*** Arthur T. Jersild. New York: Teachers College Press, 1955. p. 13.
22. ***Organizational Behavior in Education,*** Robert G. Owens. Englewood Cliffs, N.J.: Prentice-Hall, 1981. p. 182.
23. ***How We Live: an economic perspective on Americans from birth to death,*** Victor R. Fuchs. Cambridge, Mass.: Harvard University Press, 1983. p. 104.
24. ***The Person: his development throughout the life cycle,*** Theodore Lidz. New York: Basic Books, 1968. p. 355.
25. ***Everything You Always Wanted To Know about Sex,*** David Reuben. New York: McKay, 1969. pp. 270-71.
26. "A Cultural Analysis of Sex Role in the School," Patrick C. Lee and Nancy Gropper. In ***Journal of Teacher Education.*** Winter 1975 (Vol. 26, #4). pp. 335-39.
27. ***Condition of Education,*** 1984 ed., NCES. p. 62.
28. ***A Statistical Portrait of the American People,*** Andrew Hacker, ed. New York: Viking, 1983. p. 64.

29. ***Condition of Education,*** 1984 ed., NCES. p. 62.
30. ***Statistical Abstract of the United States, 1984,*** 104th ed. U.S. Department of Commerce. Washington, D.C.: Bureau of the Census, 1984. p. 558.
31. ***The Literary Hoax,*** Copperman. p. 166. Copperman cites as his source ***Television and the Public,*** R. Brower. New York: Holt, Rinehart, and Winston, 1973.
32. ***Statistical Abstract of the U.S., 1984.*** pp. 156 and 169.
33. ***Condition of Education,*** 1984. pp. 152, 172-73.
34. "The Silicon Age and Education," Harold G. Shane. In ***Phi Delta Kappan.*** January 1985 (Vol. 63, #5). pp. 303-8. Reproduced in ***Curriculum Planning,*** Hass. p. 94.
35. The cultural aspects of popular songs are discussed in ***Love, Marriage, and Family Themes in the Popular Song: a comparison of the years 1940 and 1965,*** Jerry Michael Bucci (Ed. D. dissertation, Teachers College of Columbia University, 1968) and ***Rhythm and Harmony in the Music of the Beatles,*** Steven C. Porter (Ph. D. dissertation, City University of New York, 1979. UM 7913156).
36. ***The Troubled Crusade,*** Ravitch. pp. 327-28.
37. ***Progress and Its Discontents,*** Gabriel A. Almond, Marvin Chodorow, and Roy Harvey Pearce. Berkeley: Univ. of California Press, 1982. p. 411.
38. ***Statistical Abstract, 1984.*** p. 180.
39. ***A Statistical Portrait,*** Hacker. p. 222.
40. ***A Statistical Portrait,*** Hacker. p. 70.
41. ***Statistical Abstract, 1984.*** p. 83.
42. ***A Statistical Portrait,*** Hacker. pp. 106-8
43. ***Super Mafia: organized crime threatens America,*** Jonathan Harris. New York: Julian Messner, 1984. p. 32.
44. ***The Underground Empire: where crime and governments embrace,*** James Mills. Garden City, N.Y.: Doubleday, 1986. p. 3 ff.
45. ***American Violence and Public Policy: an update of the National Commission on the Causes and Prevention of Violence,*** Lynn A. Curtis, ed. New Haven: Yale University Press, 1985. pp. 80-81.
46. ***International Drug Traffic,*** Edward F. Dolan, Jr. New York: Franklin Watts, 1985. p. 7; and ***The Addicted Society: pleasure-seeking and punishment revisited,*** Joel Fort, M.D. New York: Grove Press, 1981. p. 84.
47. ***A Statistical Portrait,*** Hacker. pp. 75-79.
48. ***Statistical Abstract, 1984.*** pp. 209-15 provide some documentation. Nathan Rosenberg discusses the issue in his essay on resource limits and economic progress in ***Progress and Its Discontents,*** pp. 313-15.
49. ***Finding Your Best Place To Live in America,*** Dr. Thomas R. Bowman, Dr. George A. Guiliani, Dr. M. Ronald Minge. New York: Red Lion Books, 1981. pp. 225-32.
50. ***America in the 1980's,*** William V. Thomas. Editorial Research Reports. Washington, D.C.: Congressional Quarterly, 1980. pp. 30-40.
51. ***America in the 1980's,*** pp. 103-4 ff.
52. ***The Gallup Poll: public opinion 1972-77,*** Dr. George H. Gallup, Director. Wilmington, Delaware: Scholarly Resources, Inc. 1978. pp. 131-2.
53. ***Reasonable Doubt,*** Henry Hurt. New York: Holt, Rinehart, and Winston, 1985. p. 439.
54. ***America in the 1980's,*** Thomas. p. 35.
55. ***Future Shock,*** Alvin Toffler. New York: Random House, 1970. p. 305.
56. ***Future Shock,*** Toffler. pp. 309-26.
57. ***The Condition of Education,*** 1986 ed., Joyce D. Stern and Mary Frase Williams, eds. Washington, D.C.: Center for Educational Statistics, U.S. Dept. of Education, 1986. pp. 84-85.
58. ***Condition of Education,*** 1986 ed. pp 62-65.

59. ***Condition of Education,*** 1986 ed. pp 66-67.
60. ***Condition of Education,*** 1986 ed. pp 66-67.
61. ***America in the 1980's,*** Thomas. pp. 48-49.
62. "Monitoring the Future: a Continuing Study of the Lifestyles and Values of Youth," Jerald G. Bachman, Lloyd D. Johnston, and Patrick M. O'Malley. In ***Research on the Quality of Life.*** ed. by Frank M. Andrews. Ann Arbor: Institute for Social Research, Univ. of Michigan, 1986. pp. 215-34.
63. ***Condition of Education,*** 1986 ed. pp. 162-63.
64. ***Statistical Abstract, 1984.*** p. 144.

Chapter Two

The Structure and Governance of American Public Education

Chapter Two

The Structure and Governance of American Public Education

SOME OF THE problems of American education today arise from the way in which it is organized throughout the nation. The lack of a central national system, the great variety between state systems, the vagaries of local control all impact sharply on the total educational picture. In this chapter we will look briefly at the structure and governance of American education. What are their philosophical and historical roots? What are the repercussions of the present day system? What may be done to improve the way in which education is organized?

A philosophical perspective

Let me tell you a little about the Trobriand Islands. Located in Melanesia north of Australia and a bit to the east of New Guinea, they housed (until World War II and the influences of "modern culture" destroyed it) a most interesting society. In the early portion of the twentieth century that society was visited by Polish anthropologist Bronislaw Malinowski, and it is largely through him that we have gained our knowledge of Trobriand life. The information below comes primarily from his book, *Sex and Repression in Savage Society.*[1] The fascination with Trobriand life stems from the fact that for Trobrianders there was no connection between sexual intercourse and childbirth. Thus, from the biological viewpoint, for these people there was no concept of the word "father." For them children were inserted into the mother's womb by the spirit of a deceased kinswoman. Infants were spiritually, not physically, conceived, and as products of the spirit world, they were held in a kind of religious reverence.

In such a state of affairs, one can easily understand that the society was matrilineal. That is, kinship was reckoned through the mother and the mother's family. The concept of motherhood was, of course, acknowledged since the baby could be seen emanating from the mother. The concepts of brother and sister were also acknowledged. Babies of the same mother were siblings born from a common human being. Likewise, the concepts of husband and wife were acknowledged. Couples paired off and shared a common house. In most aspects, then, the Trobriand family was like the Western family. The difference was simply that the husband of the wife was not regarded as the father of her children.

I say "simply." Actually, that is quite a distinction. Let us consider why. In the Western family, children are understood to be the product of the union of husband and wife. It is a matter of biology, not religious speculation, and thus the children are considered in both the legal and philosophical sense to be the "property" of mother and father. In the Trobriands, children were treated much more as "gifts" from a source with supernatural and mystical origins. The husband felt no ownership of them at all, and while the mother acknowledged them as hers, she did so not because they were the products of *her* will—*her* desire to have them—but because they had been given *to* her by the spirit world.

The repercussions of these differences on the way in which the children of both cultures could grow are dramatic and profound. In the Western world, children are forced to do their parents' bidding. They are weaned, toilet trained, schooled, told how and how not to develop by their parents in virtually every area from sexual behavior to career choice. Moreover, they are controlled in these ways by adults who feel it their *right* to exercise that control, and to do so through a variety of means which may include economic coercion and violence as often as they include reason and kindness. As the Western child reaches puberty and begins to venture toward the autonomous world of an adult, the conflicts between his or her will and the control exercised by parents or parent figures (schools, legal authorities, etc.) frequently become sharper. As we know, they can result in all kinds of problems from occasional hostility, to crime, to adolescent suicide.

In the Trobriands, childhood growth tended to be a good deal less harsh. Because the children were not considered "possessions" in the Western sense, the attitude of adults toward them was far more benevolent. They were given more space, more time, more natural freedom to develop. They were weaned later, cleansed without much of the shame or guilt often associated with Western toilet training. They were instructed in skills not because they were going to live out the unfulfilled dreams of a mother or father, but because they themselves needed the skills. They were not repressed in the exploration of their sexuality because any resultant pregnancy was not seen as the "effect" of a sexual "cause." Rather, it was a new spiritual visitation bestowed on yet another Trobriand maiden. As a result of the more harmonious relations between Trobriand children and their parents, Trobrianders experienced far less than their Western counterparts by way of the crime, violence, and self-destructive behavior we often associate with our young.

On the other hand, Trobrianders did not build bridges, invent cars and TV sets, develop aspirin or write novels. In fact, it has been suggested by more than one great psychologist that many of the benefits of what we call "civilization" derive from civilization's rechanneling of the energies it represses. In less repressed societies, there is thus less dynamic development.[2] So to say that Trobriand life had fewer social problems than Western life is not to advocate that we level our great cities to the ground and return to the forest primeval. Why then this story of Melanesia? What has it to do with modern American schooling?

Much. I tell you the story of the Trobriand Islands to say that what we do and what we have done historically in the organization of our schools stems in large measure from our desire to control our children and from a psychology which justifies that control in legal, moral, and physical terms.

How the psychology of parental and societal control visits itself upon our schools can be seen again and again. At the instant I am writing this, over the radio comes the newscast of a legal battle in the nearby city of Elmira, New York. A resident is petitioning the library for the removal of a book on adolescent sexuality stating that it encourages adults to engage in sex with children. In the school at which I teach, a parent demands that his child not be graded in music because he does not want the child to be a fine arts major in college. In Tennessee, a controversy rages between people who wish to teach Darwinian evolution and people who wish their children to believe that the world was created according to the Book of Genesis. We shall see in the pages below that such conflicts have deep historical roots in America.

They emanate from fundamental religious and economic concerns and extend far beyond the limits of family, school, or local community.

We will return to discuss many of the individual instances above in later chapters. For now I urge you not to leap to conclusions as to how problems in sex education, grading, or teaching biology may best be handled. Simply be aware that they exist and that they stem from a culture whose fundamental psychology forces them upon us. Whatever the details for working out any single conflict may be, there is a more basic point to consider at this stage of our investigation, and it is this: none of these conflicts will be successfully resolved until we replace the attitude which seeks to "control" our children with one which seeks to "inform" them.

In a free society such as ours, in order to remain free, whatever the course of action our citizenry decides to take relative to a given issue, citizens cannot successfully make those decisions from a position of ignorance. An educational system which, on the one hand, withholds information because those in control think it to be contrary to their own beliefs, or, on the other hand, propagandizes information because those in control wish to promote their own beliefs, will soon destroy the ability of its children to think and act for themselves. It is within this philosophical context that we will view many of the issues which attend modern American public education, and it is with this perspective that we turn to the historical roots of present-day educational structure.

Some historical roots of American educational governance

> The powers not delegated to the United States by the Constitution, nor prohibited by it to the States, are reserved to the States respectively, or to the people.

So reads the Tenth Amendment to the Constitution of the United States, the last of the ten original amendments, our "Bill of Rights." By the terms of this amendment, because no provision for the control and maintenance of education was delegated to any federal authority, each state claims the power to educate its own people. How we came to such a Constitutional end and what we have done since the adoption of the Constitution are matters of important historical study, and with apologies to educational historians who devote whole volumes to such study, we shall try to trace through the main points of our educational development in the pages immediately below. Bear in mind as we do that we are not looking at the development of educational subject matter. That will come somewhat later in this text. We are, rather, looking at the development of educational governance, at the structure of who controls and runs our schools.

We will divide this excursion into five historical eras: colonial times; the ages between the Revolutionary and Civil Wars (1776-1865); the era stretching from the Civil War to World War I (1865-1918); the years between the two world wars (1918-1945); and the post-1945 era.

Colonial times. It must be remembered that the early colonial settlers were people who felt the sting of religious persecution in the various European homelands from which they had come. For them it was of paramount importance that the religious organizations to which they belonged be free to pass that religion unhindered to the children of the colony. The resultant social and economic makeup of colonial society was thus quite dependent upon placing educational control in the church which dominated any particular region.

Since the colonies were not free and autonomous political agents, it was up to the king, colonial governor, proprietor, or colonial legislature to grant educational charters to the churches of any given locale. These charters enabled the churches to establish local schools, to set the curricular content of those schools, and to staff them with teachers who would impart the curriculum in such a way as to maintain the religious indoctrination of the colony.

Modifications to the church-dominated system of education began to appear when settlements arose whose primary point of view was economic survival as opposed to religious indoctrination. A group of settlers, for example, would leave the "mother colony" to establish a secondary village or simply to strike out on their own. Their sociological thrust, so to speak, would not so much be the establishment of an unencumbered worship environment as the survival of a new social and economic community. To insure that survival, it was very important that the youngsters of the settlement be taught the trades and skills which would keep the new community going. It is not that religious training suddenly did not matter, but that teachers schooled primarily in church-related curricula would not be the best choices for imparting the more immediate vocational skills needed by the new settlement.

For such communities charters were gradually granted not to the church which ministered to the community but to the town itself or to a private agency whose function it was to provide the community with educational services.

Whether chartering occurred through church, town, or private agency, the clear tradition being established in colonial life was that the control of education was to be vested in organizations which were responsible and responsive to the local community. Serving the immediate needs and philosophies of that community was the prime—at times, the sole—function of education.

In order to insure that the interests of the local community were, in fact, being served, it soon became customary to establish a mechanism for overseeing the educational process. More often than not, the mechanism proved to be a board of governors with the power to regulate curricula, hire or fire teachers, and levy school taxes from both the town and the individual parents. This body was the forerunner of our present-day board of education. In some communities the powers of the board of governors were vested in one person, and that person became the forerunner of our modern superintendent.

For the early colonial years, the systems of school governance above worked well. They did so principally because early communities were homogeneous in makeup. However, as Butts and Cremin write, "It very soon developed that government control of public schools could not be achieved in a colony where mixed religious beliefs developed into hostile sectarian rivalry."[3] For communities such as these, it fell more and more upon private schools to educate the young in ways compatible with parental will and the desire of parents to instill their values and their wishes in their offspring. The private school system grew in importance, reaching a peak in the years just prior to the Revolution.

From the Revolution to the Civil War (1776-1865). The preeminence of private schooling may have fit the character of colonial America, but once the colonies became an autonomous nation, it was no longer a viable system. The reason was a growing, abiding commitment to the preservation of the democracy which had been established by the war.

From the end of the Revolution onward into the nineteenth century more and more people came to see education not simply as a way to reflect the values of a local community but as the process by which the citizens of a free democracy might be trained to accept and carry out the duties of citizenship. The general argument of the times was that if an individual failed to receive an education, it was not only he but the entire society which would suffer, for how could an ignorant citizen read, or think, or vote for the things upon which the fate of the nation might rest? This new experiment in human society, this democracy, had come with a price, and it was the maintenance of an enlightened electorate.

No one in the post-Revolutionary era saw these issues more clearly than Thomas Jefferson. Not only did Jefferson see the necessity of an educated electorate, he also saw that because the Constitution clearly separated the powers of state from those of church, education would have to come from public rather than private sources. In 1779 Jefferson petitioned his native state of Virginia for a revision of its educational system. His petition included a comprehensive plan from elementary school to university which outlined not only the structure of a public educational system but its curriculum as well. Though his ideas met with opposition from special interest groups, eventually most of them were adopted and became a paradigm for other states to follow.

Jefferson's model was taken up by some of the most prominent educators of the time. Men like James Carter, Henry Barnard, and Horace Mann argued that not only should public education be in the control of state and local governments (as opposed to either the federal government on the one hand, or private religious and sectarian agencies on the other), but also that it should be supported by public funds raised through the tax structures of the community. Mann particularly argued that the state should be dominant in its relationship with smaller jurisdictions, that it should be a centralized force which would set the minimum curricular and financial standards for every local district.

It was not surprising that Mann's ideas met with strong opposition from special interests (both sacred and secular) who feared that state controls would ultimately erode their power. Charges were leveled that centralized education would "Prussianize" learning and run the risk of establishing totalitarian regimes. To some extent, as we shall see, the battle between state and local control has never been resolved, but the general trend of post-Revolutionary governance was inexorably toward Mann's position.

With ordinances in both 1789 and 1826, Massachusetts officially adopted publicly funded education. Taxes were levied, schools built, curricula established, overseeing committees appointed, individuals hired all according to a centralized state law. Vermont followed suit in 1854, Connecticut in 1856. In addition to laws establishing public educational systems, many of the states began to create central state boards of education and state superintendencies to regulate and coordinate local districts. New York State created the first superintendency in 1812, and between 1830 and 1850 most of the northern and some southern states followed New York's lead. In 1784 New York had established the first state education board, its Board of Regents, and that, too, became the model for others to emulate. Massachusetts created an eight-person board in 1837 with Horace Mann serving as Secretary. Virginia, South Carolina, Vermont, and Missouri quickly followed.

Concomitant with these developments was a growing trend to put into local law an expression of the desire to separate church and state authority with respect to education. Again, New York led the way with legislation passed in 1842 stating that no school in which any religious sectarian doctrine or tenet was taught would be eligible for public funds.

The one region of the post-Revolutionary nation where state centralization occurred both more slowly and more cautiously was the South. A slave economy and an agricultural base requiring decentralized settlements placed unique pressures on the South, pressures which made it, as Butts and Cremin write, "a section apart."[4] The enormous importance of local control to the southern way of life manifested itself, as far as education was concerned, in the dominance of county authority over state authority. To some extent this was also true in rural northern areas where decentralized settlements made state agencies less prominent because many rural communities were less accessible. The early pattern of southern education with its strong local controls and its relegation of blacks to the status of second-class citizens would not change substantially until well into the twentieth century. There are arguments that in some respects it has not changed to this day.

From the Civil War to World War I (1865-1918). The fifty or so years from the Civil War to World War I were characterized by urbanization, a growing population marked by a large influx of immigrants, an inexorable movement to the West, and a tremendous increase in industrial capacity. Each of these factors played its part to influence the development of American public education.

Where states and the local communities within them grew in population and complexity, the prevailing view of educational governance was that the state should assume responsibility for providing whatever would meet the complete needs of its people. In the regions of the nation which were newly settled where statehood was newly acquired and central state governments newly formed, the prevailing attitude was one of partnership. The state should play a limited role with respect to funding and curriculum development while leaving the bulk of educational authority to local jurisdictions. Finally, where local control was fiercely guarded (for example, in land freshly pioneered, rural, or tied to the traditions of the Old South), the prevailing view was that any state control was a violation of the fundamental rights of parenthood.

With predictable opposition from special interest religious and sectarian groups, the vast majority of American communities subscribed to the second view while continuing to build stronger central state education agencies. An 1880 study by the Federal Bureau of Education indicated that each of the then thirty-eight states of the Union had a chief educational officer either directly elected or appointed by some state official (a governor, state legislature, or state education board). Twenty-four of the thirty-eight states had by 1880 formed state boards of education to work with the chief educational officer in overseeing public schooling.[5]

Local districts continued to be administered by local boards of education on either a town or county districting plan, and there were thousands of them across the nation. As communities grew, the clear trend for both economic and political reasons was district consolidation. It was a trend which, as we have already noted, continued into the modern era when the 100,000 or so districts existing at the end of World War II shrank to the 16,000 that exist today.

It was during the years between the Civil War and World War I that many of the cities across the nation, now fleshed out by higher birth rates and waves of immigration, established systems of educational governance which could administer learning in large, complex, urban settings. City boards varied greatly as an 1885 study from the Bureau of Education showed. Some had as few as six members; some as many as one hundred. Some, like Pittsburgh, had well-defined and somewhat restricted powers; others, like New York and St. Louis, had broad, almost absolute, authority.[6]

By the end of the First World War, American public schooling had pretty much defined the patterns of governance and structure which it would maintain throughout the century. Local boards and superintendents organized on a town, city, or county districting plan would shoulder the day-to-day running of the schools. States, led by statewide boards and chief state officers, would guide the local districts through the establishment of central standards and regulations. Where conflicts between state and local authorities arose, the state view would generally dominate. Educational funding would, like governance, reflect a partnership between state support and local property taxation. Finally, public schooling would remain free of influences from religious or sectarian groups.

With these tenets firmly in place, American public education emerged from World War I to face the challenges of the twentieth century.

Between the wars (1918-1945). The changes which awaited education in the years following 1918 were not ones of governance or structure. Rather they were ones which began to address through our school systems social and legal developments of dynamic, dramatic importance. No clearer examples of this trend exist than the struggle for equal education in the nation's black population and the insistence of private religious and sectarian groups on the right to educate their children free from governmental interference.

A desire for isolation from the international arena was not the only legacy of World War I. There was also a rekindled desire on the part of black Americans to achieve educational opportunities equal to those available for whites. The war had given many blacks a chance to work at jobs both in and out of the military which they would not have been able to obtain in peacetime economy. Ironically, the manpower shortage created by the war had forced America to eschew its own racism and tap the black population pool in ways quite different from those of previous decades.

Having spilled their blood shoulder-to-shoulder with white comrades, having assumed wartime occupations in many instances equal to white workers, it was only fitting that the nation they had helped "save for democracy" give to blacks equal educational opportunities after the fighting was over. Injustices which had been accepted before the war were now intolerable.

In both the North and the South, civil rights organizations began to attack the Ku Klux Klan with greater vigor and greater openness. In Washington, President Roosevelt began to speak with greater frequency against segregation in employment and schooling. The push against discrimination in education eventually made its way to the U.S. Supreme Court with the case of Gaines versus the University of Missouri in 1938. Here, under the doctrine of the Fourteenth Amendment that all citizens have equal rights before the law, it was argued that the University of Missouri was constitutionally required to provide law school training for Negro students because it provided such training for whites.

The Gaines decision did not address the phenomenon of separate educational facilities for blacks. There was nothing about it which required integrated education, only equal educational opportunity. However, it was a harbinger of the 1947 Civil Rights Commission appointed by the Truman Administration and the landmark Supreme Court rulings of 1954.

In the area of public versus private education, battle lines were being drawn which would lead to significant developments in the years between the First and Second World Wars. Between 1917 and 1921 thirty-one states passed laws requiring public education to be given using English as the language of instruction. In 1919 the state of Nebraska went a step further by passing a law requiring the use of English in its private schools as well. The law was challenged with the case (Meyer vs. Nebraska) eventually reaching the U.S. Supreme Court in 1923.

The Court declared the law unconstitutional, stating that the Fourteenth Amendment guaranteed the right of teachers and parents to educate children in the "common occupations of life" (in this case, the speaking of German as a primary language). The ruling went on to say that, while states have the right to compel attendance at some school and to establish reasonable regulations for *all* schools, they could not interfere with the parental right to educate children in private religious or cultural doctrine.

A similar case (Pierce vs. the Society of Sisters) came to the Supreme Court in 1924 from the state of Oregon. Here, in order to be accorded the right to attend private, parochial school, the state law mandated that each child pass an examination given by the county superintendent. The court struck down the law, declaring that it unreasonably interfered with the right of parents to direct their children's education. "Rights guaranteed by the Constitution," declared the court, "may not be abridged by legislation which has no reasonable relation to some purpose within the competency of the State."[7]

These early decisions were an augury that the legitimate protection of constitutional liberties could and would be used as a means of preserving two educational systems in the United States, one public, the other private. While some people applauded this development, many prominent educators saw it with apprehension. J.L. Childs of Columbia Teachers College and James B. Conant, the President of Harvard, were particularly outspoken on the issue. They opposed the public/private schism not because they wished to abridge civil liberties. Far from it. Both men and many of their colleagues were passionate civil libertarians. Rather they feared the creation of a dual system which would permanently divide American society into classes cut along both religious and economic lines. Indeed, their fears were justified, for those parents either passionate or wealthy enough to remove their children from public school to avoid curricula, or association with minorities, or (in recent years) exposure to declining standards, have continued to do so.

As we shall see, neither the issue of minority rights in education nor the preservation of private schools diminished in prominence as the century moved on. If anything they intensified and were joined by other thorny problems in the post-1945 era.

The post-World War II era (1945-present). If any word typifies the condition of educational governance since 1945 that word is probably "conflict": conflict between state and local authority, conflict between federal mandate and private inclination, conflict between board of education and superintendent, conflict between student and teacher, union and taxpayer, parent and administrator. Not so much in the structure of public education but rather in the push-pull between factions intent on controlling educational content and practice, we have created an environment of increasing tension. Exacerbated by sociological and political polarizations, these tensions have surfaced with ever greater frequency in our state and federal courts. America has become a litigious society, and it is thus often in our legal systems that we find the manifestations of present-day educational trends. In the pages below we will investigate some of the more prominent ones, but let us begin more benignly with a look at present-day structure.

Oddly enough, in the area of educational organization, our system has been surprisingly stable. The make-up and selection of our state and local governing bodies have remained pretty much the same since 1945, though, as we shall see, there is considerable variety from region to region.

State boards and chief state officers continue to be the preeminent governing agencies of the American system. Every state but one (Wisconsin) has a state board, all states have departments of education, and all have some kind of chief state officer (a commissioner, superintendent, or overseer).

The most common governance structure today is one in which a governor, elected by the people, appoints a state board which in turn appoints a chief officer. This system has been adopted in fifteen states including Alaska, Connecticut, Iowa, and West Virginia. In eleven states the voters elect the state board directly. The board then appoints a chief officer. This system is used in Alabama, Hawaii, Kansas, Ohio, Utah, and Nebraska, among others. In yet another model, the chief officer is elected while the state board is appointed by the governor. This system is used in twelve states, including California, Kentucky, and Wyoming. Five states have both board and chief officer appointed by the governor (Maine, New Jersey, Pennsylvania, Tennessee, and Virginia). Florida, Mississippi, Wisconsin, New York, Louisiana, and South Carolina have governance structures unique to themselves.[8]

The number of members on state boards varies from state to state as does the length of a member's term of office. In no case are there more than twenty-four members, and in no case is the term less than four years. Perhaps of more importance is the constituency of state boards. 66% of the membership were men in 1983. 88% were over forty years of age. More than 90% were college educated, with 56.8% holding graduate degrees. 84% were Caucasian, 10% black, 2.8% Hispanic, 2.3% native American, and less than 1% Asian. Most were managers, administrators, or professionals (74.1%). Two-thirds were full-time workers. 25% were either retired or out of the work force. 12.1% were homemakers.[9]

On the local level, district boards of education exhibit an enormous variety in terms of their membership and the factors which go into their selection. In some instances the characteristics of a local board are determined by state regulation. In other cases, local ordinance or a combination of state and local regulations is used. With fifty states and sixteen thousand districts, the picture of local educational governance nationwide is a patchwork quilt of statistics. Here are some examples.

In 1985, over 93% of local board members were white. Only 3% were black with even lower representation for Hispanics, American Indians, and Asians. 64% were men, 76% were over the age of forty, and almost 80% had annual incomes greater than $30,000.

54% of boards presided over districts which were characterized as "suburban" with 35% ministering to "small town or rural" areas and only 11% to "cities." The overwhelming majority (95%) was elected rather than appointed, and 82% of our local board members served terms of office ranging from four to eight years.

36% served on five-member boards; 35% on seven-member boards; 33% on nine-member boards. Over 71% of local board members were college graduates. 70% were not compensated for their board work, and surprisingly well over 60% served even though family members were district employees.[10]

The qualifications for local board membership are even more variable. Generally, the one common thread among all 16,000 school districts currently governed by a local board of education is the requirement that each board member be a resident of the district. However, the length of time used to determine residency differs markedly from state to state. In Alaska, it is only thirty days. In New Jersey, it is two years. In Connecticut, while state statute says three months, local town ordinance may override to reduce that figure. In Texas, it is six months in the district but one year in the state. In Missouri, residency requirements differ depending on whether the district is rural or urban.[11] There are almost as many variations as there are states.

Other determinants for local board membership found from district to district are age requirements, voter qualification regulations, financial disclosure regulations, U.S. citizenship status, and general fitness criteria. As one may imagine, the national picture as regards these items is a hodgepodge of statutes.

Alabama, for example, has no financial disclosure requirement for board members, but a statement must be filed for any campaign contribution of ten dollars or more. California requires all board members to file personal financial statements on all sources of income, including gifts and loans. New York does not require personal financial disclosure, but for board candidates who receive more than five hundred dollars in campaign contributions, disclosure statements must be filed ten days before and twenty days after the election.[12]

In Colorado, the law states that to run for a local board of education, one must be eighteen years of age or older, a qualified and registered voter, and a U.S. citizen. In Kansas, the law simply requires that one be over eighteen. In New Jersey, board candidates do not have to be registered voters, but they must be over eighteen, U.S. citizens, and able to read and write. In South Carolina, they must believe in God.[13]

Perhaps even more significant than the great variety of statutes is the fact that no state requires any special training or knowledge of education for candidates seeking school board office.

To add to the confusion, many educational jurisdictions have appointed as opposed to elected board members. While thirty-one states and the District of Columbia elect their local board members in all districts, eighteen states have local governing systems which are elected here and appointed there. In one state, Virginia, all districts have local board members appointed either by a city council, a selection commission, or a board of supervisors. Generally, appointments are made in larger jurisdictions (large cities or counties), and they are usually made by a chief government official (a mayor, for instance) or a chief governing body (such as a city council).[14]

The debate over whether appointed boards perform better than elected boards is one of those modern conflicts of governance which has dogged education in the post-1945 era. Mark Hurwitz, former director of the New Jersey School Boards Association, comments that voters in a school district really do not have the direct *right* to choose local board members either by election or appointment. "It is the state legislature that prescribes the method of selection because, from a technical point of view, school board members are state rather than local officials," he writes, and goes on to say that, while appointed board members are often more competent, neither selection method "guarantees" a good board.[15]

District superintendents of schools—most of them white males over the age of forty—have continued in the post-1945 era to act as the chief educational administrator on the local level, though as we shall see they are subject to pressures from a variety of union, social, and political sources.

Generally, superintendents are more comprehensively trained now than in past years. A 1982 study showed that over 33% have degrees at the doctoral and post-doctoral levels as compared with only 15% in 1971.[16] Surprisingly, however, this increased training has not led to longer tenures of office. While superintendencies are more stable than most cursory opinion suggests, there has been a decline in the length of time superintendents remain in a given district. In the early 1970's the average was 6.5 years. By 1982 that figure had dropped to 5.9 years, just a bit longer than the 5.4 year average of a local board member.[17]

This decrease in tenure-of-office at a time when superintendents are experiencing a marked increase in academic training is one of the indicators that there are factors outside of the governance structure of post-World War II schools which are having an unsettling influence. Now that we have viewed that structure a bit, it is time to address at least some of those factors which have led to increased conflict in our public school systems. We can begin with the superintendent/local board relationship.

F.M.Wirt noted in a 1976 study that while the relationship between local boards and superintendents had clearly in the past been dominated by the latter, in recent years superintendents have been held more and more accountable. He argued that the data suggest an erosion of the superintendent's power, a kind of "transformation of administrative authority."[18] More current research has supported Wirt's finding. The work of Cistone, Iannaccone, Lutz, Mitchell, Jennings, Zeigler and other prominent educational investigators reveals that relatively placid board/superintendent relationships in the pre-1960 years have developed into hotbeds of controversy due to accelerated rates of social change and politicization. As the society goes through its various paroxysms, expectations arise in the local district that national or regional issues will be addressed. When they are not—at least not to the satisfaction of local power blocs—conflicts erupt which create shifts in board/superintendent relationships even to the point of the replacement of personnel. The problems are exacerbated when board members not trained to deal with education or to see local occurrences as manifestations of national trends fail to react properly to local situations. Zeigler and Jennings state as one conclusion of their studies that any board will continue to be a sub-par democratic institution until we "provide it with the institutional linkage to the political process which it currently lacks."[19]

Recent major issues which have rent superintendents from their boards—attempts at racial balance, sex education, bilingual education, budgetary concerns, meeting state and federal mandates, prayer and creationism in schools, affirmative action policies, etc.—have pervaded most if not all of America's districts since 1945. Caught between legally mandated policies and personal opinions, between the desire to uphold the law and a temptation to inculcate a child or community with a preconceived viewpoint, many superintendents and boards have lost the ability to communicate effectively with each other. In the absence of meaningful dialogue, wrestling matches often arise to determine who will have the power to run the district and address the issues. Such power wars are in many instances conducted sub-rosa so that meetings which once had an air of cooperation become antagonistic proceedings with hidden agendas and unpleasant innuendos. In 1986, probably because each organization sensed a national trend in disaffected superintendent/board relations, the American Association of School Administrators and the National School Board Association combined forces to study the problem. A survey was conducted of superintendents and board presidents, and it was discovered that "lack of communication" and "lack of trust" were cited most frequently as elements most likely to undermine governance relationships.[20]

The push-pull between boards and superintendents surfaces in many more places than the NSBA/AASA survey. In 1982 Gordon Cawelti, the Executive Director of the Association for Supervision and Curriculum Development in Washington, D.C., published a study of urban superintendents and their boards. While nearly 80% of the superintendents gave their board members grades of "A" or "B," Cawelti warned, "Don't uncork the champagne just yet..." Superintendents also described board members as being politically ambitious and overly oriented to pleasing their constituency rather than to managing schools effectively. In addition Cawelti found that many superintendents as well as board members have in recent years been hamstrung by court rulings which have taken governance authority away from local personnel.[21]

Superintendent David F. Kipp of Byers, Colorado is less kind to board members in his reaction to Cawelti's assessments, perhaps because he is speaking of non-urban districts where board members are elected rather than appointed. "Isn't it grand," Kipp writes, "that urban superintendents think so highly of their employers?...In the interest of fair play, here's my own personal list of school board members who make life miserable for superintendents." He then goes on to describe "know-it-alls," "ax-grinders," "jellyfish," "trendists," "seekers of personal favors," members who want hiring/firing power over the professional staff, and members who can't keep their mouths shut.[22] Clearly, he depicts a frequently adversarial tone.

The debate over where local governance power should reside has become increasingly strident since 1945, and there is no shortage of evidence for this statement in current literature. In November of 1982, R. Winfield Smith, President of the National School Board Association in 1968-69, wrote the following: "The authority to control our schools has become embedded...in the superintendency...The contemporary balance between the school board and the superintendent is abominable."[23] Smith laments the fact that boards which in the nineteenth century protected education from corrupt politicians have gradually seen their power usurped by the professionals. He rejects the idea that the professionals are more able to deal with the technical nature of modern education. He writes:

> Education decisions are technical and should be left to the superintendent. We hear this notion voiced in many quarters, but there is little evidence to support it. Innovations popular among professional educators during recent decades—open classrooms, community schools, team teaching, and so on—have had little salutary effect on education. In fact, some of these concepts appear to have had an adverse effect on what students learn. In any case, it is clear that superintendents have no monopoly on wisdom.[24]

Smith is, of course, opposed by administrators who reject the notion that local boards are losing power, who see current trends more in the mold of the research by Wirt and Cistone (discussed above). Paul Salmon, Executive Director of the American Association of School Administrators, argues that educational governance is a partnership where ultimate authority between board and superintendent should be variable according to place, time, and issue.[25] James Kutkat, Superintendent of the community schools of Williamsfield, Illinois, takes a much more vigorous stand against many local board members. There are times, he claims, when board members must be stopped from committing acts which are improper or even illegal. Board members who react in knee-jerk fashion to shibboleths like "back to basics," those who would fire the coach for getting drunk on Saturday night without giving him due process, members who wish to cave in to misguided community pressure or who insist on preferential treatment for friends and relatives—these individuals for Kutkat must clearly be opposed.[26]

Kutkat's opposition to board members who abuse their position is not without some substantiation. Contemporary boards in many instances have clear lines to the power groups in their communities, and there are several studies which confirm that, as Peter Cistone writes, "Whatever the particular configuration of power in a given community, it has been demonstrated to have a conditioning effect on board behavior."[27] In extreme instances, where districts have become the fiefdoms of private citizens or power blocs, the pressure exerted upon local governance has been sufficient to cause calamities. Let us consider three examples which gained national prominence in the post-1945 era.

During the 1946-47 school year, the board and superintendent of McCook, Nebraska engaged in an arbitrary, politically-inspired round of teacher firings, most of them with no hearings or statements of appropriate cause. Community mass meetings, student strikes, protest petitions, and staff resignations ensued on a wide scale, following the board's actions. The National Education Association was called in to investigate, and eventually the McCook board was charged with neglect of duty and unethical conduct. Whatever restitutions were finally made, the board had succeeded in leaving its educational community in a shambles.[28]

In the same year in North College Hill, Ohio, the local board fired its superintendent for causes which were clearly motivated by political and sectarian religious concerns. District teachers resigned and students struck in protest. Local parents then petitioned the board for redress, and when the board stonewalled the parents, both the NEA and the Ohio Education Association were called in to investigate. Both agencies found that the board had acted in an unwarranted, tyrannical, and improper manner. By then, however, the district had already been torn asunder.[29]

A perhaps more famous case occurred in New York City during the 1966-67 school year. In an atmosphere of rising black militancy, community members in Harlem began to agitate for control of Intermediate School 201. Their aim was to assume a more direct role in the education of young blacks, particularly in the area of adopting curricula and hiring staff members more reflective of black views. The tumult became so great that the New York City Board of Education agreed in the summer of 1967 to create three "demonstration districts" to be run by local governing boards. It was the beginning of a decentralization movement in the city aimed at diffusing the power of the central board in favor of local boards theoretically more in tune with the wishes and needs of the immediate community. What happened is described by Diane Ravitch as follows:

> In short order the local boards became increasingly radical in their demands for total control and in their attacks on the "white power structure" and the predominantly Jewish teachers' union.[30]

The resultant chaos had to be mitigated eventually by state legislation which abolished the demonstration districts and dissipated any prospects of local control by autonomous community boards. Again, the state was forced to come to grips with what I regard as an axiom of the Western family structure and the psychology of childrearing which it produces: namely, that underlying the highfalutin talk about community involvement and educational excellence is the simple desire on the part of parents to control what goes into the minds of their children. It should not take a genius to figure out that in a community of fundamentalist Christians there is going to be a resistance to the teaching of the theory of evolution over that of creationism. It should not take great effort to know that in a city as racially and ethnically polarized as New York was in the late 1960's, the blacks of Harlem or the Jews of Williamsburgh, or for that matter the Italians or Irish of Queens, would want their ideas, their cultures, their philosophies to be the dominant elements of the curricula of their schools. The problem with acquiescing to power blocs, as the City and State of New York found out, is that it drives education down a long, dark road where knowledge and independent thought is sacrificed as a goal of learning in favor of locally controlled propaganda.

The case of IS 201 leads us into another area of conflict seen in schools of the post-1945 era, the conflict between local control on the one hand, and state and federal statute on the other.

In 1980, B.C. DeSpain, Superintendent of the Hollow Rock-Bruceton Special School District of Bruceton, Tennessee, wrote the following:

> For at least three decades now, local school boards have seen their decision-making powers reduced in favor of other agencies. This constant erosion has left boards with a great deal of responsibility, perhaps as much or more than they ever had, but with only a shell of the authority they once had. Many superintendents, including myself, frequently find that a board meeting agenda contains not a single item of moderate importance over which the local board has real control. No wonder board members are frustrated.[31]

In 1982, Byron Love, Deputy Superintendent for the Pontiac, Michigan School District, wrote the following:

> Local control is the result of a subtraction process. It is what is left after all the other agencies and factors have taken their share. For example, the board of a wealthy district serving an affluent, low-need student population doesn't worry about federal control and very little about state control. By contrast...a district serving a high-need student population which qualifies for many compensatory state and federal funds and, in addition, is under a federal court order to desegregate its schools has much less control over its operations.[32]

Finally, in 1982 C. Philip Kearney, Professor of Education at the University of Michigan, wrote:

> I begin with a simple premise. As we enter the decade of the 1980's, local school board members and administrators find themselves enmeshed in new and different, often confusing, patterns of decision making. In effect, they must function within a new context, a different context than in the past. And unless board members and administrators understand that changing context, that larger environment, they are going to be unable to effectively perform their tasks...They need to understand and take account of influences at work in the external environment. It is these influences, more than any other factor, that define the limits of local decision-making authority.[33]

Dr. Kearney went on to state precisely those external influences which have forced more and more decision-making out of the hands of local agencies—or, to put it another way—have forced local agencies to do the bidding of state and federal authority. They were:

1. Textbook publishers, national curriculum movements, external testing programs, and the powerful nationalizing influence created by the high mobility rate of American families

2. Collective bargaining with its ultimate objective of involvement of the bargaining group in the decision-making process

3. The increasing role of the state in matters of public education through state-mandated and categorical programs

4. The increasing role of state and federal courts in matters of public education

5. The expanding role of the federal government in education, particularly since 1965.

There are few people involved in contemporary education who would contradict the statements of DeSpain, Love, and Kearney. Quite the opposite. The literature fairly overflows with articles and research showing how power has shifted away from the local level since 1945. Michael Kirst, Professor of Education at Stanford University, for example, writes that since the recent spate of reports criticizing American public education ("A Nation at Risk," the report of the Twentieth Century Foundation, reports from the Carnegie Foundation, etc.), many states are scrambling to reorganize local education by one mandate after another. He notes that textbooks and curricula have been revised in twenty-one states, longer school days tested in sixteen states, pilot programs established for lengthening the school year from 180 to 200 days, and aid to education boosted by hundreds of millions of dollars in states from New York to California and Alaska to Texas.[34]

Michael Killian of North Texas State University reports that the state legislature of Texas has mandated sweeping changes in public education;[35] Gordon Ambach, former New York State Commissioner of Education, has presided over the "Regents Action Plan," one of the most comprehensive educational reform packages ever passed down from Albany to the local districts;[36] Larry Cuban of Stanford decries the wholesale, state-mandated changes brought about by California Law SB 813;[37] Beverly Anderson and Chris Pipho of the Education Commission of the States in Denver warn that new state-mandated testing is becoming the current means of forcing academic reform at the same time that it is blurring the lines between local and state control;[38] Evan Jenkins, reporter for the New York Times, writes, "If any clear pattern is discernible in American education today, it is a growing shift of responsibility back to the states;"[39] James Gutherie and Paula Skene of Berkeley see an escalation of state power in an atmosphere of growing educational politicization and declining local control.[40] On and on it goes.

It is not that the roles assigned to state and local agencies before 1945 have changed. In substance, they have not. The local board is still charged with the day-in, day-out running of the schools. It must still develop the local school budget, approve the hiring and firing of staff, provide facilities, approve contracts, set educational goals, and assess programs. The state must still define the size, kind, and power of local units; define the powers of local boards and superintendents; distribute aid and define the taxing formulas which will fund the schools; set requirements for length of school year and attendance; set minimum criteria for curriculum, facilities, and certification of personnel. None of this has altered radically since World War II. But to this list has come a host of regulations passed down from either federal or state agencies to the local level, regulations which effectively force local districts to adopt certain programs and spend certain funds.

Mandated testing and revisions in minimum curricular standards are but two of a long list of items now imposed on local schools by state and federal fiat. Developing programs which allow equal access by women to the educational mainstream, providing for the education of the handicapped and impaired, assuring equal opportunities for minorities in staffing as well as student participation, assuring minimal curricular offerings for districts with large percentages of their population on welfare or in poverty—these all require districts to adopt programs, expend funds, or go through the processes necessary to receive funds from state and federal sources. They may cause a wheelchair ramp to be built so that access to a building is provided for the handicapped; they may mandate the adoption of a hot lunch program for indigent children; they may lead to the recruitment of a minority staff member, alter a social studies course to include units on black history, require the establishment of a women's softball team where in 1930 or 1945 or 1960 there was none, establish procedures whereby emotionally impaired youngsters are mainstreamed into an elementary music or art class.

In the face of developments such as these, it is not surprising that many advocates of strong local governance have come into conflict with state and federal agencies. Consider the following thoughts presented by Joan Parent, President of the National School Boards Association, in a speech before the National Forum on Excellence in Education.

> State legislatures which delegate authority to local school boards increasingly are prone to whittle away many of the local options through a multitude of laws affecting local control of education. Having an increasing impact on American education at the federal level are laws and appropriations enacted by Congress, guidelines and regulations issued by the courts. Added to this mix are other important factors, such as teacher union power, parent power, student power, and the power of many special interest groups—all of whom in varying degrees challenge the legal authority of local school boards. In many areas of the country, collective bargaining agreements have resulted in limiting the school boards' independent decision-making, and therefore reducing control by the citizenry at large. Especially is this true in the area of personnel policies, class size, homework, and teachers' extracurricular activities.[41]

At the heart of many post-1945 educational conflicts and crises are federal court rulings which have impacted on the general area we call "civil rights." No assessment of current conditions would be complete without looking at one or two examples, the ramifications of which have already been alluded to in the quotes above. We begin with the hysteria which swept America in the years immediately following the Second World War, the hysteria created by the fear of Communist subversion.

Between 1945 and 1955, fanned by the histrionics of men like Senator Joseph McCarthy, people who were suspected of left wing sympathies came under close scrutiny. In the educational community many states passed so-called "anti-subversive laws," giving them the power to inquire about the beliefs and associations of teachers. New York's "Feinberg Law" of 1949 was a prime example. The law authorized the New York State Board of Regents to prepare a list of subversive organizations and then draw up a set of regulations giving local boards and administrators the right to conduct investigations of all school personnel with a view toward preferring charges against those who appeared to be associated with the organizations on the state list. The law was declared unconstitutional by a ruling of the New York State District Court in Albany handed down in November of 1949. However, exactly one year later the District Court decision was reversed by the New York State Court of Appeals, and in March of 1952, by a six-to-three vote, the law was upheld by the U.S. Supreme Court.

As if to contradict its own opinion, however, the Supreme Court also ruled in 1952 that it was unconstitutional for the state of Oklahoma to require teachers to take a loyalty oath as a condition of employment on the grounds that the Oklahoma statute violated the First and Fourteenth Amendments (Wieman vs. Updegraff).[42]

Such apparently contradictory court rulings are not unusual in the post-1945 era. The tremendous social and political pressures unleashed upon America in recent years have often established statutes which lead to confusion rather than clarification. When laws are passed or court rulings handed down which react to these pressures in seemingly nonsensical ways, we should remember that our legislators and judges—indeed, all of us—are not gods with the ability to hammer out perfect creations on the forges of government. We often stumble through the decades, victims of our prejudices and oversensitivities in spite of our good intentions. There is perhaps no clearer example of this than the post-1945 developments in equal rights legislation and the impact of that legislation on our schools.

In 1896 (Plessy vs. Ferguson), the United State Supreme Court held that the state of Louisiana could maintain separate railroad facilities for whites and blacks as long as they were equal. The "separate but equal" doctrine was upheld in the Gaines case of 1938 where it was applied to education. However, in 1952 the National Association for the Advancement of Colored People challenged that doctrine in perhaps the most important case of the post-1945 era, Brown vs. the Board of Education.

Here, the NAACP argued that it was unconstitutional to draw school district lines or assign children to local schools on the basis of race or color. In a landmark decision, the Supreme Court agreed, stating that "in the field of public education 'separate but equal' has no place. Separate educational facilities are inherently unequal."[43] The flood of rulings and procedures which followed Brown, as district after district wrestled with compliance, changed the landscape of American public education dramatically. Equal opportunity statutes; busing policies; equal employment laws; open enrollment policies; the extension of Brown to include not only race and color but gender, ethnicity, and age as unconstitutional criteria for discrimination—all these became ubiquitous issues across the nation. And they were not issues without great controversy, great conflict, and great challenge. Nor, in the wake of that challenge, were they issues without great confusion.

As we follow the tide of civil rights legislation downstream to the 1970's, we see that the Brown decision had aged into the national fabric, spawning as it did many affirmative action programs aimed at providing equal representation in schools and work places for minorities and women. Then came the case of Allan Bakke.

In 1974 Bakke had applied for admission to medical school at the University of California campus in Davis. He was denied admission as a white man even though his credentials and M-CAT scores were superior to some blacks who had been granted admission ahead of him. This puzzling situation had come about as a result of UC/Davis's attempt to comply with affirmative action statutes which had followed the Brown decision. In short, in order to *assure* equal representation of minorities on the campus, the university had adopted a dual admission policy. On the one hand, there were eighty-four student positions for which candidates competed in the normal manner. On the other hand, however, the university provided sixteen student openings available *only* to disadvantaged minorities. Given this system it was quite possible for a white applicant like Bakke to score higher than any of the sixteen minority selectees, yet still fall below the scores of the eighty-four non-minority candidates.

Bakke challenged his rejection in the courts, claiming that since his credentials were superior to blacks who had been admitted over him, he was being denied his civil rights because he was white. The California Supreme Court found six-to-one for Bakke, but UC/Davis appealed to the Supreme Court in Washington, D.C. The 1978 decision of the court was, to say the least, inconclusive. Four of the nine justices sided with UC/Davis in favor of their affirmative action program. Four justices sided with Bakke, holding that "reverse discrimination" had deprived him of his rights under Title VI of the Civil Rights Act. Justice Lewis Powell cast the deciding vote in a compromise position neither fish nor fowl. In substance, Powell declared that it *was* constitutional to allow race to be a factor in admissions policy but that the UC/Davis program constituted a quota system which was *unconstitutional.* He charged the university to admit Bakke and revise its admissions policy so that affirmative action might occur without specific minority quotas.

The number of policy changes wrought by the Bakke decision is anybody's guess, but in the area of affirmative action, cases still reach the Supreme Court today—now arguing that a minority or a woman has been abused, now arguing that a non-minority or a man has been denied due process because of preferential treatment to others. What is more certain is the reaction of American citizens to the whole issue, and in a nutshell, ninety percent are suspicious of affirmative action.

> While federal civil rights agencies shared a strong consensus about their mission, public opinion polls showed an equally strong consensus in opposition. In late 1980 (Dec. 5-7)...only ten percent of the Gallup Poll's sample believed that race, sex, and national origin should determine decisions about employment or college entry. The idea of group rights, regulated by government, apparently was a political concept that most Americans—even most blacks and women—disliked.[44]

We will return to this topic in a later chapter. For the present, we conclude our brief history of educational governance and turn to a comparison of American governance structure with structures in other nations of contemporary importance.

Comparisons of educational governance

Now that we have a better understanding of educational governance in the United States, it is possible for us to compare the American system with the systems of other nations around the world. Such comparisons are not simply exercises in academic rhetoric. America is in serious competition with these nations, competition which will determine her economic, military, and geo-political future. If we in America wish to truly understand why our trade relations, our military competence, or our global clout have waned since World War II, we will have to look at education for at least part of the answer—perhaps a very large part.

When Japan produces products which outsell ours, when West Germany develops an economy more vibrant than ours, when the Soviet Union begins to threaten our superiority in space technology, it is time for us to look at how they teach their kids, because when kids grow up they apply the skills and work habits of their childhood to the adult world. If, in comparison to the children of other nations, our children read less well, compute less accurately, think less skillfully, we should not be surprised to find our automobile sales slumping, our space shuttles exploding, or our strategic posture slipping.

That we lag behind the educational achievements of other nations is no longer a hypothesis but a proven reality. President Reagan's Commission on Excellence in Education reported that reality as the first factor placing America at risk in today's world. They wrote:

> The educational dimensions of the risk before us have been amply documented in testimony received by the Commission. For example: international comparisons of student achievement completed a decade ago reveal that on 19 academic tests, American students were never first or second and, in comparison with other industrialized nations, were last seven times.[45]

In looking at the governance and structure of the schools of other nations, we will be forced to view some of the curricular concerns of those nations as well, for in many of them curriculum, governance, and structure are inextricably bound. We will deal with our own curricula in a later chapter and at that time it will be important to recall some of the information presented below. Let us begin our comparison with some facts about our own system not touched upon thus far.

School structure in the United States. In America, children usually begin attending school at the age of five with some sort of kindergarten. In recent years there has been a strong attempt at earlier childhood education—particularly where there are working mothers who cannot be with their babies in the first four years—but as a rule, schooling begins at five. There then follow six years of elementary school and six years of secondary school leading to a high school diploma. After that, two-year college, four-year college, technical school, the armed services, or the work force are all possible choices. For students attending two-year colleges there are associate degrees. For those attending four-year colleges there are baccalaureate degrees. Finally, for those qualified there are post-baccalaureate degrees (masters, doctorates, etc.) in specialized post-graduate studies.

The way in which an American student chooses a college is variable and somewhat beyond the scope of this topic. Suffice it to say that college is a valued, commonly-sought option and that the nation has made an attempt (albeit in an uncoordinated and haphazard way) to provide colleges for every student from the academically gifted to the academically disadvantaged. But let us turn back to the public school years—the focus of our discussion—to see how the six secondary grades are divided.

The most common secondary grade structures are a 7-8 junior high/9-12 high school, or a 7-9 junior high/10-12 high school. There are other variations seen from time to time, however—for example, a 6-7-8 middle school/9-12 high school, or a 1-7 elementary/8-12 secondary program. The table below provides an accurate picture of the national grade structure in 1981.[46]

SECONDARY SCHOOLS IN U.S. — 1981

Grades	Number of Schools
7-8 and 7-9	5,890
7-12	3,677
8-12	516
9-12	8,175
10-12	2,583
Others	1,778
Total	22,619

Perhaps even more important than the actual grade structure of the secondary program is the curricular philosophy behind it. In this respect, the most universal American model is the comprehensive high school. This is a school, as Wayne Riddle writes, "serving all public secondary pupils in a given geographical area, whatever their academic ability or interests."[47]

During the post-1945 era, the grouping of students regardless of ability (as opposed to tracking them in special programs or schools by ability) has been a major source of educational debate. So has the grade structure chosen by a given school district. We will return to these topics in detail later in this text. For now, it is important only to note the phenomena and to realize that often the surface choices of a district belie a deeper reality or mask an ulterior motive.

Let me give you two examples. I knew of a district which had experienced a sharp drop in student population during the 1970's. This occurred at a time when inflation and high rates of unemployment were eroding its tax base and causing many of its businesses to shut down. All in all, it was a terrible economic scene—one common to many districts during the 1970's.

The ramifications of this district's predicament were far-reaching. Old political regimes were voted out of office, civic programs were abandoned, many teachers were let go either through the excessing of positions or through the elimination of job vacancies brought on by retirements.

In an effort to save educational expenditures on the one hand, and generate tax revenues on the other, a number of elementary schools were closed. Their buildings were sold and their pupils moved into the elementary schools which were kept open. At the time all this was occurring, the grade structure of the district was K-6 elementary, 7-9 junior high, and 10-12 high school (one of the more common national models).

Shortly after the closing of the schools, however, the district began to develop problems with overcrowding in the elementary schools which had been forced to absorb more students. The crowded conditions quickly led to artificially inflated class sizes with predictable results. Teacher work loads became unmanageable, individual attention to student problems declined, learning began to suffer, test scores began to drop, discipline in halls and classrooms began to erode. Clearly something was needed.

That something turned out to be a wholesale grade restructuring which was aimed at alleviating the crowded conditions. Elementary schools were changed from

K-6 to K-5. The 7-9 junior high schools were replaced by 6-8 "middle" schools. The district's two 10-12 high schools were consolidated into one large 9-12 high school. All of this required tremendous changes in curricula and scheduling. It required moving dozens of staff from here to there, and it required the expenditure of millions of dollars to retrofit the existing schools for their new populations.

When the problems and expense of the district's restructuring decision began to surface, the problem of overcrowding was replaced by a new problem—public relations. Having embarked on its scheme of closing schools and restructuring grades, the board and superintendent now had to justify the present state of affairs. They did so through a well-orchestrated campaign centered around extolling the educational value of the middle school concept. If they could sell that, the rest of the restructuring would be easy to accept.

So in came the experts and up went the banners. Seminar after seminar, lecture after lecture rained down upon the community telling everyone how bloc scheduling, team-teaching, and the 6-8 population grouping were really the way it should have been done all the time. The coffee and donut concessions of the district made a fortune.

Only one thing was wrong. The arguments weren't true. In fact, many teachers hated the concept. Bloc scheduling was inflexible. According to New York State, the sixth grade was to be treated as an elementary grade with self-contained classrooms and common branch teachers, while grades 7 and 8 were required to rotate classes in the manner of a junior or senior high. The original concept of blending grades 6 through 8 together was impossible under these strictures, so the middle schools really became two schools in one: a sixth grade class-bound elementary school and a 7-8 grade junior high.

The problems really became acute when the new Regents Action Plan, aimed at improving student performance, mandated wholesale program changes in grades 7 and 8. Now stuck with a 6-8 population and a virtually inflexible scheduling system, the district had to expend months of time and effort figuring out how to meet the new mandates. In the end, it applied to the State Education Department for a variance in the middle school program.

That all this might have been avoided with a more reasoned policy of school closing was beside the point to the educational governance of the district. The point now was to play "The Emperor's New Clothes" game, to convince the public and staff that things were really good, that temporary aberrations would disappear. To this day that is their policy, and to this day the community accepts it with the same discomfort experienced by the man who buys shoes which are too tight but suffers through wearing them because he's too stubborn to admit he made a mistake.

The moral of the story is that the grade structure you see may not be there for purely educational reasons. It may not involve education at all, but rather economics, politics, and public relations ploys. But this is not unexpected. People in power who make decisions and must at times take the heat for those decisions are bound to develop public relations gimmicks to convince the public that all things are wonderful. In some districts it has become an art form. I know of the superintendent of a district who puts on an opening-day-of-school show complete with staged lighting effects and a finale which consists of all the district's handicapped students limping or rolling in wheelchairs onto the stage as the high school band plays "You'll Never

Walk Alone." Most districts are not that gauche. Most simply hire a "community relations" expert or put out a newsletter to each taxpayer with a title like "Our Schools," telling them how wonderful things are and how much they're getting for their money.

But let me return to the other example of educational masking, the example of tracking. Remember that the ubiquitous secondary model is that of the comprehensive high school where—according to much post-1960 dogma—tracking is socioeconomically and psychologically stigmatizing. Without getting into the debate over whether or not that is true (we will discuss that later on), let us look at the reality. Again, I quote Mr. Riddle:

> In terms of curriculum, the almost universal American model is the comprehensive high school...In practice, however, at least four factors limit the comprehensive nature of school enrollment. First, the geographic area covered by a school may be rather homogeneous economically or socially, thus limiting the goal of mixing pupils of very different socioeconomic groups in each school. Second, many families may opt for private schools, reducing the comprehensiveness of public school enrollment. Third, in certain localities, "magnet" or other specialized secondary schools have been established which emphasize certain curricula (e.g., vocational education, science, the arts) and may have competitive entrance requirements. Finally, within most comprehensive American senior high schools, pupils are placed on one of (usually) three "tracks" on the basis of their interests and/or abilities.[48]

Certainly in my own experience Riddle's scenario holds true. I recall one high school which really played the tracking game to the hilt. It was a high school in a fashionable area, part of a community of education-conscious upwardly-mobile middle class Americans who were often caught between their professed penchant for egalitarianism and their desire to have each of their kids go to Harvard. The egalitarianism bid them adopt an outward policy of "no tracking" because it "stereotypes our children." The desire for Harvard, however, meant that when it came to *their* kids, they wanted enriched social studies, advanced placement English, a select choir, and all the other goodies which would make their children more competitive in the college jungle.

Fortunately, the State Education Department had given them the wherewithal to practice their peculiar brand of hypocrisy. The state allowed high school students the option of acquiring either of two diplomas: a "local" diploma for students not academically able to master the state syllabus or take the state examinations in English, mathematics, science, foreign language, and social studies; and a state diploma for academically capable students who would be able to handle the state exams. Consequently, the district developed three "tracks" for every single "major subject area" course: a "general level" class, a "state level" class, and—for those destined not only for Harvard but for the Supreme Court and the White House as well—an "enriched level" class which would go even beyond state standards.

Well, the district loved it. First of all, it made the parents of "state" and "enriched" kids properly proud. (Let's not discuss how it made the "general level" people feel.) Secondly, it insured that only academically capable students would take the state exams. This, of course, led to a higher passing percentage, a fact which was trumpeted in the "Our Schools" newsletter, making great PR and raising local real estate values. Finally, it did all this under the guise of an educational banner which read "But we don't believe in tracking."

Again, the moral is that educational surfaces in the post-1945 era are often deceptive. They require looking at not only the facts which are offered but those behind the scenes as well.

The question now before us is, how do other nations organize the structure and governance of their schools, and to those nations we now turn.

School governance and structure in England. Education in Great Britain is directed, as it is in almost every modern nation *except* the United States, by a central government agency. To be sure, in many nations this kind of centralized authority is flexible enough to allow varying degrees of local control, but nowhere except in America is there the lack of a unifying, coordinating national perspective.

Great Britain is in actuality the confluence of four autonomous nation-states: England, Scotland, Northern Ireland, and Wales. Thus, its educational governance reflects that structure. The British Ministry of Education and Science directs the education in England and Wales (though Wales has its own Educational Office as well). The Scottish Education Department ministers to the schools of Scotland. The Ministry of Education in Belfast oversees the schools of Northern Ireland. For the sake of our purposes here, we will confine ourselves to structure and governance in England.

By the provisions of the Education Act of 1944, the central Department of Education and Science gave direct administrative responsibility to Local Education Authorities (so-called "LEA's"). LEA members, who are appointed by the elected officials of town and borough councils, form various committees which act like American boards of education to oversee day-to-day schools of a given region. The task of running any particular school is given to the headmaster who functions like an American principal albeit with much greater authority in setting and carrying out school policy.

Though local governance does allow for some flexibility from region to region, national offices nonetheless distribute syllabi, see to teacher welfare, and determine teacher certification requirements. The national department also sends out inspectors (so called "HMI's") who see to it that money is spent wisely and that the central agencies are kept informed of local goings-on.

English students begin a six-year primary program at the age of five. Sometimes this takes place in a single school; often it occurs in two schools, an "infant school" for the first three years, a "junior school" for the next three. According to the Education Act of 1944 which mandated universal secondary education to the age of sixteen, students were to be tested after primary school to determine what kind of secondary education would be best. The results of the so-called "11-plus" exams would be placement in one of three types of secondary schools: a "grammar" school designed for university-bound, academically astute students; a "technical" school which provided vocational education; or a "modern" school which offered a general education for non-university-bound pupils. Tracking was thus built into the national system.

At the time this configuration was in effect (1944 to the late 1960's), most of

England's secondary schools were state-funded, though there were also many privately-funded independent schools as well as a number of so-called "direct grant schools," institutions run by private agencies but subsidized by public funds and required to meet governmental standards. All of this—structure, funding, curricula—began to change, however, with the passage of several education acts in 1965 and 1976. By these acts localities were required to replace the old secondary system with comprehensive secondary schools which housed academic, vocational, and general programs in one facility. In addition, public funding of direct-grant schools was withdrawn, forcing those schools to choose between becoming wholly public or wholly private.

There is no uniform grade structure to the present-day English comprehensive secondary schools. Some cover ages 12-18 in a single school, while others provide a facility for ages 12-16 with an optional two years (the so-called "sixth form college") for students who wish to prepare for university studies. There is even a middle school structure for ages 12-14, followed by a comprehensive upper secondary school for ages 15-18. What is universal now in England is the cessation of the comprehensive secondary school mandate.

For many reasons—economic, political, educational, sociological—when the present conservative government came into office in 1979, the comprehensive secondary directive was withdrawn in favor of one allowing local agencies to choose their own secondary structures (subject to the approval of the national Ministry of Education). Widespread dissatisfaction with the comprehensive structure led some districts to readopt the old system. Many more districts which were slow to convert to the comprehensive system were, as of 1979, relieved of the burden of doing so and opted to retain the old system. According to Riddle, by 1979 85% of the secondary students in England were in comprehensive schools. He lists the actual breakdown as follows:[49]

SECONDARY SCHOOLS IN ENGLAND — 1979

Type of School	Number of Schools
Comprehensive	3,203
Modern	536
Grammar	254
Technical	19
Total	4,012

To this picture, however, one must add the approximately 2,200 independent elementary and secondary schools of England. These private institutions account for about 6% of the nation's student population. While that is a small portion of the total, it must be understood that 15% of final-year secondary pupils, 25% of post-secondary pupils, and 50% of pupils attending Oxford and Cambridge Universities come from the private school sector. It is thus evident that a kind of "tracking by social class" is taking place in England. Those with the means to send their children outside the public sector do so with statistically elegant results in terms of college preparation and admission.[50]

The switch to comprehensive secondary schools in England was intended by its advocates to promote a more egalitarian atmosphere and an interaction between different social and ability groups in a nation noted for its class stratification. In reality, the comprehensive schools never fully realized that goal largely because students are still "streamed" by ability level in much the same way they are grouped in many American programs. In 1975 it was reported that 17% of all fourteen-year-olds were streamed on the basis of overall ability, 30% on ability in English, and 35% on other academic abilities. That compares roughly with a 1980 study of American high school seniors which found that 38% were grouped into "academic" tracks, 24% in "vocational" tracks, and 36% into "general" tracks.[51]

The educational direction of post-secondary students in England is thus greatly dependent (as it is in America) on the secondary stream into which one is placed. Students who receive education directed toward vocational training usually take the national exam for the Certificate of Secondary Education. Those who receive the general secondary curriculum usually take the so-called "O level" (ordinary level) national exam leading to the General Certificate. Both these tests are administered at age 16 (the end of the compulsory educational period). Students who wish to attend universities continue to study to age 18 when they take a series of "A level" (advanced level) national exams which not only accord them Certificates of Education but make them eligible for admission to the more prestigious institutions of higher education as well.

School governance and structure in France. By comparison with England, France has a good deal more centralized authority and control in the administration of public education. At the top of the governance hierarchy is a Ministry of Education headed by a National Minister who is an appointee of the Prime Minister. The National Minister of Education presides over a country divided into twenty-seven educational regions. Each region is administered by an "academy rector" who is responsible for elementary and secondary education, both public and private. The rector is represented in each locality by an "academy inspector" who works with local officials and school boards to oversee the daily operation of the schools.

About 50% of the revenue for schools comes from local taxation. The rest is provided by national allocations. This is true of private as well as public schools. Thus, in exchange for their public subsidies, the private schools relinquish a substantial amount of control to the national agency.

Education in France is compulsory from ages 6-16. A five-year primary program is followed by four years of compulsory secondary schooling. Following this program, additional secondary work is available at either a "vocational lycee" or a "regular lycee," the former offering two- or three-year programs of training for skilled trades, the latter offering a three-year academic preparation for students hoping to enter a university or advanced technical school. Though the "lycee" years are not compulsory, about 80% of French students opt to take them. The remaining 20% choose to enter the work force or engage in other vocational training after the compulsory period. Riddle reports that in 1979 45% of the total secondary population opted to attend the "regular lycee," while 35% opted for the "vocational lycee."[52]

At the end of the "lycee" years, students take one of three national exams. Eligibility for university is determined by passing the Baccalaureate exam. Eligibility for post-secondary technical study is determined by passing the exam for the National Technical Diploma. The third exam is for special occupations and, when passed, yields an Occupational Certificate. It is of some interest to note that there are substantial failure rates for these exams as the table for 1979 indicates.[53]

RESULTS OF LYCEE EXAMINATIONS IN FRANCE — 1979

Exam	Taken	Passed	Failed
Baccalaureate*	225,969	154,081	32%
National Technical Diploma*	97,400	59,800	39%
Occupation Certificates**	524,900	305,047	42%

* Taken at a "regular lycee"
** Taken at a "vocational lycee"

It is also important to note about French schools that they are for the most part comprehensive institutions which do not attempt tracking and offer substantial remedial programs for students with academic difficulty. During the first two years of the compulsory secondary schooling, students are monitored for achievement and ability. There is some tracking that takes place subsequently in the next two years, but there are few elective courses, and the differentiation between academic and vocational courses is not overwhelming. The real tracking occurs at the "lycee" level and beyond. Moreover, students are not assigned to a "lycee" by performance on an examination. It is the academy inspector who makes the determination, taking into account both teacher recommendation and family preference.

School governance and structure in Japan. The governance of Japan's education system was established through directives issued by U.S. Occupation Forces after the Japanese surrender at the end of World War II. Educational policy is directed through a central Ministry of Education to regional prefects and, finally, local jurisdictions. Though the American plan for Japan called for a centralized national agency (a feature notably lacking in America's own system), the aim of the plan was to concentrate real power at the local level.

The central ministry—divided into divisions for elementary and secondary education; higher education and science; social education; research; and administration—was in theory designed to pass laws, allocate funds, and set policy in only a general way. Prefects were supposed to control upper secondary education, special schools, teacher certification, private schooling, and textbook selection. Local agencies were to control elementary and lower secondary education through elected school boards.

In practice, the Japanese resisted attempts at meaningful decentralization. Candidates refused to run for local boards and attempts to support the schools through local taxation also failed. Today local boards are mostly appointed and educational funding supplied mainly from the central ministry, thus creating a kind of de facto shift away from local control. To be sure, there is less centralization than before 1945, and there are forces still pressing for greater local control, but for the most part Japan must be viewed as a nation whose educational governance is fundamentally centralized.

The grade structure of education in Japan closely follows one of the common American models, the 6-3-3 pattern. That is, following a six-year elementary program for pupils aged 5-11, Japanese students enter a two-tiered secondary program, each three years in duration. They first attend a lower secondary school (grades 7-9 for pupils aged 12-14), then an upper secondary school (grades 10-12 for pupils ages 15-17). In this system only the first nine years (that is, elementary and lower secondary schools) are compulsory. In reality, however, recent studies have shown that 97% of Japanese pupils attend upper secondary schools.[54]

The nature of the elementary and lower secondary schools in Japan is comprehensive with little or no ability grouping. This is due not only to the deliberate educational policy of promoting social egalitarianism but also to a deep conviction in the homogeneous Japanese society that effort rather than ability is the main ingredient in success. Teacher expectations are high for all children, and high levels of achievement are a noted feature of the great mass of Japanese students. We shall investigate in a later chapter the high correlation between teacher expectation and student outcome. For now it is important to see that in Japan, a nation which rose from defeat in 1945 to a position of economic and industrial power, high educational expectations are accompanied by high levels of student achievement.

While tracking is not a part of the first nine years of compulsory education, it becomes decidedly important as the Japanese child enters upper secondary school. Each geographical region has several upper secondary schools. These offer two types of curricula: general academic and vocational. Moreover, each school is ranked by the local population. Those schools which succeed in placing their graduates into topflight universities are ranked highest. Those which have low rates of post-secondary placement are ranked low. Placement in an upper secondary school is accomplished chiefly through examinations taken at the end of the compulsory period (ninth grade), though grades and teacher recommendation are also considered. Upper secondary exams are not nationally uniform but rather specific to each school. Those tests for the most rigorous upper secondary schools are thus apt to be the most rigorous tests.

There is an extreme amount of pressure to be accepted by upper secondary schools of high status. The stress and pressure brought to bear on the children taking upper secondary tests have been causes of widespread concern both within Japan and for those studying the Japanese system. These pressures, however, are even greater when, at the end of upper secondary school, students take the examinations for entrance to universities. It is here that Japan encounters its high rates of adolescent suicide and violence.

Ad hoc advisory councils have been at work in Japan since 1984 to try to address not only the problem of student stress but also the criticism that a preponderance of rote learning experience by most Japanese students has stifled their ability to think creatively and to form more balanced personalities. Some of these councils have suggested a revision of the upper secondary system to forego status-conscious tracking in favor of the comprehensive, heterogeneous approach. Thus far, this change has been successfully resisted.

Relatively current figures indicate that about two-thirds of Japan's upper secondary students are in schools emphasizing the general academic curriculum, while the remaining one-third are in vocationally-oriented schools. About 25% of the upper secondary population is enrolled in private schools, but it must be understood that in contradistinction to some private schools in the U.S. or England, private schools have relatively low status in Japan. Often they are alternative schools for students unable to obtain admission to a public school of their choice. Recently, however, some localities have opted for expensive private schools of high status, a development which is, as Riddle states, "disturbing to those who consider the current, 'meritocratic' system...to be economically egalitarian."[55]

School governance and structure in the Soviet Union. Oddly enough, in terms of its population and geographical organization, the Soviet Union is in two major respects much like the United States. First, it is a polyglot of diverse cultures, languages and ethnic backgrounds. Second, it is a nation made out of a union of separate republics in ways similar to the union of states in America. The systems of both nations, however, differ markedly in their treatment of these conditions.

Soviet educational policy is directed by the Central Committee of the Communist Party. Who holds office, what textbooks are used, what courses are taught, who is to serve on local education boards, how many students will attend technical schools or institutions of higher education—these and all other major policy decisions must meet the approval of the Central Committee. Two national education agencies administer Central Committee policy. A Ministry of Education coordinates the educational activities of the fifteen Soviet republics in the areas of elementary and general secondary learning. A Ministry of Higher and Specialized Secondary Education does the same for all universities, technical schools, and teacher-training institutes.

Governance authority passes from Central Committee to National Ministry to a central Ministry of Education in each republic. The republics then delegate authority along geographical lines depending on the demographics of the given republic. One may find an urban governance, a territorial or regional one, a local governing board, or combinations of all three, depending upon the geography and population distribution at hand. The important thing to remember about Soviet educational governance is that authority is exercised from the top down in a system referred to as "democratic centralism." Whatever policies are made at the local level, they must be sent up the line for regional, republic, and central national approval.

In contradistinction to the U.S., the people in the Soviet hierarchy of educational governance are selected rather than elected by direct popular vote. The Central Committee approves the directors of the republic ministries who, in turn, approve the directors of local agencies and the selection of local board members. Local boards select building principals who, in turn, select the teaching staff. Every school has an overseeing council made up of principal, teachers, and parents; and throughout the entire system there are inspectors who report on the running of the schools to their superiors in the educational chain of command.

Because of the diversity of Soviet culture, particularly the linguistic diversity, all primary and secondary schools are taught in the local vernacular with Russian added to the curriculum as a compulsory linguistic study. The cultural idiosyncrasies of each geographical area are also preserved as part of the educational curriculum.

It is in the specialized secondary schools and institutions of higher education that regionalisms disappear in favor of a homogeneous language and curriculum.

The grade structure of Soviet schools has undergone several changes in recent years. Just after the war, education was compulsory for eight years (ages 7-15) in a system which saw four elementary years followed by four secondary ones. In 1972 the eight-year program was changed to a ten-year one (7-17) in which the first three were elementary and the last seven secondary. Recent educational reforms in 1984 have extended compulsory education to eleven years, adding another year of secondary school to the national requirement.

In the area of ability grouping, Soviet education presents a complex picture. On the surface it appears that pupils attend comprehensive schools with little differentiation in course offerings for the first eight years of the program (that is, the three primary years plus the initial five years of secondary school). At this point students must choose to attend one of three kinds of upper secondary school: a general academic school, a specialized technical school, or a vocational school. According to Riddle, in 1980 60% of the upper secondary pupils were in academic schools, 10% in specialized technical schools, and 30% in vocational schools, assignments being made on the basis of previous academic record, test scores, and (to a lesser extent) student and family preference.[56]

There is a kind of elite substratum of pupils which belies this general picture, however. In several areas of study (e.g. mathematics, science, foreign language, drama, ballet, music, and military studies), there are highly select schools which siphon off the cream of Soviet talent. Admitting pupils only by rigorous examination, these schools vary in structure. Some may include training from grade two onward, some only on the upper secondary level. In all instances, however, the training is as advanced as possible. It is difficult to know what percentage of Soviet youth attends such schools, but they are available to all regardless of geography or socioeconomic considerations, and, like all Soviet schools, they are completely state-supported. One may assume these schools are something like the elite private schools of England or the magnet schools for gifted and talented children in the U.S. If that assumption is correct, then it is reasonable to estimate that they serve about 5% of the total school population. In any event, they stand in direct philosophical opposition to the comprehensive schools which—rather than being overly rigorous—exercise a good deal of grade inflation to effect a near-100% rate of passing.[57]

Following upper secondary school, Soviet students may go on to university, to polytechnical, or to vocational education. It must be understood, however, that the university programs are extremely difficult to get into. In all, only about 25% of the secondary population ever make it to a university campus and that group only on the basis of highly competitive national examinations and recommendations from key educational and political officials (teachers, trade union leaders, members of the armed forces, leaders of the Komsomol or Communist Youth League).

It seems apparent that the current Soviet system is desirous of strictly limiting university enrollment. However, it also seems that since about 1984 there has been a concerted effort to redirect the priorities of Soviet primary and secondary education.

The economy of the Soviet Union has in many ways failed to live up to the expectation of its progenitors. Shortages in food supplies and a noticeable lack of consumer goods (by Western standards) have been a recurrent theme of post-1945 Soviet life. The recent regime in Moscow has begun openly to acknowledge these conditions and with them to acknowledge deficiencies in Soviet workmanship and in the educational system which produces the Soviet worker. As early as 1984 articles calling for significant educational reform have appeared in the Soviet press, and there is little doubt that major educational changes are already underway.[58]

Riddle notes that many of the aspects of the new Soviet program are familiar topics of the American educational scene: "improving the quality, status, and pay of teachers; upgrading and updating of curricula and texts; improving career guidance; emphasizing developments in high technology; reducing class size; focusing on moral aspects of education; attempting to increase student discipline and improve attitudes toward labor (both as students and as future workers); reducing bureaucratic intrusions into the instructional work of the schools; improving teacher assessment activities; and increasing the quality and degree of implementation of educational research."[59]

The major focus of the Soviet reform package seems to be an effort to increase the vocational training of Soviet youth. Programs emphasizing work-study curricula and those seeking to give a new and higher status to the upper secondary vocational schools will be fundamental to Soviet education through the turn of the century. As opposed to the United States, where recent educational reforms have called for more rigorous academic training for all students, the Soviet plan is clearly seeking to reduce the number of pupils in secondary academic schools and to raise the proportion of youth in vocational and technical schools. Riddle estimates that the aim is to increase vocational school enrollment by 50% so that 60% of the total Soviet student population will be in educational programs designed to make them skilled workers. He also notes than an initial $14 billion has been spent on this effort with an additional $3.5 billion per year allocated for teacher salary increases alone.[60]

It will be interesting at the very least to see what fruits the Soviet plan will bear. It will be especially so since education in the United States seems to be taking a much different direction. While America has chosen to give less status to "blue collar" trades, the Soviets appear to be heading for a kind of vocational egalitarianism. Where this will lead in the decades ahead is going to be a matter of great concern.

School governance and structure in West Germany. Education in pre-World War II Germany, renowned for its quality, was greatly restructured following the Nazi surrender in 1945. Initially, when the nation was split into four occupation zones, four separate educational systems resulted. Ultimately, however, when the East and West German nations were formed, the constitution of 1949 brought a more unified system to the Western sector. This system (which includes West Berlin) vests each of the eleven West German Lander or states with autonomous control of the education within its territory. Each has a Ministry of Education which sets policies and standards from elementary school to university.

On the surface it thus appears that West Germany, like the United States, has no national educational governance. In reality, however, that is not really the case. In an effort to counteract the fragmentary effects of the Lander system imposed upon them, West German educational authorities succeeded in organizing a Permanent Conference of Ministers of Education. Through this conference, regional differences between Lander, while not eliminated, are reduced, and a national educational perspective is achieved. The one area in which localities seem indeed to be autonomous is the university system where independence and academic freedom have been coveted educational values dating as far back as the Middle Ages.

West German primary school begins at the age of six and lasts for four years (six years in the West Berlin system). Following elementary training, West German students are assigned to one of four types of secondary school. Assignments are made on the basis of grades, teacher recommendations, and achievement test scores. The Hauptschule is a vocationally-oriented secondary school, accommodating grades 5-9 in most of the Lander. In Berlin and the North Rhine-Westphalia districts, the grade structure is 7-10. The Realschule is geared to technical training for highly skilled professions. It begins at grade 5 (7 in Berlin) and lasts through grade 10. The Gymnasium is an academic institution serving pupils bound for university study. It begins at grade 5 (7 in Berlin) and extends all the way through grade 13. To these three types of secondary schools the West German system adds a limited number (about 200) of experimental Gesamtschule. The Gesamtschule are comprehensive schools offering the same curriculum for lower secondary pupils and differentiating only at the upper secondary grades. Some Gesamtschule do not differentiate curricula at any grade level.

As the information above indicates, tracking occurs early and is a pronounced feature of West German secondary schooling. There are, however, some flexibilities built into the system. All four types of secondary schools make some attempt to coordinate the early secondary curricula so that the first two or three years of secondary study constitute a kind of "orientation phase" with subjects fairly common to all schools. It is during this early secondary stage that students may more easily transfer from one kind of school to another. Such transfers become much more difficult and thus less frequent as the curricula differentiate at the upper secondary levels.

Graduates from the Gymnasium are admitted to universities on the basis of the Arbitur exam. By the time students take this exam they have already begun to specialize in advanced secondary studies at the Gymnasium. Typical areas of specialization are math, science, economics, social science, modern language, fine arts and music.

Graduates from the Hauptschule and Realschule may enter the work force, continue study in any number of post-secondary vocational and technical schools, or engage in a combination of work and post-secondary study.

Until 1960 or so, the great majority (70%) of West German students attended Hauptschule. In 1960 only 11% were in Realschule and only 15% in Gymnasium (the remaining 4% going to the Gesamtschule). By 1978, those figures had changed dramatically. Hauptschule now claimed only 40% with 24% in Realschule, 25% in Gymnasium, and 11% in Gesamtschule.

Critics of the West German system claim that it stereotypes children far too early in their development, that it offers only limited chances to move from one type of secondary school to another, and that it favors the higher socioeconomic strata by making Gymnasium and thus university teaching more available to the upper classes. Proponents of the system claim that it is the most efficient and effective way of exposing students to programs which fit their needs and abilities. They point to the high level of West German workmanship, the high standard of West German life and the resurrection of the West German economy from disaster in 1945 to a current position of great strength as proofs that the educational tracking of secondary students works well. Thus far, the proponents of differentiated secondary education seem to hold sway.[61]

Comments, suggestions and thoughts

Having digested a fair quantity of information about educational structure and governance in America and in some of the more powerful nations of the post-1945 world, the question now before us is, what do we do with the information? Are there adverse repercussions of present governance in our system and, if so, what can be done about it?

Before coming to grips with these issues, I would like to throw two names at you: Newt Gingrich and Rensis Likert. Gingrich is a member of the U.S. House of Representatives (R-Ga.) Likert is a widely respected social scientist whose work on organizational management has achieved much attention. Both have expressed views which I believe to be of fundamental importance in dealing with issues of change in public policy, and before going into my thoughts about educational governance, I would like to set the philosophical table, so to speak.

In 1987, on March 9th and again on May 11th to be precise, Gingrich was invited to address the American Jewish Congress. His speeches dealt with many topics but concentrated particularly on the nature of substantive change. If we are truly to move our society forward, he said—and I am paraphrasing—we must distinguish between cosmetic change and meaningful change. He gave the analogy of a person wishing to develop a way of going from Washington, D.C. to Los Angeles. Plans which get you to Baltimore or even Pittsburgh or Chicago, no matter how appealing or beautifully packaged, must be rejected because they simply do not address the goal—Los Angeles. If you follow such plans, you may arrive in Pittsburgh or Chicago, but then you'll have to go through another process and possibly several others after that.

In short, you must look for programs which meet your agenda. And there may be many of them. You can walk from Washington to L.A., take a bus, drive a car, fly a plane. It may be a private plane, a military plane, a commercial airline. It may even refuel in Pittsburgh or Chicago. What plan you choose may depend upon many things: your finances, how much time you have to spend, your fear or love of flying. But no plan which does not have Los Angeles as its goal is worth consideration.

At the outset of this book, I stated that many times reports on education are cosmetic because the reporter is representing part of the problem. In our topic here, you are not going to find much research by the National Association of School Boards or the American Association of School Administrators telling you that school boards or school administrators have screwed up American education. And if changes are proposed, too often the instincts of self-preservation will make them changes which go to Pittsburgh instead of Los Angeles.

When you read the suggestions below, therefore, realize that I am not shilling for any educational power bloc, and that my eye is on Los Angeles, not on a cosmetic way-station. Try to resist the temptation to say, "Oh, that can't work—it's too idealistic, too radical." Such quotes are the shibboleths which maintain the status quo and drive us deeper and deeper toward unsolvable crises. They are the way people consumed by either laziness, hopelessness, or the selfish desire to maintain their own power, try to control the progress of others. They were not the way of the founding fathers who forged a new republic and a new constitution; they were not the way of the Edisons or Beethovens or Einsteins who built from blank paper things which have reshaped the history of us all. As you read further, give a thought now and then to Mr. Gingrich.

Among the many theories of educational management and organization expounded and researched by Rensis Likert is one known as the "time-lag concept."[62] In this theory Likert states that a considerable amount of time is necessary for the managerial policies and styles of an organization to bear fruit. On the surface that seems a benign, perhaps even self-evident, observation. However, when coupled with what we know about the longevity of a board member or superintendent, it is an observation with important significance. The relatively small amount of time spent in positions of leadership by those in much of the educational governance structure, coupled with Likert's observation about the lag between the inception of a policy and its fruition, means that often boards of education and superintendents are presiding over situations not of their own making and presumably not to their own liking.

What does this imply for educational governance?—that "quick fix" approaches have little chance of success and that a continuous turnover in governance personnel condemns districts to be forever out of sync between performance and policy.

Reports from colleagues in the field tend to substantiate Likert's observations. In one district I was told of, there were three superintendents and several board turnovers in four years. In another there were also three superintendents and several board changes in a period of less than three years. The succession of altered policies, broken promises, outright misrepresentations, and wasted work in both districts led to wholesale staff demoralization and the poorest of education for the children involved. Likert's work did not reverse the damage, but it explained it and pointed to some solutions for problems in American educational governance. As you read further, think also from time to time about Rensis Likert.

Board member qualifications. In order to be hired in my present position, in addition to verifying my degrees, I had to meet the requirements for N.Y. certification as a teacher and an administrator. I had to have my urine checked (presumably for drugs—I was never told), my blood checked (presumably for contagious or venereal diseases—I was never told), and I had to pass a general physical. My references were scrutinized. My former employers were called. I'm not trying to play the martyr here. These are standard procedures applied to everyone in the education game. Everyone, that is, except members of the Board of Education.

I am not against what I had to do to be acceptable in the eyes of educational governance, although, as I will discuss in later chapters, much of the training necessary to win my credentials was entirely inappropriate for the jobs I have held. But that aside, I am very much in favor of credentials for professionals. What I find incomprehensible and unconscionable is the fact that any boob off the street can run for a school board. That I have known many a boob who has won election is less to the point than the inconceivably inept system which has allowed incompetents to come to power.

We are told by the hundredfold—and it is in my mind an accurate tale—that education has declined mightily since 1945, and particularly since 1965. The blame has been placed on teachers, on students, on society, on government, on parents. I've said before, and repeat here, there is blame aplenty for all to share. But I wish to point out that the decline has been accompanied by greater local board involvement, by less power in the hands of superintendents, by more power in the hands of lay boards. For me the research in this area is quite clear. True, local boards have been inundated by hosts of new regulations, union and community pressures, complexities of all kinds in the social fabric of the nation. But the bottom line is that they have been in charge, that the failures of education are theirs first and foremost.

I am not against lay boards. Far from it. I think it is healthy to have people from different walks of life representing the totality of the educational community in any given locale. I am simply against untrained boards, and I believe that this lack of training, occurring particularly as it has since 1945 in an era of complex change, has significantly contributed to the erosion of our schools and of our entire society.

Teachers who affect only the children they meet in class, administrators who affect only their separate departments, have to be trained to be proper professionals. How much more, then, should board members who affect everyone have to be trained? We take more care with our drivers' licenses and pet registrations. I think it is long past time we do so with our educational governance.

What I propose is a program of university study to be established for all those who aspire to be local or state board members. The course should be one in educational governance. It should contain the history of American governance, a study of governance in foreign countries, studies in educational law and educational ethics. It should have courses in management, educational finance, curriculum, and social perspective. It should lead to a graduate degree in educational governance, and it should be a prerequisite for board candidacy.

Perhaps such a program would not eliminate all of the incompetents, all of the egomaniacs, all of the shallow thinkers, power bloc shills, and political aspirants we now have. Perhaps not, but it would root out a lot of them. The time required for such a venture (I suggest thirty graduate credits, the same amount of time required for my administrator's certificate), the expense, the level of commitment, the ability to even function on the graduate level of a university would surely yield a better crop of educational governors.

As it stands now, I know nothing about the board members who run my life and the lives of my staff and the children we are pledged to serve. They want me university trained? I want them university trained. They want me certified? I want them certified. What's sauce for the goose is sauce for the gander, and I tell you now that until such measures are enacted, America is merely toying at the process of education.

Time in office. While the normal three-year probationary period is probably sufficient for teachers and some administrators, Likert's concept of time-lag I believe indicates that upper level administrators and board members should have longer terms of office in order to establish some kind of stability and continuity in the governance structure.

My experiences have taught me that it takes a year at least, more often two, to understand the rhythm of a district, learn its strengths and weaknesses, get to know its people. Proposals of significant change are foolish before these things are done. In a second two-year phase, armed with the perspective gained by the first years of observation, changes can rationally be introduced. The passage of these four early years also allows old memories and styles to ebb, thus reducing the time-lag between past management and present performance. As a former high school choral director I can tell you that I never considered a choir truly mine until four years had elapsed. It took that long for the singers trained under a previous director to be graduated and a new crop of singers to be brought along using my own methods. Finally, it takes at least two years to evaluate changes once they have been institutionalized.

For these reasons, I believe board members, superintendents, and building principals should have six-year terms of office or periods of probation. This length of time, the length agreed upon for the office of U.S. Senator by our founding fathers, also mitigates against the syndrome I have come to call the "sour grapes effect." I'll explain.

One district I knew of had a large, complex high school with a rather inhospitable, mediocre staff and an active, aggressive union headed by a leader who, in addition to having the reputation of being a poor teacher, was as arrogant and hostile as could be. The Principal, an intelligent workaholic, left his post to become the district's Assistant Superintendent. Everyone got behind the high school's Assistant Principal, pushing for him to fill the vacancy. He was, after all, one of them, an insider who would tolerate if not cater to the peccadillos of the staff. In a surprise move, however, the board hired an outsider. He was affable, down to earth, a delegator of authority—in short, everything the high school staff didn't want.

What happened was a kind of prolonged job action. Rumors were started vilifying the new man, petitions were circulated behind his back. If anyone had a problem, they would rarely give him the courtesy of addressing it. Instead, they went either under him to the Assistant Principal or over him to the Assistant Superintendent, their old boss. The school began to suffer and in the end, the new man—a fine educator and decent human being—was hung out to dry.

Had he a six-year contract, the inhuman treatment he received, if it happened at all, would have ended fairly quickly because the staff would have known that he was a more or less permanent fixture who ultimately would have to be reckoned with on his own terms. The same would be true for a central office administrator or a board member.

The six-year time period would have another benefit. It would help those in educational governance to keep their word. So often in education promises are made which, because they aren't in writing, are never kept. "Come work for us, and we'll make sure to fund your programs," the board says. "I have no intention of using this job as a stepping stone," the administrator pledges. Then, of course, the board changes and the administrator sees the chance to make a good career move. The funds are withdrawn; the resumes dispatched; the programs abandoned. I've seen it happen dozens of times. A guarantee on the part of a newly hired administrator or newly elected board member to remain in office for six years would improve that situation.

But even more, so would the placing of promises, conditions of employment, job descriptions and the like in writing at the commencement of a term of office or period of tenure. To the extent such things are left to vague verbal assurances, they are open invitations to bad faith and deceit. The promises of those in governance must be binding on successors if trust and progress are ever to be permanent fixtures in American education.

Finally, in this regard, if long-term periods of employment or board membership are adopted, conditions must be defined and procedures established for the removal of people clearly shown to be acting contrary to law or to established district policy. Provisions for the recall of a board member or the removal of an administrator before the initial term of service has ended are only appropriate safeguards for the educational system.

Just what would constitute a recall or how one might occur are matters best decided by the localities involved, perhaps with the aid of state guidelines or statutes. The important thing is that recall procedures be available and known to all parties at the time educational service begins.

Guarantee of chain-of-command procedures. You are, say, a department chairperson routinely going about the business of your day. Suddenly your phone rings. It is a member of the board of education. "What's this about Sally Smith not going on the English trip?" the voice snaps. You are at a loss. You don't know Sally or any of the details of the situation. You fumble for an answer and end up promising to look into it right away.

Common? You bet it is, and it's the worst thing that can happen in the governance of a school district. Nothing so undermines the process of education or the people engaged in it as does the unwarranted imposition of authority, the abrogation of chain-of-command procedures. It makes false demigods of board members and castrates the effectiveness of those charged with the daily management of school affairs.

If Sally has a beef about the English trip, it is up to her and to her parents or guardians to take that beef to the teacher involved. Only if that remedy fails to satisfy should the next step be taken, and that not to a board member but to the teacher's immediate supervisor (department chairperson, assistant principal, or principal, whichever the case may be). If redress is still not forthcoming, only then should action proceed to a central office administrator (assistant superintendent or superintendent). Finally, only if this fails to achieve results should a board member be called.

District policy should insist that the educational chain-of-command be honored. There is simply no other way to insure the fair and proper functioning of the system. If anyone in the chain receives a complaint, his or her first question should be, "Have you talked to the person directly in charge of the situation?" If the answer to that question is "no," then the appropriate appointments should be made before any upper-echelon action is taken.

Moreover, it should be a matter of district policy that any person in the command chain who violates it should be subject to severe action. In the case of a board member, I believe such a violation should be grounds for removal from office. If this policy were in effect, board members would rarely be able to become fronts for special interests, hidden agendas, or political power blocs, and education would proceed in a far more orderly and statesmanlike way.

Independent, honest reporting. The desire for those in educational governance to stay in power and, even more, to placate the special interests to whom they are beholden or by whom they are besieged has led to public relations double talk at levels which I consider dangerous. Like so many of the politicians we hear tell us that two plus two is five or that statistics which say "X" really mean "Y," educational leaders have become skilled at misrepresenting and misinforming their constituents.

It is a malicious game played by every school I've ever known or worked in. There was the Long Island district, a tourist center intent on maintaining high levels of property value, which told its citizens that a ten-year decline in SAT scores and state Regents exam grades represented a "high level of educational excellence." There was the rural district which argued away its last-place regional standing on state exam scores by telling the public that it was nonetheless doing better than the statewide average. There was the district which excused its high dropout/poor student graduation rate by expounding publicly that the fault lay in a high percentage of low-income minorities.

Public deception, like all forms of self-deception, is antithetical to educational development. Indeed, it is antithetical to the progress of a democracy. No meaningful improvement is possible without criticism, and criticism is not possible without honesty. I therefore recommend that districts be reviewed by reporters of the local press who are trained to know the ins and outs of education. In fact, there are other ways of getting out the truth as well. State evaluations and evaluations by independent educational observers should be required for each district every year. Reports from such evaluations should be required mailing from the district to every taxpayer.

Only when independent, honest assessments of our schools reach the local citizen will the inaccuracies and misrepresentations of present governance be overcome. On the list of things we can do to *really* reverse our educational decline, telling the truth to each other is perhaps the first and most needed step.

A national perspective. The preservation of regional controls which lies at the heart of American educational governance was desirable to Colonial citizens. It allowed religions to inculcate the young with particular brands of dogma; it allowed the South to maintain a slave economy; it gave parents dominion over the minds of their offspring. For me, none of these are noble goals, but they were ones desired by our ancestors and in the earliest days of our land they were less absurd than they are today.

I say this because people were not as mobile then, society not as complex, and the pressures of education not as pervasive or inescapable. It is to me still a monumental mistake to program children so that they think and act as their fathers and mothers do, so that they goose-step down the paths of life according to precepts laid down by others. But the remedies for that syndrome are curricular, not structural. Propaganda can just as easily—perhaps more easily—come from a national source as from a local one or a religious one. We will deal with this underlying aspect of American educational governance in a later chapter on curriculum. For now my plea for a national perspective has more to do with the practical realities of our society. Let me explain.

The ease of transportation, the fluctuations of job markets, the general mobility of families either because they are driven by disintegration or economics, have made us a much more heterogeneous society. The child born in Boston is not necessarily going to remain in Boston, certainly not with the same frequency he or she might have during the 1700's or 1800's. It is commonplace today for children to experience more than one educational district during their public school years. Often we find children coming into a new area not just from another location within the same state but from a separate state or even a foreign country.

Certainly this kind of geographical mixing is prevalent on the college level to a much greater extent. Many colleges and universities, in fact, take a conscious pride in selecting a nationally and internationally representative student body. It is rare today to find institutions of higher learning whose student population is drawn wholly from a single state. Even state universities have become beacons which attract students from surrounding states, indeed, from across the nation.

These realities place a tremendous burden on our colleges because America lacks a national educational perspective. Think about it for a moment. You are an admissions officer at a college. You have openings for, let's say, 1000 freshmen. You receive 5000 applications from all over the country. How do you choose who will attend your college in the fall? If you use high school grades, how do you know that an "A" from a high school in California means the same level of achievement as an "A" from a high school in New York? With 16,000 school districts how can you know the real worth of all of the high schools in the country, and with each state and each locality free to set its own curricular and academic standards, how can you assess the quality of education from area to area?

Perhaps, then, you try to adopt a kind of substitute national perspective by looking at the SAT (Scholastic Aptitude Test) scores of your applicants. The SAT is, after all, a national test which tries to rate academic worth regardless of geography. But SAT scores, useful as they are, are limited in two distinct and important ways. First, as a one-time test, they can't provide a comprehensive view of a student. A poor test-taker, a kid taking the test with a fever or on the day his grandma died will not give you an accurate accounting of his or her potential. It will not tell you if the child is responsible or irresponsible, courteous or discourteous, an over-achiever or an under-achiever—things very important to success in college and beyond. Second, the child taking the test is to a large extent at the mercy of the educational and cultural system which has prepared him or her. In a good system with rigorous training and broad cultural exposure, we find higher SAT scores. In a weaker system with limited cultural exposure, the scores are lower. And yet the children may in reality have the same potential for success in college.

How much saner would things be if we had a national curricular core from which each state and locality might build. And surely there are needs for regional differences. I do not mean to minimize that in arguing for a national perspective. I remember in the 1970's being invited to do some work in Havre, Montana. Havre is a small city not far from the Canadian border. The college and high school in Havre cater to a local population whose economic thrust is ranching and farming. It was entirely appropriate, then, for Havre High School to teach courses in agriculture and animal husbandry. It was not at all out of place (though delightfully unusual) to see a high school student come to school not in Dad's Pontiac but mounted on a neatly groomed horse. It was necessary from an economic viewpoint for the school calendar to end in time for kids to help with the local crop harvest or spring round-up. It was necessary to schedule football practice so that a tailback who lived forty miles away could get home at a decent hour.

Obviously, the practices of Havre High School were different from those one might find at Erasmus High in Brooklyn, New York. No one goes to Erasmus on a pony or lives forty miles away from school.

But regional differences do not abolish the consummate need for some national uniformity in curricula, in standards, in the per capita expenditure of funds. The latter is particularly troublesome to me. Some states are wealthy and give lots of aid to each district. Some districts are wealthy and spend like drunken sailors on their schools. Some are not, and that hits a kid below the belt through no fault of his own. The differential (and we'll go into it in detail in our chapter dealing with educational economics) can be enormous. New York, for example, spends $5,492 per capita on its students. Mississippi spends $2,357.[63] Obviously the child from Mississippi is going to be at a disadvantage when the SAT tests are handed out. With only half the revenues of New York, how many textbooks will that child have read, how many symphonies will he have heard, how many field trips will he have taken in comparison to students in wealthier areas?

And if we try to pooh-pooh the problem by saying, "Well, it's Mississippi's burden—we in New York have other fish to fry," we are only deluding ourselves. The kid from Biloxi could just as easily wind up working in New York some day as he could staying in Biloxi. In a mobile society, the dilution of any part is a dilution of the whole. Our Armed Forces serve us all, and they are manned by kids from Biloxi and kids from Havre and kids from Brooklyn. Many of our businesses are national in scope with branch offices in Mississippi, Montana, and New York. The world is too integrated today for regional prejudices. Biloxi's problem is our problem. New York's dilemmas are the nation's dilemmas.

There is yet one more reason for a national perspective, and it is the ease and speed with which we can change versus the rates of change in nations with whom we must compete. The 1984 modifications of Soviet education, the 1979 reconsiderations of England were able to become ubiquitous institutional practices because both countries have governance structures which can exercise authority over the entire nation. America as it is presently constituted cannot do that, and we are at a tremendous disadvantage as a result.

We have already seen that the educational governances of the U.S.S.R., Japan, England, and France are predicated upon national authority. We have seen that even West Germany has found a way (through a permanent conference of ministries) to create a national perspective. Many, many more nations in the modern world have a centralized educational system as compared with the fragmented, uncoordinated one we see in the U.S. Even if, in our present haphazard condition, we could arrive at a consensus for things like core curricula, core examinations, uniform teacher certification requirements, and universal per capita pupil expenditures, it would take us forever to adopt it in the fifty separate statehouses of our land.

To add to this unhappy condition, we have of late been governed by national political leaders whose thrust has been to weaken rather than strengthen Federal educational authority. At least one President went so far as to propose the abolishment of the Federal Department of Education. I suspect it is born not from a foundation of reason but rather as the result of the same states' rights/local control dogma which generated our system in Colonial times, a dogma which has at its core not really the desire to educate children but the desire to propagandize them so that institutions of power can be maintained and masses of minds more easily controlled.

A national perspective need not abrogate local flexibility—indeed it should not—but unless we find a way to institute such a perspective, I fear we will fall more and more behind other nations. Clearly, a national perspective of genuine proportions would require a Constitutional Amendment stating that core standards of elementary and secondary education be established by Federal authority. In Gingrich's terms this would be a real rather than a cosmetic change. However, in our democracy it is a change which—if it ever did come about—would require such a battle royal and such a large amount of time that it might be wiser to try another approach first. I suggest the following: a strengthening of the Federal Department of Education and the creation of an Educational Congress. Let me explain.

What I envision is a panel of educational representatives (perhaps one from each state) chosen either by election or appointment (according to the will of each state) which would convene in Washington, D.C. The panel would be a part of the Department of Education with access to the facilities and research data of the Federal government. The job of the panel would be to establish and then monitor core national standards for curricula, tests, teacher qualifications, and per-pupil capital expenditures in elementary and secondary education. Perhaps eventually higher education might be included.

The panel would work as Congress works, with committees assigned to special tasks, and with policies established through the process of democratic voting. In the absence of Constitutional authority, however, the recommendations of the panel would not be binding on state and local educational agencies. Compliance with panel policy would have to be achieved through financial incentive rather than the force of law. Therefore, the Federal government would allocate revenue to those state and local areas which adhered to panel standards. Those which did not would, of course, retain their educational autonomy but would be ineligible for the special Federal funds appropriated. Needless to say, any program required by Federal legal statute through such a system (for example, Title IX programs or programs for the handicapped or disabled) would need Federal funding to enable state and local compliance.

I do not consider this proposal to be a panacea, nor do I think it would be inexpensive in the financial view of things. However, it is hard to think of a more necessary way of spending money, and I would even favor fair and reasonable taxes as a means of public support. We have little choice. We can either find the will and the revenue to develop a meaningful national education perspective, or we will go the way of Rome. The choice is ours, and it will need to be made quickly by historical terms, perhaps before the end of the century.

Topics for consideration and debate. There are many topics which have not been covered in this discussion. Should local and state board members be paid or volunteer? Should they be elected or appointed? If degrees in educational governance are required for board members, should members be reimbursed for the cost of such degrees? Perhaps funds could be set aside to pay for such training. If board members are themselves paid, perhaps they should bear the costs of their own training—just as teachers and administrators do. How can we protect our schools more adequately against conflicts of interest in educational governance? How do we avoid favoritism for children of board members? How do we prevent board patronage of cronies? Should a board member be allowed to serve if a spouse or relative is a district employee? If a National Education Congress ever did become a part of the governance picture, how might it best be structured? What mechanisms in the Federal government would administrate it?

These are just a few of the many questions which face us if we are to deal meaningfully with improvements in the governance of American education. There are many more in the areas of funding, the grade structure of our schools, the curricula we teach. Some of these topics will be approached again in the pages ahead. For now they are raised to make the reader more aware of their presence in the total picture of education and to stimulate thought for real rather than cosmetic improvement of our schools.

With that in mind, we turn to our next topic, unionism in American education.

References for Chapter Two

1. ***Sex and Repression in Savage Society,*** Bronislaw Malinowski. New York: Humanities Press, 1953. Reprinted from the 1927 original edition. Distillation in ***Man in Contemporary Society,*** G.T. Matthews et al., eds. New York: Columbia University Press, 1955. pp. 162-91.
2. ***Civilization and Its Discontents,*** Sigmund Freud. London: The Hogarth Press, 1930. This reference contains the original definitive discussion of artistic and scientific progress as forms of repression or sublimation.
3. ***A History of Education in American Culture,*** R.F. Butts and L.A. Cremin. New York: Henry Holt & Co., 1953. p. 88.
4. ***A History of Education in American Culture,*** p. 160.
5. ***A History of Education in American Culture,*** p. 430.
6. ***A History of Education in American Culture,*** p. 431.
7. ***A History of Education in American Culture,*** pp. 534-35. Source cited as Pierce vs. Society of Sisters, 268 U.S. 510 (1924).
8. ***State Boards of Education: quality leadership,*** Dinah Wiley. Alexandria, Virginia: National Association of State Boards of Education, 1983. pp. 19-36.
9. ***State Boards of Education,*** Wiley. pp. 15-18.
10. ***School Boards: strengthening grass-roots leadership,*** Lila N. Carol, Luvern L. Cunningham, et al. Washington D.C.: Institute for Educational Leadership, 1986. pp. 3-9. These statistics were compiled from a research study which sampled 1,468 local board members from across the nation.
11. "For Your Information" section of ***The New Jersey School Leader,*** June, 1974. p. 21.
12. "Personal Financial Disclosure: is it your civic duty or indecent exposure?" Ellen Ficklin. In ***The American School Board Journal,*** February, 1985. pp. 23-28. The article contains a compendium of financial disclosure requirements for each state.
13. "For Your Information," ***New Jersey School Leader.*** p. 21.
14. "States with Appointed School Boards by Appointment Characteristics," information sheet prepared by the National School Board Association, June, 1984. Data source: U.S. Dept. of Commerce, Bureau of the Census. ***1982 Census of Governments. Vol. 1: Governmental Organizations.*** Washington, D.C.: Government Printing Office, 1983.
15. "What Works Best: an elected or an appointed school board?" Mark W. Hurwitz. In ***The American School Board Journal.*** July, 1972. pp. 21-23.
16. ***The American School Superintendency, 1982: a full report,*** Luvern L. Cunningham and Joseph Hentges, eds. Arlington, Va.: American Association of School Administrators, 1983. p. 14. The report was based on a survey which sampled 2,533 of the 15,214 superintendents in 1982.
17. ***The American School Superintendency,*** Cunningham and Hentges. pp. 14 and 73.
18. "Political Turbulence and Administrative Authority in the Schools," F.M. Wirt. In ***The New Urban Politics,*** L.H. Masotti and R. L. Lineberry, eds. Cambridge, Mass.: Ballinger, 1976. p. 62.
19. ***Governing American Schools,*** L.H. Zeigler and M.K. Jennings. North Scituate, Mass: Duxbury, 1974. p. 249. These and related issues are discussed in the sources which follow. "Educational Governance: contradictions and tendencies," P.J. Cistone and L. Iannaccone. In ***Education and Urban Society,*** 1980, pp. 407-40. ***Politics, Power and Policy,*** L. Iannaccone and F.W. Lutz. Columbus, Ohio: Merrill. 1970. ***Public Participation in Local School Districts,*** F.W. Lutz and L. Iannaccone, eds. Lexington, Mass: Heath. 1978. "Measurements and Methodological Issues Related to Research on

Incumbent Defeat and Superintendent Turnover," D.E. Mitchell. In ***Public Participation in Local School Districts*** (cited above).

20. "An Overview of the NSBA/AASA Survey of School Board/Superintendent Relations," prepared by the Educational Research Service, Arlington, Virginia. Spring, 1986. Nancy Protheroe, supervisor.
21. "Guess What? Big City Superintendents Say Their School Boards Are Splendid," Gordon Cawelti. In ***The American School Board Journal,*** March, 1982. pp. 33-35.
22. "But These Board Members Drive Superintendents Crazy," David F. Kipp. In ***The American School Board Journal,*** March, 1982. p. 35.
23. "Who Runs Our Schools? Superintendents—But That Must Change," R. Winfield Smith. In ***The American School Board Journal,*** November, 1982. p. 27.
24. "Who Runs Our Schools?...," R. Winfield Smith. In ***The American School Board Journal,*** November, 1982. p. 28.
25. "Who Runs Our Schools? A Definitive Answer Is Impossible," Paul Salmon. In ***The American School Board Journal,*** November, 1982. pp. 29-31.
26. "Clash: Superintendents Oppose Boards," James H. Kutkat. In ***The American School Board Journal,*** May, 1981. p. 37.
27. ***Encyclopedia of Educational Research,*** 5th ed. Harold E. Metzel, editor-in-chief. New York: The Free Press. 1982. Article on "School Boards" by Peter J. Cistone. p. 1642. In ***Governing American Schools*** (North Scituate, Mass: Duxbury, 1974), authors Zeigler and Jennings add that pressure groups tend to exert more influence in cities while individual pressure appears greater in suburban and rural areas.
28. ***A History of Education in American Culture,*** Butts and Cremin. p. 575.
29. ***A History of Education in American Culture,*** Butts and Cremin. pp. 575-76.
30. ***The Troubled Crusade,*** Ravitch. pp. 173-74.
31. "On Local Control: Who Is in Charge?" Byron Love. In ***The Michigan School Board Journal,*** February, 1982. p. 8. The source cited was an article by B.C. DeSpain in ***Educational Leadership,*** the Journal of the Association for Supervision and Curriculum Development, November, 1980. p. 106.
32. "On Local Control — Part III: Who Is in Charge?" Byron Love. In ***The Michigan School Board Journal,*** April, 1982. p. 12.
33. "On Local Control: Who Is in Charge?" C. Philip Kearney. In ***The Michigan School Board Journal,*** February, 1982. p. 9.
34. "The Changing Balance in State and Local Power To Control Education," Michael W. Kirst. In ***Phi Delta Kappan.*** November, 1984. pp. 189-91.
35. "Local Control — The Vanishing Myth in Texas," Michael G. Killian. In ***Phi Delta Kappan.*** November, 1984. pp. 191-95.
36. "State and Local Action for Education in New York," Gordon M. Ambach. In ***Phi Delta Kappan.*** November, 1984. pp. 202-04.
37. "School Reform by Remote Control," Larry Cuban. In ***Phi Delta Kappan.*** November, 1984. pp. 213-15.
38. "State-mandated Testing and the Fate of Local Control," Beverly Anderson and Chris Pipho. In ***Phi Delta Kappan.*** November, 1984. pp. 209-11.
39. "Educational Power Shift — I: The States Have Come a Long Way," Evan Jenkins. In ***Compact.*** March/April, 1974. p. 13.
40. "Educational Power Shift — II: Local Control Gives Way," James W. Gutherie and Paula H. Skene. In ***Compact.*** March/April, 1974. pp. 17-20.
41. "Roles and Responsibilities of Local School Districts." Speech given by M. Joan Parent, President of the National School Boards Association, before the National Forum on Excellence in Education. December 8, 1983. Indianapolis, Indiana. The text is printed by and available from the NSBA. Quote is taken from p. 5 of printed text.

42. See ***A History of Education in American Culture,*** Butts and Cremin, pp. 551-58 and ***The Troubled Crusade,*** Ravitch, pp. 81-113.
43. ***The Troubled Crusade,*** Ravitch. p. 127. The issue is discussed in depth on pp. 114-44.
44. ***The Troubled Crusade,*** Ravitch. p. 292. Ravitch cites the Gallup Polls of December 5-7, 1980 as her source.
45. ***A Nation at Risk: the imperative for educational reform.*** The National Commission on Excellence in Education (David P. Gardner, Chairman). Washington, D.C.: The U.S. Department of Education, 1983. p. 8.
46. "Public Secondary Education Systems in England, France, Japan, the Soviet Union, the United States and West Germany: a comparative analysis," Wayne Riddle. Washington, D.C.: Congressional Research Service, Library of Congress, Education and Public Welfare Division, December 7, 1984. p. 4. The source cited is the U.S. Department of Education, Digest of Education Statistics, 1983-84, p. 66.
47. "Public Secondary Education Systems...," Riddle. p. 4.
48. "Public Secondary Education Systems...," Riddle. p. 4.
49. "Public Secondary Education Systems...," Riddle. pp. 8-9.
50. "Public Secondary Education Systems...," Riddle. pp. 9-10. Riddle goes on to state that government aid through the so-called "assisted places" program is making private school available to students who might otherwise not be able to afford it. He also compares the 6% private enrollment in England with 16% in France and 10% each in West Germany and the United States.
51. "Public Secondary Education Systems...," Riddle. pp. 6 and 10.
52. "Public Secondary Education Systems...," Riddle. p. 15.
53. "Public Secondary Education Systems...," Riddle. p. 16.
54. "Public Secondary Education Systems...," Riddle. p. 17. Riddle cites as his source the 1981 Mombusho report from the Japanese Ministry of Education, Science, and Culture in Tokyo, p. 17.
55. "Public Secondary Education Systems...," Riddle. p. 19.
56. "Public Secondary Education Systems...," Riddle. pp. 22-23.
57. ***Education in the U.S.S.R.*** Joseph I. Zadja. Oxford, England: Pergammon Press, 1980. p. 20.
58. "Basic Guidelines for the School Reform," ***Current Digest of the Soviet Press.*** May, 1984. pp. 12-20.
59. "Public Secondary Education Systems...," Riddle. pp. 24-25.
60. "Public Secondary Education Systems...," Riddle. pp. 25-28.
61. ***Analytic Comparison of Education Systems: an overview of purposes, policies, structures, and outcome,*** Christopher J. Hurn and Barbara B. Burn. Washington, D.C.: National Commission on Excellence in Education, February, 1982. p. 68. passim.
62. The time-lag concept as well as other work by Likert may be found in the sources listed below. ***New Patterns of Management,*** Rensis Likert. New York: McGraw Hill, 1961. "The Likert School Profile Measurements of Human Organization," Albert F. Siepert and Rensis Likert. Paper presented at the National Convention of the American Educational Research Association, February 23, 1973. ***The Human Organization: its management and value,*** Rensis Likert. New York: McGraw Hill, 1967. ***New Ways of Managing Conflict,*** Rensis Likert and Jane Gibson Likert. New York: McGraw Hill, 1976. ***Organizational Behavior,*** Fred Luthans. New York, McGraw Hill, 1977.
63. "State Education Statistics Supplement." Prepared by the U.S. Department of Education, Office of Planning, Budget, and Evaluation. February, 1987.

Chapter Three

Unions and American Education

Chapter Three

Unions and American Education

BEFORE DELVING INTO the subject of unionism in American education, it might be useful to get a kind of thumbnail statistical perspective of the educational landscape in which today's unions function. The facts and figures below come principally from 1986 data disseminated by the National School Board Association using information from the National Center for Education Statistics, the U.S. Bureau of Census, the Education Commission of the States, and the Educational Research Service.

- There are 15,912 public school districts in America of which 15,601 are operational.

- 90% of the districts are financially independent, that is, the revenue needed to run them comes from their own tax base plus state and federal funds.

- School enrollment in public elementary and secondary programs is 40.9 million. This is down from the record 45.9 million in 1971, but an increase to about 42 million is projected by around 1992. Specifically, there are 27.6 million students in grades K-8 and 13.3 million in grades 9-12.

- The average school district enrollment is 2,600 students. About 73% of all districts have an enrollment of under 5,000.

- The 167 largest urban districts—that is, cities with populations of 100,000 or more—account for almost 22% of all students (about 9 million of the 41 million total).

- The total 1986 expenditures for all 16,000 American school districts was $150 billion, about one-half of the Defense Department budget.

- The sources of public school funding are as follows: 50.1% from state sources, 43.5% from local sources, and 6.4% from federal sources.

- The average per-pupil expenditure is $3,677 for a year of schooling.

- The total public school population is serviced by an instructional staff of 2.2 million of whom 1.2 million teach in elementary schools and 1 million in secondary schools. The ratio of students to teachers is thus about 18 to 1. In addition to instructional staff, there are 1.5 million people serving in support capacities (guidance counselors, psychologists, administrators, aides, secretaries, etc.). The total instructional and support staff salaries for the 3.7 million educational workers account for about 80% of the average school budget (the rest going for supplies, plant operations, debt services, etc.).

- There are 3.98 million students in American schools classified as either mentally, emotionally, or physically handicapped. The average annual expenditure for these students is $4,898, ranging from $2,253 for speech impaired pupils to $9,664 for those who are blind.

- There are 95,000 board of education members governing America's schools. 90% of these are directly elected; the remainder are appointed by elected officials. The average number of board members per district is 6 (from 5-7).

- The average superintendent's salary is $46,664. The average high school principal's salary is $34,776. The average elementary school principal's salary is $30,242. The average classroom teacher's salary is $25,313.

- The two largest teacher unions in the nation are the American Federation of Teachers and the National Education Association. The AFT has about 580,000 members; the NEA claims 1.6 million members. Thus, 2.18 million teachers of the 2.2 million total are union members. There are, in addition, unions which cover most of the administrative and support personnel.

- In 1986, about 69% of Americans were high school graduates. This compares with 52% in 1970.

- There are 21,000 private elementary and secondary schools in America with a total enrollment of 5 million pupils. Of these, 64% are Catholic, 21% non-Catholic, and 15% non-affiliated. The ratio of students to teachers in non-public schools is 18 to 1.[1]

How did education unions come to be?

There is the temptation in an educational environment as polarized as today's to see the struggles between teachers and communities in overly simplistic terms. Union diehards blame everything wrong on anyone but the teacher. Community rednecks see the unions as the sole stumbling block to quality education. Such views are not only wrong, they are fundamental obstacles to educational progress. Teacher associations have a long and important history, and it is necessary to understand that history in order to accurately assess the current educational reality and move forward.

Fortunately, there are scholars who have enabled us to do this. Among the writing of modern educational historians is the work of Marshall Donley whose doctoral dissertation traced the development of American educational unions from Colonial days to the post-1945 era. Professor Donley capsulized his work in the book *Power to the Teacher*, and it is principally (though not exclusively) from his writing that we draw the information below.

The early days. Teacher militancy during the Colonial era and the first one hundred fifty years of the Republic was extremely infrequent. In 1666 one Ezekiel Cheever complained to the elders of Charlestown, Massachusetts that his salary as the town mentor was not being paid on schedule. Caleb Bingham did the same around

1790. In 1802 Tom Peugh refused to unlock the schoolhouse door until the town committee promised him one afternoon off per month, and in 1823 Connecticut teacher William Alcott had the audacity to publish some of his grievances in the New Haven *Register*. But these were the exceptions, not the rule. "Until at least the early 1900's, the typical teacher was humble and uncomplaining. He was expected to be religiously orthodox, loyal to the government, and morally acceptable,"[2] and many state and local laws were passed to ensure that point of view.

The first American educational association, the Society of Associated Teachers of New York City, was founded in 1794. It was followed by the School Association of Middlesex County (Connecticut) in 1799 and the Boston Instructors of Youth in 1812. Between 1840 and 1861, thirty state teacher associations were formed. All of these groups had a dichotomy of purpose—to serve the community and to improve the lot of the teacher—a dichotomy often in conflict with itself both then and now. It is important to note that the leaders of these early organizations rarely, if ever, came from teachers "in the day-to-day trenches." Rather they were school superintendents or college administrators somewhat removed from the pressures and perspectives of the ordinary public school educator. It is also important to note that women, who constituted the majority of the working public school profession, were, in these early days, not even accorded the right of full membership. All this, of course, would change in time.

By 1857 a National Teachers Association had been formed. When, during the 1870's, it merged with the National Association of School Superintendents and the American Normal School Association, it was renamed the National Education Association (NEA), the title it has carried to this day. The NEA charter announced that the organization would exist "to elevate the character and advance the interests of the profession of teaching, and to promote the cause of popular education in the United States."[3] In reality, however, the organization did little to promote the well-being of educational professionals in its early days. Dominated by superintendents and college professors it was more a forum for esoteric speeches than a wellspring of meaningful action. Not until the 1920's would the NEA begin to move toward the forefront of meaningful educational reform.

It did, however, enjoy two significant successes in its early days. First, it successfully pressed for the formation of a federal Department of Education. Second, it organized a series of state affiliates which did manage to achieve some educational reform. The Illinois Education Association secured a state mandate in 1870 providing free school for all children. In 1872 the New Hampshire Education Association backed the first compulsory school attendance law. The New Mexico Education Association was able to secure the passage of an 1891 law allowing schools to glean financial support from local property taxation. The New York Teachers Association was able to establish a uniform procedure for licensing teachers from 1887 onward. Finally, in the decade before 1900, the New Jersey Education Association was able to address in its talks with management issues such as retirement pay, tenure, minimum salary schedules, and legal defense for teachers whose rights were abused. Substantive progress on these issues would not come for at least a quarter century, but the ball was rolling and the direction of the NEA and its affiliates was charted.

From 1900 to World War II. Progress for the American teacher was anything but swift in the first two decades of the century. To be sure, there was some—a salary victory in Saline County, Illinois in 1904; a public demonstration by Virginia teachers in 1908; the 1916 affiliation of the Scranton (Pennsylvania) Teachers Association with the American Federation of Labor (AFL); the unionization of New York City teachers in 1916; a 1918 strike by Memphis teachers which brought a ten dollar monthly salary hike. But these were atypical of the national picture. As Donley writes, "...poorly paid and ill-prepared, the American teacher gained little money and less respect from society. He was expected to be cheerful, meek, loyal, and most of all quiet."[4]

The NEA remained a relatively inactive, relatively ineffective force between the turn of the century and the end of World War I, despite voices like Margaret Haley's (President of the National Federation of Teachers) and John Dewey's urging professionals to take a direct hand in shaping curricula and improving their own lot. In part, the failures of the NEA were due to the fact that very few educators were even members. In 1900, the organization boasted but 2,332 members or about 0.6% of the teaching work force. By 1910 membership was up to 6,909 (1.3% of the work force), but that was hardly enough to represent the profession as a whole. In 1919, 7% of American teachers were NEA members. While that represented an improvement, it was really on the state level that membership gains were being made. By 1916, 34% of the nation's public school teachers (188,730 individuals) were members of state NEA affiliates. It is thus not surprising that most of the progress of teachers vis-a-vis tenure and salary increases took place on the state level.

In 1908 New Jersey passed the first tenure law. In 1913 Montana enacted a "continuous contract" law. Tenure laws were passed for Massachusetts in 1914 and New York in 1917. By the end of the world war, minimum salary laws had been enacted in Iowa, West Virginia, and Massachusetts. Georgia, Alabama, and California adopted teacher codes of ethics, and by 1919 there were teacher retirement provisions in New Jersey, Illinois, Minnesota, New Hampshire, West Virginia, and Pennsylvania.

With all of this came another important development, the appearance of strong city associations. In 1902 both the San Antonio and Chicago teacher groups affiliated with the AFL. By 1916 a new national teacher association was formed, the American Federation of Teachers (AFT). Unlike the NEA, the AFT was directly and inextricably tied to the labor unions of the nation and it was from those unions that it adopted many of its tactics and drew much of its financial underpinning. The first eight chapters of the AFT came from Chicago and Gary, Indiana, and it would be principally from cities such as these that it would draw its future membership.

Between 1920 and the beginning of World War II, teachers remained in a relatively low-pay, low-status posture. During these years, however, national membership in the NEA grew significantly from 8,466 in 1917 to 141,212 in 1927 to over 200,000 by 1940. Gradually, the national organization became more representative of the average teacher and thus more willing to address issues affecting the average teacher—issues like secure sources of school revenue, salary hikes, tenure guarantees, and education legislation. By the start of World War II, the NEA had established a national office in Washington, D.C. run by a staff of trained professionals. Every state had an NEA affiliate, and every classroom teacher was accorded full membership status. A representative assembly with delegates from each state was formed to set NEA policy. Thus, if not for its militant actions, then for its growth and organization, the NEA made significant strides in these years.

Assertive militancy between 1920 and 1940 occurred much more on the state level through the various state NEA affiliates. Sparked by the economic hardships of the Great Depression, state organizations attracted more and more members and gradually wrested more and more leadership control from the superintendents and college professors who had once thoroughly dominated them.

Meanwhile, the AFT was experiencing a noticeable decline in membership. The 10,000 teachers it claimed in 1920 dropped to 5,000 in 1928. Only a few big cities (New York, Chicago, Atlanta, and San Francisco in particular) seemed able to sustain AFT support. Even the Depression failed to attract large numbers to the cause. By 1938 AFT membership was still only 32,000. The reason for the decline was the infiltration of communists into the labor unions of the land, an infiltration which quickly spread to the AFT, a labor union affiliate. All through the 1930's and early 1940's the debate raged through the AFT: "Do we accept the presence of communist influences or do we kick the communists out?"

The 1935 AFT convention saw a call from the floor for the revocation of union charters in locals where communists had gained clear and significant influence. Particularly cited were five New York City locals, and while no definite action occurred in 1935, within a few years the charters of those locals were withdrawn by a vote of 11,000 to 8,000.

It was not the issue of communism, however, which would dominate the education labor movement of the U.S. Important an issue as that was it would be the monumental effects of World War II and its aftermath which would propel the movement forward.

From 1940 to 1960. The decades during and immediately following World War II were characterized by a sharp increase in teacher militancy. Where strikes before the war had been few and far between, from 1942 to 1959 there were over one hundred. They occurred in all parts of the nation, in small districts and those as large as Buffalo and Minneapolis. For the most part, the cause of the strikes centered on the extremely low wages being paid most teachers, especially in the wake of wartime inflation. Even though the post-war baby boom created a shortage of educators, salaries were simply not rising to bring in new professional blood. The statistics which follow provide accurate (if painful) verification.

At the start of World War II, 26 of the 48 states were paying teachers less than $600 per year with only two states and the District of Columbia paying more than $1,200. Staff turnover ran as high as 35% per year in many states. Teacher shortages abounded. In the 1945-46 school year, for example, 110,000 emergency teaching certificates were issued to fill the void. The profession was simply not attracting candidates of calibre. In 1936, for instance, 16% of all college students were education majors. By 1945 that figure had dropped to a paltry 7%—and this at a time of increasing childbirth rates. Wartime and post-war inflation produced rising salaries in almost every major industry except education. Factory worker income, for example, rose 80%; farm income increased 300% over pre-war figures while teacher pay during the same period rose only 10%. The average teacher salary in 1947 was but $2,380 a year. It climbed to $3,080 in 1951 but this figure was still 4% less than the $3,200 earned by the average American worker.[5]

In view of statistics such as these, it is hardly surprising that teacher associations became more and more militant. The strikes of the 1950's succeeded in raising the average teacher salary to $5,313, a figure then slightly above the annual wage of the average U.S. worker. The strikes, however, also succeeded in creating a negative reaction among the taxpaying public and state legislators who were footing the educational bill.

No clearer example of this reaction exists than the passage of the Condon-Wadlin Law in New York State. The teacher strike in Buffalo was supported by more than the teachers themselves. As an AFL affiliate, the Buffalo teachers' union was able to call on the resources and cooperation of other unions in the American Federation of Labor. Thus, when the 2,400 members of the Buffalo teachers' union withdrew their services from the schools, so did sympathetic union members who served the schools in indirect yet vital ways. To name just one example, the truckers who delivered food to the cafeterias of the Buffalo public schools refused to cross the picket lines, thus exacerbating the situation by forcing even greater hardship on the students and administrators who were trying to keep the schools open.

That workers charged with a public trust would abandon that trust for self-interest was an occurrence which infuriated some members of the New York State legislature. Their ire was enough to draft and pass the Condon-Wadlin Act which outlawed the right to strike by public employees. Though Condon-Wadlin would not survive in its original form (it would be replaced by New York's Taylor Law in 1967), it was nonetheless a harbinger of the backlash which awaited educational unionism, a backlash which is alive and perhaps growing today.

Despite a few gains and over fifty years of existence, however, most education associations were still relatively weak. The NEA had spent decades lobbying unsuccessfully for broader federal education support, but it was not until the launching of Sputnik I by Russia (1957) and the subsequent passage of the National Defense Education Act (NDEA) that Washington heeded the call. Nor in the decades following 1960 did major federal programs emerge to continue the NDEA thrust. Notwithstanding, the NEA continued to build its organizational base. By 1957 it had a central staff in Washington of over 440 people with thirteen separate divisions and over thirty departments. It adopted as its philosophy the concepts that "better service must go with higher salaries" and that "no one wins in a strike."[6]

By contrast, the AFT remained comparatively inactive between 1940 and 1960. With power bases primarily in New York and Chicago, it claimed only 54,817 members by 1959 or about 3.8% of the nation's public school teaching force. Although adopting an outward posture which deplored strikes, the AFT was certainly more prone to use the strike as a tactic than the NEA. By 1960 the stage was set in many districts for bitter inter-union struggles over the right to represent teachers in the bargaining process. No struggle was as significant as the one in New York City.

The 1960's in New York City. By any measure, the decade of the '60's was a turbulent time. Civil rights demonstrations; the war in Vietnam; the assassination of American political leaders; and a radical shift in the nation's social, moral, and sexual behavior created a confrontational atmosphere which made activities on the labor front delicate and potentially volatile. This was even more true in New York City for two reasons. First, the city itself was (as it had always been) a racial, religious, and ethnic polyglot. Black, Hispanic, Jewish, Irish, Italian, Middle Eastern, and Eastern European communities lived in close proximity. At times of racial, ethnic, or religious polarization, there was bound to be friction. Second, the city schools had become a testing ground between the NEA and the United Federation of Teachers (UFT), the local unit of the AFT. The prize for winning control was the right to represent the 50,000 teachers of the city system and thereby gain a commanding voice in the union affairs of the state.

At the beginning of the decade, the edge was clearly in the UFT camp. The NEA, which at one time had 10,000 city teachers to its credit, enrolled only 700 in 1960. The UFT was determined to hold onto its power base, and it had both the blessing and support of its national parent (the AFT) as well as the entire AFL-CIO with which the AFT was affiliated. In fact, this was no small issue for the AFL-CIO. Traditionally a representative of blue-collar workers, it saw the AFT and UFT as a way to open American labor unions to white-collar employees. That, in turn, would mean a tremendous increase in union power. It could potentially bring the threat of strikes not only to the schools with teachers but to the hospitals with doctors, the courts with lawyers, the banks, the insurance companies, the commercial marketplace as well.

The decade opened with a teacher strike in 1960. The UFT mobilized members to support the strike; the NEA argued against it. It was a rough-and-tumble debate with several dirty tricks along the way, mostly on the part of the UFT. (Among other things, Donley mentions tactics like stealing NEA mail and sabotaging NEA meetings.) In the end, the teachers voted three-to-one to support the UFT position, and from 1961 onward, the UFT was accorded the right to represent the teachers of New York City in all labor negotiations.

This UFT victory sparked a rise in AFT power throughout the nation. Ironically, however, it also forced the NEA's 7,500 locals and 1,300,000 members into positions of greater militancy and led to an NEA campaign aimed at recruiting members in the big cities of the nation.

In 1962 the UFT of New York City called a second strike, one which Donley describes as "an almost totally unnecessary act that brought a tirade of editorial blasts at teacher unionism."[7]

The strike, called because of a bureaucratic snag in the payment of a salary hike, was illegal according to the provisions of the Condon-Wadlin Law. Even though it was settled in a single day by a quick unraveling of the monetary snafu, it left a bitter taste in many mouths. The NEA was among the first to denounce the strike. In general, strikes were not part of the NEA gestalt. A more genteel organization than its AFT counterpart, in most situations the NEA urged its members to continue to work until negotiations (usually with settlements retroactive to the expiration of previous contracts) had been completed. The UFT, however, saw the incident in positive terms. Now dominated by leaders who accepted the more militant tactics of the UFT's parent organization, the AFL-CIO, UFT members argued that muscle-flexing was the only language the New York City Board of Education understood.

In 1963 UFT President Charles Cogen threatened yet another strike, declaring that the Condon-Wadlin Law was in violation of basic civil rights and that public employees had a constitutional right to strike. He particularly pointed to a difference between teachers and other public workers in that a strike by police, firemen, sanitation workers, or transportation crews might create conditions which threatened civil life and limb, while a teacher strike would cause only inconvenience. The 1963 strike was averted, but another occurred in 1964 and yet another in September of 1967, just before the opening of school.

Initially, the 1967 strike was over money. The UFT demanded a $7,000 starting salary. The city countered with a $6,200 offer. The settlement was a three-year package giving the union $6,200 in 1967; $6,600 in 1968; and $6,750 in 1969. It was not money, however, which became the central issue but rather the right of teachers to deal with unruly students—even over the authority of building principals.

The American society had, by the 1967 strike, already changed radically. Social unrest over Vietnam, militant civil disobedience, increased drug use, and a liberalized moral standard had worked their way through the national fabric and found particularly strong expression in American high schools and colleges. Many teachers began to experience severe breakdowns of classroom discipline, and in New York City this entire social malaise was accompanied by overtones of racism.

The UFT was predominantly white, predominantly Jewish. Many of the schools in which student behavior had become disruptive were heavily black and/or Puerto Rican. The minority communities began to look upon the UFT demands for greater disciplinary authority as the racist domination of an anti-black, anti-Hispanic society. They saw the school principal—particularly when he or she was a minority member—as a safeguard against the racial abuses of the white/Jewish establishment, and thus they were militantly opposed to circumventing the principal's authority in matters of discipline by giving teachers the power to expel students.

The strike lasted two weeks, and in the end the UFT won only the right to appeal a principal's decision where disruptive students were concerned. However, the issue was far from over. 1967 proved to be only a mild precursor of what was to come.

It was clear by the end of the 1967 strike that the Condon-Wadlin Law was not working. In short order, a new one, the Taylor Law, replaced it. The Taylor Law also prohibited strikes by public employees, but it was more easily applied than its predecessor, and it contained a series of procedures designed to facilitate negotiation and head off public strikes. Where normal union/management bargaining failed, the new law provided for declarations of impasse, the appointment of state mediators, fact-finding procedures, and even legislative action to avert school closings.

It was also clear by the end of the 1967 strike that things in New York City were going to get worse before they got better. Strong leadership in the UFT hierarchy was going to be a must, and it came to the fore in the person of Albert Shanker, a man who would dominate educational unionism for the next quarter century.

A volatile atmosphere, the new Taylor Law, a new man at the helm of the UFT—the stage was set for 1968.

Shanker began the year with a warning that he would "close down the entire district" where any teacher was dismissed or punished "without the benefit of an impartial review."[8] At the heart of his threat, of course, was the growing polarization between the white teachers and the minority constituents they served.

Things came to a head in the Ocean Hill-Brownsville district, a primarily black community in which ten UFT teachers were dismissed for failing to teach relevant material. The union struck, exacerbating what the New York Times called "the worst of the city's racial fears and prejudices."[9] The teachers stayed out until October 1st when the dismissed staff members were reinstated with neutral observers and police assigned to keep community harassment to a minimum.

The presence of observers and police, however, did not calm the Ocean Hill-Brownsville residents who proceeded to riot with many people injured. Again, the teachers walked out, closing the schools a second time. Violence and strikes continued well into the fall. Finally, the State of New York agreed to take over the city district as a trusteeship. Only then, with the guarantee of state protection, did the teachers vote (17,658 to 2,738) to return. It was an uneasy peace at best, one with educational and sociological scars which would last well into the 1970's and beyond.

There were many who resented the militancy of the UFT during the 1968 strikes, and in order to curb future union actions, the Taylor Law was strengthened with much stiffer penalties, including two days loss of pay for every one day of strike, plus the possible imposition of jail sentences and dismissal procedures. Rather than being intimidated by the new legal provisions, however, the UFT became even more forceful under the leadership of Albert Shanker. Membership increased, and lucrative contracts were negotiated in 1972 and again in 1975. The latter secured a $20,000 salary for teachers with 7½ years of experience, plus fringe benefits which ranged from a generous retirement pension to college tuition incentive payments. Clearly, the star of Albert Shanker was on the rise.

The 1960's nationwide. Despite the power of the UFT in New York, most teachers nationwide were NEA members during the decade of the '60's, a trend which would also hold true in the 70's and 80's as well. What the UFT did more than snare teachers away from the NEA was force the NEA and its state affiliates into positions of greater militancy. The NEA still called for bargaining with mediation and retroactive settlements rather than strikes, but beginning in the early '60's, it also began to apply sanctions against districts which were particularly intractable in the negotiations process.

A sanction could take any of several forms: refusal to do extracurricular work, statewide or national publicity against a given district, refusal to serve on school committees, etc. In 1962, sanctions were applied in Utah, Wisconsin, California, Connecticut, Kansas, Michigan, and Minnesota, and in fairly short order the NEA's reputation for toughness began to spread, even to the point where it won the right to bargain over AFT unions in a few large cities (Long Beach, California and Denver, Colorado being two notable examples.)

To add to the NEA's position, both the courts and President Kennedy supported the right of teacher associations to apply sanctions as leverage in negotiations. The court also upheld the right of teachers to seek arbitration in the resolution of grievances and to form (or not form) professional associations which could represent them in the bargaining process.

The AFT did not react to the NEA's advances with passivity. In fact, during the first half of the decade, the AFT embarked upon a concerted campaign to overtake the NEA district by district. Donley describes the AFT's three-stage tactic as follows:

> First Stage—drive a wedge between the teacher and his professional organization...Everything that is wrong with the teaching profession is blamed

> on the professional organization...The unions then promise to correct all the ills...Second Stage—seek equal rights with professional organizations. Third Stage—after winning election...work with big labor unions in the city...No longer (wanting) equal terms with professional associations...force non-union teachers to join the union or leave the system.[10]

Although the AFT campaign did not succeed everywhere, by 1963 it had managed to increase membership to 81,798 or approximately 4.9% of the national teaching work force. In the same year, the AFT also passed a resolution recognizing the right of AFT locals to strike and urging AFL-CIO affiliates to support such strikes.

Again, the NEA countered the AFT pressure with a reassertion of its own guidelines and a redoubling of its efforts as a negotiator in districts where there were labor/management disputes. By March of 1963 it had successfully resolved some twenty disputes in seven separate states with nine more agreements to come from the state of Washington alone. However, its biggest success occurred in Denver where teacher salaries were raised from their low level to an annual top wage of $10,000. The NEA claimed the settlement an eloquent testimony to the effectiveness of its leadership and a vindication of its professional approach to problems.

For awhile the application of sanctions by the AFT and its state affiliates seemed to be working. In 1964 they were applied, for example, by the Utah Education Association as leverage in bargaining for higher wages. The UEA declared a two-day "recess" of schools, and the NEA urged that no 1964-65 contracts be signed in Utah until the wage issue was settled. The NEA also asked that no out-of-state teacher apply for vacant in-state jobs until negotiations were successfully completed. In the face of these pressures, Utah teachers won substantial gains in both salaries and school conditions. Sanctions were applied again in 1965 when Oklahoma teachers sought more money for wages and the upgrading of school conditions. Once more the OEA was supported by its NEA parent, and once more the tactic worked. Before the end of September, state legislative action was taken allowing for an increase in local school levies to pay for the teachers' demands.

In 1967, however, the sanction principle ran into a snag. NEA sanctions were applied against the state of Florida in support of Florida Education Association demands for improved school conditions. Specifically, the NEA published national condemnations of the Florida school system and Florida Governor Claude Kirk. The NEA went on to issue a warning that individuals not then in the Florida state system who took Florida jobs would be subject to NEA unethical conduct charges. In September the teachers of Broward County "recessed" for seven days. The county quickly appropriated money for higher salaries and school improvements and urged Governor Kirk to find a statewide settlement. There followed a series of legislative delays after which the NEA collected some 32,000 resignation forms from the Florida membership. On February 19, 1968 some 26,000 Florida teachers failed to report to class. The NEA sent $2 million for teacher support and legal fees. When a resolution of the crisis finally passed the legislature without a veto from Governor Kirk, the teachers returned. However, during the strike many counties had hired substitute teachers. Some of these counties refused to reinstate the regular teachers, and despite all the NEA could do, over 500 teachers lost their jobs permanently. In all it was a mixed victory. On the one hand, Florida apportioned $446.2 million in additional education revenue, raising average salaries by $2,000. On the other hand, the public clearly resented the strike, and 500 jobs were lost.

From the Florida crisis on, the NEA opted more and more to apply the tactic of local strikes against selected districts over that of statewide sanctions. It was learning that as salaries were increasing, public sympathy for teachers would decrease in almost direct proportion.

The relatively small number of teacher strikes which occurred in the early 1960's began to burgeon rapidly from 1967 onward. In 1966, for example, there were 33 such strikes. In 1967 there were 105. Even with calls from more moderate leaders that collective bargaining mechanisms be employed, the trend was a clear one. And so was the trend of public opinion. As the public experienced the inconvenience of strikes and the imposition of higher taxes which were the inevitable result of strike settlements, its support for the strike tactic and for teachers in general began to wane. A Gallup poll conducted in March of 1968 showed 57% of the people against the right of teachers to strike. A follow-up study in December showed that the figure had increased to 60%. By comparison, in 1965 only 53% of teachers favored using the strike as a bargaining tactic. By 1968 that figure had grown into a solid 68% majority. Clearly, the profession and the public were on a collision course as the nation emerged into the 1970's. 1969, for example, saw a record 131 teacher strikes in 24 states plus the District of Columbia.

The 1970's and beyond. The decade of the '70's was marked both by severe economic recession and a precipitous decline in the number of public school students. In an already confrontational atmosphere, these new developments brought educational labor/management relations to the breaking point in district after district across the nation. In 1970 alone, for example, there was a record 171 strikes. The repercussions of these conditions were seen in two key areas. First, both the NEA and AFT sought the passage of "right-to-strike" laws, and second, in an effort to consolidate and increase bargaining power, many educators began to advocate an NEA/AFT merger.

The model laws for the prohibition of strikes by public employees had been New York's Condon-Wadlin Act and its successor, the Taylor Law. However, in 1968 the U.S. Court of Appeals ruled that the Constitution gave teachers the right to engage in union activities and that any teacher so involved "could not be dismissed for exercising that right whether or not he had tenure."[11] While not legally condoning public employee strikes, the ruling nonetheless encouraged the passage of "Taylor-type" laws in states other than New York, laws which would guarantee public workers some kind of bargaining process while trying to avert actual work stoppages.

In 1970 Hawaii teachers with the support of the NEA gained the right to strike like any private employee. A similar ruling was issued in the state of Pennsylvania, and Vermont followed with a law limiting injunctions against striking teachers. Strikes in Hawaii and the city of Philadelphia were soon called to test the new laws. The Philadelphia strike revealed a particularly important scenario as far as the decade of the 1970's was concerned. The financial conditions of the city were chaotic at best. Deficits mounted in the wake of the recession, topping the $50 million mark in the 1972-73 school year. When the teachers went out, there was really nothing the city could do. Union militancy, no matter how forcefully applied, was simply no way to restore the city's economy. The teachers remained out of work for ten weeks, nearly one-quarter of the school year, and in the end they returned to work with no economic gains. It was a strike in which everyone lost, but it was one which carried a clear and important message: in the absence of an economic climate capable of sustaining increased educational expenditures, strikes hurt both labor and management without yielding any gains to either.

Much more constructive than strikes in the decade of recession and enrollment decline were collective bargaining procedures which would attempt to provide settlements without walkouts or school closings. Encouraged by the format of New York's Taylor Law, Alaska, New Hampshire, Wisconsin, California, Florida, Massachusetts, New Jersey, Oregon, and Connecticut soon enacted similar legislation. Not that the entire educational community looked favorably upon the Taylor Law and its legal brethren. Many denounced the law as biased against the worker, not only because it prohibited strikes but also because it did not assure through compulsory arbitration that the recommendation of impartial fact-finders would be adopted. Be this as it may, by 1974 "Taylor-type" laws existed in twenty-six states, and through them over 1.4 million teachers were covered by negotiated agreements. Beyond 1974, the latter half of the decade and most of the 1980's saw a variety of tactics used in the negotiations process. At times retroactive bargaining without strikes was sufficient to solve local labor/management disputes. At other times strikes of varying dimensions were called. The rule of thumb in such matters was to apply the tactic which seemed to work best in any given district.

Just as the collective bargaining laws enacted after 1970 held no panacea for American education, neither did the proposals for NEA/AFT merger. As we have already seen, the rivalry between the NEA and the AFT had gone on since the beginning of the century. Only briefly in 1966 was there talk of joining the two, and when nothing came of it, the idea faded into the background. It surfaced again in 1968 when a weakened financial position led the AFT to propose the institution of merger talks. However, NEA President Elizabeth Koontz declined the invitation, citing the AFT's financial position and declaring that there would be no advantage to the NEA if a merger took place. Again the issue faded. It was resurrected briefly in 1970 when NEA and AFT affiliates joined in the city of Los Angeles to form the United Teachers of Los Angeles. The new association promptly launched a five-week strike which ended without the teachers getting the funds they were seeking. Predictably, a new round of NEA/AFT rivalries ensued. By 1972 the NEA had won negotiated contracts in 3,891 districts, the AFT in just 126.

Far behind in the race for new members, the AFT again pushed for a merger. This time there were two powerful personalities to help move things along, the AFT national president, David Selden, and Albert Shanker, the ubiquitous leader of New York City's United Federation of Teachers. The thrust of Selden's campaign was to approach the NEA national leaders, feel them out, as it were, and try for some kind of accommodation. Shanker's tactic was to try to effect a merger in New York State between NEA and AFT affiliates. It was a move which many believed was designed as much for his own advancement as for the cause of NEA/AFT unity. People argued that by bringing off a state merger, Shanker would become the new state union president, representing some 200,000 teachers. From this base, to use Donley's words, he would "outflank Selden, represent the majority of AFT teachers in the nation, and eventually replace Selden as AFT national president."[12]

In fact, whether by design or happenstance, much of that scenario came to be. Shanker succeeded in winning over Thomas Hobart, New York's NEA affiliate president, by arguing that a merger of NEA and AFT power would present a more solid front in negotiations with the state legislature. Accordingly, a loose merger was consummated in 1972 when New York's NEA and AFT affiliates joined to become NYSUT, the New York State United Teachers. NYSUT was organized with Shanker and Hobart as co-leaders and with affiliation ties to both the NEA and AFL-CIO. There were many who prophesied a Shanker takeover and who warned that the New York deal was really a capitulation of NEA power to the AFL-CIO. When NEA executive Sam Lambert voiced these concerns, the NEA heeded his words by passing Business Item #20 which stated that "in the future, the NEA and its affiliates would not enter into a merger requiring affiliation with the AFL-CIO."[13]

National merger talks took place from October of 1973 to February of 1974. At the time, the NEA had 1.5 million members and a national president, Terry Herndon, whose manner was described as "quietly competent." The AFT membership was about 300,000, and AFT leader David Selden was being challenged for power by Albert Shanker, labelled as the "aggressive" protege of AFL/CIO chief George Meany.[14]

The position of Meany, Shanker and the AFT was intransigent on the issue of affiliation. Any merger would have to recognize the AFL-CIO as a political and economic parent organization. The NEA offered a compromise. Members could join the AFL-CIO or be free to decline in writing. On this sticking point if not the conflicting personalities of Herndon and Shanker, the merger talks bogged down and eventually collapsed. Shanker then resolved to bring about a merger by making the AFT so strong that it would not be ignored. In specific, he set out to win California, Puerto Rico, and Florida to the AFT camp. The battles, particularly those in Florida, became bitter, so much so that in 1975 the NEA began to disassociate itself from the NYSUT merger in New York State. The erosion of NEA support for NYSUT—the most tangible example of NEA/AFT unity—continued for the rest of the 1970's and into the 1980's. By 1987 the NEA was completely divorced from NYSUT. Now an AFT affiliate, NYSUT claimed about 125,000 members while the NEA/NY association claimed around 25,000. With the New York merger a lost cause, national unity between the NEA and AFT became a moot issue.

To be sure, strikes on the one hand and attempts at merger on the other were not the only things which occupied American education associations in the years which followed 1970. A third stream of activity began to surface with greater frequency and vehemence, the stream of political action. As teachers became better trained, as more men joined the ranks of teachers, and as the social and economic context of education became more complex, teaching associations began to assert themselves in arenas which were not directly connected to schools per se.[15]

Examples of post-1970 political action are many. A concerted, if futile, support of George McGovern for President in 1972 was perhaps the most dramatic early one, but there were others. There was the boycott of Farah brand clothes because Farah was a non-union shop; protests against President Nixon's policies in Vietnam; opposition to the nominations of Clement Haynsworth and G. Harold Carswell for

Supreme Court Justice. By the mid-1970's NEA and AFT Political Action Committees had been formed and were busily at work supporting candidates and causes which were deemed compatible with the best interests of teachers and education in general.

Over and over again, both NEA and AFT power was brought to bear in the major political movements of the nation. There was, for example, tremendous support, both political and monetary, for the desegregation edicts which followed the Supreme Court rulings of the 1960's. In general, education unions supported busing to achieve racial balance, and between 1970 and 1973, $750,000 was sent by the NEA to the NAACP to help fight discrimination in the hiring of black teachers. Unions fought for the right of teachers to wear beards; for the preservation of works such as *For Whom the Bell Tolls, The Zoo Story,* and *Midnight Cowboy* in schools where the banning of American art forms had become a conservative fashion; for the right of women everywhere to receive job protection when they became pregnant.

If mergers did not continue as a dominant union theme into the decade of the 1980's, certainly militancy and political action did, and the major question of the decade became not so much "what are teaching unions going to do" but "how is the public going to react to them." To that question we now turn.

Public views of teacher unions in the 1980's

Let us concede at the outset of this section of our investigation of unionism in American education that assessing the effects of educational unions is not an exact science. Many serious studies of the subject have, for example, concluded that unions seem to have different impacts in different districts. Many researchers warn that because educational trends are so dynamic, momentary conclusions about the effect of unions are often "time-bound." That is, the conclusions are products of data which are constantly changing. If a district, for example, experiences a strike, it is only normal to expect views of the union involved to be much more negative during and immediately after the strike. More valuable are assessments which try to see broader pictures and longer trends. So with Robert Doherty's caveat in mind that "one cannot avoid a certain amount of untidiness when talking about the effects of collective bargaining on educational outcomes,"[16] we will try to draw upon a researched and reasoned perspective in the discussion below.

Susan Moore Johnson has devoted some considerable time and effort to the study of the impact of unions on the process of education. Following a career both as a teacher and an administrator, she speaks for many present-day researchers when she observes that fair-minded analyses see both positive and negative influences in the union/management relationship. Moreover, by studying a number of districts, she documents that the effects of unionism are variable, that it is not so much the processes of labor/management relations per se which impact on our school but rather the quality of the people involved. Where reasonable, intelligent leadership exists on both sides of the union/management debate, results are apt to be reasonable and intelligent. Where leadership is stubborn, pigheaded, and arbitrary, results can be calamitous.[17]

Without categorizing them as "good" or "bad," Johnson and other researchers such as Perry and Wildman pretty much agree that the great bulk of educational collective bargaining has produced four fairly ubiquitous results:

1. It has increased the formal authority of teachers while restricting the formal authority of principals.
2. It has centralized and standardized school practices.
3. It has redefined, codified, and to some extent reduced teacher work obligations (in the case of the latter through the hiring of aides, paraprofessionals, and outside specialists who may run any of the various extracurricular functions of a school).
4. It has increased teacher pay and job protection.[18]

All of which is not to say that everyone inside and outside education views these results in a sanguine way. Johnson is quick to point to studies by McDonnell, Pascal, Kerchner, and Mitchell which indicate that "many practitioners and educational commentators are disturbed by these effects."[19] Reallocations of authority from principal to teacher have, for many, made our schools less effective. Centralization of standards and practices are often seen as unwise and excessive formalizations of the educational environment. In the detailed defining of teachers' work obligations, many see the reduction of services to unsatisfactory levels. By increasing job protection—not only for teachers but for administrators and support staff through their unions—many argue that we have made it virtually impossible to get incompetent workers out of the system.

Thus, the gains made by unions over the course of the century may quite legitimately be viewed in diametrically opposite ways. A tenure law may truly protect a good teacher from arbitrary dismissal at the very same time it assures the retention of a mediocre one. In the world of educational unionism there may be many mixed blessings. The price of a gain in one area may often be a loss in another. To paraphrase *Inherit the Wind,* if we want to fly, the clouds may sometimes smell of gasoline, and the birds may sometimes lose their wonder.

Differences in educational perspectives are not dispassionate things. You can read the generalizations of a text and never get a feeling for the human realities behind the words. I do not want you to leave the pages of this book in that way, and so I am going to tell you two anecdotes which I hope bring home the generalizations of the research cited here.

Case #1. For a union, saving a member from dismissal is viewed as a prime objective. For many in the public, such objectives have a demeaning effect, undermining professionalism and protecting incompetents. To quote *Newsweek*, often unions are seen as "a source of considerable friction"[20] rather than an element of professional expression. I can think of a vivid case in point, a case in which a union sought to save from dismissal a member who was clearly regarded as a hazard to the school.

The district was a small, upper-middle class community. It had a history of bitter political fighting in its educational governance, and this had helped cultivate an active, aggressive teachers' union. In the years just prior to the incident to be described, enrollment declines and recession had eroded an already small faculty. To make matters worse, student performance relative to surrounding districts (some of which spent considerably less per capita on education) was disappointingly low. The net result of all these conditions was a community overly-critical of its teachers and a union overly protective of an aging, beleaguered membership.

Enter Teacher X, a high school staff member of mediocre reputation with severe emotional problems. The problems became worse and manifested themselves through an inordinate fascination with firearms. One day, the teacher brought a loaded handgun to school, gave it to a student of questionable judgment who discharged it in the hall grazing the head of a passing fellow pupil. Needless to say, the weapon was immediately confiscated and the teacher swiftly suspended from duties—with pay—until an investigation and due process judgment could be rendered.

The position of management in this case was that the teacher should be summarily dismissed and remediated with psychiatric care. The position of the union was that the teacher had suffered a temporary aberration and was, in fact, a fine member of the profession who ought to be retained. Meanwhile, the teacher—still collecting pay—began to take per diem jobs as a substitute in some of the surrounding school systems.

Negotiations on the fate of Teacher X dragged on for months with the union producing document after document proclaiming the teacher a professional of competent standing. Then, one day, word came that the teacher had been discovered in a car filled with weapons. Supposedly, the discovery had occurred in the parking lot of a school where the teacher had been substituting. It became clear at this point that the behavior involved was no temporary condition and that the union position was inaccurate and untenable. The teacher was quickly dismissed and assigned by the courts to a psychiatric center for treatment.

In the aftermath of this incident, the union protested that by trying to protect Teacher X, it was only doing its job. Indeed, had Teacher X been an emotionally normal individual, such protection would have been regarded not only as proper but as just. The public, however, did not buy the union position. Something had to be wrong with a system which offered safe haven for a clearly undesirable person. Whether it be the tenure laws or the dismissal procedures, administrative supervision or poor hiring practices, something would have to change.

In fact, however, nothing did change, and the district simply drifted, as so many do, into an era of greater mutual suspicion and more intense mutual frustration.

Case #2. The push-pull between union, management, and the public can often be quite involved. Battle lines are not always clearly drawn, and if you are a "union man," the enemy may not always be outside the union. Consider the next case which again occurred in a middle class bedroom community.

It was during the difficult mid-1970's and this was a particularly rambunctious seventh grade class. The school was a small 7-8-9 junior high with a wonderful, self-motivated faculty of about fifty teachers. The principal of the building was still in his period of probation, and the union rep was a veteran teacher with his eye on the career ladder. In general, the community supported its schools well. However, because it was something of a resort community with extremely high real estate values, it greatly feared adverse publicity where the schools were concerned. Adverse publicity lowers realty prices and tends to diminish tourism.

Not too far into the school year, it became apparent to the staff that the behavior of some of the seventh grade boys was far beyond normal limits. Tires were being slashed and antennas ripped from faculty cars. Classroom windows were being broken at a record pace. Verbal disrespect became commonplace, and all in all the tone of the school began to change from one of open conviviality to one of fear and anger. When a bag of M-80 firecrackers was set off in front of the door to the home of a faculty member known to have a weak heart, it was clear the time for action had come.

At their monthly faculty meeting, the staff agreed to form a Standards Committee which would look into the matter of student discipline and report back at a later date. The committee worked diligently over the summer and in the fall presented a comprehensive plan which included parent meetings, student counseling, after-school detentions, written behavior codes, uniform disciplinary procedures, and even psychological testing. The plan was approved by the staff unanimously and sanctioned by the building Parent-Teacher Association. It was implemented throughout the year with a noticeable and welcome effect. If not a cure-all, it was a message to students and adults alike that the school would no longer tolerate the abuses it had endured in the past.

A happy ending, you say? Well, the story is not quite over. The Standards Committee plan eventually reached the newspapers. It then became a matter of public knowledge that the school was encountering severe behavior problems with some of its kids. Questions started to be asked of the central administration. Administrators became uneasy. People whose livelihood depended upon selling the good name of the town and its schools became fearful that adverse publicity would hurt them economically. Meetings were held and finally it was agreed that the Standards Committee and its plan would go.

The committee chairperson was summoned at the start of the following year to an informal chat. The principal was there as was the building's union rep.

"The teachers aren't being paid for their after-school time," the rep said. "From the union point of view, especially in a contract negotiations year, that's not good."

"Discipline is the province of the administration," the principal said. "It is not wise to give it up to a faculty committee."

Well, what could the staff do? The union wouldn't support them. The administration wouldn't support them. They did nothing, and the signal which had been sent to the kids was now gone. In short order the school began to revert to its former condition. But that was merely the beginning.

Within five years, many members of that wonderful staff had left the school. Many had left the district. A few had left teaching altogether. The seventh graders grew up, as they are wont to do, and became high school students. Now older, their behavioral abnormalities increased in severity. Soon they formed a teenage, devil-worship cult, and in the madness of a ceremony killed a fellow student and dismembered parts of his body.

Now, of course, there was no stopping the press. But it was too late for that dead youngster. The two ringleaders of the cult were arrested. One hanged himself in the cell of his jail. The other was sentenced to prison.

The union rep eventually became a building principal. The principal eventually became a superintendent.

These cases are severe, dramatic. I chose them for that reason. They are, however, not isolated examples of the dichotomy between the union's perception of its duty and the public's perception of the unions. I could tell you of the union leader who tried to use the work of other teachers above and beyond the contract as a wedge to reopen contract negotiations in the year of his retirement for the purpose of adding a generous retirement incentive clause. I could tell you of the association president who obstructed the transfer of a poor high school teacher to an elementary position even though the retention of the teacher would mean the loss of jobs because students would simply not sign up for the teacher's classes. I could tell you of deals between union and administration to undermine, harass, and even dismiss fine teachers in exchange for personal favors. I could tell you of union pressure brought to bear against union members who were working above and beyond the contract because it was feared that lazy faculty would suffer by comparison.

All of which is not to leave you with the impression that unions are evil, wrong, or unnecessary. In the wake of miserable treatment and even more miserable pay, unions were an inevitability and remain today the only agent pledged to safeguard and advance the welfare of the teacher. But it is to say that with this pledge comes the responsibility to assure a high quality of workmanship. When such assurances are not forthcoming, the reactions against unions become more severe and their positions ultimately become weaker, eventually running the risk of real impotence—an inevitability to me unthinkable, for it would leave teachers virtually defenseless. Already many educators themselves see the danger.

Mario Fantini, formerly Professor and Dean of Education at the State University of New York (New Paltz campus), was also an officer of the Ford Foundation and a seasoned researcher in the area of teacher/public relations. In his book, *What's Best for the Children,* he observes that the post-1970 public, now tired of strikes and higher taxes, has started to look at teacher unions with a somewhat jaundiced eye.[21] Fantini writes:

> Naturally, teachers' organizations oppose any legislative attempts that may jeopardize the interests of their members. The case is crystal clear on the matter of teacher tenure. Once a teacher passes his or her probation period, he or she is entitled to tenure. Tenure protects the teacher from arbitrary or unwarranted dismissal and [safeguards] established academic freedom. Few would argue these rights. However, certain teachers view tenure as guaranteed lifetime employment. Assured of continuing employment and job security, they tend to fall into patterns of mediocrity. It is extremely difficult to deal with these matters after the granting of tenure. Yet many parents, students, and school administrators know that certain teachers are not producing. Some parents and students go so far as stating that these teachers are "incompetent" and should be removed. But the legal appeals are extremely complicated. The limited number of teachers whose continuing contract has been terminated attests to the difficulties in dealing with non-productive teachers.
>
> While there are various reasons why inferior teachers have been placed on tenure (the manpower strain imposed by previous decades of teacher shortages and improper evaluation by administrators during the probationary period), the fact remains that many experienced teachers are not enhancing the learning process with children. These same teachers are protected by teachers'

organizations. Since the first set of objectives for any present professional association is to protect its members, the results are against the interests of children and the public.[22]

Fantini is not alone in his observation. Consider the following from Robert Braun, education editor of the *Newark Star Ledger:*

> Because it [the AFT] is a union first and foremost, its organization is geared to war, to servicing strikes, to collecting new members, to protecting teachers—whether or not they deserve protection—never considering the possibility that teachers, as surrogate parents, should really derive their true protection from the pure love they provide for their children and the respect they earn in a community, a neighborhood, or a town. AFT leadership behaves like the leadership of any other established union—that is, with an eye to staying in power as long as possible...Although it pays considerable lip service to local autonomy and union democracy, the national [organization] trains its reps to mold opinion, to exploit fears, if necessary, to promote paranoia and hysteria and even racism among its teachers, for the war must be won.[23]

That Braun would think as he does is all the more significant because he is more than an educational researcher. He is also a newspaperman with access to and influence upon public perception. It is because public perception is so important in the public education of a free society that we must take it greatly into account in assessing where we are and where we wish to go. In this regard, two important questions arise: (1) is public perception of education and its teachers justified, and (2) how widely held are these public opinions? Let us address the second question first.

It seems apparent that since 1970 (when the economy declined, student enrollment fell, and pupil outcomes dropped), the public has become more critical of its schools. The following quotes from New York City are typical of the syndrome.

> At a time of extreme fiscal austerity and extraordinary need for instructional and administrative improvement in the public schools, a settlement acceptable to the people of this city must give assurance that additional expenditures are inseparably linked to improved quality.[24]

> The parents and public who pay for [education]...seem unsure that they are getting their money's worth.[25]

A more scientific and more up-to-date documentation of the public's attitude can be seen in recent Gallup polls. Asked to grade their local schools, the 1986 Gallup sample responded with an A-rating in only 11% of the cases. 30% responded with a B-rating and 44% with ratings of C or lower. 85% of the respondents were in favor of competency tests for teachers, apparently feeling uneasy at best about the quality of their children's education.[26]

The 1987 Gallup survey showed similar results. Asked if the public schools had improved over the five-year period from 1982-87, the sample responded "yes" in only 25% of the cases. 36% said that schools had remained the same. 22% said they were worse. 17% could not make any judgments. When asked to grade the schools, only 12% gave an A-rating. 31% rated them B. 43% rated them C or below. 14%

did not offer an opinion. Teachers themselves did not fair much better. Only 15% of the sample gave teachers an A-rating. 34% gave a B-rating. 34% gave ratings of C or less. 17% responded "don't know." Virtually the same percentages were true for principals and administrators (14%-A; 29%-B; 39%-C or less; 18%-no opinion). Perhaps even more telling were the responses stating what people wish to see. 71% wished to give parents the right to choose their child's school, and a plurality (44%) were in favor of adopting a "voucher system" of education where the government allocates a certain amount of money per student per year and parents spend it on public, private, or parochial school as they wish. (41% were against this plan and 15% offered no opinion.)[27]

Consistently, then, in the 1980's a very large percentage of respondents place American schools and educators in categories of mediocrity. The question we must now address is their justification for doing so. One way of accomplishing this is to compare student outcomes with teacher incomes, a common public practice. "If I'm going to pay more," the public seems to say, "my kid should be better because I'm getting better teachers and better instruction." While not a year-for-year comparison, the table below at least allows us to look simultaneously at long-term trends in teachers' wages and SAT scores.[28]

TEACHER WAGES/SAT SCORES

Year	Average Teacher Salary	Year	National SAT Scores (1951-1987)	New York SAT Scores (1974-1987)
1951-52	$3,080	1952	476-V / 494-M (970 combined)	
1968-69	$7,295	1963	478-V / 502-M (980 combined)	
1974-75	$11,000	1977	429-V / 470-M (899 combined)	435-V / 480-M (915 combined)
1986-87	$25,313	1987	430-V / 476-M (906 combined)	425-V / 469-M (894 combined)

During the 1950's and at least part of the 1960's we see that the two trends are parallel. Average teacher salaries rise and SAT scores increase—not drastically, but they do go up. During the late 1960's, and 1970's, and through most of the 1980's, however, the pattern changes dramatically. Salaries rise over $18,000 while nationwide SAT scores fall precipitously. The picture in New York is even bleaker. As AFT and NYSUT power increases, student outcomes drop even below the national average. Clearly, for the last quarter century, there is a painful dichotomy between what we are paying and what we are getting.

Consider what this means to a taxpayer in a heavily taxed state such as New York. The teacher's salary goes up from $7,000 to $25,000 while the student's SAT score drops from 980 to 894. The income rise is greater than 250%. The student performance is a decline of 86 points or 14.3%.[29] It is a shocking disparity.

A 250% salary hike is understandable to us as an enormous increase. A 14.3% drop in performance may be a bit more difficult to assess because of the way SAT's are scored. We can bring the decline into clearer perspective, however, with a grading analogy. We are all familiar with our high school grading system, a 100-point scale on which a passing grade is usually 65. An "A" is generally considered to be anything above 90, and an average score is generally considered to be something between 75 and 80. What the SAT decline says, in effect, is that a student doing average work in 1987, getting 75's on most of his or her tests and papers, would have been getting 61's (or 14.3% less in the 100-point grade scale) in 1963. To say this in another way using alpha-grade terminology, a "C" student in high school today would have been an "F" student in 1963, and an "A" grade of 93 or 94 today would have been worth only a "C+" then. That is quite a difference in performance.

There are some educators, however, who do not see the SAT decline as being a true indicator of long-term student performance trends. They argue that public education today seeks to train a broader clientele than it did a quarter century ago and that many more students of lesser academic ability take the test today, thereby lowering the average score. There are also many who claim that the test itself is "culture-bound," unfair to minorities, and only one of many possible indicators of a student's ability.

Some of this is true. An SAT score indicates performance on only one day and one test in the career of a student. It will not tell you if the child is thorough or slipshod, an overachiever or an underachiever, responsible or irresponsible. But it is one of only a handful of national standards by which we may measure how our children perform relative to each other and to other generations regardless of geographical or socioeconomic differences. Great care has been taken to keep the test consistent over the years and to minimize the effects which cultural backgrounds have on outcomes. As for the number and kind of student taking the test, it is interesting to read Copperman's analysis:

> The pattern after 1952 is very clear in its message. Verbal and math aptitudes vary somewhat over the next few years but show 2- and 8-point gains respectively by 1963. This increase took place despite a high school dropout rate which declined from 40 to 30 percent and despite a sharp increase in the percentage of high school graduates taking the SAT, up from less than 7 percent in 1952 to approximately 30 percent in 1963. As both of these factors would tend to make the test-taking population significantly less selective, we can reasonably infer that America's high school seniors significantly increased their academic achievement during this period.[30]

Copperman goes on to point out that three separate studies between 1966 and 1977 determined not only that the tests themselves were valid ones, but that scoring procedures were not in error. In fact, the 1977 study concluded that somewhat more lenient scoring allowed for both verbal and math scores to drift ten points higher than more stringent scoring methods. He also indicates that the decline from 1970 to 1977 was accompanied by stable dropout rates, a decline in the percentage of high school graduates taking the test, a constant percentage of minority students, and an increase in SAT-taker family income—all of which would tend to raise, not lower, the scores.[31]

Might the SAT be "culture-bound?" Yes, but in the face of the studies on validity and the acumen of the CEEB, not likely. Besides, a really culturally biased test would probably show much greater declines in the verbal score than the math score, the latter involving concepts and vocabulary ubiquitous in the nation regardless of socioeconomic influences. In fact, both declined precipitously. Is the SAT a true picture of any student? No. One should also look at a total grade-point average and the anecdotal assessment of teachers. But the SAT and ACT tests are virtually the only national standardized tests of our high school seniors, and they are the ones cited by both colleges and the U.S. Department of Education as indicators of student performance. Thus, in the composite view of student outcomes they cannot be ignored and should not be underestimated.

Whatever weaknesses there are in the SAT, and no test anywhere is perfect, it seems apparent that it is a reasonable measuring device, and it is incontrovertible that declines in SAT scores occurred concomitantly with a rise in teacher union militancy and enormous gains in teacher salaries. No minority group objection that SAT's are "racist," no union protest that SAT-takers are somehow less competent now than they were in 1963 can change the reality. Propagandized though the facts may be—and you must decide in your own mind whose statistical interpretations you prefer—I maintain that the trends do coincide and that the public has ample justification for its suspicions about what it is getting for its educational buck. Even more, I believe that the face-saving protestations of union and/or community apologists are extremely dangerous because they seek to downplay the declines we have suffered and divert us from desperately needed corrective action.

I say this not only because of the SAT score decline. We fare terribly on international tests in comparison with other countries, as the *Nation at Risk* document pointed out, and our measurements of teacher competency continue to show alarming results as teacher salaries continue to climb. Consider the following.

A recent federal report was issued giving the results of teacher competency tests. "Despite extremely low passing requirements, 17 percent of prospective public school teachers are failing certification exams that most states now require for those applying for classroom jobs."[32] All states except Iowa and Alaska require some teacher test, either for admission to a college of education or (more often) to secure a teaching license. The federal study indicates that the failure rates are occurring everywhere even though most of the tests concentrate not on higher-order intellectual skills but simple minimum-level reading and writing ability. To quote from the study itself, "Given that the tests are not difficult and that the passing scores appear to be relatively low, one would expect virtually everyone to pass teacher certification examinations. Yet, this is not the case."[33]

The passing standard for many tests makes the 17% failure rate truly alarming. In ten states, for example, teachers receive passing grades for answering only 47 of 104 questions correctly. To make matters worse, minority test-takers do more poorly than whites. In California, for example, only 26% of blacks passed the 1983 test. Only 33% passed it in 1985. The 1983 passing rate for Mexican-Americans was but 39%. In 1985 it was still only 46%. The 1983 passing rate for whites was 76%. In 1985 it was 81%. And mind you, as Finn points out, these are only crude tests of teacher ability. "They cannot guarantee that an individual who passes will be a good teacher...In principle, however, they can guarantee that an individual who passes is literate and/or knows the subject matter."[34]

Compare the competency results with current wage trends. Gary Putka reports in *The Wall Street Journal* that in the late 1980's and into the 1990's salaries will increase at incredible rates. A new New York City teachers' contract raises maximum salaries to $50,000. The minimum average salary raise of Connecticut teachers with M.A. degrees was up 31% over 1987 levels by September 1988. The AFT reports mean annual earnings at $26,698 in the 1987-88 school year. Rochester (N.Y.) teachers will gain a 52% increase over a three-year period to a $70,000 maximum salary level. The UFT contracts call for an increase in starting salaries to $25,000 by the end of the 1980's.[35]

I do not throw these statistics at you because I believe teachers should not be paid high wages. I believe higher wages will, in fact, be the only significant way we will attract better teachers to the profession. I don't tell you that minorities do poorly on tests because I wish to denigrate minorities. There is no modern thinking person who accepts any doctrine which holds that minorities are inferior academically or in any other way. Certainly, I don't hold any such notions. I don't give you the information because I wish to promote panic in our schools or homes. I collect and publish the data because they are warnings which must be heeded. Like the productivity declines of our industries, the federal budget and trade deficits of our economy, the increase in drug-related behavior on our streets, or the epidemic of venereal disease in our bedrooms, they are harbingers that, unless we face our problems squarely, we stand to lose our nation.

I tell you these facts, these stories, these things because I greatly love this land and because I fear for its tomorrow. I believe that if America fails to right itself, not only will its own people have a bleak future, but the entire portion of the world which seeks protection under our economic, military, and political umbrella will also have a bleak future. I am convinced not only of the majesty of the American creed—of the equal chance we wish for every person because we believe that all of us are created equal—but also of the probability that if that creed does not survive in this nuclear age, mankind itself will not survive.

Putting our heads in the sand now will not solve our problems. Playing "The Emperor's New Clothes" will only insure the worst. The union which cannot improve quality and productivity as it demands more money will have to face the public wrath when, after the money is spent, the children still do not learn. A 52% increase in wages which is not accompanied by, if not a 52%, then at least a significant increase in SAT performance, will ultimately lead to the lowering of wages and the loss of union power and protection. That would be a recipe for disaster. The minority which tries to ascribe poor student performance to an unjustified, unsubstantiated racial cause simply fails to give its children what they need to rise above the poverties and prejudices which are indeed real. If blacks or Hispanics or anyone else continue to say "we can't learn because 'whitey' hates us," then they merely provide a smokescreen to hide the failure of minority students. Even worse, they do nothing to improve the schools and inspire the kids whom they profess to care for.

We will come back to these topics in a future chapter. For now, we turn to issues which need addressing and to some more suggestions as to how we may make real progress in the upgrading of American public education.

Issues and suggestions for educational unionism

It seems clear that American education unions have several important issues to address in the decade of the 1990's. We shall list some of the more pressing ones below and deal with each in turn.

1. Tenure
2. Seniority
3. Differentiated staffing
4. Differentiated pay
5. Membership selectivity
6. Union/management conflict of interests
7. A continuing voice in teacher training, curricular reforms, school management, and school financing

Tenure. That teachers (or any worker) should be protected from unwarranted dismissal, that they should be accorded due process in any proceeding against them, that their academic freedom within a proscribed curricular and legal framework should be protected are all axiomatic to education in a free society. To the extent that tenure laws do these things they are right and proper and should be preserved. That is not simply the opinion of this author, but the law of the land as well. In Keyishian vs. Board of Regents (1967) U.S. Supreme Court Justice William O. Douglas writes as follows:

> Our nation is deeply committed to safeguarding academic freedom, which is a transcendent value to all of us and not merely to the teachers concerned. That freedom is therefore a special concern of the First Amendment which does not tolerate laws that cast a pall of orthodoxy over the classroom.[36]

However, that there are, as Fischer writes, "disadvantages to the operation of tenure"[37] is also true, for tenure laws have in practice been clearly used to shield pedagogical mediocrity. Such a perversion of the intent of tenure laws is greatly at the heart of our present academic problems, and I maintain that every link in the educational chain—administrators, legislators, parents, students, and teachers through their unions—must address the issue honestly if real educational progress is to come. In fact, many educators have begun to do just that. The observations of Fantini (cited earlier) are not isolated ones in the literature of recent years. Respected pedagogues such as Richard Sartore, Jerry Curtis, Shirley Neill, J. Leo Friewald, and Barbara Guthrie-Morse have forthrightly written about the sometimes adverse effect of tenure laws on our schools.[38]

The question which faces us today is what to do about the situation. How do we, on the one hand, protect the academic and personal liberties which tenure is designed to guarantee while, on the other, eliminate the shielding of incompetence which tenure so often promotes? It is not an easy question. There are many well-meaning intellects on both sides of the fence. Many educators of great good will have argued both sides of the issue. Ted Elsberg, President of the New York City Council of Supervisors, for example, states that without the security of tenure, administrators would not be psychologically free to make the difficult decisions needed for effective education. Remove the protection of tenure, he says, and you greatly increase the chance that decisions which might involve controversy will never be made because of the fear of personal reprisal.[39] Yet whole school systems like the one in Dade County, Florida have opted for the removal of tenure laws because they are tired of the educational mediocrity which often results due to them.[40]

I would like here to offer a compromise solution, one which neither eliminates tenure nor sees its unlimited use become the instrument for protecting poor teachers. It is a system of probation and tenure similar to what exists today but with periodic reviews of performance for both teachers and administrators which could lead either to an extension of tenure or a new period of probation. Below is a more detailed scenario.

Educator X is hired and placed on probation for a three-year period. If performance is unsatisfactory, he/she is terminated at any time appropriate during the probationary period. If performance is satisfactory, tenure is granted for a period of five years after which a second tenure evaluation is conducted. If the worker has performed satisfactorily over the five-year tenure period, an extension of tenure for another ten years is granted. If performance has lapsed into mediocrity or worse, a second two-year probationary period is imposed during which the worker must demonstrate improvement. Following the second probationary period the disposition of the worker will be either dismissal if work continues to be poor or the granting of tenure for five more years until another performance review. The worker who successfully obtained a tenure extension of ten years after the initial tenure period would also receive a review after the ten years were over. This would lead, as in the case above, to either another ten-year extension or another period of probation.

A visual flowchart of the process of periodic review appears on the following page.

SYSTEM OF TENURE REVIEW

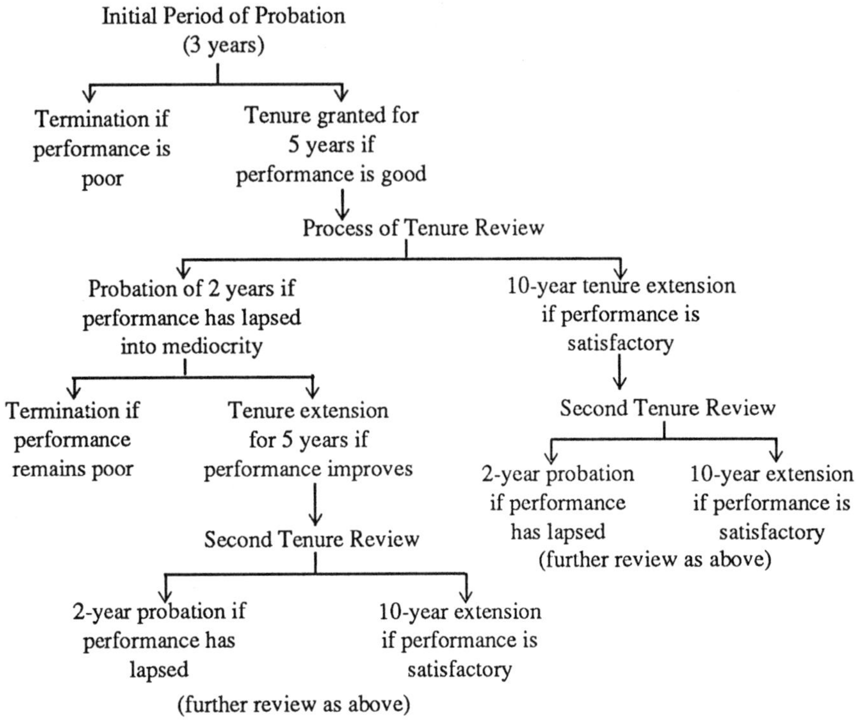

There are several features of this plan which need amplification: (a) built-in administrative accountability, (b) the courtesy of time to change performance or seek new employment, (c) credit for previously received tenure in cases of voluntary changes of employment, (d) fiscal safeguards against abuses by districts for fiscal gain, (e) review criteria, and (f) appeal.

(a) Accountability. The system of tenure review is designed to reduce (if not eliminate) the smugness which says "I'm secure in my job for life—go ahead and try to get me to improve." However, because it would be applied to administrators as well as teachers, it would also guard against the administrator anxious to remove a teacher for personal rather than professional reasons. The vendetta-oriented administrator who drove a good teacher from the rolls would himself/herself be forced to answer for it in his/her own tenure review. As the administrator's vocational well-being would be tied directly to the maintenance of a productive staff, the tenure reviews would of necessity tend to be more fair than unfair.

(b) The courtesy of time. Educators are professionals. They gain employment only after years of preparation. Once an initial period of probation has been successfully completed, the review system suggested here would take that professionalism into account by allowing the educator time to regain his/her competence if it had, indeed, slipped to a level of non-productivity. Even if initial tenure were erroneously granted by a poor administrator, the courtesy of a second probationary period as opposed to outright dismissal says to the individual, "You are a professional and we wish to treat you as such. Let us help you regain your pride as well as your performance level—or at the least, let us give you a decent period of time to relocate in another place or another career."

(c) Tenure credit. The system proposed here would, as do present systems, allow for shorter periods of probation for educators who had been granted tenure in previous jobs. Educator X, for example, has served ten years in a previous school district where he/she successfully completed initial probation, the initial five-year tenure review, and two years of the second ten-year tenure period. Upon entering the new job a one-or two-year probation might then be followed with a ten-year tenure appointment. Such procedures not only credit educators for previous accomplishments, they also make it easier to remain mobile as an employee. Mobility is good for the profession for it acts as an incentive for professionals to grow from one assignment to another and it allows districts to recruit veteran personnel more easily.

(d) Fiscal safeguards. There are those districts which rule by the buck, whose every decision is predicated first and foremost by economics. Such management is not only insane on the face of it but can lead to terrible abuses for which there must be safeguards. Let me put the case of Teacher X, a veteran of such a district for seventeen years. He/she has passed the initial probation, first tenure review, and now comes up for a second review and the final ten years of a twenty-seven year career, leading hopefully to a peaceful and healthy retirement. Being a seventeen-year veteran, Teacher X now commands a salary many thousands of dollars more than the starting salary of a new teacher straight out of college about to begin the initial three-year probation. Were there no safeguards against it, this money-mad district might well deny Teacher X his/her final years of tenure simply to avoid paying the higher salary. Even in the face of due process hearings the district might conspire to build a "paper trail" of evidence against the veteran which no union or private lawyer could gainsay.

To avoid this syndrome, the following is suggested: when an educator is dismissed and replaced by another (as opposed to dismissed with the entire position eliminated in program-cutting attritions), the district would be legally bound to spend the equivalent of the veteran teacher's salary (or a greater amount) in the process of personnel replacement. Should the new educator be hired for less than the outgoing one, the salary differential would have to be equally distributed among all district personnel. In this way, it could never be to a district's financial interest to dismiss a staff member. The decisions for or against tenure would thus have to rest on purely pedagogical grounds.

(e) Review criteria. It is said that there are no valid ways to evaluate the performance of an educator. As a teacher I doubted that, thinking it to be a smokescreen for avoiding educational accountability. As an administrator I now know it to be pure hogwash. Since tenure would be granted on such evaluations, it behooves us to mention for both teacher and administrator at least some of the more important criteria which would be used in the review process.

The criteria for evaluating a teacher are neither obscure nor immeasurable. They should include at least the following: (1) expertise in the subject area; (2) the ability to communicate material clearly; (3) a developed sense of organization in the preparation of lessons, the handling of materials, and the arranging of facilities; (4) prompt disposition of paperwork; (5) the ability to control a class effectively; (6) a sensitivity to the individual needs and differences of students; (7) the ability to work with peers for the good of school or department; and (8) an analysis of student outcomes.

Most of these criteria are rather straightforward and fairly non-controversial. If you ask a teacher for a quarterly report on student progress and it comes in two weeks late, if a class visitation reveals unruly students and a disheveled atmosphere, if parents or students or colleagues continually complain about the inability to work with the teacher, you may be virtually certain that this is not a teacher about to get tenure. If all these things are excellent, you may be equally sure in the opposite direction.

Perhaps the most controversial of the criteria is the one involving student outcomes. "How can I," the teacher often asks, "be accountable for the performance of a student? I am only one link in a learning chain. Even if I'm the best teacher in the world, I can't overcome the effects of a broken home, a drug-ridden student, a lazy child who will not study." Yes, all that is true, and in using student outcomes to judge teacher performance, one must be extra careful to take such factors into account. However, over a range of years and in comparison to other teachers teaching the same courses to students of like ability, the aggregate outcomes of pupils can well reflect the quality of instruction. If Teacher X teaches 10th grade English for three years to children heterogeneously grouped, and Teacher Y does the same in a similar environment, and all the students take the same departmental or state exams, the outcomes of the pupils of Teacher X should be reasonably close to those of Teacher Y. However, if the three-year average shows that 60% of the students of Teacher X are passing the course while 90% of Teacher Y's students are passing, then the performance of Teacher X is legitimately called into question.

The criteria for evaluating administrators are also fairly self-evident. Schaefer and Read state them in the following five points: (1) a measurement of goal accomplishments; (2) performance of assigned duties; (3) peer rating; (4) rating of subordinates; and (5) evidence of professional growth.[41] One can be reasonably sure that if these ratings are high, the candidate is justified in receiving tenure, and if they are low, tenure should be withheld. In any event, they constitute at least a point of departure in the establishment of evaluative criteria.

(f) The right of appeal. Finally, the proper administration of a tenure system should incorporate the right of an educator to appeal a negative decision. In such an appeal process, the educator should be allowed union representation as well as legal representation, and the appeal board should consist of at least one administrator and one board of education member familiar with the district but not party to the original decision.

In all of this, it should be understood that no system is foolproof. A particularly cantankerous staff member of mine is ever ready to point out that in any system, no matter how carefully or conscientiously contrived, people will find a way to subvert it. "Why are you always such a pessimist?" I growl at him, and he answers (with a twinkle in his eye because he is a good and caring teacher), "It's not pessimism; it's realism." Perhaps he's right, but even if he is, we must continue to try to better the system, for the alternative to trying will certainly ensure the worst. Progress, if it ever comes, is usually in fits and starts.

Seniority. Tenure at least has the motive of protecting the worker against abuse. Seniority claims no other purpose but an arbitrary aggrandizement of those in power. That someone should be retained simply because he has been around longer is a doctrine which must be eliminated if schools are to improve. Longevity in and of itself is not a justification for, nor a proper measure of, competence, and when it is used as such in our schools the results can often be disastrous.

During times of population growth and/or fiscal prosperity educational staffs tend to increase. In such atmospheres, while seniority may be used to hand out perks, it does not play a role in staff dismissals simply because there are no dismissals. The problems come when staff reductions have to be made, and these are usually done on the basis of seniority. The last hired is generally the first fired. The most senior is generally the most secure—regardless of competence. That is a policy of sheer lunacy, for if the younger staffers happen to be better educators, the policy forces the elimination of excellence and the retention and promotion of mediocrity. The determinant for dismissal should be merit and job competence (or the lack of it) measured by the same criteria as those used for tenure.

There is an interesting sidelight to dismissals caused by the excessing (elimination) of positions in times of enrollment decline or fiscal trouble. Having living through such a period in the 1970's when many of my colleagues' jobs were done away with, I remember repeatedly asking my union to save them by voluntarily accepting less of an increase in our newly negotiated contracts—the money thus saved to go toward the retention of our fellow workers. "We just got a 6% increase," I said. "There are over 500 of us in this district. If we each donate 2% of our wages to the general fund, we will have enough to save the jobs of the ten teachers who are being let go."

I was laughed out of the hall. It was a laugh tinged with the prejudices of seniority. You see, the union leaders were not rookie teachers but workers with the most service in terms of years in the district. Their salaries were thus among the highest. When they negotiated wage increments they always did so in percentages rather than flat dollar figures because percentages gave them much more money. If you are earning $30,000, a 6% salary hike increases your pay by $1,800. The guy or gal with little seniority making only $15,000 gets only a $900 raise. Had a blanket $1,000 increase been negotiated, it would have been much fairer, but remember that union negotiators had the honey of seniority dripping from their lips, and so they were eager to skew the distribution of the larder to their own advantage.

This syndrome of union elders feeding off the flesh of younger brethren is dangerous on two grounds. First, it promotes internal inequity and thus internal dissension. Secondly, and much more damaging, it acts as a powerful disincentive for young, bright educators to enter the field. If there is any place in which the unions should look to the cleaning of their houses, it is here.

Having said all this, however, there is a major problem which emerges when seniority is eliminated. In its absence, greedy employers (they exist, too, you know) may be tempted to let senior staffers go simply *because* their salaries are higher. "We don't care about competence," they reason. "Teacher X earns more than Teacher Y. If we have to reduce the staff, Teacher X goes." That is not merely a theoretical problem. It happens in many industries, and without proper safeguards it would happen in education, too, people being what they are.

The safeguard is the same fiscal policy discussed in the section on tenure (above), that is, the forced redistribution of salary differentials. Say Teacher X with seniority earns $30,000 while Teacher Y earns $20,000. A position is going to be eliminated and because Teacher X is far less competent, it will be Teacher X who goes. The difference between the two salaries ($10,000) would have to be distributed equally among all district staff members under the fiscal safeguard proposed here. In that way, even though the district would save a full salary by the excessing of a position, it would be the salary of Teacher Y, not the salary of Teacher X. This procedure would insure that if a senior staff member like Teacher X were let go it would be for reasons of incompetence and not ones of pure economics.

All of which is not to say that seniority should *never* be a factor in dealing with educational personnel. In matters of forced elimination of jobs, involuntary transfer of assignments, selecting who gets to go to a conference or convention, *if all other factors are equal* between competing staff members, seniority may be the only reasonable way to decide things. It should, however, be the instrument of last, not first, resort simply because the ultimate goal in education should always be to take the pedagogically, not economically or politically, soundest course.

If unions have a difficult time swallowing that message, I believe it best for them to remember that higher quality makes for a stronger union. Ultimately, if unions merely stand for the protection of incompetence, the public will react as they did in the 1967 Florida strike when five hundred jobs were lost. Already the "pay more for less" attitude of many unions has caused a shrinkage of membership and concomitant loss of power in the American labor movement of the 1970's and 1980's. That is very unfortunate, for with all my criticisms of them, I still remain convinced that unions represent the best worker protection we have and a vital link in the chain of economic checks and balances available to a free marketplace.

Differentiated staffing. Most workers have areas of strengths and weaknesses. Certainly it is not often one finds an educator who is outstanding in every aspect of his/her field, and for that matter it is not likely that one will be weak in all areas of endeavor. The science department usually has members who excel in biology or chemistry or physics but rarely all three. The music department may have specialists in band or orchestra or chorus, but it is not often one finds expertise for each area in the same teacher. Similarly, some educators may be long on organizational skills but short on classroom management, excellent teachers but poor supervisors, wonderful in dealing with students but sluggish on curriculum development. To the extent that teacher certification procedures can pinpoint expertise as opposed to creating bland generalists, they can help in the eventual improvement of American education. But if certification is not the vehicle available for the maximization of staff performance, differentiated staffing assignments certainly can be.

There is a good deal of literature on the subject, much of it greatly in favor of more intelligent ways of assigning educational personnel than those currently in use. Gideonse suggests a hierarchy of entry level, staff level, and master level teachers.[42] Goodlad speaks favorably of differentiated staffing, albeit with the caveat that present systems may be difficult to change.[43] Koehler proposes two separate kinds of educational training, one specializing in the arts of teaching and curriculum development, the other in the arts of educational management (much as hospitals have doctors who are medical practitioners and executives who are medical administrators).[44] Trump suggests that just as education often is best when it is personalized or individualized for the student, so it may be most effective when assignments are personalized or individualized for the staff.[45]

The notion of differentiated staffing is not new to the 1980's. Several educators began pioneering the concept as far back as twenty years ago and more. In 1968 Rand and English were already field-testing models of differentiated staffing in California, apparently with positive results.[46] In 1970 Olivero and Buffie edited several articles on differentiated staffing in their work entitled *Educational Manpower*,[47] and in 1971 units of the Bureau of Cooperative Educational Services (BOCES) of New York State compiled an extensive compendium of over fifty articles on the subject.[48]

To be sure, not all educators are enthusiastic about the idea. Spillane, for example, sees the master teacher concept as a usurpation of the authority and function of trained educational administrators,[49] while Supranovich claims that differentiated staffing is a further "bureaucratization of a profession which already rewards those practitioners furthest removed from its clients."[50] To the extent that its problems can be managed, however, and to the extent that unions can work with school administrators to develop mutually satisfactory plans, differentiated staffing is certainly one way to improve the use of personnel and thereby the outcomes of students.

Differentiated pay. There is a teacher who has been working for about ten years. He earns $25,000. He has a fairly good relationship with his students. He teaches fairly well. Occasionally his paperwork is late. His room and materials are pretty decently organized. He rarely stays beyond the final bell. He never volunteers for any extra assignment which would benefit the department whether or not there is pay attached to it. There is another teacher who has also been working about ten years. The kids love her. Her energy is boundless. She is always ready to work for the betterment of the students and the program in general. Her paperwork is always early, her room well-organized, her teaching superb. She is also paid about $25,000. I think it's a crime.

The present regime in the Soviet Union is coming to grips with the painful reality that as it is constituted Soviet socialist communism does not make for a vital economy. We have already seen that since 1984 the U.S.S.R. has embarked upon a massive and costly reform of its educational system to try to improve its economic future. Along with that reform is an openness which is finally addressing the self-criticism that lies at the heart of any serious attempt at improvement. It is no unimportant matter that a key element in this self-criticism (and we see it also in the People's Republic of China) is the acknowledgement that where there are disincentives to personal gain there is a lack of productivity. Russia and China are beginning to accept openly and politically that working simply for the good of a vague societal well-being is just not motivation enough for most people. Why must we run our schools with the same ethic which has failed our economic opposites and which they now admit does not work?

It is maddening for good teachers who care and try, who stay late and arrive early, who strive to be and do become excellent to see their mediocre, often lazy, sometimes incompetent colleagues receiving the same wages, the same benefits year upon year. The praises are ubiquitous. "We're really proud of a fine staff," the superintendent says on opening day. "We will negotiate a fixed percentage raise for all of us," the union leader exhorts. Meanwhile, we all know the truth. Some of us *are* fine. Some of us deserve that raise—and more. And others of us ought to be selling shoes instead of corrupting the educational landscape.

More often than not, the broad brush with which unions and administrators so often paint is made even worse by pressure to slack off, lest by comparison a hardworking teacher make the laggard look bad. I have seen it firsthand. Don't doubt it; it's real. I've heard the union rep say, "We resent your staying until 5 o'clock," and the superintendent whisper, "We've got to slow that guy down." It's an ass-backwards system, and it need not be.

If not for the rank or job title they hold (for positions with greater responsibility generally merit a higher base pay), then for the *quality* of the work they do, educators should be compensated by wages which differentiate them according to merit. Such a philosophy is an incentive for diligence and a protection against sloth. It replaces the Marxian ethic "from each according to his ability, to each according to his need" with a much more real one: "from each according to his level of commitment, to each according to his level of achievement." How much more honest is this ethic? How much finer example is it for the students whom these educators serve?

Are there dangers with merit pay? Yes, and they should be addressed. How do you determine merit? How do you avoid political favoritism and administrate a merit plan so that staff members are not unduly embarrassed? How does a union negotiate in the light of a merit pay system? Let us consider each question in turn.

The determination of merit can rest not only on the criteria of performance discussed for both teachers and administrators in the section on tenure (above), but on factors which lie beyond the normal parameters of educational job descriptions. Miller and Say, in their discussion of merit pay in the Houston public school system, indicate that pay may increase for teachers who accept assignments in curricular areas where there are staff shortages as well as for those who show clear evidence of professional growth or educational progress.[51] What might one consider "professional growth and educational progress?" Many things. The successful completion of an in-service program or the successful completion of a graduate degree are two which readily come to mind, but there are others. If a staff member prepares a special report, chairs a special committee, accepts professional statewide or regional assignments, reviews materials for a school or department, attends conferences for the purpose of reporting back to home staff, then he or she is functioning far beyond the bounds of a normal assignment, and rewards should be forthcoming.

There are still other factors which might enter the merit pay evaluation. Let us say that an educator receives an award for service or special accomplishment. The recognition thus gained from others might well be translated into a merit pay increase. If an educator is able to publish materials which enhance the field, he or she has taken a step which only a small percentage of educators takes. Such initiative and ability should be rewarded, for as the star of the educator rises, so the reputation of his/her home educational community ascends as well.

There is a growing body of evidence that criteria such as the ones above are being successfully used in merit pay systems. Besides Houston, Texas, state colleges in New Jersey and school districts in California also report positive programs.[52] It is, moreover, interesting to note that such programs appear to be working not only with teachers but with administrators as well.[53] Stoddard even reports on a superintendent whose performance in five key areas (leadership, finance, organization, management, and employee morale) is graded by his board of education on an A - F scale. Grades of A, B, or C yield bonuses of between $500 and $1,000. Grades of D or F require salary forfeitures of $500 and $1,000 respectively.[54]

Just as workable evaluative criteria appear to exist, there seems to be a built-in safeguard against any unfair politicization in the administration of merit pay systems. The safeguard is that those who, on the one hand, dispense the merit pay of subordinates are, on the other hand, accountable for the performance of those subordinates in receiving their own merit pay. If the judgment of, say, a department chairperson is wrong in assigning merit increases to his or her staff, the morale of the staff and thus its performance will more than likely suffer. This, in turn, will mean a lower rating for the chairperson. To be sure, this is a safeguard which is hardly foolproof. For example, errors in judgment may be as much a product of honest misassessment as of deliberate politicization, and even if there is fair and just objectivity in the dispensing of increases, there may still be hard feelings which create intra-departmental tensions and individual demoralizations.

There have been some educational researchers and theorists who, in anticipation of such problems, have offered a range of interesting suggestions. Schrag, for example, sees the possibility of merit pay based on achieving the rank of "distinguished teacher" where the rank is bestowed by a panel of parents, peers, administrators, and former students.[55] Others, such as Burke, feel that confidentiality is a key factor in making merit systems work.[56]

My advocacy for the merit proposals here is thus not accompanied by the naive notion that such systems would be perfect. The debate on the topic within the educational community is a lively one,[57] and in trying to start any such system it is worth noting that in some teacher-preference polls on the subject, many prefer to leave things as they are—that is, pay without the merit policy.[58] My point is, rather, that merit pay is a stimulus for greater educational productivity which is well worth trying, with all the proper safeguards we can devise, of course. The alternative is continuing in our present mold, and that is the least acceptable of all.

How would a union negotiate a merit increase? Let me repeat an interesting idea which came from former New York Yankee broadcaster Bill White. I don't remember what team they were playing, but it started to rain, forcing the Yanks off the field. As the grounds crew got our their tarp, Bill White and his broadcast partner, former Yankee great Phil Rizzuto, began a conversation to fill up the time. It centered on the enormous differences in salary between what White and Rizzuto had made in their playing days, and what is being dispensed today to players of similar (or lesser) ability.

White commented that it has made many players egomaniacal as opposed to team-oriented people (an observation echoed by many other former greats such as basketball's Bob Couzy), but even more, that the salaries are doled out *before* the season's performance. Thus, he argued, one frequently sees a player earning a million dollars or more for a mediocre year, hardly an incentive for lower-paid athletes to put forth greater efforts. Rizzuto asked White if he had a better system, and the intelligent Hiram College graduate said that he did. He suggested that Yankee owner George Steinbrenner set aside however many millions he had allocated for player salaries in a given year. Pay everyone a decent baseline wage, White went on, and then devise an increment scale based upon *both* individual and team performance. For so many team wins beyond 82 (50% of the total games of the season), all players would receive bonuses. The more wins, the higher the bonuses. For individual achievements beyond baseline expectations (more than 10 wins for a starting pitcher, higher batting averages than .250 for a hitter, etc.), individual raises would be granted. The greater the achievements, the greater the raises.

White argued that such a system would not only be fairer to the players, but that it would also set a wonderful example for future players and for the kids of the nation who, after all, so often look to pro athletes for the ethical examples expected of a role model.

I don't know what Mr. Steinbrenner thinks of White's idea, but personally I love it, and I can easily see how it might be adapted into the educational arena with respect to union/management contract negotiations. The union and district would bargain for a percentage increase above current salary levels. This would, in turn, increase the total dollar pool allocated for the next year's wages. The district would be legally bound to use up that money, but the district's merit formula would determine who received a raise and how much it would be. A Utopia? No, but a good deal better than the present systems which reward industry and sloth, excellence and mediocrity with equal recognition.

Membership selectivity. The guilds which arose in Medieval and Renaissance Europe did not have as their aim merely the protection and well-being of the artisans who populated them. They also sought the maintenance of the standards of workmanship which their crafts demanded. For many occupations, this assurance of quality was passed on to the American workplace by the early Colonial settlers. The silversmiths and cabinetmakers, printers and foundrymen who labored here had in many instances an enormous sense of pride in product and a sense of duty about keeping the value of products high. It was no small thing when a Paul Revere stamped his name into the silver of a dish or tray, and it was no light decision for workers like Revere to accept a youngster as an apprentice.

In some respects, we may still see the ethic of the guilds at work: a hand-crafted piano, a piece of china, the loving care of a seamstress. Unfortunately, we see it all too seldom in education, and not at all in the educational unions—at least not the ones I've known or studied. A rookie comes out of college, lands a job, and the union fairly trips over itself to get the kid signed up. After all, they're playing hardball. Memberships mean money and power. "It's not our job," one union rep said to me, "to evaluate the calibre of our membership. That's for the administrators. It's our job to protect them and get what we can for them." Well, in part, I agree. It is certainly the job of a union to fight for its constituents, and it is certainly the role of the administration to evaluate teaching performance—especially in the probationary years before tenure. However, it is cynically shortsighted, counterproductive to the well-being of the profession, and counterproductive to the well-being of the union itself to turn a deaf ear or a blind eye to the incompetence of a member.

What I suggest to deal with the issue is a reawakening of the attitude of quality workmanship on the part of educational unions. If they are going to accept automatically any worker hired by the district (and for purposes of bargaining, I can see that as a kind of sine qua non), then I suggest that they have their own period of probation, a period in which members might be counseled by veterans and observed by peers with the idea that performance can be improved. Perhaps union reviews of performance, periodic workshops in new techniques and materials (run jointly with the management of the district) would also be reflective of a new order, a new educational partnership. Finally, I believe that in the face of clear evidence, incompetent members should be asked to leave the union and, if need be, to bargain for themselves in the negotiations process.

If things like this do not begin to happen, I can see two dire consequences: one, that union support in the public sector will continue to erode, and two, that educators longing for a more responsible professional organization may bolt existing unions, further fragmenting, complicating, and weakening the national educational fabric.

Union/management conflicts of interest. In government there are explicit statutes against conflicts of interest. Judges are not supposed to render decisions in cases where they have a personal involvement; elected or appointed officials are asked to place individual assets in trusts before assuming office. There are few things more maddening to the taxpayer or more corrosive to the framework of a democracy than the Secretary of Commerce who leaves office to head up an airline or the lumber company executive who becomes a big deal for the Department of the Interior and throws a lot of million dollar contracts to his old firm.

Where it exists in education, the union leader who "plays ball" with management at the expense of the educational community in order to climb the corporate ladder is an abomination. Perhaps we will never stop this kind of thing, but we ought to pass some sort of legislation restricting and discouraging it. For example, how about a statute which says that anyone holding union office in a state or local jurisdiction would be required to wait five years from the leaving of that office before assuming an administrative position in the same jurisdiction? I'm not a constitutional lawyer, but if such a statute were not a violation of civil liberties, it would go a long way toward ending the kind of collusion which ruins many a school.

A continuing voice. To the extent that education unions have promoted educational well-being in addition to things like wage hikes and benefits, they are to be applauded. As education moves into the twenty-first century I hope that the union voice will not be still on this score. Improvements in areas such as curriculum, school management, and educational financing are apt to be much more meaningful if they come from those who are in daily contact with the processes of education. It is also important that with all the criticism of them, we understand that union voices are an indispensable counterweight in the checks and balances of a free democracy.

If constructive in nature, criticisms are not acts of rebuke but ones of concern. The parent willing to point out the flaws of the child, the teacher willing to point out the errors of the student are far from being the enemies. On the contrary, if done for the purposes of strengthening the child, such criticisms are acts of love, more powerful and far more important than cotton candy praises or gratuitous acceptance. This is no less true of collective institutions such as education or government, especially in a free society. In the final analysis, that is what America's founding fathers had in mind when they gave us the amendment process. It says, in effect, find out where you are weak or wrong and change things so that the problems are fixed: don't be afraid of self-investigation and growth, for they are the true mechanisms we have to adapt to the dynamic conditions of time. They are our best chance of survival.

References for Chapter Three

1. Some of the statistics supplied by the NSBA have been updated here by 1987 figures from the U.S. Department of Education Office of Planning, Budget, and Evaluation in its February 1987 report. In a few cases the updates are significant. For example, the NSBA reports the average 1986 teacher salary as $19,272, while the Department of Education reports it as $25,313 and breaks that down by state. The NSBA reports the pupil-teacher ratio in public schools as 18.9 to 1. The Department of Education puts it at 17.9 to 1. Where possible, the statistics in this text are the latest available at the time of writing.
2. ***Power to the Teacher: how America's educators became militant,*** Marshall O. Donley. Bloomington, Indiana: Indiana Univ. Press, 1976. p. 5.
3. ***Power to the Teacher,*** Donley. p. 11.
4. ***Power to the Teacher,*** Donley. p. 17.
5. ***Power to the Teacher,*** Donley. All these statistics may be found on pp. 39-40 ff.
6. ***Power to the Teacher,*** Donley. p. 44.
7. ***Power to the Teacher,*** Donley. p. 50.
8. ***Power to the Teacher,*** Donley. p. 55.
9. ***Power to the Teacher,*** Donley. p. 55.
10. ***Power to the Teacher,*** Donley. pp. 74-75.
11. ***Power to the Teacher,*** Donley. p. 138.
12. ***Power to the Teacher,*** Donley. p. 166.
13. ***Power to the Teacher,*** Donley. p. 168.
14. ***Power to the Teacher,*** Donley. p. 170.
15. ***Power to the Teacher,*** Donley. p. 195. Donley cites the rise of association political action with statistics involving both greater amounts of higher education and increases in male teachers. In 1947, for example, only 44% of teachers had bachelor's degrees and only 15% advanced degrees. By 1955 it was 52% and 25%, respectively. By 1965 over 90% were college graduates. Similarly, in the mid-1920's only 17% of public school teachers were men. By 1965 it was 30%, and between 1954 and 1964 the number of male teachers grew three times as fast as the number of female teachers.
16. "Does Teacher Bargaining Effect Student Achievement?" Robert E. Doherty. In ***Faculty and Teacher Bargaining: the impact of unions on education,*** George W. Angell, ed. Lexington, Mass.: Lexington Books, 1981. p. 64.
17. ***Teacher Unions in Schools,*** Susan Moore Johnson. Philadelphia: Temple University Press, 1984. passim.
18. ***The Impact of Negotiations in Public Education: the evidence from the schools,*** Charles R. Perry and W.A. Wildman. Worthington, Ohio: Jones Pub. Co., 1970.
19. ***Teacher Unions in Schools,*** Johnson. p. 5. Johnson cites the following sources: ***Organized Teachers in American Schools,*** Lorraine McDonnell and Anthony Pascal. Santa Monica, Ca.: Rand Corp., 1979; ***The Dynamics of Public School Bargaining and Its Impact on Governance, Administration, and Teaching,*** Charles T. Kerchner and Douglas E. Mitchell. Washington, D.C.: National Institute of Education, 1981.
20. "Teachers Are in Trouble," Dennis A. Williams et al. In *Newsweek.* April 27, 1981. See also "Teacher Bargaining: an autopsy," Myron Lieberman. In ***Phi Delta Kappan.*** December 1981 (Vol. 63, #4); and "After Twenty Years, Lieberman's Vision is Failing," Albert Shanker. In ***Phi Delta Kappan.*** December 1981 (Vol. 63, #4).
21. ***What's Best for the Children: resolving the power struggle between parents and teachers,*** Mario D. Fantini. Garden City, N.Y.: Anchor Press/Doubleday, 1975. pp. 55-137 passim.

22. ***What's Best for the Children,*** Fantini. p. 106.
23. ***Teachers and Power: the story of the American Federation of Teachers,*** Robert Braun. New York: Simon and Schuster, 1972. p. 252.
24. ***New York Times.*** September 7, 1972.
25. ***New York Times.*** September 12, 1973.
26. "The 18th Annual Gallup Poll of the Public's Attitudes toward the Public Schools," Alec M. Gallup. In ***Phi Delta Kappan.*** September 1986 (Vol. 68, #1). pp. 43-59.
27. "The 19th Annual Gallup Poll of the Public's Attitudes toward the Public Schools," Alec M. Gallup and David L. Clark. In ***Phi Delta Kappan.*** September 1987 (Vol. 69, #1). pp. 17-30.
28. The wage figures for 1951-52, 1968-69, and 1974-75 come from ***Power to the Teacher,*** Donley, pp. 40, 192, and 222. Wage figures for 1986 come from the "Statement and Fourth Annual Wallchart of State Educational Statistics." U.S. Dept. of Education. February, 1987. The 1952, 1963, and 1977 SAT scores may be found in ***The Literacy Hoax,*** Copperman, p. 38. The 1987 SAT data come from the U.S. Dept. of Education's 1987 "Wallchart."
29. SAT scores are based on a minimum score of 200 and a maximum of 800. The 86 point drop thus represents 14.3% of the 600 point variance from maximum low to maximum high.
30. ***The Literacy Hoax,*** Copperman. p. 39. Copperman cites as his sources: ***On Further Investigation: report of the advisory panel on the Scholastic Aptitude Test score decline.*** New York: College Entrance Examination Board, 1977. ***Achievement Test Score Decline: do we need to worry?*** D. Wiley and A. Harnischfeger. Chicago: Cemrel, Inc. 1975.
31. ***The Literacy Hoax,*** Copperman. p. 40.
32. "Seventeen Percent of Teachers Flunk Exam." Associated Press wire story in ***The Kennebec Journal.*** Augusta, Maine: August 27, 1987. The study referred to is entitled "What's Happening in Teacher Testing" and was conducted by the Office of Educational Research and Improvement for the U.S. Department of Education. Washington, D.C.: 1987. The director of the project was Chester Finn, Jr., Education Department research chief.
33. "What's Happening in Teacher Testing?" Federal report on teacher competency tests. Chester Finn, Jr., chief researcher. Washington, D.C.: Department of Education, 1987.
34. "Seventeen Percent of Teachers Flunk Exam," ***The Kennebec Journal.*** Augusta, Maine: August 27, 1987.
35. "Teachers Get More Pay and Power in the Wake of Reform Movements," Gary Putka. In ***The Wall Street Journal.*** September 21, 1987.
36. "Academic Freedom and Tenure," Louis Fischer. In ***Encyclopedia of Educational Research,*** 5th ed. Harold E. Mitzel, ed. in chief. New York: The Free Press, 1982. p. 4. From Keyishian vs. Board of Regents, 385 U.S. 589, 1967.
37. "Academic Freedom and Tenure," Fischer. In ***Encyclopedia of Educational Research,*** 5th ed. p. 6.
38. See the following: "Tenure Laws: another look," Richard L. Sartore. In ***Illinois Schools Journal,*** Winter 1978-79 (Vol. 58, #4). pp. 8-11; "Staff Dismissal: problems and solutions," Jerry Curtis and Shirley B. Neill. Arlington, Virginia: American Association of School Administrators, 1978; "Tenure — Another Sacred Cow about To Bite the Dust," J. Leo Friewald. In ***Phi Delta Kappan,*** September 1979 (Vol. 61, #1); "Assessing the Impact of Faculty Unions: the financial implications of collective bargaining," Barbara Gutherie-Morse et al. In ***Journal of Higher Education,*** May 1980 (Vol. 52, #3). pp. 237-55.

39. "Schools Need Tenured Leaders," Ted Elsberg. In ***The New York Times.*** November 13, 1982.
40. See "Tenure — Another Sacred Cow about To Bite the Dust," Friewald cited above. Dade County replaced its tenure system with a "just cause/due process" procedure in which teachers have the rights of union representation and appeal.
41. "Use This Plan To Evaluate and Pay Administrators," William Schaefer and Bruce Read. In ***Executive Educator,*** July 1982 (Vol. 4, #7). pp. 22-24.
42. "The Necessary Revolution in Teacher Education," Hendrick D. Gideonse. In ***Phi Delta Kappan,*** September 1982 (Vol. 64, #1). pp. 15-18.
43. "Let's Get On with the Reconstruction," John I. Goodlad. In ***Phi Delta Kappan,*** September 1982 (Vol. 64, #1). pp. 19-20.
44. "Schools without Lowerarchies: are they possible?" Michael D. Koehler. In ***Clearing House,*** May 1979 (Vol. 52, #9). pp. 434-35.
45. "A School for Everyone," J. Lloyd Trump. Reston, Virginia: National Association of Secondary School Principals, 1977. pp. 20-21 ff, 52-53 ff, and 200-11 ff.
46. "Towards a Differentiated Teaching Staff," M. John Rand and Fenwick English. In ***Phi Delta Kappan,*** January 1968 (Vol. 49, #5). pp. 264-68.
47. ***Educational Manpower,*** James L. Olivero and G. Buffie, eds. Bloomington, Indiana: Indiana University Press, 1970. Chapter 11 is an article generally favorable to the concept of differentiated staffing. It is entitled "A Differentiated Staff: putting teaching talent to work," and was written by Dwight W. Allen. Chapter 13 contains further information on field testing the concept by Fenwick English.
48. ***Differentiated Staffing.*** Central New York Regional Office for Educational Planning and Nassau Regional Office of Educational Planning (BOCES), 1971.
49. "Some Unfortunate Assumptions," Robert Spillane. In ***Phi Delta Kappan.*** September 1982 (Vol. 64, #1). p. 21.
50. "Differentiated Staffing Revisited," Beth Bond Supranovich. In ***Phi Delta Kappan.*** September 1982 (Vol. 64, #1). pp. 20-21.
51. "This Bold Incentive Pay Plan Pits Capitalism against Teacher Shortages," Leslie Miller and Elaine Say. In ***American School Board Journal.*** September 1982. pp. 24-25.
52. "Paying Faculty Members What They Are Worth," Robert Breslin and Leo F. Klagholz. In ***Education Record.*** Winter 1980 (Vol. 61). pp. 43-44; and "Merit Pay for Teachers: Round Valley may have the answer," Brian T. Burke. In ***Phi Delta Kappan.*** December 1982 (Vol. 64, #4). pp. 265-66.
53. See "If You Follow These Proven Guidelines, Merit Pay for Administrators Can Succeed," Philip E. Geiger and Gerald Toscano. In ***American School Board Journal.*** January 1980 (Vol. 167, #1). pp. 31-32; and "Administrator Merit Pay — Theory into Practice," Larry G. Ruttan. In ***Thrust for Educational Leadership.*** May 1979 (Vol. 8, #5). pp. 28-30.
54. "This Board Hired a Superintendent Who Requested a Merit Pay Plan for Himself," Robert Stoddard. In ***American School Board Journal.*** January 1979 (Vol. 166, #1). p. 41.
55. "It's Time for Merit Pay," Francis Schrag. In ***Learning.*** March 1983 (Vol. 11, #8). p. 28.
56. See "Merit Pay for Teachers: Round Valley may have the answer," Brian T. Burke. In ***Phi Delta Kappan.*** December 1982 (Vol. 64, #4). pp. 265-66.
57. To cite just some participants in the merit pay debate, on the "pro-merit" side, see "Is There Merit in Merit Increases?" Jane T. Brinks. In ***Personnel Administrator.*** May 1980 (Vol. 25, #5). pp. 59-64; and "Would Bear Bryant Teach in Public School?" William F. Casey. In ***Phi Delta Kappan.*** March 1979 (Vol. 60, #7). pp. 500-01. For views against merit systems, see "Why Not Merit Pay?" Lawrence J. Dennis. In

Contemporary Education. Fall 1982 (Vol. 56, #6). pp. 18-21; and "What Ever Happened to Kalamazoo's Merit Pay Plan?" Richard R. Doremus. In ***Phi Delta Kappan.*** February 1982 (Vol. 63, #6). pp. 409-10. For views both pro and con, see "Salary Scales: pros and cons," Maryse Eymonerie. In ***Academy Bulletin of the AAUP.*** March 1980 (Vol. 66, #2). pp. 118-19.

58. "Teachers' Preference Toward Alternate Systems of Salary Increment," Cheryl E. Bogie and Donald W. Bogie. In ***Education.*** Winter 1978 (Vol. 99, #2). pp. 215-20.

Chapter Four

Behind the Scenes —
Beyond the Classroom

Chapter Four

Behind the Scenes — Beyond the Classroom

BEFORE THE CHILD and teacher walk into the classroom, a host of things has happened which will to a significant degree affect the learning process. How the teacher has been prepared, how the educational dollar has been divided, how the child has been manipulated by government intervention—these and much more will set the framework in which learning will (or will not) occur. Thus, before we investigate the details of curriculum and student behavior within the school, it behooves us to look at the educational atmosphere outside it. In doing so, we will concentrate on four broad topics:

1. Educational economics
2. Teacher training and evaluation
3. The impact of religion on schooling
4. Educational social engineering

To some extent we have touched upon aspects of these subjects already. One cannot talk of unionism and avoid economics. One cannot look at the history of American educational governance and avoid religion. The realities of current American education are too complex and too interwoven to neatly separate one topic from another. However, there is more to investigate in these areas than previous pages have done, and we will try not to cover old ground.

It is also important before we look at these topics to understand that we are going to set some working boundaries for our discussion. First, the topics themselves constitute a boundary. They are not the only forces at work beyond the classroom. To name just a few more, there are the family, the media, and the culture at large (all of which we have discussed cursorily in Chapter One). The topics chosen for this chapter, however, constitute powerful educational influences which bear deeper investigation. Second, each topic is itself worthy of a separate volume. Our investigations will thus be general ones, confined to specific issues as opposed to comprehensive treatments. The reader is asked to understand the need for these parameters and to judge the things which are discussed rather than to bemoan the things which are left unsaid.

Educational economics

There are two aspects of educational economics with which we shall deal. The first is the visible economic environment of American public education. The second is the less visible way in which economics affects the educational process. For the first, we shall delve more deeply into the manner in which education in America is funded. We will look at the sources of that funding and the economic pressures which are increasingly being applied to our schools. For the second, we will look behind the scenes at some fiscal aspects of our educational system which, while important, are often kept hidden from view.

Visible economic realities in American public education. You hear it over and over again. "We don't spend enough on our schools." If you are a property taxpayer, or if you are currently sending a child or two through college, you probably disagree with that. Are you right? Just what does the educational economic landscape look like?

Using 1986 and 1987 figures, which at the time of this writing are the most complete ones available, and using round numbers so as not to overburden you with economic minutia, the picture looks something like this.

The gross national product of the entire country was $4 trillion. The federal budget was $1 trillion. Federal expenditure for defense was slightly short of $300 billion. The total school district expenditure for elementary and secondary public education was $150 billion. The federal expenditure for education was about $15 billion.[1] By no reckoning can these statistics lead any thinking person to conclude that public education in America is a fiscal priority. It simply is not. We spend as an entire nation on all our elementary and secondary schools combined only one-half of the federal defense budget. Our public school expenditures amount to only 3.75% of our GNP. The federal government allocates only 1.6% of its trillion-dollar budget to education.

As a nation America has an economic agenda in which basic schooling takes a back seat to many other things. To give you an idea, in the same year (1986) we spent $150 billion on our public schools, we spent $170 billion on automobiles from the "big three" manufacturers alone (Ford, GM, and Chrysler). Cars are a national necessity, you say? We also spent an estimated $120 billion on illegal drugs. Even in our charitable giving, education was an also-ran. Dale Mann of Columbia Teachers College reports that while religious institutions received about $28 billion (which was over 46% of all charitable giving), educational institutions received only $8.5 billion—and 95% of that went not to public schooling but to colleges and universities.[2]

According to the U.S. Department of Education, the average per-pupil expenditure for public school students in 1986 was $3,677. About 50% of this money came from state taxes, 43.5% from local taxes, and 6.5% from federal revenues. By far, the greatest bulk of the local educational dollar came from the property tax. A recent fifty-state task force impaneled by the National Conference of State Legislatures reported that 50% of municipal, 76% of county, and 94% of township revenue still comes from local property taxes.[3] The problem with using local property taxes as a major source of educational funding lies in the substantial differences one finds in the assessments of property from area to area. Researcher Martin Carnoy points out that these variations have led to inequities not only from one state to another but between different localities within the same state. As a result, a rash of post-1970 court challenges to the property tax system are already spurring changes in the way in which public education will be supported in the future.[4] For example, in some states such as Wisconsin, major reforms are now under consideration to abolish the property tax as a means of funding schools. In other states like Colorado, some residents are being allowed to reduce portions of their property tax bills by working for local county governments.[5]

However, it is not only in the local property tax system that inequities can occur. The vagaries of international, national, and regional economics can make paupers or princes out of many states. When the funding of education is tied—as it inevitably is—to the taxes of those states, schools can ride a fiscal roller coaster from boom to bust and back again with little or no relationship to purely educational phenomena.

Consider the recent hard times encountered by the agricultural heartland of the United States. With many family farms on the auction block, midwestern communities are being forced into new arrangements in order to keep their educational heads afloat. One common practice currently being reported in rural states such as Iowa, Montana, Nebraska, Utah, Vermont, Wisconsin, and Minnesota is the sharing of services from district to district. In Iowa, for example, 86 of the 436 districts in the state have fewer than 300 students. It is simply no longer economically possible for each of these small districts to function independently. 75 of them have therefore begun to cooperate with nearby districts in the mutual funding of shared programs and personnel. Many districts share a school nurse, for example. Several have combined athletic teams. 24 of the districts even share their superintendents. For the most part, rural state education departments have encouraged such practices. In some instances, they have even offered economic incentives to promote cooperative financing. Iowa, for example, offers a 5% state aid bonus for districts which share superintendents.[6]

Of course, economic hard times are not the only side of the picture. Occasionally, there are state windfalls such as the one experienced recently in Louisiana where a court ruling gave the state hundreds of millions of dollars in unanticipated revenue from off-shore oil drilling royalties in the Gulf of Mexico. The money enabled the state to establish a $540 million trust fund which nets the schools of Louisiana a cool $30 million per year in additional revenues.[7]

The god of oil, however, is a fickle god. He can taketh away just as easily as he giveth—probably more so. Decreases in the price of oil hit both Texas and Alaska very hard. For every $1 decline in the price of a barrel of oil, Texas loses $100 million in state revenue, and 1986 price drops contributed to a $3.5 billion deficit and a consequent rise in state sales and gasoline taxes. The effect in Alaska was a 15% reduction in the state budget with concomitant cuts in services.[8]

Finally, state and regional inequities can be triggered not only by general economic trends but by changes in federal law as well. Consider the recently restructured federal tax codes. The reduced federal tax rates have been accompanied by the elimination of some previously deductible items. For 35 states this set of circumstances translates into higher state taxes since the net taxable incomes of state residents will be higher as a consequence of fewer deductions. However, in other states such as Nebraska, Rhode Island, and North Dakota, where the state income tax is a flat percentage of federal income tax, reduced federal tax rates will mean less state money and a tighter squeeze of the educational belt. Just to make the patchwork quilt of educational funding more complex, states like Alaska, Florida, and Texas with no state income taxes will not be affected one way or the other by new federal codes.[9]

Hovering above this economic hodgepodge are two powerful realities—realities with which we will be dealing until at least the turn of the century—realities with pressing economic agendas of their own. They are the issue of American economic competitiveness and the institution of desperately needed educational reforms.

It has seemed to me in my lifetime that America responds to nothing so much as crisis. Perhaps it would be more accurate to say nothing *but* crisis. Perhaps we have always been that way, and perhaps not, but it surely appears that we have a penchant for keeping our heads in the sand until the eleventh hour and then rising up in some national furor to address what might have—should have—been addressed long before. The first of our post-1945 educational crises was precipitated by the launching of Russia's Sputnik I satellite in 1957. The second and current crisis is our inability to retain the economic competitiveness and influence we once had both nationally and internationally. Indeed, John Jennings, the counsel for the Committee on Education and Labor of the U.S. House of Representatives, has dubbed our current plight "the Sputnik of the eighties."[10]

America is now a debtor nation. Our stock market crashes and groans; our trade imbalances threaten us; our federal budget deficits have made interest payments on the national debt larger than the entire federal budget of JFK's inaugural year. At home, our productivity wanes. Abroad, we find our dollar weakened to post-war lows and our preeminence in industries like steel and automobiles replaced by the Japanese and West Germans. Having languished through the educational declines of the sixties, seventies, and eighties, we are only now beginning to acknowledge openly what many of us knew in our hearts all along to be true: the tie between "educational attainment and economic competitiveness," as Jennings puts it, is real and irrevocable.[11]

After years of cutbacks, we are finally beginning to fund education in increasing amounts with the hope that it is not too late to restore the nation to its former economic posture. In this effort we have cast our eyes to Japan particularly since the Japanese have been out-producing us in large measure because of an educational system which receives tremendous governmental and parental support and which, as a result, achieves an enormously high level of student outcomes. In the early 1980's, for example, the New York Stock Exchange commissioned a report on Japanese business. It concluded that "one of the things the Japanese do right is...schooling their people: the extraordinary effectiveness of their schools is one relatively neglected reason for their high productivity." The report went on to note that it was not simply the Japanese intellectual elite which excelled in school but the average child as well. Thus productivity gains were seen not only in the industrial leadership but also in the output of the average worker.[12]

Moved by findings such as those of the New York Stock Exchange, we have between 1980 and 1986 added $4.2 billion in constant dollars to state and local public school expenditures.[13] Educational professionals, however, are quick to point out that this increase has merely counteracted a $4.2 billion cut in federal educational spending. Overall federal cuts were 11% in constant dollars between 1980 and 1986.[14] Only now is Congress beginning to think in terms of a new National Defense Education Act which will finally increase funds for things like the National Science Foundation, Chapter 1 programs for the disadvantaged, and aid to the education of children with handicapping conditions.

Competitiveness is thus acting as a catalyst for reforms to the educational system. To attract better teachers we will need higher teaching salaries. To train a better work force we will need programs which can more effectively educate all our children, especially those from disadvantaged backgrounds. Bilingual education courses which can make foreign language-speaking students more conversant with English, programs which prevent school dropouts, projects which lower teenage pregnancy and substance abuse—all these and more will have a direct bearing on America's future economic potential, and all these come with a price tag.

That price tag is no small item. Allen Odden of the University of Southern California estimates that reforms will cost about 20% of current expenditures,[15] and when one factors in the demographics of the issue, it is possible to project much higher amounts. Consider some recent research on the student population to whom our educational reforms will be applied. The socioeconomic practices of the 1960's and 1970's, the recent upsurge of immigration due to foreign turmoil (both military and economic) in areas such as Southeast Asia and Latin America, and the high birthrates among many of the nation's disadvantaged have combined to produce some very sobering figures. 14% of today's students are "illegitimate." 40% will live in single-parent homes by the age of 18. 30% are now "latchkey children" with no one at home at the end of the school day. 20% live below the poverty line. 15% are either physically or mentally handicapped. 10% have parents who are not minimally educated.[16]

As bone-chilling as these statistics are, they are still milder than what awaits us. Harold Hodgkinson, former director of the National Institute of Education and now senior fellow at the American Council on Education in Washington, D.C., recently served up the following information. The four-year-old population of 1986 will be the entering college freshman class of the year 2000. Here is what the demographic reports say of them. They number 3.6 million. 24% of them now live below the poverty line. One-third of them belong to groups classified as "minorities." 45% will have been raised in a single-parent household by 2000. 54% have working mothers. 24% of the girls are projected to become pregnant by the age of 18. Many of them currently do not speak English as a native language. Many more do not speak English at all. An increasing number of them (more than 15%) are projected to develop physical and/or mental handicaps.[17]

Estimates of the price of educational reform are apt to grow larger than the projected 20% of current costs if the demographic data above prove true. Whatever the ultimate costs, however, the trend to generate more revenue for education is clearly at hand, and of the three traditional sources of educational funding (local taxes, state taxes and federal grants), it is largely the states which have taken the initiative.

We have already noted that federal funding for educational programs during the Reagan Administration declined. Odden points out that the declines were particularly hard-hitting since they occurred at the same time per-pupil expenditures were rising. From 1982 to 1985, for example, expenditures rose 15.8% (7.2% real growth when adjusted for inflation) while federal spending declined by $1 billion (as measured in constant dollars).[18] Thus, any rise in federal education outlays during the final years of the decade will probably serve only to recapture past program levels rather than fund new ones.

Odden also notes that "local property taxes, the main source of funding on the local level, have not been substantially increased to cover the costs of the reforms of the 1980's." In his study of reform financing in eleven states, he goes on to say that while local taxes rose in some areas (notably Arkansas, Florida and Texas), "the property tax is still an unpopular tax, and efforts to increase its use, except in times of severe fiscal stress, are likely to produce a backlash."[19] Indeed, the backlash has already been painfully visible in some states, the most noteworthy example probably being California's passage of Proposition 13 which placed a limit on the amount of money that could be raised through local property taxes.[20] Some local areas are trying to increase educational revenue through things other than the property tax. It is estimated that as much as 9% of a district's budget can be obtained through programs such as donor contribution, the leasing of school facilities, and the sharing of facilities, but these are not likely to generate the kind of cash needed for the remainder of the century.[21]

In the absence of massive federal funding, property tax increases and local alternatives to the property tax, it has been the state education programs which have thus far shouldered the burden. Michael Kirst of Stanford University points out that from 1970 to 1980 alone, state educational spending rose from $16.6 billion to $46.5 billion, a whopping 44.5% even when measured in "real" dollars. Where once state sources funded only 37% of the cost of public education, they now fund over 50%.[22] And in the decade of the 80's, states have continued to supply greater and greater amounts to local districts. They have done it both by enacting new funding formulas which distribute state aid in such a way as to promote fiscal equality between districts and by instituting tax increases specifically earmarked for the schools. Arkansas, South Carolina, and Tennessee, for example, have increased state sales taxes with revenues mandated for education. A one-penny increase in the Tennessee sales tax was able to generate over $67 million in school funding in its first year alone. The second year brought in $155 million. Even greater gains were seen in South Carolina ($242 million per year by 1987). In Missouri, a state education sales tax not only raised school aid by 18%, it also lowered property taxes on the local level. New gasoline, franchise, and corporation taxes in Texas were able to generate $4.8 billion of which $2.7 billion was designated for Texas public schools. A state lottery in New York made $43 million more than anticipated and contributed to a $2.3 billion increase in state aid to education between 1982 and 1986.[23]

As impressive as these figures are, Kirst is quick to note that they will soon reach their limits. A drop in high school enrollments, an increasingly older tax base as senior citizens (with no children in school) become a greater percentage of the population, declines in commodity prices, public alienation and dissatisfaction with public schools, growing child care needs in single-parent and working-mother families, and federal budget problems are all likely to cause a "return to neglect."[24] As we approach the new century, education dollars are apt to be more and more tied to cost-effectiveness analyses, program evaluations, and education prejudices. The class for gifted children which serves only five students may not continue if it is cost effective to maintain a pupil-teacher ratio of 20:1. The mainstreaming program for a blind child may have to be dropped if a new economic recession flows from the trade and budget deficits of Washington. The music program may need to be cut back if the educational prejudices of a community decide that it is more important to stimulate mathematics.

However the trends go, it will still be necessary for us to remember the principles of Rensis Likert. The educational dollar we plant today may bear no visible fruit for years. There is a time lag which is inevitable and profound between the expenditure of money in a school and its return to the society. The dollar we give a disadvantaged child which may in 1990 keep him or her in school will not show its true worth until ten or twenty years have passed when the child—now grown into a functioning, useful citizen—contributes through labor and taxes to the nation which had the wisdom to offer a helping hand years before.

In addition to remembering Likert, it is also important to bear in mind that merely throwing money at our schools will not insure their true regeneration. The changes in teacher retention policies and educational governance which we have already discussed are not ones with large price tags. Some changes have no price tags at all. If we were to double or even triple our education budgets tomorrow without addressing these non-fiscal issues—and others which we have yet to investigate—we would not substantially improve our present condition. Paying a poor teacher twice his or her salary will not give you a good teacher, and raising the revenue of a school district on whose board of education sits an uninformed idiot will only endanger greater sums of money.

Hidden economic realities in American public education. What you see in the business of education is often not what you get. Behind the neatly arrayed budget figures of your local school district there are games being played and things going on which have a powerful effect on the nation. Yet because these things are not nice to talk about, they are largely kept hidden from view by the establishments which control the flow of educational information. Some of the hidden economics of our school system are outright criminal. There is the district clerk who embezzles tax funds, the director of food services who arranges kickback schemes with local distributors, the board member who engages in bid-rigging to assure that a relative or political ally is awarded a contract. Education involves big money, and where there is big money there is the temptation to abuse the system.

I do not want to talk about these kinds of things (except to mention them in passing), however, because as bad as they are, they are not built into the system. Embezzlement, kickbacks, bid-rigging and the like are crimes. They occur as temporary (and, for the most part, infrequent) aberrations of the educational scene They are the products of individual rather than systemic corruption, and they are usually dealt with by a legal system whose justice is generally if not perfectly dispensed. It is not these things I mean to discuss, but rather practices which are more ubiquitous and so nefarious that they permeate the very fiber of our schools and spread poisons which attack the very soul of our nation. In specific, I would like to discuss three such practices by way of example. The are (a) the "college game"—particularly the "doctorate game," (b) the "teacher hiring game," and (c) the "industry hype game." Let us consider each in turn.

(a) The "college game." College tuition rates are growing faster than the cost of living. It can take as much as $40,000 to get a bachelor's degree at a state-supported college, and as much as $100,000 at some of the more exclusive private ones. The average debt incurred by a graduate of a public college is $8,950.[25] Such figures are forcing parents into second mortgages, dictating student career choices (so that they can land jobs which allow them to pay back the cost of their education), and further reducing the ability of poor children to go to college at all (thus condemning them to a cycle of poverty generation after generation).

Hodgkinson tells us that already the percentage of minority students and staff in higher education is "underwhelming," and that "their success rates are even lower."[26] The ability to pay for college, he says, is becoming an increasing requirement while academic ability is becoming a decreasing one. In an effort to help parents plan for their children's higher education, some states are even setting up trust funds into which parents can pre-pay college tuition. (Illinois Law SB-17 and Florida Law HB-17 are two examples.)

The questions which arise from this state of affairs are essentially two in nature. First, how do we make college affordable, and second, what are we getting for our money in the realm of higher education? I will leave the first question for a bit later when I discuss some proposed remedies for our educational economic difficulties. It is the second question which bears answering now, and the answer is truly dismal.

We bemoan public school dropout rates which slide beyond 10%. The 25% national rate of 1985 is considered a virtual disaster. Yet, as incredible as it sounds, for the past twenty years, American colleges have failed to graduate 50% of their students.[27] Moreover, the quality of education at many colleges has sunk so low that, as Hodgkinson puts it, "freshmen at some institutions know more at entry level than graduating seniors from other institutions."[28] However, it is the economic reality of the job market which really epitomizes the disgrace of the "college game." Having given college their money and time and along with them the hope that the money and time will yield a brighter economic future, the Bureau of Labor Statistics tells college students that fully 20% of them will end up working at jobs requiring no college at all.[29] Even worse, many college students who major in "non-glamorous" subjects such as art history or musicology find themselves virtually unemployable in their fields upon graduation simply because the American economy has little use for them.

Nowhere is this abomination more pronounced than in American graduate schools, particularly at the doctoral level. Hodgkinson reports that "during the 1980's, 18,000 doctorates will be awarded in the humanities while only a handful of jobs will be available in these fields." LeCroy adds that from 1980 to 1995, between 25,000 and 30,000 doctoral degrees will be awarded annually, while only 100,000 jobs will be available for Ph.D.'s during the same period. Many Ph.D. candidates now seek employment in public schools where, ironically, they find themselves both overpriced and under-prepared.[30] Many more students consider much of their study a waste of time—unchallenging, irrelevant, and ritualistic. "Maybe the purpose of doctoral programs is simply to get my 'ticket punched'...and that makes me mad," writes one student lamenting what appears to be a common graduate school opinion.[31]

Actually, the game is a good deal more sinister than mere "ticket punching." It goes something like this. Things have value relative to their scarcity. Generally, the rarer something is, the more it is worth. In order to keep their Ph.D.'s valuable as degrees, it behooves institutions of higher education to make them hard to get. Yet, in order to justify faculty positions, in order to attract big grant money, in order to maintain glamorous facilities, doctoral programs have to attract fairly large numbers of students. Hence, the game. Attract enough doctoral candidates to fill your classrooms and your coffers, then find ways of getting rid of them before awarding them the degrees whose continued scarcity insures a continuing high value.

The resultant horror stories among doctoral candidates are commonplace. A student takes thirty or sixty graduate credits at enormous expense, but now, having outlived fiscal usefulness as a name on the roster books, the student is bombarded by a series of maddening requirements. Let me give you, by way of example, my own experiences which I assure you are not unusual in the "doctorate game." Having completed my coursework I had to run an academic gauntlet of questionable value, and I had to do it in a certain order. First there were two language exams. Next there was a series of so-called "qualifying exams." These consisted of a written research project, a written examination, and an oral examination. The research project required a lengthy paper "ready for publication" within a two-week period. The topic was obtained by picking it out of a fishbowl. I was not permitted one of my own choosing. The written exam was several hours in duration and was, as the saying goes, "open-ended." That means the questions could cover literally any aspect of my discipline. Finally, the oral examination consisted of a battery of questions, again open-ended, from a collection of the professors on the staff. One had to pass the languages to get to the research component, the research to get to the written, the written to get to the oral.

And that was just to "qualify for candidacy." Next came choosing a dissertation topic, writing a dissertation proposal, and having both topic and proposal approved by a faculty committee. Then came writing the dissertation itself with approval of every chapter required not only from a dissertation advisor but from two faculty readers as well. Finally, there was an oral defense of the dissertation in front of another committee.

Frequently, these kinds of processes take many years to complete, and equally as frequently they are made to be both emotionally and physically brutal. They are also from time to time laced with deliberate attempts to force students out of the program. I could tell you of the candidate purposely failed on a qualifying exam who appealed for a review. The reviewer passed the candidate but was made to recant his judgment in the name of "departmental solidarity." I could tell you of another candidate who, having completed his dissertation, experienced the great misfortune of having his advisor die shortly before the final dissertation defense. The new advisor—who wished to use the candidate as his own research lackey—declared the dissertation unsatisfactory and forced the candidate to rewrite on a topic for which the advisor needed current research. I could tell you of the candidate who was requested—subtly, of course—to provide stock market tips to an advisor, or of the female candidate who was "told" in the roundabout way it is usually done that sexual friendship would not hurt her chances of success. I could tell you how many dozens of candidates dropped out (which, of course, is the point of the game), or how one had a nervous breakdown and another attempted suicide.

It is not the obvious surface injustice of the game which is most irksome, however. It is that many fine candidates get "wiped out" of programs for reasons having nothing whatsoever to do with their academic ability. When that happens, the quality of educational leadership changes from one dominated by educational worth to one dominated by either obstinacy or the ability to "play ball." Since Ph.D.'s become the leaders of our system, either as commissioners, superintendents, or college faculty whose function it is to train tomorrow's teachers and do tomorrow's research, Ph.D.'s must be our *best.* Not our most obstinate. Not our most compliant. Our *best.*

To indicate how educationally damaging the game is, let me tell you that in all my doctoral years, I was never once asked to demonstrate knowledge or skill in the art of teaching—and neither were any of my colleagues. No courses, no assignments, no requirements of any kind existed in that area. Yet almost all the successful candidates ended up in teaching positions. Is it any wonder that so many of our colleges have professors who are classroom duds? Could you think of a greater piece of lunacy than to put these duds in charge of training the educators of tomorrow?

We will talk much more of teacher training in the pages ahead, and I will offer some remedies for the "college game." For now, there is another game to consider: the game of teacher hiring.

(b) The "teacher hiring game." Pretend for the moment that you are the chairperson of a department in a public school district. You are going to have several staff openings next year, and your superiors have given you the task of finding some outstanding teachers to fill the vacancies. Being an astute administrator you realize that there is no more important task you can perform for your district. Any momentary bit of brilliance you may show as a program innovator or supervisor cannot compare to the long-range good you do by selecting a great teacher who over the course of a twenty or thirty year career will positively affect the lives of hundreds if not thousands of students.

You therefore plan your hiring strategy. You will advertise in the trade journals and the education section of *The New York Times,* plow through the dozens of applications you receive, restructure your schedule to allow for interviews and observations. You may even arrange for the finalists to come in for a "teaching audition." You trod over to the personnel office, fired with enthusiasm, and present your plan. Here, finally, is your chance to do something truly meaningful for your program.

Well, not quite. "You understand, of course," the personnel director begins, "that the contract we negotiated with the union says we can't offer more than the base starting salary."

A cloud begins to creep onto your horizon. "But what about credit for years of service?"

"Our contract allows $500 for every year of previous accredited teaching..." A light begins to brighten your face once more. "...But only up to ten years."

"Ten years?" you groan. "That's only $5,000. Our base starting pay is $20,000. How can I get a good teacher to apply for $25,000? Anyone decent who's been teaching for ten years is going to be making more than that. Besides, to come here they'd be giving up tenure...seniority...They'd be moving, maybe buying and selling a house...And suppose they come from another state. How can we expect them to leave a vested retirement system for that kind of salary? What kind of teacher can I find for us with these restrictions?"

"Well," the personnel director smiles, "those are the rules. We have a contract, and the board policy is 'no exceptions.' You'll just have to do the best you can."

In the world of private industry, if you wish to attract good people to your staff, you are free to apply just about any salary or fringe benefit conditions you need in order to succeed. Oh, you may have fiscal limits and political or corporate boundaries over which you cannot step, but the latitude you encounter has the expansiveness of the universe in comparison with the restrictions of public education. One of the reasons we don't attract good teachers—existing teachers—to programs is that we have boxed ourselves into unrealistic hiring policies. Not only are the salaries we offer restricted and often unattractive, we have developed non-transferable state retirement systems which, after a teacher has been working a few years, literally shackle him or her to a geographical range of action which virtually precludes the possibility of upward mobility.

The results of this game are a twofold disaster. Disaster number one is that in order to move upward to better paying jobs or greener educational pastures, many teachers find it necessary to leave the classroom. They either become administrators or leave the profession altogether. Disaster number two is that they quit inside. Tied to where they are by the so-called "golden handcuff" and unable to exercise the options of a free agent in an open market because of restrictive hiring covenants, they stay put and die a little each day.

(c) The "industry hype game." Let me throw a few items at you. The hula-hoop. The CB radio. The cabbage patch doll. We are a nation of fads. Things, phrases, people bubble up in our national consciousness. They burn meteorically for a few weeks or months or even years, then wane into the amorphous societal stew from which they came. In and of itself the phenomenon of fadism is not all that alarming. However, when it is coupled with the greed of the marketplace and the gullibility and stupidity of the consumer, it can become a damaging phenomenon indeed. Take that cabbage patch doll. Whilst the fire of cabbage-patchism burned with the fervor of a dog in heat, people willingly—happily—shelled out a hundred dollars or more for a doll whose net worth in material goods was a mere fraction of the price tag. Now that the fever has gone, you can pick up a doll for ten or twenty bucks.

So what has this to do with education? The sad truth is that because educational governance is, in many instances, so poorly prepared, because those who hold the purse-strings of our schools have not been trained in curricula, philosophy, or economics, our schools play the cabbage patch doll game year after year. They play it not only with our dollars but, even more tragically, with the values of our children. Let me give you but two of many examples—two current examples which hopefully strike home: the computer and the science textbook.

The electronics age is upon us, and in the mindless acceptance of fadism our schools all rush to dance the computer dance. Everyone needs a "PC (that's "personal computer" for those of you who aren't up on the latest fad phrases). Why? Don't ask (though we will in our chapter on curriculum). It's here. It's in, "good buddy," and we all need it "for sure." The school system without computer literacy programs is not playing the game. So along come the salesmen, the software, the hardware, the program changes, the classroom alterations, the staff development seminars. The hype is upon the board, and it becomes fashionable to buy. More than that. It becomes heretical not to.

All of a sudden—without quite knowing how a computer trains a better musician, or how it teaches a sloppy teacher to be neater, or how it develops a reverence for intrinsic as opposed to extrinsic rewards (p.s.: it does none of these)—millions upon millions are spent in the name of "quality education." Educators feel no choice in the matter. It is like swearing allegiance to the king. "It's not a question of can I afford to do this?" writes one superintendent. "It's a question of can I afford not to?"[32]

By the 1980-81 academic year, U.S. school systems had purchased 400,000 microcomputers or about one unit for every 100 children grades K-12. Software sales exceeded $10 million that year, leapt to $35 million in 1981-82, and climbed steadily ever since. Not that I am against the computer. I'm not. But the unthinking knee-jerk reaction to the "industry hype" which preys upon a fadistic mentality leads to an incredible amount of wasteful spending. Think, if you will, of that firecracker, hot dog company of the early computer days, Texas Instruments Corporation. When TIC went into bankruptcy, what happened to all those computers it sold? When they wore out or were misused, where did the service come from? Who supplied the spare parts? How many districts were left holding the bag? "The reason for this sad situation," comments Gene Geisert of St. John's University, "is that most school administrators rely on software producers and their sales forces—people who have no idea of what educators need..."[33]

But perhaps you, too, are a computer ideologue, and I have gored your sacred cow. Alright, then. Let's choose another example—the science textbook of the Reagan age. When Reagan came to power, he did so on a tidal wave of "new conservatism." I'm not one for political labels, but let's cut through a lot of semantic arguing and agree at least to the fact that he was supported by many fundamentalist Christians who saw his landslide election as the cue to "come out of the closet," so to speak. What followed, as you all know, was a great controversy about the teaching of science—particularly the theory of evolution—in our public schools. We will get into that controversy in some detail later in this chapter, and as I have so many times before, I urge you not to leap to any knee-jerk conclusions of your own. Putting aside questions of religion, however, the strength of the "creationist" movement began to have a very potent economic effect on the publishing industry, an effect which itself had consequences, both financial and curricular, in our schools.

Consider the following comments from an editor of one of America's largest textbook publishers, Holt, Rinehart, and Winston. "If our books aren't listed on state-approved textbook lists—and they won't be if we pay too much attention to Darwin and not enough to creationism—then we simply can't compete in states that have statewide textbook adoption procedures."[34]

The necessity which publishers feel to patronize a political faction whose point of view happens to be prominent is, of course, one of the most damaging things that can befall education in a free society. It makes the exchange of ideas not a function of curricular insight, but rather one of economics and power politics. That publishers do feel the pressure, however, is really no longer in doubt. Consider the following statements by two publishers, both of whom asked that their names not be used for fear of academic reprisal. The first says this:

> Creationism has no place in biology books, but, after all, we're in the business of selling textbooks. And if our books don't sell in Texas and California, the

> two largest purchasers of textbooks and two strongholds of the scientific creationists, it's certain that we're not going to make a profit.

The second writes:

> Once a publisher includes creationism in his textbooks, he's opening a can of worms...For several years, if I found a creationism reference in a competitor's textbook, I'd make sure that everyone knew about it. And for awhile, school boards and textbook committees listened; they were adamant in their desire to keep science and theology separate. Now, however, their attitudes are changing. They're rejecting textbooks that reflect solid scientific discipline and inquiry in favor of textbooks that, like television, pander to those who make the most noise.[35]

The question really no longer centers on whether or not some of these economic practices exist, but rather on what we can do to make educational economics work more for the benefit of education.

Some suggestions for a better system. The economics of American public education are not beyond improving. Here are some ideas which can help.

(a) A greater federal role. It seems both unlikely and unwise for America at this juncture to increase the federal budget. The deficits are enormous and can no longer be tolerated. Clearly, to reduce them some combination of spending cuts and tax increases will be needed. Thus an increased federal role in educational funding probably will not and should not come from the imposition of higher budgets. It certainly can come, however, from the reapportionment of existing revenues, and here there is much that can be done. There are rail, farm and similar subsidies which have long proven counter-productive. Perhaps some of these can be dealt with partially by eliminating them and partially by rechanneling their monies to education. Fraud in the receipt of federal welfare programs has been considerable. It has also been noted that many on welfare might be brought off it through so-called "work-fare" programs. Certainly there are sources of educational revenue here. Pork-barrel legislation which wastes enormous sums can be devoted to education, but most of all, defense spending can be used for education.

In a certain sense, education *is* defense spending, perhaps the wisest kind of defense spending. An uninformed electorate, an unproductive electorate, can weaken a democracy more quickly and far more mortally than the reduction-in-force of an aircraft carrier or a ballistic missile. Such an electorate is far less capable of negotiating peace treaties or analyzing unnecessary cost overruns. It is far less capable of maintaining the economic and sociopolitical strength which is at the heart of every military system. But these points aside, as it stands now, the increase in American defense spending during the Reagan years has been huge, as have the instances of military waste and corporate misdeeds in the fulfillment of military contracts. Accounting for no more than these items, it should be relatively easy to take 10% of the defense budget and give it to education. If applied only to make college loans available to indigent Americans, the resultant $30 billion or so would insure a kind of national security no nuclear warhead could ever buy. Just a portion of such a sum applied to the educational Congress discussed in Chapter Two would yield benefits for generations to come.

This nation will not reverse the course of its post-World War II slide until it begins to apply its federal budget more toward learning and less toward killing, for there are more than mere dollars at stake in the equation. There is also the moral, philosophical and political destiny of the people who choose between the alternatives.

(b) Greater and more equitable state and local funding. The federal government, inadequate as it is in the area of educational finances, cannot be considered the lone culprit, nor can it be asked to shoulder the burdens of economic reform by itself. We must remind ourselves that whatever the federal role, the rest of us spend less than 4% of the GNP on our public schools. Realizing that we spend nearly the same on cocaine and alcohol, there is really no excuse to avoid a greater state and local commitment to our schools. The problem is to make that commitment in a way which is equitable to all students, all districts, rich and poor alike.

The use of local property taxes as a significant means of funding only insures inequity. It is an extremely unpopular tax which unequally distributes the school burden among the citizenry. Even more, it allows districts to vote yea or nay on their local budgets as if education were a flow of water which should be stopped and started by local public opinion. The on-again, off-again budget vote becomes even more dangerous as our population ages because many senior citizens begin to care less about schools when their own children grow and are graduated—not that the senior citizen, who may be trapped by a fixed income on the one hand and an inflationary economy on the other, doesn't have a legitimate problem.

I submit that the educational system is larger and more important than the special interests of a district or a citizen group. Putting the economic control of education into the hands of special interests not only insures fiscal inequities, but also promotes the feeling that those groups should have curricular powers as well. Already we have seen many instances across the nation of citizen tax revolts which have expressed discontent with the property levy as a means of school funding. The 1978 passage of Proposition 13 in California, for example, was followed by a resolution in 1979 limiting increases in educational expenditure. In 1980, a similar law was passed in Massachusetts cutting property taxes by 40%—and this at a time when President Reagan was supporting a 25% cut in federal education expenditures.[36] We have also noted that economic pressures can be (and sometimes are) applied by special interests to use classroom curricula and textual materials for the promotion of certain intellectual prejudices. Later in this chapter we will see that phenomenon again with legal as well as fiscal ramifications.

For now, it is interesting to note the general opinion of Americans relative to property taxes and school financing as measured by the 1986 Gallup Poll. When asked the best way of funding public schools, only 24% of the respondents selected the property tax. 33% selected state taxes. The remainder opted for federal taxes or replied "don't know." When asked if they were in favor of tax increases to pay for new educational programs, only 37% replied in the affirmative. (It is interesting to note that in 1969 over 45% had said "yes.") Finally, the sample was asked what taxes should be increased if increases were absolutely necessary. The answers were most illuminating. 79% said cigarette and tobacco taxes; 78% responded that state lotteries should be used. Only 33% mentioned the property tax, while 28% said gasoline taxes and 27% income taxes.[37]

Perhaps there is some collective wisdom in the public's disenchantment with the property tax. I believe there is and suggest that schools be funded virtually entirely from state revenues. What might happen is that state education departments would establish a minimum per-student figure necessary for *quality* education. That figure would be multiplied by the number of students in a given district to obtain the district's base budget. The base could then be augmented by variations in costs of living which might apply from region to region within a state. Beyond this formula, I suggest districts be left free to levy local taxes or float local bonds to cover the costs of new facilities, new equipment, higher salaries, etc. in excess of the state minimum, should they wish to do so. The only caveat in the local levy would be that the tax must apply equally to all district residents.

In this funding structure, sales taxes, lotteries, income taxes, user fees, and other non-regressive ways of raising revenue would be acceptable. What would not be acceptable would be taxes such as the property tax which could vary from area to area or person to person with little rhyme or reason. Finally, such a structure would never leave a district at the mercy of a budget vote. The per-pupil allotment—already designed to provide *quality* education, and capable itself of being adjusted for rates of inflation or deflation—would be guaranteed by the state. Moreover, any district wishing more than the quality standard set by the state could enhance its revenue by any means which was equitably imposed on its tax-paying citizens.

(c) "Truth in advertising" for colleges. The "college game" can be cleaned up largely by instituting practices which, on the one hand, tell students the truth and, on the other, develop programs which are meaningfully goal-oriented. Let us consider the second first.

Whatever else one gains from an undergraduate or graduate program—educational broadening, social development, intellectual training, etc.—colleges should have as their primary responsibility the vocational training of the student to a point where the student is either marketable or successfully prepared for further study. To accept students into programs which leave them unmarketable in the absence of information to that effect is unconscionable and should not be tolerated. Having accepted this principle, a whole host of "truth in advertising" mandates logically follows:

1. Major-by-major, colleges should be required to publish employment statistics based on the latest demographic data. For example, "Art history majors will have a 15% chance of employment in the field of art history upon graduation," or "Government majors stand a 1-in-3 chance of landing a job in their field upon completion of a bachelor's degree."

2. Major-by-major, colleges should be required to give statistics of *their own graduates* for the decade past. For example, "Of the English majors who have graduated between 1978 and 1988, 50% are currently employed in fields unrelated to English, 40% are in graduate school, 5% are unaccounted for, 5% are unemployed, etc."

3. Colleges should be required to post their dropout rates. For example, "Of the entering freshman classes of the last decade, 40% do not return for a sophomore year, 52% successfully graduate, etc." This should also be broken down major-by-major.

4. Transfer credit data ought to be published informing students of what happens if they leave one college for another. For example, "Of those who transfer out of our college, 57% of our courses are accepted for credit by other institutions—43% are not. For those transferring into our college, we accept 61% of the courses taken at accredited universities, etc."

5. Colleges should provide "success quotients" of their graduates by major. For example, "Our math majors earn an average of $31,000 per year within five years of graduation."

6. Colleges should be required to make alumni names available to prospective students so that students can talk to consenting alumni to gain first-hand knowledge of the results of their schooling.

7. Graduate schools ought to be required to find employment for all graduates or to place them in programs granting even higher degrees unless the student waived this condition in writing. Such a policy would force an end to the economic usury discussed above because it would assure that getting into a program would be a tougher requirement than getting out of it. It would force graduate schools to accept only the best candidates and only enough of them that could be reasonably expected to find work in the field. The endless stream of "qualifying exams," used to drive students out of a program once their fiscal usefulness was gone, might instead be used as part of the criteria for accepting them. In tandem with a graduate school's published figures on the percentage of entrants who eventually are graduated, this policy would offer at least some protection to graduate students. They would enter programs more fully aware of their chances of success and leave them more gainfully employed.

Compliance on the part of colleges and universities with these policies could be obtained relatively easily if failure to do so would mean the loss of any federal, state, or municipal revenue.

(d) Interstate retirement transfers. Reciprocal arrangements between the teacher retirement systems of all states should be effected to make it more possible for teachers to move from one state to another. The loss of retirement benefits in every field is nothing short of a national scandal. Perhaps, in addition to getting its own house in order, such an educational policy might pave the way for a national policy to benefit any worker in any field. Wouldn't that be wonderful? No longer the poor dope fired after 24 years, just one year short of the 25-year pension. Instead, the years of service given in "job A" could be transferred to "job B" so that a worker might receive credit for every year of honest labor.

(e) **Free bargaining rights for veteran teacher transfers.** Here, the teacher earning a relatively high wage who is recruited by another district would be able to enter the district at a salary level agreed upon by the bargaining parties, not one set by a third-party contract. Once the transferring teacher had joined the new district, yearly increments and conditions of employment contained in the district contract would apply. This procedure would allow veteran teachers of high quality to truly enjoy the benefits of a free market. It would give them an economic "leg up" in the search for better jobs and it would also make districts less "cock-sure" of their best staff, staff who are now held in a kind of pedagogical servitude by the "golden handcuff." Perhaps if some districts knew they might more easily lose their best teachers, they would take them a little less for granted.

(f) **Ending the game of "industrial hype."** I wish there were a way to do this with the passage of a law or the institution of a policy. Unfortunately, I don't think there is. The only real protection against buying computers you don't need or textbooks which placate the special interest groups of your community is to hire intelligent, honest, courageous educators and elect intelligent, honest, courageous board members. And as those things largely depend upon training, it is to the issue of teacher training and evaluation we now turn.

Teacher training and evaluation

Whether a child is gifted or below average, eager to learn or hostile toward school, supported by the home or abandoned, he or she is but half the basic educational equation. The other half is the teacher. How the teacher is prepared for the tasks of education will to a tremendous degree affect student outcomes. Teachers can't do everything. They cannot be held fully responsible for a student's final product, but they can make a powerful difference. They can tip the scales of learning in either direction, and in this section of our study of American public education after World War II we will investigate some current ideas on the education of our educators. We will look first at some contemporary theories of teacher training, then turn our attention to processes of teacher evaluation and staff development. Finally, we will explore some suggestions which may help to improve the quality of our teaching force.

Some current ideas on teacher training. Paul Woodring, formerly an advisor to the Ford Foundation and now Distinguished Service Professor Emeritus at Western Washington University, speaks for many critics of modern education when he says that the calibre of teacher training programs is woefully low. "The underlying problem," he writes, "is the hostile climate of opinion in prestigious colleges and universities toward teacher education of any kind."

> Professors are prone to say, "You are too bright to be a teacher." It takes a tough-minded student to hold out against that kind of pressure...Professional courses for teachers have never been highly regarded in U.S. universities and have often been targets of ridicule. Professors of education bear some portion of the blame for this state of affairs. They have permitted undergraduate

> courses in education to multiply beyond all reason, making an enormous amount of duplication inevitable. They have permitted standards for entrance to teacher education programs to remain much too low, even in periods marked by teacher surplus. Teacher education programs in some universities still admit some students who score just above 400 on the verbal section of the Scholastic Aptitude Test—a level lower than the mean score of the high school juniors whom some of these prospective teachers hope eventually to teach.[38]

Woodring in a nutshell articulates the bipartite troubles of contemporary teacher education. In the first instance, teacher candidates are of generally low calibre; in the second, they receive generally low-level instruction in an environment which places little value on education programs. That his assessment is correct is supported by a host of corroborative sources, as we shall now see.

A 1986 study of 76 institutions by the American Association of Colleges of Teacher Education (AACTE) revealed that SAT scores for elementary education majors were a pitiful 927, and that after completing 135 undergraduate credits, grade averages for all education majors were under 3.0 on the 4-point college scale.[39] Hodgkinson concludes that the main mode of college instruction, the lecture, is a poor method for such students. It encourages little interaction between student and teacher, and provides little opportunity for teachers to work individually with students in need of special attention. It seems, he laments, that many colleges are more attracted to the high television profits which have helped to keep scandal and drugs a part of their athletic programs than they are to meaningful methods of educational instruction.[40]

Gollnick and Kunkel of the National Council for Accreditation of Teacher Education (NCATE) report that NCATE has recently moved to shore up the process by which it evaluates the colleges which train our teachers. Key among NCATE's new approach are sharper looks at college education curricula, the relationship between colleges and the practical world of public education, admissions standards, and evaluation of college faculty. The idea is both to raise the standards of colleges of education and to make them more uniform throughout the nation.[41] Though the reaction of NCATE's initiative is mixed,[42] there are practically no voices in education today which oppose NCATE's goals or think them ill-considered.

Recently, two significant appraisals of teacher training in America have taken place, one by the so-called "Holmes Group," the other by a task force from the Carnegie Foundation. Because both studies were conducted with some of the best educational brainpower around, and because both found fundamentally the same things, it behooves us to go into them as part of our discussion on current thought in this critical area.

The Holmes Group (named after Henry Holmes, former Dean of the Graduate School of Education at Harvard University) is a consortium of deans of some of the largest, most prestigious American universities. Led by Dean Judith Lanier of Michigan State University, the group studied many institutions of teacher training and issued a report entitled "Tomorrow's Teachers" which was particularly critical about "the content, cohesiveness, and quality of instruction provided to prospective teachers..." The report stated that many education courses are "dumbed down and boring."[43] To remedy this situation, the group advocates not only the strengthening of liberal arts requirements for education majors and the establishing of more rigorous teacher licensing procedures, but the abolishing of undergraduate education majors entirely in favor of programs requiring greater subject competency. Education courses, the group says, should occur on the graduate level and should encourage differentiated teacher career paths (classroom vs. research vs. administration, etc.) based on the varying degrees of competency among students.

The views of the Holmes Group—especially the recommendation to replace undergraduate education programs—are not without controversy both pro and con. Frank Murray, Dean of the School of Education at the University of Delaware, and David Imig, Executive Director of the American Association of Colleges of Teacher Education, for example, both write in support of the Holmes Group recommendation.[44] They are joined by many others. Edwin Meyer, a practicing high school English teacher, for instance, writes in an educational journal that his pedagogical training was "worse than worthless. A practical step toward raising the quality of teaching," he goes on, "would be to eliminate all education requirements for teacher certification, thereby eliminating the departments of education in colleges and universities that have for so long been an unproductive and self-serving blight on U.S. schools."[45] Meyer claims that most education courses waste time which would be better spent on building subject competence, that most ed. majors lack both intellect and ambition, that most good educators view ed. courses with contempt, and that teacher training curricula should be replaced with a year of "guided internship" (at half salary) somewhat in the manner of medical school training. While not quite as strident as Meyer, respected researchers such as W. Robert Houston and Katherine Newman also concede that existing teacher training programs since World War II have not been as productive as they could be.[46]

Wholehearted acceptance of the Holmes Group report, however, is anything but universal. Howard Mehlinger, Dean of the School of Education at Indiana University, sees the elimination of education studies as very unwise. He argues that in and of itself it will not raise the admission standards of many colleges, and even more, by forcing would-be educators into extended graduate training to develop teacher skills, it will put a career in education further out of the reach of many minority candidates. Most of all, Mehlinger argues that it is a blanket solution to a problem which, because of the differences between states, lacks any uniform pattern. "I recognize that the Holmes Group plan is not designed to fit any single state," he writes. "Yet, in our decentralized system of education, all national plans are merely rhetoric until they are tuned to fit the particular circumstances that exist in each state, university and school district."[47]

Edward Nussel, Associate Dean at the College of Education, University of Toledo, is even more critical than Mehlinger. He calls the report "naive" and "vague," particularly in its suggestions for implementation.

> Although the Holmes Group recognizes that "the student teaching course is one of the few predictors of teaching success," they choose to replace current models of field experience with an entity they call a "professional school"—an arrangement rather common in good teacher education programs that nevertheless seems innovative to the Holmes Group...In reality, the...report is a reactionary document. Its graduate curriculum still looks like a traditional bachelor's degree.[48]

The report of the Carnegie Task Force, entitled "A Nation Prepared: teachers for the 21st century," is in some respects more specific than the Holmes Group report. For example, it gives some financial estimates for the cost of proposed reforms (about 2.8% of current expenditures per year for the next ten years), and suggests a National Board for Professional Training to set and maintain standards of teacher education. Generally, however, it agrees with the Holmes Group that current schools of education need to go further in attracting minority candidates and improving the quality of all prospective teachers. The Carnegie report offers a very straightforward set of student outcomes as a means of verifying teacher quality. They are standardized tests, rates of attendance, dropout rates, job placement rates, and college acceptances. If these indicators are high, the report says, then the teachers and schools can be counted as successful. To the extent the indicators drop, the success of the educational system also falls.[49]

One might well argue that these same criteria would make a meaningful set of standards for colleges of teacher education as well as public schools. Indeed, in the pages below we shall suggest criteria for evaluating the performance of both teachers and the colleges which produce them that draw on the work of the Carnegie Task Force. For now, it is important to note how widely the criticism of teacher training institutions ranges and how many voices, not outside but within the profession itself, are raised in calls for improvement.

In an effort to shore-up the slipping standards of teacher education experienced in recent years, many new programs for teacher certification and competency testing have begun to surface. By 1986, thirty-six states were already administering competency tests in programs with new certification and even re-certification requirements. Seventeen of these states opted for the newly-written National Teacher Exam (NTE). Another nine developed their own tests, while the remainder used a variety of measuring instruments.[50] It seems fairly certain that as pressures for education reform continue, tests to assure higher standards of teacher quality will be around for a long time. What is less certain is how effective these tests are, and again there are opinions pro and con.

George Madaus is the Director of the Center for the Study of Testing, Evaluation, and Educational Policy at Boston College. He writes with colleague Diana Pullin that the NTE may not accurately reflect the competence of a teacher nor reliably predict the teacher's chances of classroom success. In particular, Madaus—not an opponent of competency testing—fears that the short-answer nature of the test and the content material of some test questions do not sufficiently probe the ability levels of the test takers.[51] His views are somewhat supported by researchers such as Lee Shulman, Director of the Teacher Assessment Project at Stanford University. Shulman not only sees a need to develop better tests for both prospective and veteran teachers but also sees testing as only one of several means of teacher assessment. He contends that such things as supervised field activities and direct observations should accompany testing in an on-going, continuous process of staff evaluation.[52]

On the other side of the coin, competency tests are defended by many in the profession. Popham and Kirby, for instance, contend that it is the right of every child in the American democracy to be taught by a literate teacher, and it is thus the obligation of state officials to mandate tests of instructional competency both in the veteran and prospective teacher corps.[53] Superintendent Russell Joki (Nampa,

Idaho) writes that competency and accountability for quality should be written board of education policies and should cover administrators as well as teachers.[54] Researcher Joel Burdin notes that, with certain variations, all states now require at least a bachelor's degree for teacher certification, virtually all states require a test, and some require post-graduate degrees.[55] Finally, Gregory Anrig, President of the Educational Testing Service, the agency which wrote the National Teacher Examination, answers critics of the test by reminding us that the test is only a measure of minimal competency. It cannot measure interpersonal quality, nor can it substitute for the observation and guidance of experienced administrators in the process of teacher assessment. Moreover, Anrig adds, there are constant efforts to improve the test. New questions on communications skills, essay-writing, reading comprehension, as well as revised questions on professional educational knowledge and liberal arts subject areas, are already going into updated versions of the NTE. In addition, the test was submitted for comment to over 3,000 school deans, parents, teachers, and board members, of whom 50% responded—many with high praise as well as suggested improvements.[56]

It would seem hard to dispute the necessity for some kind of competency measurement given the acknowledged weakness of many teacher training programs and the dreadfully low scores of many prospective teachers (discussed previously). As irksome as this issue is, however, it is bound to become even more so in the immediate future because of the projected teacher shortages about to descend upon us. The reason is that shortages have in the past been accompanied by the relaxation, not the tightening, of standards. The issuance of so-called "emergency certificates" during these periods has given us many teachers who are both pedagogically unprepared and who frequently find themselves teaching in an area other than their primary area of expertise. Grabbing a body for a classroom by issuing alternative routes to certification or lowering certification standards for so-called "emergency purposes" is a practice which can only insure the continuing decline of the American system. As Robert Roth, Director of the Center for Research on Teaching at the University of South Florida, writes, "a profession is only as strong as its practitioners are competent," and by the AFT's own estimates, at least 200,000 current teachers are substandard in either pedagogical or subject area expertise.[57]

By 1992, we are projected to have only 65.6% of the teachers we will require, and from existing teacher unions as well as educational researchers we are hearing a plea that certification standards be kept high in the face of this shortfall. Gary Watts, Assistant Executive Director of the NEA, for example, writes that it would be better to "leave the classrooms vacant rather than fill them with lower-quality substitutes,"[58] and Willis Hawley, Dean of the Peabody College for Teachers at Vanderbilt University, argues that we may have to consider enticing former teachers to re-enter the profession if we are going to meet the coming shortage without a drop in standards.[59]

Hawley goes further than mere programs of re-entry, however, and it would be wise to heed his comprehensive view of things, for he links training standards with economics, and economics with demographic trends, in a total strategy which interweaves many of the seemingly diverse strands of our current system. Citing figures from the National Center for Education Statistics, Hawley writes that between 1989 and 1993 America will need as many as one million new teachers.[60]

Yet at this time of need, enrollments in schools of education are down due to a variety of factors, including low pay, increased opportunities for women and minorities in other fields, increased certification requirements, and the decline of schools as a wholesome working environment. Traditionally, increases in salary and decreases in certification standards have been used to cope with such shortages. Now, however, Hawley believes these tactics will not work for two important reasons. First, standards are already low and cannot be dropped any further. Second, it would take a 40% rise in teacher salaries to make them competitive with other professional fields.[61] Policies which increase the preparation period for teachers or make certification a more rigorous process, while they may be pedagogically sound, will probably not attract more people to the profession. They may, in fact, reduce the number of teacher candidates. Thus, for Hawley, things such as paid internships during graduate school, increased starting salaries to some level below the 40% career differential, merit pay raises after being hired, the facilitation of both interstate and interdistrict movement, an upgrading of the school environment, differentiated career positions, and a greater voice in school policy decisions become extremely important to the process of attracting high-quality candidates without lowering standards.[62] We will return to suggestions such as Hawley's later in this chapter. For now, we move on to other ways of judging and molding educational personnel.

Some current ideas on teacher evaluation and staff development. Training the teacher of tomorrow will not in and of itself improve the education of today because, like it or not, we must live with the teachers who are already in the system, particularly those with tenure who fully expect to teach until retirement. We cannot "train" these individuals. That has already occurred. But we can evaluate them and try to help them develop into better teachers. Toward those ends a veritable torrent of ideas has poured onto the modern educational landscape.

In viewing the topics of staff evaluation and staff development, it is probably wisest to begin with a realization that they are not—or, rather, *should* not—be separate entities. When intelligently practiced, the various methods of evaluating educational personnel contain provisions for improving teacher performance as well as criticizing it. Indeed, criticism has little value unless accompanied by constructive suggestions for improvement.[63] Accordingly, most modern educators practice a form of evaluation known in the business as "clinical supervision."

With apologies to educators like Cogen, Goldhammer, and Sullivan whose books on the subject cover it in exquisite detail,[64] clinical supervision is a system of monitoring and evaluation which involves very specific procedures and an atmosphere designed to be non-threatening and developmental. There are three stages to the process: planning, observation, and evaluation. During the planning stage, a "clinical relationship" is built between supervisor and teacher. In a pre-observation conference, they plan the lesson (or a series of lessons) to be observed. They discuss various aspects of the class and the material, finally agreeing on the goals and objectives which ought to be met in the actual teaching. In the observation phase, the teacher teaches while the supervisor watches, taking notes which will be used later during the evaluation.

For many supervisors notetaking is an art which can range from verbatim data to offhand impressions. It is important, for example, to know what to look for and to be able to jot it down during the sometimes heated flow of a class. The orderliness of the teaching environment, the relationship between students and teacher (often called the "psychological environment"), the organization of the lesson, the manner in which it is presented, the response of the students, the teacher's control of the classroom, the way in which interruptions are handled if they occur—all these and more should be part of the notetaking repertoire. Following the observation, the second stage concludes with an analysis of the data collected and planning for the post-observation conference. In the last stage of the process, teacher and supervisor meet again. They discuss the lesson in relationship to the goals and objectives they had previously established, noting what was successful and what was not. Based on their assessments, an evaluation is written and future plans for improvement are made. For poorer teachers these plans may be very specific and can involve things as fundamental as "learn your subject matter so that you can present accurate information." For master teachers they may involve things like video-taping a lesson to share with other staff members for their development.

Every supervisor, of course, does not follow the blueprint above robotically. There are those who modify the regimen to fit personal views; there are those who simply don't have the time to apply the regimen fully; and there are those who disagree with aspects of the clinical process, preferring to use other criteria or other procedures. Arthur Costa, Professor of Education at California State University/Sacramento, for example, accepts the basic format of clinical supervision but sees it more as a way of getting teachers to think and behave intelligently than as a means of mere performance evaluation.[65] Famed educator Madeline Hunter rejects procedures such as the pre-observation conference. She writes that it is "not only a waste of time but it can create bias in both observer and teacher which interferes with objective observation of teacher performance...,"[66] and her opinions are not without controversy.[67] Finally, there are educators whose research indicates that criteria other than those found in traditional clinical supervision more accurately reflect the reality of an educator's performance, and, indeed, that a preoccupation with so-called "humanistic" teaching and supervision has actually hurt modern education.

Consider, for example, the work of Coker, Medley, and Soar. Their two-year study revealed that many tenets of the "humanistic" education which teacher training and clinical supervision programs encourage result in poorer student outcomes than older, more traditional methods. In the study, five hundred teachers from Texas, Ohio, Louisiana, and Canada covering grades 3-8 were asked to state the teaching techniques they thought to be most effective. Responses such as "pause to let students answer," "respond to student questions," "practice good listening skills," "praise students," "use rewards," etc. were collected in a list. Teachers were then observed and evaluated based on how well they adhered to the criteria on the list. Meanwhile, the students were tested at both the start and end of each school year (four tests in all) using the Iowa Test of Basic Skills. "The upsetting [conclusion]," writes Prof. Coker, "was many of the things [teachers] said were important were not significant, and of those that were significant, more than half were counterproductive." The authors of the study blame teacher-training institutions for the miseducation of both teachers and supervisors, especially since, when confronted with the evidence of the study, "they react in anger, in disgust—always in disbelief." Schools need to return, the authors claim, to an atmosphere of "businesslike" behavior where neither false praise nor abuse is tolerated, for businesslike behavior and an insistence on classroom participation were the greatest predictors of high student outcomes. Short of these realizations, writes Coker, all of the hoopla of modernism and reform is "merely rearranging deck chairs on the Titanic."[68]

Coker and Medley went on to conduct another study of supervisors alone. This time their work showed that there is little if any correlation between a principal's judgment of teacher effectiveness and student outcomes. They argue for observation procedures which will more accurately reflect the actual achievements of the classroom.[69] Nor is the work of Coker and Medley isolated. Aretha Pigford, Associate Professor in the College of Education at the University of South Carolina, recalls her days as a building principal. At first, regardless of student outcomes, all her teachers rated themselves "outstanding" or "above average." "No teacher rated himself or herself 'average' or 'below average.' My first evaluation of teachers," she writes, "proved to be little more than a game with the teachers as controlling players." Eventually, she replaced the labels and systems with four goal-oriented questions: "where are we," "where do we want to go," "how do we get there," and "did we make it." She found this evaluative scheme far more meaningful for her own work, the work of her teachers, and—most importantly—the education of her students.[70]

Without belaboring the point by citing additional thoughts on staff assessments,[71] evaluation has many faces in today's complex picture, most of them aimed at both staff development and the improvement of student outcomes. Besides evaluation tools, however, most districts today are engaged in staff development projects in an effort to upgrade and/or extend the work of the teacher-training colleges. Many such staff development projects stem from deficiencies discovered in the evaluation process. Others are attempts to help teachers keep abreast of new educational ideas and methods. We will look briefly at some of the more popular current trends in staff development.

One of the most widely encountered staff development programs is the teaching-learning series developed by Madeline Hunter at UCLA. Again, with apologies to Dr. Hunter, whose own writing explains the teaching-learning process in exquisite detail, the process stresses that the work one observes in the classroom should have roots and repercussions in an education context much broader than the actual lesson.[72] The first step in the Hunter process is identifying what lesson ought to be taught in the unfolding of a curriculum. The next steps are to determine the needs of the class and the intellectual level on which the students are functioning and then to decide on the intellectual level(s) on which the lesson will be taught.[73] Finally, the process ends with the teaching of the lesson and an evaluation of the results. There is much more to the work of Hunter than this, however, most of it involving the specific steps of teaching a given lesson.

A Madeline Hunter lesson contains seven ingredients, the first of which is referred to as "the anticipatory set." Here the teacher introduces the topic, its purpose, and what the student can expect to be accountable for. Next, the teacher imparts the basic information of the lesson (the so-called "input" stage). In the third phase, the teacher presents examples of the information ("modeling"), and in the fourth, the teacher checks for student understanding, usually through questions which force some sort of class participation. Participation continues in phase five as the teacher guides the students through some kind of practice with the information he/she has imparted. In the sixth phase of a lesson, the teacher asks the students to work alone using the newly-learned material. Often, this so-called "independent practice" stage is in the form of homework. Finally, in the "feedback stage" the homework is reviewed and criticized, while the teacher sums up the point of the lesson in a statement usually referred to as "closure."

During the decade of the 1980's Hunter's theories have been presented to countless thousands of teachers in staff development workshops run largely by the districts in which the teachers work. But the Mastery Teaching syllabus of Madeline Hunter is only one of several staff development plans currently popular. Showers, Servatius, and Young, for example, write about peer coaching workshops in which teachers trained to do so act as coaches to upgrade and develop the performance of fellow teachers.[74] Kindsvatter and Wilen describe self-evaluation charts on which supervisors are encouraged to build conference skills.[75] Dodd and Rosenbaum advocate "learning communities" in which teachers work together in small groups to improve themselves.[76] The Madison Workshops in Mansfield, Ohio bring noted educators such as John Goodlad, Mario Fantini, and William Glassner to work with Madison School District staff in fifteen-hour workshops jointly funded by the district and Ashland College.[77] F.W. Parkay writes about student test scores rising following staff development seminars run jointly by six schools and the University of Texas.[78] Finally, Kerman and Martin, working in California, have produced a series of courses for staff development based on teacher expectation. Their idea, and it is supported by considerable research, is that student outcomes rise as teachers learn to expect and demand better student performance.[79] Supportive work with supervisors likewise indicates that as a principal's curricular vision broadens and his/her expectations of staff increase, students achieve more. Workshops to encourage such instructional leadership among school administrators are thus becoming more and more frequent.[80]

With all of this research and activity going on, one wonders why our schools have not achieved more. The answer lies, I believe, in the fact that much of the work is overrated and much downright irrelevant to the push-pull activities in the trenches of the daily educational battleground. In the final section of this topic I will elaborate on that statement and offer some suggestions for improving the training, evaluation, and development of our teachers.

Some suggestions for teacher training and evaluation. Below are some ideas which I hope will yield a better teaching force than the one which has serviced America's children since 1945.

(a) Curriculum in teacher training. One can be driven crazy with pedagogical controversy. Arguments between supporters of the Holmes Group and those of the Carnegie Task Force sometimes become more important to the educational environment than solving our problem of poor teacher training. What I would like to advocate here is a general curriculum which can be implemented in any number of ways. Whether in a two-year program, a four-year one, or a six-year one, whether in a school of education or a liberal arts college, whether in an undergraduate or graduate environment, it is the mastery of the curriculum which is important.

A good teacher must possess four qualities: competence in a given subject area; a general literacy with respect to the world around him or her; a deep and conscious self-knowledge; and the ability to teach. Nothing less will do.

It seems almost silly to say that subject competency is axiomatic for a teacher, but in America we often put our worst practitioners in schools while leaving our best to inhabit the industrial marketplace. In this we ought to take a lesson from the Soviet Union. When an Olga Korbut has won her gold medals in gymnastics or a Sviatoslav Richter has finished his touring career as a concert pianist, they teach. In America, when American athletes finish their careers, they make television commercials. We never require our best to give back what they've taken, to pass the baton on to the next generation in mankind's relay race, and we systematically expect our teachers to be the least competent of our professionals. It is tragically usual to find a high school choral director who can't read a score or play the piano, a public school drama coach who has never studied drama, a middle school earth science teacher who has never done any original scientific research, or a high school creative writing teacher who has never once written so much as a short story. On the other hand, how often does a Hemingway or Steinbeck walk into a school, a Salk teach a biology course, or a Julius Irving coach a high school basketball team? However it is addressed, subject competency is the sine qua non of the educational process, and we had better address it.

It is now somewhat more common to hear that general literacy should be a prerequisite for a teacher, though just what constitutes that literacy is a bit more vague. In any event, it is a trend I applaud, for life is the integration of disciplines, and no teacher can really exist in an intellectual vacuum and still be a good teacher. The scientist who teaches nuclear technology had better develop the ability to think morally and ethically, lest his students learn only how to make the bombs and not how to deter their use. Of what good is the literature teacher who assigns a reading on Jim Thorpe but is ignorant of athletics? Basic reading and writing skills are not enough, though they are fundamentally necessary. There is a cultural literacy which goes beyond the basics that must become part of every teacher's repertoire. When Hirsch writes that "cultural literacy constitutes the only sure avenue of opportunity";[81] when Bloom laments the passing of a liberal arts curriculum which once required what he calls "humane learning" in addition to career preparation;[82] when Adler argues that education in a democracy must provide all students with learning which not only trains them for careers but also prepares them for the duties and responsibilities of citizenship and allows for their personal self-development;[83] they speak to the heart of what real educational training must become. Side-by-side with subject competence, then, a meaningful teacher-training curriculum must require the student to be conversant with and able to think rationally about man's general culture—historically and in the present. Later, in our investigation of curricula, we will spell that out in more detail.

To my way of thinking, people who see little or no value in pedagogy courses are crazy. They have either never faced the real world of teaching or are ignorant of how complex that world is. The work of people such as Madeline Hunter is anything but superfluous to the learning process, nor can one be expected to "divine" it without pedagogical training. You might just as well tell a surgeon to "wing it" in the operating room. And preparing a lesson is only one of a host of pedagogical skills which a good teacher needs. The organizational techniques of writing a syllabus or keeping a room neat, the ability to understand different student learning patterns and adjust to them, learning how to build wholesome student relationships, learning how to deal with peers or administrators or parents, being taught how to grade and how to get the tons of educational paperwork done on time and well, and applying all this to a given subject area is a major undertaking which requires schooling. It is inconceivable that we could significantly improve our teacher crop without such training. Just to know how to speak to a group or mix humor with data in this television age is enough to constitute a course in "stand-up teaching skills." If you doubt it, try stepping into a seventh-grade math class and see what happens to your communication and classroom management without any professional preparation. You would most likely be lucky to get out alive much less successfully teach a lesson.

Finally, a good teacher must have a deep and conscious knowledge of self in order to face real students today. Let me give you an idea of what I mean. What do you do when an angry youngster tells you to "go fuck yourself" when you ask him to step to the board? How do you respond to the high school girl who comes to you frightened out of her mind because she has just had oral sex with a drug user and needs to be tested for AIDS? What do you say to the eighth-grade boy who tells you with tears in his eyes that he can't face his father because he is a homosexual? How do you react to the child who has been beaten because his dyslexia has "set off" an alcoholic parent? What do you do to comfort the girl whose mother and father are fighting over her in a divorce case? Rare occurrences? Don't kid yourself. They happen every day in today's schools, and they require the attention of teachers whose own psychological make-up is strong and—above all—known to them.

When Jersild asked teachers to "face themselves,"[84] he was aware that there is a human side to the student-teacher relationship which often transcends the simple transfer of subject data. How teachers cope with anxiety, loneliness, meaninglessness, attitudes toward authority, attitudes toward sex, hostility, feelings of hopelessness, perceptions of reality and much more, will directly affect the way they teach and interact with their students.

What do you think the male teacher who himself has fears about homosexuality will be able to do for that eighth-grade boy? How will the educator who grew up in a home which "hated niggers" react to the black child in class? How can the teacher who grew up fearful of his parents be able to tolerate or control the student who insists on challenging classroom authority?

Courses in educational psychology, particularly ones which ask teachers to confront and work through their own problems before becoming professionals who might inflict those problems on students or allow them to inhibit the process of education, are essential. To the extent many teachers never receive training of this kind, they are time bombs waiting for the wrong situation to explode.

To assure that standards in subject competency, cultural literacy, pedagogical skills, and personal psychological training have been met, tests are axiomatic. Exactly what form they take (especially in the last area) is really up to the teacher-training institutions, though again, a national education congress such as the one proposed earlier might provide a great service by establishing minimum guidelines. I can only hope that the tests will be rigorous and that no educational jurisdiction will license any teacher without them.

(b) Practical preparation and career steps. There is great wisdom in the ideas of Willis Hawley, particularly as they relate to the practical preparation of teachers through paid internships. It is not that traditional student teaching components should be done away with; it is that they are not sufficient. Too many teachers are ill-prepared when they first hit the classroom simply because there is just too much to learn about the practical, daily business of teaching. In this regard we should take our cue from medicine. It is after medical school that the doctor must spend two, three, sometimes four years in internship and residency programs before a full-fledged practice can be set up. That is because there is a gap between the classroom course—even with its practical components—and the daily flow of a hospital, a gap which can only be filled by practical experience. So it is with teaching.

What I propose is a year of paid internship which follows the field component of student teaching courses and which bridges the gap between school and the real world of education. But more than that, I believe the internship should be the first rung of a career ladder which teachers can climb by dint of the competence they achieve. From intern to a no-nonsense, three-year probationary status; from there to the rank of "professional teacher"; and finally to the rank of "master teacher"; an educator should be able to advance with recognition, pay increases, modification of schedule to allow time for individual projects, and coherent criteria for upward mobility.

That last part is essential. Upward mobility in this scenario cannot merely be based upon years of service if the teaching corp is to become strong. It cannot be the automatic reward of seniority dispensed by administrators too lazy or too cowardly to apply predetermined standards of excellence to teachers in their jurisdiction. There are criteria (and we have already discussed them) which can and must be applied to insure high standards of education. The probationary teacher whose class control is poor, whose lesson plans are disorganized, whose paperwork is overdue, whose teaching and subject competency are lacking, whose room is disorderly, whose relationships with students and peers is less than sound, or whose student outcomes are sub-par is no candidate for retention, no matter what the teacher shortage. The "professional teacher" whose work never achieves excellence, who never publishes, who never gets that grant, who hasn't put in more than the contract hours, who has never received peer recognition, whose student outcomes have never become exemplary should not be a candidate for "master status." To those ends, there is no substitute for astute supervision—and that brings us to the training of administrators.

(c) Administrator training. If the career ladder is a viable scenario for a teacher, it is indispensable for an administrator. There should be no administrator who has not attained the competence of a master teacher. It is only after that degree of achievement that the nuts and bolts of supervision, finance control, teacher hiring, and the other jobs of an administrator can be applied intelligently to the daily flow of education. Therefore, master teacher status should be made a requirement for administrator certification. If it is not, we will only end up with mediocre teachers becoming mediocre supervisors who hire more mediocre teachers.

There is another thing we must insist upon in the area of educational administration and that is a continuing involvement by the administrator with the daily business of teaching. The complaint that administrators often lose the feel of the classroom is a just one. As this happens, administrators begin to pontificate instead of advise, to grow insensitive to problems rather than more sensitive to them. Thus, it should be a requirement of all public school administrators either to teach a class or to supervise an ongoing student activity. In this way they would not lose the feel of the daily environment in which others labor, and because they, too, would have to obey their own pronouncements, they would become instantly aware of their own wisdom or folly.

(d) Decalcifying the "ivory tower." The same principle applied to administrators above should also be applied to college professors who teach our teachers. What could be more detrimental to the process of teacher training than to have the professors responsible for it ignorant or out-of-touch with the reality of it? Already, the weakness of the system has become apparent. As noted above, NCATE proposes that the relationship between the college and the practicing world of the teacher be an important criterion in the evaluation of the college program.[85] Andrew Porter, Co-director of the Institute for Research on Teaching at Michigan State University, sees an even greater problem in the area of educational research. "Teachers provide the insight, wisdom, judgment, and experience possible only from one who interacts daily with children and learning," he writes. "Too easily the researcher becomes the sole originator of the research while the practitioner becomes simply the object of study rather than an instigator as well."[86]

To solve the "ivory tower dilemma," I propose that all professors of education be required to teach a class or run an ongoing student activity in a K-12 environment. To supply that environment, colleges of education should institute "university public schools" to service the children of their local area. The great majority of the staff of these schools would, of course, be regular "front-line" teachers, but the professors would have to be "in the trenches" as well. Many fine universities have such programs now. My suggestion is that they become required and that the college professors who train our teachers use them to come face-to-face with their own theories in a real, working environment.

(e) Real evaluation, real supervision, real staff development. Every time I have attended a clinical supervision workshop or a class in mastery teaching, a little voice has crept into my mind saying "this is not the way it is." During the breaks in these sessions, I frequently found myself talking to other class members who have also heard the voice. I believe the little voice is there because it is saying something true, something we had better pay attention to if we really intend to straighten out our schools.

There is in the staff development/teacher evaluation game being peddled today an assumption that every teacher can be improved and, even more, that honest, direct, sometimes forceful criticism is a "no-no" which so deeply bruises the psyche that nothing positive can happen. By the way, this same assumption occurs with students, too, and you might as well know that I think it is wrong—wrong both for the children and the staff.

I am not for brutality of any kind, neither physical nor emotional. But in the name of avoiding psychic damage we have, since World War II, lost the ability to be honest with ourselves. We cloak every negative comment in shields of platitudes so thick that positives lose their meaning and true growth never occurs. In the clinical supervision game we are taught never to say, "Miss Jones, that was a poor lesson." Instead we say, "There were several positive aspects to your lesson, Miss Jones, and perhaps some which may need attention." In his book, *How Children Fail*, John Holt discusses this problem in great detail. He states, and I agree, that kids *want* to be told when they are wrong or doing poorly. The honesty is worth ten times the hypocrisy of soft-soaping reality both in terms of improved performance and in the development of trustworthy relationships.[87] In this regard, I do not think there is much difference between kids and adults.

To bring the point home in concrete terms, let me describe observation and evaluation forms I have been required to use with my own staff. The observation form has a section for simply describing the lesson, one for noting what was well done, and one for noting what was not well done. The supervisor is virtually required to say something positive, even if there was little or no positive aspect to the lesson. But, even more, the terminology of the form deliberately avoids negatives. The section headings are "description of activity," "positive aspects," and "suggestions for improvement,"—as if the words "negative aspects" were some kind of Communist plot. Similarly, the final year-end staff evaluation form has a host of criteria ranging from room maintenance to knowledge of the subject matter. Here the evaluative categories are "superior," "satisfactory," "needs improvement," and "no data available"—again, as if the word "unsatisfactory" was a violation of union contracts.

But there is more to the real world of evaluations. On every form, the teacher is given an opportunity to respond to the supervisor's comments. In and of itself, this is fine. Responses are important, and no administrator is infallible, to say the least. However, it has become an increasingly frequent occurrence to challenge what a supervisor has written—challenge to the point of union harassment or to the point where comments are changed. Let me give you an example. Of the twenty or so criteria for which one teacher was evaluated, seventeen were listed as "superior" and three as "satisfactory." Well, the fact that everything was not "superior" threw this particular teacher into such a snit that the evaluator's administrative colleagues were bombarded by demands that the evaluation be changed. And they were changed by a higher administrator whose cowardice and hypocrisy were all too typical of the current environment. In certain quarters I have even observed administrators afraid to praise some teachers in public lest others, not mentioned, turn the slight into a vindictive war.

Beyond the necessity for the honest and open expression of criticism is a greater need, the need for meaningful criteria, and on this score I must tell you that we pay far too little attention to student outcomes and far too much to the superficial trappings of the moment. The lengthy, sometimes overly elaborate procedures of clinical supervision force both teacher and administrator to concentrate on the lesson. That is fine. The procedure (with modification for how little time we all have) is an acceptable one. But the lesson is not the forest. It is only the tree, and to pay it mind to the exclusion of the forest is to miss the real point of true evaluation.

The forest is the total achievement of the students. The lesson is the means by which that achievement occurs. True educational accountability and thus true evaluation and supervision must focus first on student outcomes. Let me give you an example from the world of music.

You are evaluating a high school chorus teacher. What do you do first? Observe the rehearsal? I submit you do not. Observe the concert. See first if the kids can sing. Are they well-dressed? Are they well-disciplined on the risers? Do they have an attentive and positive rapport with the conductor? Is the tone pleasant or harsh? Is the ensemble together or fragmented? Is the music appropriate to the group? Is it performed with musical sensitivity or mechanically? Do the students appear to enjoy their task, or are they just going through the motions? The answers to these questions will give you a feel for the teacher's work immediately. If the answers are all glowing, you may rest assured that the individual lessons are good. If the answers are not glowing, that is the time to find out where the process of education has bogged down.

It is very much like seeing the doctor. He or she checks your blood pressure. It is 180/95. Not good. *Now* is the time for the doctor to probe your life further. Reduce your salt, lose weight, stop smoking, take it easy, get your blood tested. *Now* the investigation must continue because 180/95 is not good, and that is the bottom line, the reality, the thing no "soft soaping" can change.

I have stated earlier that the teacher cannot be wholly responsible for student outcomes, and that is true. Teachers cannot force children to be attentive in class. They cannot make them do their homework. They cannot be expected to overcome the ravages of dope, a poor diet, a broken home, child abuse, alcohol, or any of the other social diseases which plague so many of our students. But, and it is a huge "but," they can and must be made accountable for the maintenance of the *average* standards of a given course in a given area. When their classes consistently and over a period of time (please note those words) achieve more than the mean, the evaluation must reflect a superior effort. When the achievement is below the mean, the evaluation must reflect a poorer-than-average effort.

The research and experiences of educators such as Coker, Medley, and Pigford cannot be shoved aside if we truly want our kids to learn. These educators have told us that to be valid, evaluation must be goal-oriented, and in the business of teaching, goals are reflected by student outcomes. There can be no fudging with that principle.

As to the matter of staff development, it is a fundamental error to assume that every teacher can or even wants to do a good job. I am greatly at odds with the plastic, Pollyanna-like attitude of the "happiness gurus" in the evaluation game. If you just adhere to the rules of the game, if you just keep smiling and play to the ego of the teacher, if you avoid negatives and stress positives, your entire staff will improve. Baloney. You may try that approach at first. And, by the way, that is the first approach you *ought* to try because the presumption of civility and competence can, indeed, inspire some people. But as sure as you live, you are going to find staff members who will take advantage of your civility and who don't want to give one ounce more than is necessary to keep getting a paycheck. That is a reality which is not just personal opinion or personal experience. It squares with the research and writing of some of the most noteworthy behavioral and managerial scholars in the field.

In 1965 and 1970, drawing on the work of many before him, Abraham Maslow published two books in which he described a hierarchy of human needs ranging from the basics of food, clothing, and shelter to the need for safety, for love, for self-esteem, and finally for complete self-actualization.[88] Maslow argued that as a person satisfies one set of needs on the lowest rung of the hierarchy, he or she can then turn to the next need in an upward quest for self-fulfillment.

The acceptance of Maslow's work triggered a tremendous amount of research into the motivational behavior of people, particularly as they might seek to develop themselves in the workplace. Lyman Porter restructured the hierarchy to include the need for autonomy,[89] and both Thomas Sergiovanni and Fred Carver applied Maslow's theories to the teachers of the 1970's and found that the greatest need of the educator was the one for self-esteem.[90] But by far the most influential apostle of Maslovian psychology was Frederick Herzberg. Herzberg challenged the notion that lower and higher order needs were separate in the individual. He argued that they reside side-by-side in a given person at the same time and to varying degrees, and that because of this, every person needs management from supervisors capable of addressing both aspects of the hierarchy, lower order needs and higher order ones.[91]

As Herzberg's work came to be accepted, it eventually spawned the realization that not all individuals stress the same hierarchical needs or stress them to the same extent. "Person A" might be extremely "security conscious" (for any of a number of reasons), content to avoid the challenges of Maslovian development and wary of any changes of behavior. "Person B," in diametric opposition, might care little about things such as job security, preferring instead to use the criticism of a supervisor as a tool in a process of development toward vocational self-actualization. "Person C" might lie somewhere in between the two extremes.

What accompanied Herzberg was a flutter of activity among social and educational psychologists which applied his work to human behavior. Robert Presthus developed a profile of people as being "upwardly mobile," "indifferent," or "ambivalent."[92] Victor Thompson stated that security-oriented people tended to be "place-bound," while more daring personalities were "career-bound."[93] Douglas MacGregor postulated a "Theory X" personality viewing the world in Hobbesian terms (slothful, given to avoiding work, needing firm direction from others) and a "Theory Y" personality viewing it in Lockian terms (self-directed, willing to assume responsibility, etc.) Argyris developed a "pattern A" management system for MacGregor's "Theory X" personality and a "pattern B" system for "Theory Y" behavior. Likert, Vroom, Blake, Mouton, Hersey, and Blanchard added other systems of management geared to various Maslovian levels; some to the maturity of people, some to the relationships needed between workers and supervisors, some to individual psychological needs.[94]

What all of this led to was a general theory of management and supervision in which individuals are treated as individuals. With certain basic assumptions of human behavior, the theory (sometimes called "contingency management" or "differentiated management") says, in effect, don't paint with a brush so broad that you lose sight of the differences between one person and another, one situation and another.[95] Robert Owens says it in more measured terms. "The contingency approach to motivation," he writes, "suggests that efforts to get the maximum cooperation and effort from individuals requires us to use approaches particularly appropriate to the specific situation."[96] The application of this theory to the special tasks of educational supervision by researchers such as Sergiovanni and Glickman has given educational administrators a wide range of criteria and behavioral options by which they can effectively manage their staffs.[97]

All of which gets us back to the fact that some teachers are going to be "developed" in one way and some in another. Let us take two examples. We'll call them Smith and Jones. Ms. Smith is a highly motivated teacher, not yet at the top of her craft either in terms of subject expertise or pedagogical acumen, but eager to grow and driven by a burning love for education. In the terminology above, she is a "Theory Y" personality, already functioning on the upper levels of the Maslovian hierarchy. Her observation and evaluation sessions are cooperative, professional, positive, and at times downright fun. The supervisional style for her is to remove as many bureaucratic impediments from her life as possible, to make only occasional suggestions for she requires no heavy-handed direction, and to reward her energy and efforts with every tool from praise to funds for new projects.

By contrast, Mr. Jones is a sour, sickly man whose classes consistently achieve less than those of his colleagues. His paperwork (grades, student evaluations, staff reports, etc.) is never in on time, his planning always a last-minute, haphazard affair. He is absent as many days as the contract allows and always manages an excuse to avoid department meetings. From a psychological viewpoint, he has long ago left the profession.

At first one may try being understanding and reasonable with Mr. Jones. Would he mind, please, trying to get his work in on time? What might be done to help improve his student outcomes? When would he like to meet to discuss his classes? If this proves ineffective, supervisional style should change to become much more directional. Please come to my office at 3:30 P.M. I will expect your grades on my desk by the end of the marking period. You've missed the last three staff meetings; please be there tomorrow.

But Mr. Jones is tenured with well over twenty years in the district and is simply biding his time to retirement. Since his work is marginally acceptable, we have no grounds to even attempt dismissal procedures, so we give up any hope he will respond to our efforts. For him, "staff development" may just be to transfer him to a position where he will do the least harm and to encourage him to do what he should have done years before—leave the profession.

The point of all of this is that real supervision and real staff development have to deal with reality, and reality includes the cloak of tenure protection and people like Mr. Jones as well as those like Ms. Smith. Either we recognize that and develop real ways of dealing with it, or we go on playing games while the students of teachers and administrators like Mr. Jones continue to waste their educational lives.

(f) Educational recognition. Finally, as a nation we ought to adopt some steps which will help bring national attention to the value of education in general and in particular to great educators whose work has enhanced us all. As cheap and crass as it may seem, a Nobel Prize or Pulitzer Prize in education is an idea which could focus attention of a public relations-conscious world on a truly noble and necessary profession. With damn little money and just a modicum of leadership, I'd love to see an American President award an educator each year with the civilian medal of honor—and do it on prime time television where millions or parents and kids could see. Why not? There are press photo sessions for World Series winners and astronauts. Why not for teachers? Why not an educator's Hall of Fame? Maybe dedicate a wing of the Smithsonian to it. Why not a $50,000 annual teacher-of-the-year award given by a grateful Congress to some deserving educator?

I'm not saying it would turn things around, but it would surely help create a feeling of pride in the educational community. And who knows? Maybe if a few million kids could see a teacher getting an award from a President, it would inspire more respect for our schools in the eyes of students. It might even inspire a few of them to become part of a profession which many of us still love and care for.

The impact of religion on contemporary schooling

The history of American public education has, as we have seen, contained powerful religious influences from the earliest Colonial days, and that has presented a somewhat peculiar problem to the American people. On the one hand, our nation was settled by immigrants whose chief concern was the establishment of a social order in which religious freedom and economic opportunity were protected by the state. Toward that end, they built many of their early schools around their various churches, interweaving religious doctrine with secular learning in a fabric where the separate threads were often indistinguishable. On the other hand, as the nation grew more pluralistic, and as the need for a common educational experience arose, it became clear that no religious viewpoint could be allowed to dominate the schools. The separation of church and state therefore developed into a legal and philosophical tenet which survives intact to this day. Thus, the nation founded on an educational interweaving of religion and schooling has obligated itself to separate the two in the reality of educational practice. That is not an easy thing for a people to do, especially when, from a psychological point of view, the society (or at least many within it) wishes to use education as a way of passing on moral, ethical, and religious dogma to the children of succeeding generations.

The conflicts arising from this American dilemma have been ongoing ones exacerbated from time to time by a new special interest group, a court ruling, a changing pattern of immigration, or the ascendancy of a particular political movement. At the time of this writing, it is the latter which seems especially to be true. The election of President Reagan in 1980 brought to the fore a conservatism which was accompanied by a powerful, significant religious fundamentalism. Indeed, the Reagan Administration sought out religious fundamentalist support and advanced it governmentally. One highly visible example was Reagan's appointment of the Reverend Robert Billings to the Department of Education. Billings, formerly the Executive Director of the Moral Majority and a lobbyist for the National Christian Action Coalition, has been counted on to promote a particular conservative, fundamentalist view within the government. Among other positions, he is on record as being strongly opposed to the creation of the very Department of Education in which he has served. He has also opposed sex education, the teaching of evolution, and texts which, as he says, "belittle the traditional role of women." He has lobbied against passage of the ERA (Equal Rights Amendment) and the Domestic Violence Bill which sought to provide shelters for battered wives and children on the grounds that such pieces of legislation are "boondoggles for special interest, extreme feminist-oriented groups to use to get the taxpayer to finance their ideology." On the other hand, he supports prayer in the schools, tuition tax credits, and the repeal of Title IX.[98]

The insistence upon an educational agenda which includes prayer in schools, tuition tax credits, and the construction of curricula that enhance specific religious views has served to polarize Americans around their schools by increasing, as Patricia Lines puts it, "the tension between cultural pluralism and the desire to establish a common cultural base."[99] What we shall do in the pages below is examine that tension and discuss some things which might help to reduce it. In doing so, we will touch upon issues such as school prayer and tuition tax credit, but concentrate mainly on the area of curriculum because it is there that the issue seems to have crystalized most clearly.

Some recent statistics on private school pupils. Perhaps it might be best to begin by getting an idea of the nature of America's non-public school population. Mary Williams notes that statistics on private school students are difficult to come by, often scanty, and frequently contradictory. With these caveats, she uses the federal government's figures from the Center for Statistics to give us the following information:

- In 1983-84 there were 5.7 million American students in private schools (about 12.6% of the total school population). This number represented an increase in non-public school pupils since 1979.

- In 1979, 1982, and 1985, about 86% of all private school students in grades 1-12 were enrolled in church-related schools. In 1965 87% of these had been Catholic schools, but Catholic school enrollments have been declining sharply: 64% in 1980 and only 56% in 1983. Concurrently, there has been a sharp increase in student enrollments at Calvinist, Lutheran, and evangelical schools.

- Historically, private schools were centered more in cities than suburban or rural areas, but since 1979 that trend has been reversing. It was also generally true that private schools educated more students in the north and northcentral part of the country. During the 1970's, however, and through the 1980's the rates in the north decreased while those in the west and south increased.

- 63% of private school students come from middle-income families whose annual earnings range from $15,000 to $49,000 a year. 23% of private school students come from upper-income families (families with more than $50,000 in earnings per year), with only 14% coming from low-income homes. In this regard it is important to note that income is much higher in *non-church-related* private school families. The educational level of parents of *non-church-related* private school pupils is also higher.

- In terms of race and ethnicity, blacks are least likely to attend private schools, Hispanics somewhat more likely. Whites form the great majority of private school students, though enrollments among both Hispanics and Asians in Catholic schools have been increasing since around 1981.

- 1985 tuition data placed median levels at $774 per year for elementary and $1,569 per year for secondary education. There is a great difference, however, between church-related and non-church-related schools. In church-related institutions, elementary tuition is an average of $692, secondary tuition an average of $1,508. In non-church-related schools, the figures are $2,282 (elementary) and $3,571 (secondary.)[100]

The figures above square, for the most part, with other sources. The NSBA's 1986 statistics claimed about 5 million non-public school students of which 64% were Catholic, 21% non-Catholic, and 15% non-religious. This enrollment represents 11% of the national K-12 population.[101] Fleming and Hunt write that parochial education has until recently been predominantly Catholic. In 1965 they list Catholic school students as 87% of a non-public school enrollment of 5.6 million. By 1982, that percentage had dropped to 64% (representing about 3 million pupils). This decline, they go on, was accompanied by a growth in schools provided by other denominations, particularly fundamentalist and evangelical sects. By 1982 there were between 9,000 and 11,000 such schools servicing about 1 million students, an increase of 627%.[102] Finally, Blaunstein agrees that while the non-public school enrollment in 1986 represented about 12.6% of total K-12 population, there is a large number of home-taught students unaccounted for in the statistics. Just how many is anyone's guess, but the figure is sure to be in the tens of thousands.[103]

It thus seems, no matter what statistical figures one chooses, that there are at least 5 million church-related private school pupils currently attending classes, that the vast majority of them are middle-class whites, and that an ever-increasing percentage of them represents fundamentalist, evangelical sects. These new parochial school demographics have begun to exert a powerful effect on the curricula of both private and public schools. Let us consider a few examples.

Some recent cases in the area of religion.

(a) **Louisiana's Balanced Treatment Act.** In June of 1980, Louisiana State Senator Bill Keith introduced legislation requiring that the theory of creationism be taught at any school in which the theory of evolution was being taught. The bill defined creationist theory as "the belief that the origin of the elements, the galaxy, the solar system, of life, of all the species of plants and animals, the origin of man, and origin of all things and their processes and relationships were created ex nihilo [from nothing] and fixed by God."[104]

After several hearings, the Louisiana legislature passed Keith's bill, entitling it the "Balanced Treatment Act of 1982." Parents, teachers, and school boards quickly brought suit against the State of Louisiana on the grounds that the law was a violation of the establishment clause of the First Amendment. The suit was upheld by the U.S. District Court for Eastern Louisiana, and when the State appealed, the suit was again upheld by the U.S. Fifth Circuit Court. The State of Louisiana appealed again, this time to the U.S. Supreme Court which rendered its decision on June 19, 1987.

By a 7-2 vote, the Court upheld the suit, thus striking down the Louisiana law. The majority opinion was written by Justice Brennan who applied a "three-pronged test" to the case. If allowed to stand, Brennan argued, the law (1) must have a non-religious purpose, (2) must as its primary effect neither advance nor inhibit a religion, and (3) must not result in excessive entanglements between government and religion. Applying these tests to the Balanced Treatment Act, Brennan held that the act exhibited "a discriminatory preference for the teaching of creation science against the teaching of evolution." He went on to explain that "the pre-eminent purpose of the Louisiana legislature was clearly to advance the point that a supernatural being created humankind..."[105]

Judges Scalia and Rehnquist strongly dissented, Scalia writing the minority opinion. Among his other points, Scalia stated that there was afoot in the land an intellectual predisposition since the Scopes trial creating "an instinctive reaction that any governmentally-imposed requirement bearing upon the teaching of evolution must be a manifestation of Christian fundamentalist repression."[106]

(b) Mozert vs. Hawkins County. Robert B. Mozert, Jr. was the Director of Citizens Organized for Better Schools, a group of parents in Hawkins County, Tennessee greatly concerned about the education their children were receiving. In a letter to the *Kingsport Times News* published on October 18, 1983, Mozert voiced his group's opposition to the use of the Holt, Rinehart, and Winston reading series by the Hawkins County schools. He wrote that the series propagandized the religion of "secular humanism," a religion he claimed as being fathered by John Dewey and holding as its two basic tenets the fostering of the Equal Rights Amendment and a desire to change "cultural ethics and values."[107] As evidence of his position, Mozert cited several passages in the series which he and his group found objectionable. In a first grade reader, Mozert objected to a picture showing a girl reading while a boy was cooking, commenting that "the religion of John Dewey is planted in the first grader's [sic] mind that there are no God-given roles for the different sexes." Objections were also found to the children's stories, "The Three Little Pigs" and "Goldilocks," on the grounds that in the former, punishment is meted out in the absence of a crime, while in the latter, "secular humanism" is advanced because Goldilocks does not pay for her "crimes" of trespassing and stealing.[108] There were many other objections cited as well, including passages from a Margaret Mead essay that "language makes us human," a dialogue exchange in *The Diary of Anne Frank* in which Anne entreats Peter to believe in "some kind" of religion, and a story involving a boy whose grandmother did not like guns.

Mozert took Hawkins County to court over the issue, claiming that the schools had no right to compel children to read material to which their parents had objections on religious and philosophical grounds. In a 1984 decision, Tennessee Judge Thomas Hull found in favor of the schools, stating that although the reading series exposed children to a wide diversity of thought, it did not compel the children to adopt any belief, nor did it hold that any one belief was better than another. Mozert returned to court in 1986 claiming again that his children's religious rights were being violated. He did not argue that the series be banned, only that his children be given the option to read alternative material acceptable to the parents, and that students not be punished for refusing to read the Holt, Rinehart series.

The 1986 appeal was also heard by Judge Hull who, in something of a surprise decision, reversed his former opinion. In the second hearing, Hull argued that the Mozert children were being "burdened" in the exercise of their religion, particularly since their refusal to read the Holt series had led to suspension from school. "This adverse treatment," he wrote "[constituted] a coercion of...students against their will and the will of their parents." Hull declared that the parental objections were on "bona fide religious grounds" and ordered that alternative material and, if necessary, an alternative reading environment be supplied to students whose parents objected to the original texts.[109]

The 1986 reversal was in large measure based on the testimony of Vicki Frost, a student who had read all the books in the Holt series. Frost testified that many of the stories she was forced to read were attempts to impregnate her mind with non-fundamentalist biases, particularly the ideas of "rebellion, secular humanism, and the notion that animals are equal to humans."[110] As an example, Frost cited for Judge Hull the story, "Freddy Found a Frog," from the second-grade reader. Freddy, finding a frog, asks neighbor Mays what he would do with it. Mays replies he would use it for bait. Freddy then asks Miss Denny, and she tells him that she would cook it. Finally, Freddy asks his mother who says that she would return it to the pond from which it came. This Freddy does and decides that the frog is beautiful there. According to Frost's testimony, this story "could seduce a child into a belief in disarmament," because "if you think it's wrong to kill an animal for food, then the inference could be made that it is wrong to kill a person in war."[111]

Confronted by Frost's testimony, Hull concluded that, taken as a whole, the Holt series might lead a child to "adopt the views of a feminist, a humanist, a pacifist, an anti-Christian, a vegetarian, or an advocate of a 'one-world government'."[112] Quite predictably, there have been many cries of protest against the 1986 reversal from the NEA and various women's groups, and it is probably safe to assume that we haven't heard the last of this case. There has also been a good deal of comment on Mozert vs. Hawkins County from some of our best education scholars, and it behooves us to view their thoughts briefly.

Edward Jenkinson, Professor of Education at the University of Indiana, writes that Hull's decision was colored by the fact that Mozert and his group had a "tendency to read everything literally" which led them "to conclusions that other people would probably not reach." Jenkinson writes:

> It is unfortunate that no literary scholar was asked to testify about the plaintiff's interpretations of the themes in the reading series...Must reading material be so narrow that it will never offend some group's sincerely held religious beliefs? Does the First Amendment guarantee the right *not* to be offended by someone else's ideas?[113]

David Remes, a lawyer specializing in First Amendment cases, speaks to these questions in the December 3, 1986 issue of *Education Week*. Drawing on Supreme Court Justice William Brennan's observation that education in our free, pluralistic society should encompass "a heritage common to all American groups and religions," Remes writes:

> That heritage is one that includes *The Diary of Anne Frank* and *Huckleberry Finn*. It is a heritage of tolerance and diversity...Public education is not and cannot be an education that instructs children in the orthodoxies of their

> parents...Nor does the fact that public school curriculum may force some fundamentalist Christian parents to pay for a private-school education mean that their rights of religious freedom have been burdened. The Supreme Court has held repeatedly that the government does not burden the exercise of a protected right by refusing to subsidize it; and the fact that some parents may not be able to send their children to private schools is immaterial. An individual's inability to pay for what he wants does not turn the government's refusal to make it available to him for nothing into a 'burden' in the constitutional sense of the term.[114]

Even Secretary of Education William Bennett, a Reagan appointee, called Judge Hull's reversal a "mistake." He says:

> If you don't like what is going on in class,...you have the right to pull your children out...The effort to achieve a consensus in what should be taught, particularly in the area of values, should not be undercut by allowing people to opt out of discussions of these things if they have disagreements with this or that.[115]

Charles Glenn, Director of Equal Opportunity for the Massachusetts Department of Education, sees the Hull reversal as "the first trickle in what might become a flood of litigation on the content of school curriculum." But he is also somewhat sympathetic to Mozert. Noting that as public school enrollment declined 17% in the 1970's while private school enrollment rose 6%, Glenn laments that it would be unfair to the Mozerts of this nation if things go "so far that...there are no depictions of [fundamental Christian values]." "Surely," he writes, "that would be a distortion of another kind—and one deeply offensive to...conservative Christians."[116] Somewhat supportive of Glenn's argument, Paul Vitz, Professor of Psychology at New York University, states that American textbooks have systematically avoided any discussions of religion at all. Vitz bases his views on a study he conducted under the aegis of the National Institute of Education. His NIE grant allowed him to examine ten social studies, six basal reading, and ten United States history texts in wide use today. The conclusion was that religion in general was not dealt with meaningfully as a topic and that Protestantism particularly was avoided.[117]

The complexities of the Balanced Treatment Act and Mozert vs. Hawkins County will be subjects for further comment below. For now, let us consider a few more examples of the influence of religion in America's schools today. We move next to Arkansas and California.

(c) **Arkansas Act 590.** This case involved Arkansas State Attorney General Steven Clark who argued before Federal District Judge William Overton that Arkansas Act 590 is constitutional and should be allowed to stand. The act, very much like Louisiana's Balanced Treatment Act, required creationism to be taught wherever evolution is taught. Clark's case was that creationism is a science and that "the concept of a creator is not necessarily inherently religious." Judge Overton, however, disagreed, declaring Act 590 unconstitutional. "No group, large or small," he wrote, "may use the organs of government, of which the public schools are the most conspicuous and influential, to force its religious beliefs on others."[118]

(d) Seagraves vs. California. In March of 1981 California Justice Irving H. Perluss rendered an interesting decision in the case of Seagraves vs. the California State Board of Education. In this case the plaintiff alleged that the teaching of evolution was a violation of the religious rights of certain pupils and their parents. Perluss disagreed stating that the exposition of Darwin's theories does not in and of itself inhibit the religious freedom of those who believe in Genesis. However, the judge went on to state that care should be taken by schools to present Darwin's ideas as theory, not as fact. "Darwinism must be changed to a conditional statement," wrote Perluss. "Science must emphasize the 'how' and not the 'ultimate cause' for the origins of man." Such a position, he went on, would be possible if teachers were to use phrases like "most scientists believe that..."[119] or "scientists hypothesize that..." instead of phrases like "the facts prove conclusively that..." We shall return to this ruling below. For now we consider our last example, the phenomenon of Accelerated Christian Education Schools.

(e) ACE School Programs. In 1970 Dr. and Mrs. Donald R. Howard developed a series of curriculum packets for their private Christian school in Texas. Since then, their "Accelerated Christian Education" (ACE) program has been adopted in over 5,000 parochial schools with the result that it now exerts a considerable influence on modern education.

The ACE program is a K-12 self-instructional regimen in which students work at their own pace and are tested at the end of each unit. Learning packets in math, English, science, social studies, languages, art, business, physical education, and the Bible are highly structured and individualized to the level of the student. In addition to basic information, the packets also contain pointed religious indoctrination because, in their own words, ACE proponents seek to give their children a "thoroughly Christian" education from which a child can "learn truth from God's point of view" in a program "that supports the word of God."[120]

To cite an example of the ACE curriculum, a seventh grade social studies unit states the following: "When you successfully complete this [unit], you should be able to recite the Ten Commandments and to recognize the facts related to the Biblical basis of government."[121] It goes on to state that the Ten Commandments are "crucial to the effective operation of any government and particularly a free government." Other units are somewhat more controversial. An eighth grade unit states that Communist "anti-Christs" are working in our government today. A unit in grade nine describes Jomo Kenyatta as engaging in bestial acts of torture and murder as part of Mau-Mau ritual. A tenth grade unit contains the following quote:

> The United Nations was created by Communists and has always been used by Communists to further Communist goals. Even most of the United States delegates to the San Francisco Convention to found the U.N. were later discovered to be members of the Communist party.[122]

As one might imagine, such statements have drawn some sharp fire from parents and educators alike who take issue with ACE points of view. In defense of his program and its materials, Ronald Johnson, Vice-President of ACE, Inc., Lewisville, Texas, cites the high test scores of ACE pupils. 7,428 students from 40 states scored between two and four grade levels higher on the California Achievement Tests than their public school counterparts, Johnson points out. In addition, he states that many ACE ninth graders achieve well above twelfth grade levels on national standardized tests, and that hundreds of ACE students have already been accepted at major colleges and universities. With regard to ACE religious philosophy, Johnson states that it is separate from "the humanistic-pluralistic curricula most often used in secular schools." In the ACE philosophy:

> Communism and socialism are seen as antithetical to theism, and the two cannot co-exist peacefully...The autonomy of governments, national identification, and the loyalty of citizens are seen as rights and responsibilities of all men...We do not believe that...the final interpretation of facts and events should be left up to immature, inexperienced minds, as mainline secular curricula do.[123]

Suggestions and comments. Having looked at some recent events in the area of religion and our schools, the questions concerning them fairly leap out of the page. What is appropriate to teach? What should be the extent of church/state separation? What do we do about curriculum, school prayer, and tuition tax credits? How do we deal with parents like Mr. Mozert? To what extent can we or should we accommodate his requests? It is to these and other issues we now turn, and we shall consider them in the following order:

a) Who speaks for God?
b) Church/state separation
c) Creationism and curriculum
d) School prayer
e) Tuition tax credit

(a) Who speaks for God? Setting aside the church/state issue for a moment, there is another element of our present condition which is greatly troubling. It is the presumption that any mortal can accurately assess "the word of God." When the ACE program states that its children will learn "truth from God's point of view" or when a Mozert declares that a book does not depict "God-given roles for the different sexes," they are skating on very thin epistemological ice. And, by the way, so is the scientist who makes the same claim of "truth" when unfolding theories concerning the "natural law" of the universe. My trouble with statements like these stems from the fact that I am a good deal more humble in the face of the grandeur of the universe than many of my fellow men in either the "religious" or "scientific" camp.

You see, I adopt the view—and I believe most of us do—that as a human being, I am by definition not a god. Gods, as we define them (or God as monotheistic religions define God) are omniscient, omnitemporal, omnipresent, omnipotent. I am none of those—at least not according to the best available evidence of the moment. I do not know everything that ever was. I do not even know everything that is. But most of all, I do not know everything that *will be*, and that is very important because it forces me to accept my knowledge as a *temporary* thing which, while it may be supported by evidence today, may also be subject to change in the light of new evidence tomorrow.

For mortals like me, it is a tremendous presumption, then, to claim a knowledge of "truth" or "the view of God," and I question both the reasoning and the motivation of those who do. How can they? How do they "know" the eternal mechanisms of the universe, and even if they stumbled upon one, how could they—not being able to survive to prove it—"know" it was eternal?

At times such presumers point to the Bible as their evidence. At times they point to the test tube. I trust neither as a final or eternal source of proof. The Bible is a book set down by men. It is published by men and subject to the interpretations of men. It is, in many instances, used by men for profit, and it exists in dozens of different wordings. The test tube operates according to the theories of the moment, theories which have changed in a historical parade of human experimentation thousands of years old. When I studied high school biology in 1959, the word "DNA" did not even appear in my textbook. Today it is the sine qua non of the subject. Science is always modifying itself. Heliocentrism replaces the medieval view of the solar system. Einstein's notion of gravity supplants Newton.

Let me give you an example from the ACE curriculum itself. The seventh grade social studies syllabus deals with the establishment of government in relation to the Ten Commandments. The Commandments are seen as "crucial" to the effective operation of government. As it happens, several years ago I was preparing a musical setting of the Ten Commandments for publication. I wanted to be sure what the words really meant, so I went to an Orthodox Jewish scholar well-known in the area for his study of the Old Testament and Talmud. He graciously gave me several weeks of his time, weeks in which I learned that the ancient languages of the Bible are often at odds with modern linguistic interpretations. I was particularly struck by the wording of the commandment, "Honor thy father and mother." When I asked the scholar rather foolishly if that was such a good commandment in an age like ours where parents are often guilty of child abuse or of giving drugs and alcohol to minors, he laughed and said, "But you don't understand the words." Then he explained. "The word 'honor' does not translate as 'obey.' It means 'to bring credit to.' The commandment doesn't mean 'obey your parents' but rather 'act in such a way that you bring credit to your house'."

I wondered then, and wonder now, how much misinterpretation surrounds anyone's knowing "the truth from God's point of view." How far might we stray from that truth with the literal interpretations of Vicki Frost? After all, the Bible is a work of literature, a work in which allegory, metaphor, and symbolism are appropriate literary techniques. If we interpret everything in the Bible literally we might find an objection to anything. The Last Supper might be symbolic of cannibalism; the Crucifixion, an invitation to kill dissenters.

The effect of my view of the epistemology of knowledge on my view of education is immediate and dynamic. Not "knowing," I feel an obligation to present all kinds of information impartially. Not having a "lock on the truth," I feel it my duty to encourage each student to come to grips with opposing viewpoints in his or her heart and mind. I say all this now because it greatly colors what I will say below about religion and later on about curriculum in general.

(b) The separation of church and state. It is a matter of law that in the U.S. there shall be no abridging of the right to establish private parochial education. It is also a matter of law that no public school can promote a belief in any given religion or require a child to accept such a belief as a part of school curriculum. On the face of it, these tenets would seem to make the separation of church and state a clearcut issue. In reality, however, it is not—nor do I think it should be—so black and white. There is an interlocking of the secular and sacred worlds both in terms of administration and curriculum. We will consider the latter below. Let us, for the moment, address the former.

The state allows for the establishment of private, parochial education, but it also mandates much of that private school activity. The question is, should it? And if it should, is the state then not obligated to support the private school to some financial degree? I answer "yes" to both questions, and there are compelling reasons for that answer.

The survival of our democracy depends (perhaps more than anything else) on the education of our citizenry. While the various states are constitutionally autonomous in determining the content of that education, there is a substantial agreement among them as to the basic courses and skills to be taught. All states mandate fundamental reading, writing, and mathematical achievement; all have the familiar math-science-English-social studies academic core; all include experiences in physical education, art, music, foreign language, business and occupational skills. When the state steps aside to allow private, parochial training, it does not divest itself of the responsibility for the non-religious part of a parochial school student's education. Indeed, since the parochial school student will take an equal place in society with students educated in public schools, the state cannot abandon its mission of non-religious education for parochial school students. States thus quite properly require parochial schools to contain services and curricula fundamental to all citizens regardless of religious or philosophical creed. That position is defensible on its own grounds, but when one considers that 12.6% of American children are not attending regular public school, the position becomes demographically necessary.

The extent of state mandates for private schools is more than most of us may realize. It goes well beyond the bounds of mere curriculum. Health and safety standards, transportation regulations, procedures for reporting grades and other data, instructional time, testing, providing services for handicapped students, providing vocational educational services, and providing special opportunities for gifted and talented pupils have all been mandated by one state or another. In addition, states and private schools have interlocked on many occasions in the areas of textbook selection, teacher licensing and certification, and zoning. The worlds are not as separate as one might think.

Given the extent to which the state mandates private school operations, it becomes appropriate to ask if the state should then contribute to the funding needed to comply with the mandates. To say "no" would be to impose such a burden on private school education that it would virtually make such education financially impossible for millions of children, and that would be a violation of the intent of the Constitution. It would be as if a parent were to say to a child, "Yes, you may go to the circus, but I will set the price of a ticket at $50,000, and you must mow all the lawns in town to earn it." In view of the consequences of saying "no" to public aid for private schools, saying "yes" seems the only reasonable course.

It is interesting to see how various states and various religions react to the educational interlocking of the two. The federal government, for example, provides funds for federally mandated programs in non-public schools through the Surplus Property Act, the Education Consolidation and Improvement Act, and the Education for All Handicapped Children Act. Some private schools welcome such aid. Others (including Seventh Day Adventists, Amish, and many evangelical Christian schools) "reject virtually all state aid in order to avoid state regulation."[124]

Just how states distribute aid to private schools varies from one state to another. Florida, for example, with 12% of its students in private schools provides no services to those schools and, aside from compulsory attendance, has no state laws regulating them. It does, however, have an educational agency which works as a liaison between the public and private school sectors in dealing with educational standards and services. Louisiana, with 17% of its pupils in private schools, has a state-supported, nine-member commission representing various sects whose job it is to coordinate private school standards with public school mandates. Similar commissions exist in Illinois, Michigan, New Hampshire, Oregon, Washington, and New York, among others.

In Ohio a state minimum standard law for private education was challenged in the 1976 State vs. Wisner case on the grounds that it burdened the free exercise of religion by leaving too little time for religious education. The Ohio Supreme Court ruled in favor of Wisner and, in 1979, the Ohio State Board of Education created a 34-member advisory committee to recommend new standards which insured the religious rights of private institutions. By 1983 a new set of standards went into effect.

Perhaps the greatest interlocking of public and private school education occurs in New York which has 17.3% of its children enrolled in non-public schools. The New York State Education Department has established an Office of Non-Public School Services which, since 1979, has acted as a coordinator between public and private sectors. In addition there is a Commissioner's Advisory Council for Non-Public Schools to administer those state policies and guidelines which affect private education. New York asserts the legal right of parents to choose alternatives to public education, but by law assists such alternative schools in the areas of health, welfare, textbooks, transportation, occupational education, education of the gifted, and education of the handicapped.[125]

(c) Creationism and curriculum. I have adopted the view that "truth," in the eternal sense of the word, is unknowable to me. I also adopt the view that as a teacher I do not have the right to foist my own beliefs on my students. Rather, I feel it my obligation to present, in as impartial a manner as I can, all the information they may need to live happy, useful, constructive lives—and to do that consistent with the subjects I teach and the educational mandates of the state in which I teach. If I can do these things and try to provide the intellectual training necessary for my students to come to their own conclusions about the data they are given, I feel I will have done the most an educator can or should be asked to do. That is an educational creed quite different from creeds which seek to indoctrinate students in one or another set of values or to bring them up according to "the views of God" or anyone else.

Oddly enough, however, my educational credo is very much offended by schools which do *not* allow the teaching of religiously controversial subjects like creationism. I feel that as a widely-held view, one with which students will *have* to deal when they become full voting members of the society, it is *incumbent* upon us to teach it. Beyond that, creationism in and of itself is a fascinating counter-argument to evolution, one well worth the intellectual time of any student regardless of his or her views or the views of his or her parents. Whether or not creationism should be discussed in a biology class is another matter. I would think a class dealing with comparative religious philosophy would be more appropriate. I am certainly, however, against any statute (such as that in Louisiana's "Balanced Treatment Act") which requires the hiring of "creationist scientists" to teach creationism. It must remain an inviolate principle that a belief in a subject not be a requirement for teaching it, and that any properly licensed teacher who has been familiarized with a given curriculum in his or her area of certification be accorded the right to teach that curriculum.

Behind my position on creationism is a broader, more important idea, the idea that explaining something is not synonymous with accepting it as an article of one's faith. Even more, I believe that withholding knowledge (in the educational sense of the word) is counter-productive to the well-being of the student and ultimately of the nation. To cite a controversial example from the social studies curriculum, one should teach American children the principles of Communism not to turn them into Communists, but to give them information vital to the world with which they must deal. I believe the withholding of such topics as creationism or Communism or sex education occurs when the educators and/or parents are themselves afraid of their own convictions (or lack of them). The irony of such fear is that, given a knowledge of Communism, American pupils might just come to appreciate democracy all the more. Given the views of both evolution and creationism a student may just come to appreciate that neither is an eternal truth, or, even more, that both may be expressions of a more unified theory—that evolution is the tool of a creative power which is seen by Darwin in the manifestations of a laboratory and by evangelical Christians in the poetry of the Bible.

(d) School prayer. It is not the existence of prayer in schools which bothers me. It is, rather, the imposition of it—either the wording of it or the time at which it occurs—that is offensive. For anyone predisposed to prayer, as long as the act of prayer does not interrupt the flow of the school's activities or inhibit the rights of others, it should be allowed. Indeed, how can it be stopped? A youngster walks into a final exam. The exam lies face down on the youngster's desk. "Please, God," the child says, "let me pass this test." It is a moment in the mind and heart of the child which causes no ill to others and into which no one else has the right to intrude. A basketball player is fouled and steps up to the foul line, pressure mounting, the game at stake. The child makes the sign of the cross before shooting the ball. Again, it is an act causing no adversity to others. It is a private prayer only for the moment on public display. Such prayers should not be stopped and probably could not be stopped even if one had a mind to. But who would be of such mind, and what would such a course of action hope to accomplish?

It is another matter, however, to mandate a time for prayer or to put the words of a prayer into the mouth of a student. For a private, parochial school, such requirements are the very purpose of the school. For a public school they are a violation of civil liberties which no governmental agency has a right to impose. In Justice Brennan's words, they have a clear religious purpose and result in an absolutely unnecessary entanglement between religion and government. I say unnecessary because any student who wishes to pray may start the day off at home with prayer, pray silently at any of dozens of times during the school day, or end the day with evening prayers. Praying at a school-appointed time or with state-chosen words neither enhances the process nor makes it more sanctified. It simply imposes it upon the school population, and I do not believe schools should have that right.

(e) Tuition tax credits. When David Remes points out that an individual's inability to pay for what he wants does not turn the government's refusal to make it available to him for nothing into a Constitutional violation, he speaks to the heart of the tax credit issue. By allowing private school parents to deduct the cost of non-public education from their taxable income, the government would, in effect, be asking the rest of the taxpayers to subsidize the private school system since the tax revenues lost as a result of such deductions would perforce be made up by increases in the taxes of others. That is clearly a violation of the church/state separation philosophy. Nor is it fair to relieve private school parents of any public school taxes, for every citizen must be accountable for a fair share of the public well-being. It is, after all, a well-being of the common good. Consider the analogy of taxes which go into the upkeep of roads or a public library. One may choose not to use the roads or visit the library, but by dint of the decision to remain in a society which supplies them to the public at large, one cannot absolve oneself of the obligation to contribute to their upkeep.

The decision to use private schooling is a decision which must be accompanied by the burden of paying for the schooling (with whatever state support is available for state-mandated programs). The same case can and should be made for higher education, either public or private. As long as the state does not mandate attendance at a college or university, the state should not allow individuals to deduct tuition costs for the personal, private decision to attend.

Having said all this, however, we must also recognize the practical necessity of higher education in today's world, and we must make it financially feasible for anyone who wishes it to obtain a college degree. To do this without tax credits, we would have to make federal, state, and private loans sufficiently available at low interest rates. Such steps are especially needed for low-income, disadvantaged students—and that brings us to the issue of educational equal opportunity and social engineering, our next topic.

Educational social engineering

The gap between what we preach and what we practice in the area of church/state separation is not the only one which haunts the American conscience. There is also a considerable gap between the principles of civil equality articulated by our laws and the reality of our treatment of women and minorities. We have touched briefly upon this phenomenon in our surveys of educational governance and the development of educational unions. It is now time to come to grips with the topic in greater detail. As we do, we shall consider the doctrine of educational equity in general and then see how that doctrine has manifested itself in recent examples of "social engineering." Finally, we will comment on some of these recent cases and offer a few suggestions for the future.

General considerations of equity in education. All men are not created equal. In two very fundamental ways there are vast differences between people. The first is ability, the second, socioeconomic inheritance. Not everyone can run a four-minute mile, write a symphony, learn to perform brain surgery, fix an automobile, or type a hundred words a minute. Not everyone is born into a comfortable home, has parents who can pay for college, or starts life off with a $50,000 bank account. We are smart and slow, rich and poor, creative and uncreative, and everything in between. It was not to our talents or our backgrounds that our founding fathers referred when they said we were created equal.

What they referred to was our ethical and legal rights and to the access to opportunity which those rights guarantee. But in the history of humankind that was quite enough to begin America's glorious experiment in democracy. To the extent our educational system provides equal access and equal opportunity, it honors the philosophical commitment of our nation. To the extent it does not, it diminishes the promise of America and allows us to fall victim to stereotypes of race, or sex, or age, or creed, or physical condition.

The pressures for educational equity ebb and flow over time and territory. They burn hot at certain historical periods or in certain geographical locations and cool down at others. This is not to say that the underlying problems which produce these pressures have been successfully eliminated. They have not. Nor is it to say that for those who have felt the sting of inequity, periods of coolness are somehow more pallatable. They are not. It is to say, however, that the consciousness of the education environment is sometimes at a peak and sometimes in a valley. We tend to address the question of equity at times of peaked consciousness. At other times we allow problems of inequity to languish and fester.

It might be appropriate here to state just how history or geography or community make-up can affect educational equity, for a recognition of such influences may aid us greatly in evaluating the present situation and help in establishing meaningful criteria for dealing with our educational future. Taking the matter of history first, we have already seen how the Plessy vs. Ferguson decision of 1896 galvanized Southerners who wanted "separate but equal" educational facilities for whites and blacks in Louisiana. Similarly, we have already seen how World War I created an impetus for racial equality in the workplaces and unions of the industrialized North. These events were early peaks in the equity consciousness of the twentieth century. They were followed by a valley of almost thirty-five years, a valley in which the Depression and the Second World War dominated both national and global attention. It was not until the Brown vs. Board of Education decision of 1954 that the issue of educational equity again gained prominence, and the case can be made that from that time to the present America has experienced a continuous surge of concern for human and minority rights.

When in 1954 the Supreme Court declared that "in the field of public education the doctrine of 'separate but equal' has no place" and that separate educational facilities are "inherently unequal," it ushered in the age of school desegregation.[126] There followed, in 1955, a court directive for districts to desegregate "with all deliberate speed." Those who applauded the court's position focused on the word "speed." Those who opposed it focused on the word "deliberate," thus giving rise to a civil rights movement led by Dr. Martin Luther King, Jr. which grew ever more impatient with the reluctance of schools in the North as well as the South to comply with the meaning of Brown vs. Board of Education. The reality of the issue clearly showed King's position to be correct. By 1964, fully a decade after *Brown*, only 1.2% of black children in the South attended desegregated schools.[127] Moreover, the cries against forced busing to achieve school racial balances were being heard not just in the South but all over the nation, and not only among anti-integration parents but also among parents who, as Woodring states, "believe deeply in racial equality and recognize the need for desegregation [but] are not willing to let their children carry the full burden."[128]

Congress, realizing the necessity to put some teeth into the 1954 Supreme Court decision, thus decided to pass the Civil Rights Act of 1964. Title IV of the act authorized the U.S. Commissioner of Education to "help" districts desegregate and further authorized the withholding of federal funds from districts which did not comply in a satisfactory manner. It was this last provision which finally began to drive the point home, and in subsequent years, the federal government would return again and again to the withholding of educational dollars as a means of assuring compliance with policies of social engineering.

The Civil Rights Act of 1964 was soon followed by others whose intent was educational equity. In 1972 Title IX of the Educational Amendments Bill was passed prohibiting sex discrimination in all educational jurisdictions receiving federal aid. The results were efforts to encourage women to participate in areas previously denied them, areas such as athletics and educational administration, and to counsel young women in career options and social roles vastly different and more extensive than their mothers and grandmothers had experienced. Then, in the 1974 Lau vs. Nichols case, the Supreme Court ruled that "failure to offer instruction in the native language of children who are not fluent in English, denies them the opportunity to participate meaningfully in the educational process, a violation of the Civil Rights Act of 1964."[129] The result was a rash of bilingual education programs and the printing and administering of state tests in languages other than English. The thrust of these programs was clearly toward the disadvantaged student population who had been earmarked by Title I funds in the 1964 Civil Rights Act for special educational treatment. Again, the government's philosophy was to overcome inequities of socio-economic inheritance and thus achieve equal access to opportunity in the immigrant and disadvantaged community.

Minorities, women, and non-English-speaking students now fell under the umbrella of educational social engineering. One group yet remained unprotected, the handicapped. The needs of this constituency were addressed in 1975 by Public Law 94-142, the Education for All Handicapped Children Act. The purpose of the law was not only to provide equal educational opportunities for students with handicapping conditions, but to do so in "the least restrictive environment" possible. The results were first and foremost a broadening of the definition of "handicapped" to include not just the obvious impairments of limb or sight, but also impairments of speech, hearing, reading, and emotional/psychological condition. Following this enlarged definition came a slew of programs. Special Education Committee reviews, Committee on the Handicapped reviews, mainstreaming projects, individualized instructional plans, barrier-free facilities all became regular parts of the public school environment. In sum, the 1954 Brown vs. Board of Education decision had, by 1975, launched an unprecedented era of educational equity consciousness the legal, social, and financial repercussions of which still affect America's schools, as we shall see later.

Historical ebb and flow are but one of the ways in which equity consciousness expresses itself. Another, perhaps equally powerful, is geography. Woodring notes, for example, that while desegregation programs occur with "painful strife" in much of the South, where there is only one school, as is the case in many northern and western rural areas, integration has occurred "usually without much protest from anyone."[130] He goes on to point out, however, that in cities with complex populations, complex demographic patterns, and complex boundaries, the problems become more severe regardless of considerations of North or South, East or West. Woodring writes:

> Desegregation of schools while housing patterns remain segregated—either by tradition or by economic levels—requires that children be assigned to schools distant from their homes...The major metropolitan areas have additional problems accentuated in recent years by the massive movement of middle-class families out of the inner cities and their replacement by poorer people, many of them black or Hispanic.[131]

The result has been that most efforts at metropolitan desegregation have failed. Thirty years after *Brown*, with whites either fleeing to white-dominated suburbs or placing their children in white-dominated private schools, many urban systems have become virtually all minority. Washington, D.C. is only 4% white, Detroit only 12%, Chicago only 19%. In fact, blacks, Hispanics, and Asians now outnumber whites in 33 of the nation's 55 largest city systems, and this is a nation where whites are 84% of the total population.[132] Establishing racial balances in these circumstances is a difficult if not impossible task, if for no other reason than the difficulty of simply defining the community to be integrated. As Woodring poses the question, "For a school in Manhattan, is the community Harlem, the entire borough of Manhattan, the five boroughs, or the New York metropolitan area, which includes parts of Connecticut and New Jersey?"[133]

Finally, beyond considerations of history and geography are those of community. The demographic makeup of a given school district will tend to skew equity consciousness to those groups which are either numerically prominent or sociopolitically active. When I taught in the New York City area, for example, my district calendar never had the schools open on Yom Kippur or Rosh Hashanah. The large, vocal Jewish population simply would not have permitted it. In another district in which I taught, however, some two hundred and fifty miles from New York City, while the school calendar acknowledged Jewish holidays in print, schools were nonetheless open. Where there are large black populations, Martin Luther King, Jr. Day is solemnly observed. In other areas it gets less play. Various places in the South honor the birthdays of Robert E. Lee and Jefferson Davis. Not many Northern locations do the same. But it is not only in the school calendar that local community considerations reveal an awareness of equity. It is also in the area of curricular policy. Bilingual programs are essential in Los Angeles, New York, and Miami with their heavy concentration of Hispanics. In Ames, Iowa or Havre, Montana, they may receive less attention. In towns like Brentwood or Roosevelt on Long Island, where black populations are high, the pressures to concentrate on black history may be considerably more intense than they are in communities just down the road such as Jericho or Northport where blacks represent a very low percentage of the school enrollments.

All of which brings us to the last topic of our general consideration of equity, the topic of stereotyping. We see the patterns of educational or sociological behavior in a district or region, and we begin to make generalizations about the people involved. The generalizations fuel our fears and prejudices, and soon we begin to think of people in stereotypical terms. If you are black, you must be this; white, that; Hispanic, something else. It is important to discuss this issue honestly because the way in which we interact in school—the courses we teach, groupings we encourage, court cases we decide—often incorporates our stereotypical concepts.

I think modern research has laid to rest the theory that any group of people is innately anything (the key word being "innately"). Jews are not by nature greedy any more than blacks are by nature better athletes or Hispanics by nature more emotionally volatile. I don't know how you feel about it, but I reject arguments of racial superiority or inferiority out of hand, and you might as well accept that if you intend reading further. However, I do believe there are characteristics and courses of action with which groups identify—not by birth but by choice or social pressure—and in education we must be aware of the phenomenon, cognizant of its reason for being, and sensitive (in the best meaning of that word) to the people who experience it.

Let me explain what I mean by this statement. One looks at a National Basketball Association game on television and sees a tremendously high percentage of black players, a percentage far higher than the 11% of the national black population. One looks at a National Hockey League game and sees practically no black players at all. It is an inescapable conclusion that as a group blacks gravitate to the one sport and not to the other. The key point for us to study is not that it happens but why it happens. One can dismiss it and say "blacks play basketball because they can jump, and they don't play hockey because their balance isn't good," but that is exactly the kind of unsubstantiated racist bigotry which began the processes of racism centuries ago. There may be other reasons for the phenomenon which have to do with the social and economic realities of black life in America. Blacks as a group lag much farther behind whites in economic achievement. As a result, they are forced into more urban settings, away from the more affluent suburban ones with their multi-thousand-dollar homes and private schools. Woodring in fact tells us that although blacks represent only 11% of the total population, they represent 16% of the public school population because they can't afford to send their children to private schools to the same degree that whites do.[134] Given the general economic condition of blacks and their resultant living environment, basketball is a more accessible game than hockey. It takes very little money for a city to put up a couple of backboards and hoops on a cement playground, far less than it takes to build an ice arena. From the point of view of equipment, all it takes to play basketball is one ball and a pair of sneakers. In hockey there is enough equipment to choke a horse. Even in a bare-bones game, the stick, puck, and skates can run into a big buck, and even if there is no fancy rink, one needs a lot of little ponds to freeze over, ponds which are not found in the middle of a large city. So black kids play basketball because it is what they find available. They begin to use it as a social as well as an athletic experience, and it becomes associated with them as a group. Thus, when they excel at it, they do so in large numbers because they are playing it in large numbers. The same is true for the white kid in Vermont or Minnesota or Toronto, Canada where hockey is a big sport. The weather makes the game accessible. The economics of it are sociologically viable. Ergo, pro hockey players tend to be white. Reverse the bigotry of racism, reverse the economics of the society, put those black kids in the suburbs and the white ones in the ghettos, and after a few generations go by you will see a lot of white basketball players and a lot of black hockey stars.

The point of this is to realize that what we see in education has much the same roots. When we read, as we did earlier in conjunction with the National Teacher Exam, that blacks and Hispanics do far worse than whites, it is not that they are by birth less capable, but that they are by life less fortunate. Racism has kept them in poverty, and poverty has deprived them of quality education. Why should they do better? How could they do better? Take the last four hundred years of American race relations and reverse it, put the whites in bondage to black plantation owners, drive the whites from the good jobs and good homes, and then see who scores well on the NTE.

Let me tell you a story from my own experience as a choral director. It took place in a town in New York State with a black population of about 20%. I was hired, in part, to make the high school chorus "nationally recognized," as my superintendent put it. Shortly after I came on board, another teacher said to me, "You ought to get more black kids involved, but I guess they don't appreciate music as much as whites." I thought at first he was joking. Visions of Marion Anderson, Andre Watts, Harry Belafonte, and scores of great jazz artists flashed through me as I laughed. Then he told me he was serious. "Just look at the facts," he said. "All these kids and you've only got one black singing." I decided to talk to my one black singer about it.

"Black kids don't join chorus," the student said, "because the last few music teachers they had here made it pretty clear they didn't like us."

"You mean if you find out I'm not a racist, we'll get some more black singers?"

"Pretty much," he replied.

"Okay," I answered. "You be my critic. If I can't cut it with you, drop out. If I can, help me get some good kids in here."

He agreed and was true to his word. Within a year the entire enrollment had swelled, including a pretty decent number of black kids. All it took was acting like a human being. There was nothing inherently pro- or anti-music in those kids. The fact that they had self-segregated themselves from chorus had nothing whatsoever to do with genetics. Nor was their entry into the program a manifestation of anything other than ordinary, understandable human behavior. I urge you to bear this in mind as we move deeper into the topic of educational equity.

Recent examples of social engineering. There has been such a plethora of activity in educational social engineering since the 1964 Civil Rights Act, it would be impossible for a text of this type to deal with every issue or every important case. What we shall do, therefore, is to "sample the menu" with a variety of topics to get at least a general look at what is going on. In doing so, we will concentrate on four areas of investigation:

a) Busing
b) Quotas in school and job applications
c) Curricular social engineering
d) Recent concerns of educational equity for women

(a) Busing. When the Supreme Court declared in 1954 that racially separate educational facilities were inherently unequal, it was establishing an educational rather than a sociological purpose for desegregation. Schools were to be integrated not primarily to promote a society where the races mixed for social reasons, but rather to insure that access to education was equal regardless of race. Thus when busing became a tool by which school desegregation could be achieved, the racial mixing of kids was not done primarily so that blacks and whites would date or marry or even become friends—though I dare speculate that friendship, at least, was a desired goal for many. It was primarily so that a black child might be able to use the same texts, libraries, theaters, and gymnasiums as a white child—so that the *quality* of education would be equal. That the football teams and marching bands, English classes and chemistry labs would result in blacks and whites seeing each other in less racial terms was an inevitable secondary by-product, but it was not a by-product which could then nor does now force people of different races to be friends or to care for each other in the deepest human sense.

Why do I mention this? I mention it because busing was able to achieve neither its primary educational nor its secondary sociological goal, and it failed in the former *because* it failed in the latter. The forced busing of children exacerbated the racial divisions of America for many, if not all, of its people. Forcing anybody to do anything usually creates feelings of hostility. Forcing children into situations clearly opposed by many of their parents merely poured salt onto the wounds of America's racist heritage. It angered parents opposed to busing on purely racial grounds and alienated parents who had concerns other than those of race. Again, let me quote Woodring.

> The problem cannot be solved by hurling the charge 'racist' against every parent who objects to having his children transported to a school far across town. The real motives are far more complex.

Safety factors, access to after-school extra-curricular activities, after-school discipline, and crime are just a few of the considerations aside from race which Woodring cites as part of the legitimate concerns of parents[135]

The results of busing are all too clear. First, it has sparked the "white flight" mentioned above so that in many districts—especially those in our larger cities—

racial mixing is practically impossible. Second, it has not been accompanied by significantly improved educational, social, or economical status for the minorities it intended to help. Finally, its failure has wasted millions of dollars and created multitudes of social problems. What I am saying here is not personal opinion, nor is it "white" opinion. Listen to the words of others both white and black. First, again from Paul Woodring:

> Busing has been ordered by the courts and school boards not because they think it educationally sound, but because they want to comply with the law and have been unable to think of an alternative...[The James S. Coleman report] "Trends in School Desegregation 1968-73" concluded that one effect of court-ordered busing has been to increase the white exodus from inner cities. When busing was ordered between inner cities and suburbs, white children...were sent by their parents to non-public schools. Consequently, forced busing was counter-productive in that it resulted in resegregation.[136]

Clarence Thomas, a black educator who is the head of the Equal Opportunity Commission and was a former Assistant Secretary for Civil Rights in the U.S. Department of Education, said the following in 1982:

> Twenty-eight years after *Brown*, the evidence on minority education...provides no reason to believe that busing or proportional representation is the route to educational quality...The controversy over busing has diverted attention away from the educational problems experienced by minorities at the elementary and secondary levels...One does not have to be against civil rights to oppose school busing.[137]

Mary Anne Raywid echoes the same sentiments five years later. In an article on alternative school programs, she writes:

> Minority demands related to schooling have shifted discernibly in recent years, due to a growing realization that access to desegregated schools is not enough to insure admission to the societal mainstream. What is essential is access to schools that *work*—to high quality education.[138]

In *The Troubled Crusade*, Diane Ravitch gives a survey of social engineering in education from 1945 to 1980. Amid discussions of *Brown* and *Bakke*, and citing the research of Derrick Bell at Columbia Teachers College, she writes that many blacks themselves "might not necessarily include the racial dispersion remedy" in the upgrading of black education. Having seen little good come from dispersion, they now prefer the "substantial improvement of their neighborhood school."[139] Famed black educator Marva Collins is living substantiation of Ravitch's observations. Preferring the development of educational excellence at her Westside Preparatory School in Chicago to the busing of students out of the inner city, Collins writes:

> Busing is another example of a self-defeating approach to black education. It only makes minority children ashamed of themselves and their neighborhoods,

> as though only schools in white neighborhoods can teach...Busing...is merely another way of side-stepping the real problem—ineffective teachers... Miseducation is not a function of a child's race or neighborhood but of the teaching methods he or she is exposed to.[140]

The reversal of the busing mandates of the 1960's and 1970's is, in fact, already upon us, the most vivid example, perhaps, being the case of Los Angeles in 1981. After two years of legal battles, the California State Supreme Court, having twice before ruled in favor of L.A. busing, refused to review (thus upholding) a lower court ruling which overturned a mandatory busing plan affecting 600,000 students of whom only 23% were white. The State Supreme Court's action upheld California Proposition One, a 1979 anti-busing amendment to the State Constitution, prohibiting busing for the purposes of achieving racial balance "unless deliberate action to discriminate by a school system or state agency can be proved."[141] This seems to have been in line with the U.S. Supreme Court's 1971 ruling in Swann vs. Charlotte-Mecklenburg Board of Education, a ruling which declared that busing is legal only to redress constitutional violations. It is interesting to note the comments of T.H. Bell, then U.S. Education Secretary. "The problem with busing," he said, "is that at the end of the bus ride, you're still back in that racially isolated neighborhood," and he went on to say that he "would certainly not oppose" a federal law or constitutional amendment to prohibit busing as a remedy for segregation.[142]

What Los Angeles experienced in 1981 seems to have been echoed in the American macrocosm by recent Gallup Polls. In 1981 the busing-for-integration issue was fairly high on the list of the biggest problems facing America's schools. By the eighteenth annual poll of attitudes toward public schools (1986), of the twenty-eight problems listed, busing ranked only thirteenth. In the 1987 poll it was fourteenth on a list of thirty headed by topics such as student drug abuse and school discipline. In both 1986 and 1987 polls, less than 4% of the respondents saw busing as a major issue.[143]

The question of busing seems to have been replaced by more concerted efforts to improve neighborhood schools, white or black, the theory being that better education is a more promising avenue to equal opportunity than forced social engineering. We will comment on this trend below. For now we turn to our second example of recent educational social engineering.

(b) Quotas in school and job applications. The systematic denial of opportunities to minorities in being admitted to colleges and to the work force is a shameful part of America's racism which has been documented all too frequently. In recent years, however, it is not the discrimination which has grabbed the headlines but rather the programs instituted to end it. Usually lumped under the name "affirmative action," these programs have led to charges that in an effort to make up for past social wrongs they now discriminate against whites or men. The *Bakke* case which we viewed earlier is but one of many instances of this so-called "reverse discrimination." It is a situation of extreme sensitivity which manifests itself in college admissions policies, educational administration hiring, teaching hiring, and job reduction policies. Consider for a moment the situation at the University of California/Berkeley. Asians, who represent a small minority of the nation (under

2%), are excelling educationally to the point where they now constitute over 20% of the enrollment on the prestigious Berkeley campus. Whites—once the agent of discrimination—are now complaining that in an effort to make opportunities available to Asian minorities, white applicants are being passed over. Asians claim that Asian students are being accepted to Berkeley not because of any affirmative action program but because they are simply outscoring whites on the admissions tests. Whites are countering that if this is true, affirmative action, applied so often since 1964 to admit less deserving minorities over more deserving whites, should now be applied to less deserving whites. "We are demographically under-represented," the whites are saying. "It is now time to let affirmative action work for us." And, predictably, the minorities see this as an open door to renewed discrimination. Having gained access to colleges and jobs through the affirmative action program, they wish not only to keep the program but also to cancel its use for the benefit of whites where it might possibly hurt deserving minority candidates.

The whole situation is a mess, and at the center of that mess stands the U.S. Supreme Court. Would that the Court had a definitive position, bus alas, its rulings are as inconsistent and confusing as the situation itself. Let us view some recent cases by way of example. For each case, lawyer Thomas Flygare writes that we should ask three questions: 1) why were racially preferential practices instituted; 2) who benefitted from them; and 3) who suffered as a result of any reverse discrimination?[144]

In its 1986 ruling of Wynant vs. Jackson (Michigan) Board of Education, the Court was asked to decide the liability of a 1972 collective bargaining agreement which exempted minority teachers from seniority-based layoffs. Two lower court opinions had held against the white plaintiffs, stating that the law was a legitimate attempt "to remedy societal discrimination by providing 'role models' for minority school children."[145] In their appeal to the Supreme Court, the white teachers argued that whatever the motive for the law, it was a violation of the equal protection clause of the Fourteenth Amendment. In a narrow 5-4 vote, the Court agreed with the plaintiffs and overturned the 1972 Michigan law. Judges Powell, Burger, Rehnquist, O'Connor, and White represented the majority. Justices Marshall, Stevens, Brennan, and Blackmun dissented.

The "swing vote" in the case was Powell, as he had been in the Bakke decision. In a similiar case, not education-related, Powell sided with Marshall, Stevens, Brennan, and Blackmun in ordering Local 28 of the Sheetmetal Workers' Union to raise minority membership to 29% because of its "egregious, contemptuous, racial discrimination." Flygare suggests that Powell's seemingly inconsistent stand was taken because the Local 28 case ruling "had less of an impact on innocent third parties."[146] Whatever the accuracy of that opinion, Justice Powell has now retired from the Court, and in future cases it will be a moot point. In the eyes of many, in fact, the new composition of the Court is apt to alter many of the close 5-4 and 6-3 votes of recent years.[147]

The inconsistency of the Court may be demonstrated even further by cases ranging from Boston to California. In the Weber case of 1979, the Court ruled that employers who wished to do so could favor women and minorities over equally qualified white males, thus upholding the doctrine of voluntary affirmative action. In the Texas Department of Community Affairs vs. Joyce Ann Burdine (1981), however, the court modified its position, stating that employers were not *compelled* to hire women or minority members instead of an equally qualified white male. In yet another case, Szewiola vs. the Los Angeles School District, it was decided that 50% of the administrative vacancies over the next decade would have to be filled by women in order to redress past discrimination. Finally, the Court refused to even hear the case of the Boston Teachers' Union vs. the City of Boston where a federal desegregation ruling had mandated a 20% black staff. When layoffs hit the Boston school system, one thousand white teachers were let go while blacks with less seniority were retained. The Court's refusal to hear the case in effect upheld the affirmative action, a position diametrically opposed to its own ruling in Wynant vs. Jackson Board of Education. All of which led the *American School Board Journal* to write, "Trying to divine why the U.S. Supreme Court accepts some cases and declines to hear others is a bit like reading goat entrails, tea leaves, or sun spots."[148]

How we might deal with this hodgepodge is a matter we will save for the commentary section of this topic. For now we move on to the phenomenon of social engineering through the curriculum.

(c) Curricular social engineering. It is not simply in subject matter alone that curriculum relates to social engineering, though it is an obvious and frequently encountered phenomenon. More subtle is the method of teaching itself. Let me explain. In an effort to make all American students aware of the contribution of minorities and women to the nation's cultural mainstream and to expose Americans more completely to the so-called "Third World" cultures of Africa, Asia, and Latin America, many new subjects have been added to the post-1960 curriculum. Asian and African history, the writings of James Baldwin, the poetry of Emily Dickinson all have a different place and stress in the post-1960 era. To the extent such curricular changes are broadening and not merely propagandistic, there is everything right with them, and they occur with little controversy. The more important engineering occurs in the ability groupings and school choices available to students.

We will cover the subject of tracking and ability grouping in much greater depth in the next chapter, for it properly belongs among the things one finds inside rather than outside the classroom. But as it has a very dynamic impact on social engineering, it bears mentioning here. The child who at an early age is placed in a remedial environment or a slower learning track is frequently locked into that track throughout the entirety of a public school career simply because the "academic distance" between that child and children who learn at more accelerated rates is usually an ever-widening one. This is not a rap at remediation; nor is it a plea to end ability grouping. It is simply a statement of educational reality. As I said, the problem is quite complex and will be dealt with in depth later. For now just hold the thought that kids in slow tracks generally stay there. The same is true with students who for a variety of reasons (economic, emotional, drug-related, etc.) do not or cannot function in the normal school environment. Assigning them to special schools at once gives them a better chance to succeed and generally keeps them out of the educational mainstream.

The results of these processes are often a kind of socioeconomic predetermination. Remediated students tend to become lower wage earners at less skilled jobs requiring less intensive education, while accelerated students tend to become higher wage earners in more skilled positions which demand greater amounts of education.[149] The way in which children are grouped thus has economic and social ramifications all their lives, and since the tests which determine such grouping have at times been viewed as unfair to minorities, tracking has been seen by some very fine educators as a phenomenon which perpetuates the cycle of poverty among blacks, Hispanics, and other disadvantaged groups.[150]

All of which is not to say that alternative learning environments for some students are necessarily bad. For example, a great deal of recent work on so-called "schools of choice" has yielded some interesting data. Alternative school programs seem to be salvaging many minority (and some non-minority) students who have dropped out of the regular school environment. They also seem to be reducing racial tensions caused by forced integration.[151] Already, Alaska, Arizona, California, Colorado, Florida, Iowa, Louisiana, Massachusetts, Missouri, Minnesota, New York, North Carolina, Virginia, Washington, and Wisconsin have some schools of choice. In certain locations (such as Buffalo, N.Y.), as much as 30% of the school population is involved in an alternative program. From the Central Park East School in Manhattan's District 4 to the Alternative Learning Center of Vancouver, Washington, alternative schools are reporting successes among students who have known only failure.[152] Mueller suggests that this is in part true because there is more parental involvement in such programs,[153] but others see an even deeper reason. Alternative schools are less apt to treat students as an undifferentiated mass of bodies and more likely to individualize schedules, curricula, tests, and teaching methods to fit very individual needs. Raywid writes eloquently on the idea:

> Clearly we must call a halt to our century-long march toward standardization. We must forget such fruitless battles as whether or not to begin all reading instruction with phonics and seek instead to match our teaching strategies to particular students—starting some youngsters with phonics and others with drastically different approaches. The evidence supporting such a strategy is extensive and certainly not new; we know for a fact that different youngsters learn in different ways and according to different patterns. When we insist on imposing a single instructional approach on all children, we succeed with some students and systematically handicap others. There is no reason (beyond our own perversity) to continue to assume that some single "right" approach exists that suits every student.[154]

With an acknowledgement that curricular content and student grouping each have an important bearing on social engineering and a promise to return to the topics of curriculum and grouping in the next chapter, we move on to considerations of educational equity for women.

(d) Recent concerns of education equity for women. It is not in admission to the educational work force that women have been denied equal access. We have already seen in our survey of educational unionism that women have long been a substantial part of the teaching force, often a majority of it. Rather it is in the area of educational advancement that women have felt the sting of denial. In 1985 women constituted 53% of the total U.S. population and 40% of the work force. They also constituted 70% of all elementary and secondary school teachers.[155] However, they represented only about 16% of public school principals (23% of elementary and 7% of secondary principalships) and an appallingly low 1.8% of school superintendents.[156] It is interesting to speculate why women have remained out of the administrative hierarchy, and for some researchers, at least, the reasons have less to do with discrimination and more to do with sociological and psychological role definitions.

From the purely biological viewpoint, women must shoulder the burdens of childbirth and surely that interrupts if not ends plans of career advancement. From the historical viewpoint, women have been counselled to be homemakers—wives and mothers first before considerations of career—and that, too, has contributed to the statistics. But it doesn't explain everything about the 1985 figures, for the past twenty years have clearly seen a reversal of much of the traditional role counselling of women. By the mid and late 1980's one would think that we should have seen more women administrators than we actually have. Porat speculates that it is a psychological barrier which must now be crossed to bring women to their full and just measure of participation in positions of educational leadership. She cites negative self-perception, lack of confidence, and low personal expectations as the three dominant factors preventing women from educational advancement.[157] Lynn Erickson goes a step further. She sees a conflict between assertiveness (normally associated with men) and nurturing (normally associated with women) in the role of the woman administrator. Women, Erickson argues, must adopt traits of assertiveness without losing their sociobiological nurturing characteristics in order to become successful administrators, and this is not easy for many women to do.[158]

It seems more and more that the thing needed at this point in women's march to educational equity is encouragement. Where programs exist to say, in effect, "you *can* do it—let us help you," it appears that women have responded successfully. The "Hot Castle Springs" project of Arizona is a good example. There, in a program funded cooperatively by the government's Title IV Project Equity, the Arizona Department of Education, and a steering committee of women administrators, women educators have been helped to overcome many of the barriers described above. The results have been an increase in the percentage of female administrators in the region.[159]

Comments and suggestions. In my own opinion and quite obviously in the opinion of some of the judges, lawyers, and educators mentioned above, America is playing a very confusing game with the equity issue. In fact, it is a dangerous game because it is polarizing, fractionalizing, and angering large segments of the population. The game, simply put, is that two wrongs make a right. They don't. They never did; they never will. Yet, when we deliberately discriminate against innocent people in the name of affirmative action, that is the game we play. No student should ever be admitted to a school, no job should ever be awarded on any basis other than merit. Whether a candidate is green or white, Hindu or Buddist, blind or sighted—it is merit and merit alone which should be the criterion for judgment. Saying to a person, "I am going to discriminate against you because two hundred years ago someone of your race or sex discriminated against someone else," is merely perpetuating the insult of discrimination. It cannot change the past, and it does little or nothing to help the present. Worst of all, it guarantees a future of diminished potential because it systematically harms the most talented among us.

Having said this, I would add two qualifiers and a warning. Qualifier number one is that the means of determining candidate merit must be as non-biased and valid as we can possibly make it. I suppose that is self-evident, but it ought to be said. The second qualifier is that where there are candidates of exactly equal worth, the choice should go to the minority or woman candidate because, at that point, social restitution becomes a viable criterion. The warning is that the affirmative action approach is going to doom the very minorities or women whom affirmative action is designed to help. I would like to explain that.

I remember when the City University of New York changed from a college system in which admissions standards were competitive to one in which admission was based simply on "open enrollment," as it was called. By the thousands sub-standard students were admitted to the campuses which formed the university system. Admissions tests were simplified, cut-off standards were lowered, and the overall quality of the university fell overnight to a shameful shadow of what it had been. It soon became apparent that few "open enrollment students" could handle college level work, so courses were "dumbed down" and remedial programs were begun in wholesale numbers. However, that did very little to solve the problem because many "open enrollment kids" had never developed the study skills or disciplines needed to master even remedial programs. The result was that such students dropped out in droves, and those who did remain were graduated with sub-standard skills. Tragic enough? Yes, but that was just the beginning, for many of these kids found, when they hit the real work force, that they couldn't hack it. Soon they were being fired or laid off or sent back to school by employers whose livelihoods depended not on a public relations game but on the bottom line ability to get the job done.

Having been miseducated to start with, these students were betrayed a second time by being misinformed as to the value of their degrees. No matter what insane gimmickry the City University of New York was using, it is not, in the final analysis, the sheepskin which constitutes an education but the skills and the knowledge of the curriculum. Open enrollment for thousands of kids was another four-year delusion: four more years of wasted time, of being lied to and used by an establishment whose primary goal was not the redemption of a failed education system but rather making itself look good in the eyes of a critical world. The trendy programs designed to lift minorities from the ghetto never addressed the real problems of learning, and the result was another generation of beaten, hopeless children. Listen, please, to the words of Marva Collins:

> When teachers turn to the education experts for help, they rarely seem to offer any practical advice. The experts are busy trying to build professional reputations based on some new gimmick. Each has had its fling: new math, teaching machines...non-graded classrooms, open classrooms...back-to-basics, black English...bilingual instruction...People seem to think that if they throw a few dollars at a problem it will go away.
>
> I remember a time, years back, when schools and teachers tried to deal with their own problems. Then federal dollars became available and suddenly everyone had a problem he couldn't solve and was writing grant proposals.

> People got billions of dollars to study problems, and when those studies didn't work out, people got more government money to do a new study to find out what went wrong with the first one.
>
> Countless studies have been done on how to teach inner-city students. To me it seems perfectly plain that inner-city children should be taught the same way other children are taught because...a ghetto child learns in the same way as any other child...I don't hold with a "ghetto approach" to teaching. The experts claim that correcting an inner-city child's grammar will damage that child's whole life. I believe that not correcting grammar will damage that child's whole life. While others lowered their standards...I made mind higher.
>
> New methods and theories are not the solution. In fact they have been the primary cause of miseducation. In the mid-1960's many educators supported a trend away from the use of books toward "experiential learning activities..." One educational psychology textbook...stated, "Today's schools probably depend far too much upon reading as a data gathering technique." Why then were educators surprised when students went all the way through school without being able to read? And why was everyone surprised when those same non-readers became teachers themselves and spawned a whole new crop of miseducated students?[160]

What Collins is saying is so obvious and powerful that it amazes me it should have to be said at all. To solve a problem, one must address the problem, not a separate issue. If there is de facto segregation because of bigotry in the real estate business, it is the real estate industry which bears scrutiny. Busing a child from here to there will not do the job. If minorities are so poorly educated that they cannot afford homes in better areas, lowering their learning standards surely is the worst way to correct the deficiency. If the competitiveness of a society fails because its citizenry is poorly trained, affirmative action will not improve the standards. In fact, to the extent that such social games are played, the disadvantaged among us, regardless of race, are doomed to remain disadvantaged.

What, then, do we do? We address the problems in real terms. If a ghetto school—or any school— is dirty, we clean it up. If it is not secure or safe, we make it safe. If it has poor teachers, we get better teachers. If it has students with few community resources, we supplement them through added resources. If it has kids from deprived or troubled homes, we provide as many of the available support services we can to compensate as much as we can. If it has disruptive students, we remove them and try to remediate them, but we clear the way for other students to learn. If it has a drug dealer on campus, we call a cop. In short, we provide every opportunity we can to help every child we can gain access to the mainstream through real achievements rather than falsified ones.

Where we ought to be spending our money is not on what Collins calls the "gimmicks," but on programs which assure disadvantaged kids who *have* made the academic grade the opportunity to advance. There is perhaps nothing more tragic nor more out-of-tune with our professed desire to help minority youth out of the cycles of poverty which so often entrap them than to be academically deserving and not have the money for college. It should therefore be a priority for both federal and state governments to make scholarship aid and low interest loans available for such students—in fact, for all students who are academically capable and financially in need. We also ought to be spending the money we waste for things such as busing on real, substantive improvements to the schools of disadvantaged areas. Larger libraries, more enriched programs, the upgrading and maintenance of physical plants, better equipment, a safer campus—these are the things which really need doing.

I am reminded of a district where gimmicks always took precedence over the practical day-in, day-out needs of teaching. Every administrator had his or her own "dog and pony show." They went through Management-By-Objective seminars, Mastery-Learning Workshops, Comprehensive School Improvement Plans (CSIP), Cooperative Grouping inservice courses, Middle States evaluations—all approved by a Board of Education who could be dazzled with anything that sounded esoteric or anyone who had a "doctor" in front of his name. Meanwhile, the dropout rate was the highest in the area, SAT scores actually declined over the decade these programs were instituted, and the school was vandalized over and over again. I can't tell you how many memos were written pleading for new locks on the auditorium doors or for the school to hire a theatrical technician both to teach and look after a facility which was being damaged almost on a monthly basis. Repairs just to the pianos in that auditorium ran over four thousand dollars. A twenty-thousand dollar organ was broken beyond fixing. Seats were torn up; fires started; even stage flooring broken. But the administration always pleaded poverty for such things, while in the next breath appropriating tens of thousands for a new gimmick. The result was an educational system constantly out of sync with its needs, constantly achieving less than its potential.

It is not that I am against Mastery Learning or CSIP programs or Middle States evaluations, but first you've got to take care of basic deficiencies. As Maslow stated, no one who must forage for food in a jungle is going to pay much attention to a regimen for building self-esteem before he eats. First put out the fire in the auditorium. Then talk to me about Madeline Hunter.

There is yet another caution to mention about our social engineering in education, and it is the abuse of well-intentioned programs. Let me give you examples from the areas of Title I funding, bilingual education courses, and maternity leave benefits.

In 1965, President Lyndon Johnson created the first federal education program specifically earmarked for disadvantaged areas and specifically aimed at breaking the cycle of poverty in those areas. Originally called "Title I of the Elementary and Secondary Education Act" (later renamed "Chapter 1" by the Reagan Administration), the program has been funded since its inception to the tune of about $45 billion (about $2 billion per year)—no small piece of change. Obviously, with dropouts, pregnancies, drug abuse, and school violence up and SAT scores down in the locations for which Title I programs were intended, one must look with some reservation upon the programs. But there is an even sadder abuse involved, and it is this: because of the poor way Title I projects are written and even poorer way they are administrated, much of the money never concentrates in the disadvantaged communities. David Savage reports that 90% of the 16,000 school districts in America receive Title I funds. 70% of America's elementary schools get Title I money, many of them containing few if any disadvantaged children. He goes on to say that the approximately $500 per child which Title I programs provide often go to remedial math and reading lessons which pull kids out of regular instruction, stigmatize them, and work in direct opposition to the mainstreaming techniques being practiced in the very same schools.[161] Perhaps fixing the programs so that they are educationally viable is a worthy goal, but it is absolutely imperative that the programs be kept in the communities for which they were intended and not used to give money to districts already well-fixed.

It is particularly critical that money meant for minority children remain in minority communities in the closing years of this century because we must provide an incentive for minority children, especially black children, to go into teaching. Why? Because there are not enough black teachers to act as positive role models for black kids, and because minorities are becoming an ever-increasing percentage of the public school population. Patricia Graham, Dean of the Graduate School of Education at Harvard University, writes extensively on this subject, and the statistics below come from her research.

Blacks are now about 12% of the U.S. population, Hispanics about 6%. By the year 2000, those figures are apt to swell by 40% due to patterns of immigration and higher birthrates in minority homes. Blacks represent 16% of today's public school population but constitute only 7% of the teaching force. Of those students who are attracted to teaching careers, far more whites are able to pass their teaching exams than blacks, especially in the South. In Louisiana, for example, 78% of whites pass the tests as compared with only 15% of blacks. In Georgia the rates are 84% for whites and 34% for blacks. It is especially important to improve these figures in the South and in states such as New York and California because of the high minority public school enrollments there. It is particularly there where we need good minority educators.

The problems of improving black education are complex for the roots of black miseducation are deep. Consider some of the shocking statistics below. In 1953 we spent $235 per child on education. In Mississippi it was only $154—and that was for white kids. Black children received a mere $46. Today 46% of black families live below the poverty line. In 1980 only 32% of black high school students chose academic-track courses which might lead to college and degrees in education. In 1982, when blacks constituted 15% of public school enrollment, nearly one-third never received high school diplomas. Between 1976 and 1985, whites scored 30-40% higher on SAT tests (110 points higher on the verbal section, 125 points higher on the math section). In 1976 only 33.5% of black high school graduates enrolled in college. By 1983 that figure had dropped to 27%, and very few of these students chose careers in education because opportunities in science, computers, and engineering were so much more attractive.[162]

In the face of these conditions, affirmative action programs which lower black student achievement goals and abuses which siphon money away from blacks are nothing short of criminal. Why can't we, instead, say to black kids, "For those of you who finish high school and choose to become teachers, we will provide scholarships, loans, and work-study programs which will guarantee the financial part of your education, and we will provide as much remediation and encouragement as we can to make sure you pass your courses and your tests and take your place as proud citizens and positive role models for other minority kids." Where are the billions for this? Why must we burn them up in the exhaust fumes of a bus whose function it is to take students needlessly from one school to another?

The bilingual program abuses are an even worse calamity than the Title I fiasco because they have too frequently become a perversion not only of education but of the concept of nationhood. There is only a handful of things which constitute the essence of a nation: a common boundary, a common economy, a common history, and a common language. To the extent these things become fractured, the nation loses its cohesion. That doesn't mean that nations should not have diversity. Diversity can be a powerful strength, creating checks and balances and adding richness to the overall culture. But no nation can endure permanently if it wars economically or linguistically or geographically within itself.

Bilingual programs were intended to help non-English-speaking students gain equal access to educational opportunity by speeding up the learning of English. Now, in far too many instances, they are used in the name of "ethnic pride" to delay the learning of English—in some cases permanently. That is an insanity which must stop immediately, for it will end in one of only two ways, each of them disastrous. Either non-English-speaking kids will be prevented from joining the linguistic mainstream of America, thus depriving them of an economic ascendancy, or the mainstream itself will disappear and with it the cohesion of a nation united by a single tongue. It is essential that the thrust of bilingual programs be an intensive indoctrination in English, not of teaching a curricula in a native language other than English. If necessary, such an indoctrination should require the isolation of foreign students from some regular classrooms so that the speed of learning English is increased with no undue academic harm. For other classes, mainstreaming can be a wonderful learning and social device. In an English class, it is a disaster for obvious reasons. In a chorus or physical education class, I have seen it work miracles.

Finally, there is the abuse of what I have come to call "the motherhood game." Before I elaborate, I'd like to make it clear that the game is not played by women any more than by men—or should I say mothers any more than fathers. I do not view it as a "women's" problem because the decision to have children is (hopefully) a joint one between man and woman, and it is perhaps there that I should start. When a couple decides to produce a child and when a woman decides to bear it, they must accept the responsibility for that child. However they do it, they must come up with a plan to feed it, clothe it, and (hopefully, again) love it. To the extent that society can aid in these things through maternity leaves and day-care centers, it certainly should. That such aid (particularly the latter) is unavailable in America is deplorable—and I say that even with some grave reservations about the psychological wisdom of leaving one's baby with strangers for most of the day or the fiscal wisdom of having a child at all if "day-care abandonment" must become a condition of childrearing. Whatever my personal preferences for having and raising babies, however, these things are not part of the abuse I wish to discuss. Rather, the abuse comes in not being honest or forthright in disclosing an impending birth.

As it is right now, I cannot as an employer ask a female candidate if she plans to have children or is pregnant at the time of an interview. I cannot ask a male candidate if he might have to reduce his hours as a teacher should he become a father. Civil rights laws do not permit such personal probings, and as a result I cannot effectively plan for the well-being of my staff or students. Let me give you an example of what I'm talking about.

After many years on the job, my secretary retired. I thus embarked upon a search for a new secretary and, following the interviews of candidates (all of whom were women provided by a civil service list in ranked order), I hired a replacement. About two months later I was informed by my new secretary that she was three months pregnant and would be taking a maternity leave later in the term. After congratulating her, I asked how long she would be out. "We're allowed a year," she replied and would elaborate no further. In due time she left, and I hired a temporary replacement. The replacement was temporary because by civil service contract the mother-to-be was guaranteed her old job for one year. In the meantime the baby was born. It was normal and healthy, and so was the mother. However, every time I asked when the mother would return I received no definite answer. Then another job opened up in the district, a permanent job, and my temporary secretary—seeing the chance to come on board as a permanent employee—applied for it. But before she did, she asked the new mother if she intended to return after the year was up. "Because if you don't," the temporary said, "I'd like to stay here and won't apply for the other opening." Once again, the mother refused to answer. Result: the temporary employee left and I had a fourth secretary within the space of that one school year.

The discourtesy, inconvenience, and waste of the situation hurt me, my staff, the students, and two other secretaries who were kept dangling while a selfish mother and father played their "women's rights/civil service" game to the hilt. It should not have been allowed and could have been prevented with a few simple procedures, the first being that as pregnancy is a condition which greatly affects the ability to work, it should be stated (if known) at the original interview. The second procedure should be that, barring an untoward medical condition, six months, not a full year, be the period for which a specific job is held. After that, for the balance of the year, it should be an "equal job at equal pay" with the employer, not the employee, given the exercise of the option. Finally, so that jobs are not taken under false pretenses, no maternity leave privileges should be allowed for the first year of employment. It is simply not the responsibility of the employer for the employee's decision to have a baby. It should thus not be a penalty upon the employer any more than a prior existing condition should be the responsibility of an insurer once a policy is signed.

The generalization here is clear, and it applies to all of the abuses of educational social engineering. Improving the lot of anyone who is the victim of systematic discrimination cannot occur at the expense of an innocent third party if we are to remain on a steady ethical and legal keel. To the extent we honor this principle, we will continue to grow as a nation. To the extent we ignore it, the confusion and anger spawned by the cases discussed in this chapter and hundreds of similar cases will continue to rip away at the soul of our schools and our nation.

References for Chapter Four

1. The figures for this paragraph and this section of text come from several sources: the National Center for Educational Statistics, the U.S. Census Bureau, the Education Commission of the States, and the Educational Research Service. See, for example, ***The Condition of Education,*** 1986 ed. Washington, D.C.: Center for Educational Statistics, U.S. Dept. of Education, 1986. pp. 52-56, 108-12. There is also a compendium of figures in the 1987 edition of ***The World Almanac.*** New York: Pharos Books, 1987. pp. 115-31. The Almanac cites the U.S. Treasury Dept. and other federal agencies as sources. Further data yielding much the same information have been made available by the National School Board Association and the ***1987 State Education Statistics Supplement*** of the U.S. Dept. of Education. The references above contain detailed citations. The figures in the text are round numbers. The more specific data appear below. GNP = $3.99 trillion. Federal budget = $936.6 billion. Defense Dept. budget = $262.9 billion. Public school district expenditures = $149.6 billion. Federal education expenditures = $16 billion.
2. "Business Involvement and Public School Improvement," Dale Mann. In ***Phi Delta Kappan.*** October 1987 (Vol. 69, #2). pp. 123-28. A chart of charitable giving appears on p. 125. Mann cites as his source the ***Giving USA*** 1983 Annual Report.
3. "States on the Lookout for New Money," Chris Pipho. In ***Phi Delta Kappan.*** April 1987 (Vol. 68, #8). pp. 574-75.
4. "Economics and Education," Martin Carnoy. In ***Encyclopedia of Educational Research,*** 5th ed. Harold E. Mitzel, editor-in-chief. New York: The Free Press, 1982. pp. 526-29. See also ***Educational Cost Differentials and Allocations of State Aid for Elementary and Secondary Education,*** J. Chambers. Stanford, Calif.: Stanford Univ., 1979.
5. "States on the Lookout for New Money," Pipho. pp. 574-75.
6. "Rural Education," Chris Pipho. In ***Phi Delta Kappan.*** October 1987 (Vol. 69, #2). pp. 6-7.
7. "Education and Economy," Chris Pipho. In ***Phi Delta Kappan.*** December 1986 (Vol. 68, #4) pp. 269-70.
8. "Education and Economy," Pipho. pp. 269-70.
9. "Education and Economy," Pipho. pp. 269-70.
10. "The Sputnik of the Eighties," John F. Jennings. In ***Phi Delta Kappan.*** October 1987 (Vol. 69, #2). pp. 104-09.
11. "The Sputnik of the Eighties," Jennings. p. 104.
12. ***People and Productivity: a challenge to corporate America.*** New York: New York Stock Exchange, Office of Economic Research. November 1982. p. 39 ff.
13. ***Estimates of School Statistics, 1985-86.*** West Haven, Conn.: National Education Association Professional Library, 1986. p. 20.
14. "The Sputnik of the Eighties," Jennings. pp. 105-06.
15. "Sources of Funding for Educational Reform," Allen Odden. In ***Phi Delta Kappan.*** January 1986 (Vol. 67, #5). pp. 335-40.
16. "Involving Low-income Parents in the Schools: a role for policy?" Milbrey Wallin McLaughlin and Patrick M. Shields. In ***Phi Delta Kappan.*** October 1987 (Vol. 69, #2). p. 157. See also "What's Ahead for Education," Harold L. Hodgkinson. In ***Principal.*** January 1986. pp. 6-11.
17. "Reform? Higher Education? Don't Be Absurd!" Harold L. Hodgkinson. In ***Phi Delta Kappan.*** December 1986 (Vol. 68, #4). pp. 271-74.

18. "Sources of Funding for Educational Reform," Odden. p. 336.
19. "Sources of Funding for Educational Reform," Odden. p. 340.
20. "Sustaining the Momentum of State Education Reform: the link between assessment and financial support," Michael W. Kirst. In ***Phi Delta Kappan.*** January 1986 (Vol. 67, #5). pp. 341-45. See also ***Public Attitudes on Governments and Taxation, 1984.*** Washington, D.C.: Advisory Commission on Intergovernment Relations, 1984; and "State Tax Increase of 1983: prelude to another tax revolt," Steven Gold. In ***National Tax Journal.*** March 1984. pp. 9-22.
21. "Sources of Funding for Educational Reform," Odden. p. 340.
22. "Sustaining the Momentum of State Education Reform...," Kirst. pp. 341-45.
23. "Sources of Funding for Educational Reform," Odden. pp. 335-40.
24. "Sustaining the Momentum of State Education Reform...," Kirst. p. 342.
25. "States on the Lookout for New Money," Pipho. pp. 574-75. See also ***The Condition of Education, 1986.*** pp. 108-21.
26. "Reform? Higher Education? Don't Be Absurd!" Hodgkinson. p. 272.
27. "Reform? Higher Education? Don't Be Absurd!" Hodgkinson. pp. 271-72.
28. "Reform? Higher Education? Don't Be Absurd!" Hodgkinson. p. 272.
29. "Reform? Higher Education? Don't Be Absurd!" Hodgkinson. p. 272.
30. See "Reform? Higher Education? Don't Be Absurd!" Hodgkinson. p. 272. See also "The Ph.D. in Public Schools: how should graduate programs adapt?" Hoyt F. LeCroy. In ***Music Educators Journal.*** January 1988 (Vol. 73, #5). pp. 42-45; and "The Ph.D. outside Academe: some appalling facts," Edward Tenner. In ***Chronicle of Higher Education.*** February 1985. p. 80.
31. "Of Hopes and Expectations," Judy Meloy. In ***Phi Delta Kappan.*** January 1986 (Vol. 67, #5). pp. 390-91.
32. "In This System the Computer Future Is Now," Dan Levin. In ***The American School Board Journal.*** May 1981 (Vol. 168, #5). pp. 27-28.
33. "How To Help Teachers Welcome Computers," Gene Geisert. In ***The American School Board Journal.*** May 1981 (Vol. 168, #5). p. 29.
34. "Creationists Limit Dogmatic Darwinism." In ***The American School Board Journal.*** May 1981 (Vol. 168, #5). pp. 17-18. See also "Making Knowledge Legitimate: power, profit, and the textbook," Michael W. Apple. In ***Current Thought on Curriculum.*** Alexandria, Va.: ASCD, 1985. pp. 73-89.
35. "Creationists Limit Dogmatic Darwinism," pp. 17-18.
36. "Economics and Education," Carnoy. pp. 526-29. See also ***Proposition 13: the campaign, the vote, the immediate aftereffects,*** J. Catterall and T. Thresher. Stanford, Calif.: Stanford Univ. Institute for Research on Educational Finance and Governance, 1979.
37. "The 18th Annual Gallup Poll of the Public's Attitude toward the Public Schools," Alec M. Gallup. In ***Phi Delta Kappan.*** September 1986. pp. 43-59.
38. "Too Bright To Be a Teacher?" Paul Woodring. In ***Phi Delta Kappan.*** April 1987 (Vol. 68, #8). pp. 617-18.
39. "Able Students Going into Teaching." In ***Phi Delta Kappan.*** April 1987. (Vol. 68, #8). p 636.
40. "Reform? Higher Education? Don't Be Absurd!" Hodgkinson. pp. 272-73.
41. "The Reform of National Accreditation," Donna M. Gollnick and Richard C. Kunkel. In ***Phi Delta Kappan.*** December 1986 (Vol. 68, #4). pp. 310-14.
42. See "Four Educators Comment on the Redesign of NCATE," Doyle Watts. In ***Phi Delta Kappan.*** December 1986 (Vol. 68, #4). pp. 315-18; and "The Faculty Dilemma: a short course," Jack Schuster. In ***Phi Delta Kappan.*** December 1986 (Vol. 68, #4). pp. 275-82.

43. "An Overview of the Holmes Group," Lynn Olson. In ***Phi Delta Kappan.*** April 1987 (Vol. 68, #8). p. 621.
44. See "The Greater Challenge," David G. Imig. In ***Phi Delta Kappan.*** September 1986 (Vol. 68, #1). pp. 32-33; and "Goals for the Reform of Teacher Education: an executive summary of the Holmes Group report," Frank B. Murray. In ***Phi Delta Kappan.*** September 1986 (Vol. 68, #1). pp. 28-32. Murray's support as a member of the group is not surprising. He is joined by the deans of Columbia University, Michigan State University, Ohio State University, SUNY Albany, SUNY Buffalo, Texas A&M, University of California/Berkeley, University of Illinois/Champaign, University of Illinois/Chicago, University of Iowa, University of Utah, University of Virginia, and University of Wisconsin.
45. "A Radical Proposal for Teacher Preparation," Edwin J. Meyer. In ***Phi Delta Kappan.*** June 1986 (Vol. 67, #10). pp. 728-29.
46. See "Teacher Education Programs," W. Robert Houston and Katherine K. Newman. In ***Encyclopedia of Educational Research,*** 5th ed. pp. 1881-93.
47. "A Risky Venture," Howard D. Mehlinger. In ***Phi Delta Kappan.*** September 1986 (Vol. 68, #1). p. 36.
48. "What the Holmes Group Report Doesn't Say," Edward J. Nussel. In ***Phi Delta Kappan.*** September 1986 (Vol. 68, #1). pp. 36-38.
49. See "A Field Guide to the Land of Teachers," Francis Keppel. In ***Phi Delta Kappan.*** September 1986 (Vol. 68, #1). pp. 18-23; and "The Carnegie Report—a Call for Redesigning the Schools," Marc Tucker and David Mandel. In ***Phi Delta Kappan.*** September 1986 (Vol. 68, #1). pp. 24-27.
50. "States Move Reform Closer to Reality," Chris Pipho. In ***Phi Delta Kappan.*** December 1986 (Vol. 68, #4). pp. K1-K8 (special section).
51. "Teacher Certification Tests: do they really measure what we need to know?" George F. Madaus and Diana Pullin. In ***Phi Delta Kappan.*** September 1987 (Vol. 69, #1). pp. 31-38.
52. "Assessment for Teaching: an initiative for the profession," Lee S. Shulman. In ***Phi Delta Kappan.*** September 1987 (Vol. 69, #1). pp. 38-44.
53. "Recertification Tests for Teachers: a defensible safeguard for society," W. James Popham and W.N. Kirby. In ***Phi Delta Kappan.*** September 1987 (Vol. 69, #1). pp. 45-49.
54. "Make Teacher Competency Your Policy," Russell A. Joki. In ***The American School Board Journal.*** November 1982 (Vol. 169, #11). pp. 32 and 52.
55. "Teacher Certification," Joel L. Burdin. In ***Encyclopedia of Educational Research,*** 5th ed. pp. 1865-69.
56. "This Revised Teacher Test Merits Attention." In ***The American School Board Journal.*** November 1982 (Vol. 169, #11). pp. 18 and 23.
57. "Emergency Certificates, Misassignment of Teachers and Other 'Dirty Little Secrets'," Robert A. Roth. In ***Phi Delta Kappan.*** June 1986 (Vol. 67, #10). pp. 725-27.
58. "And Let the Air Out of the Volleyballs," Gary D. Watts. In ***Phi Delta Kappan.*** June 1986 (Vol. 67, #10). p. 723.
59. "Toward a Comprehensive Strategy for Addressing the Teacher Shortage," Willis D. Hawley. In ***Phi Delta Kappan.*** June 1986 (Vol. 67, #10). pp. 712-18.
60. "Toward a Comprehensive Strategy for Addressing the Teacher Shortage," Hawley. pp. 712-18. Hawley cites as his source ***The Condition of Education,*** V. W. Plisko and J. Stern, eds. Washington, D.C.: U.S. Government Printing Office. 1985. p. 144. He states that the government figures tend to be conservative. For example, for 1983 the government had predicted a need of 164,000 teachers. In actuality, 230,000 were hired.

61. See "Economic and Political Trends Affecting Education," Paul E. Peterson. Paper presented to Association of Colleges and Schools of Education. Denver. February 1985; and "Academic Ability, Earnings, and the Decision To Become a Teacher," Charles F. Manski. Cambridge, Mass.: National Bureau of Economic Research, Working Paper #1539. January 1985.
62. "Toward a Comprehensive Strategy...," Hawley. pp. 716-17.
63. See "Clinical Supervision in the 1980's," Karolyn J. Snyder. In ***Educational Leadership.*** April 1981 (Vol. 38, #7). pp. 521-24.
64. See ***Clinical Supervision,*** R. Goldhammer. New York: Holt, Rinehart, and Winston, 1969; ***Clinical Supervision,*** Morris Cogen. Boston: Houghton-Mifflin, 1978; ***Clinical Supervision: a state of the art review.*** Cheryl Granade Sullivan. Alexandria, Va.: Association for Supervision and Curriculum Development, 1980; ***Developmental Supervision,*** Carl D. Glickman. Alexandria, Va.: Association for Supervision and Curriculum Development, 1981; and ***Successful Teacher Evaluation,*** Thomas L. McGreal. Alexandria, Va.: Association for Supervision and Curriculum Development, 1983.
65. See "Supervision for Intelligent Teaching," Arthur L. Costa and Robert Garmston. In ***Educational Leadership.*** February 1985. pp. 70-80; and "Who Is Right—Madeline Hunter or Art Costa?" Linda Lambert. In ***Educational Leadership.*** February 1985. pp. 68-69.
66. "Let's Eliminate the Preobservation Conference," Madeline Hunter. In ***Educational Leadership.*** March 1986. p. 69.
67. See "A Thank You and Some Questions for Madeline Hunter," Barbara N. Pavan. In ***Educational Leadership.*** March 1986. pp. 67-68; "Madeline Hunter Replies: develop collaboration; build trust," Madeline Hunter. In ***Educational Leadership.*** March 1986. p. 68; and "In Defense of the Preobservation Conference," John Lordon. In ***Educational Leadership.*** March 1986. pp. 70-71.
68. The study referred to was conducted by Homer Coker (Georgia State University), David Medley (University of Virginia), and Robert Soar (University of Florida). A synopsis report of the study appears in "Humanistic Education Is a Failure," ***The American School Board Journal.*** May 1981 (Vol. 168, #5). p. 20.
69. See "How Valid Are Principals' Judgments of Teacher Effectiveness?" Donald M. Medley and Homer Coker. In ***Phi Delta Kappan.*** October 1987 (Vol. 69, #2). pp. 138-40.
70. "Teacher Evaluation: more than a game that principals play," Aretha Butler Pigford. In ***Phi Delta Kappan.*** October 1987 (Vol. 69, #2). pp. 141-42.
71. See, for example, "Who Is Accountable for Thoughtfulness," Rexford Brown. In ***Phi Delta Kappan.*** September 1987 (Vol. 69, #1). pp. 49-52; "Evaluating Elementary Principals," Phyllis L. White. In ***Phi Delta Kappan.*** October 1987 (Vol. 69, #2). pp. 143-44; "Developing a Teacher Performance Evaluation System," Shirley B. Stow and Jim Sweeney. In ***Educational Leadership.*** April 1981 (Vol. 38, #7). pp. 538-41; and "Evaluation of Teachers," James Raths. In ***Encyclopedia of Educational Research,*** 5th ed. pp. 611-18.
72. See, for example, ***Mastery Teaching,*** Madeline Hunter. El Segundo, Calif.: TIP Publications, 1982; ***Rx for Improved Instruction,*** Madeline Hunter. El Segundo, Calif.: TIP Publications, 1976; and other books in the TIP series dealing with transfer, motivation, retention, reinforcement, etc.
73. "Intellectual levels" here refer to the various states of thinking in Bloom's Taxonomy of Cognitive Skills (knowledge, comprehension, application, analysis, synthesis, and evaluation). See the following: ***Taxonomy of Educational Objectives,*** Benjamin Bloom. New York: McKay, 1956; ***Handbook on Formative and Summative***

Evaluation of Student Learning, Benjamin Bloom. New York, 1960; and ***Human Characteristics and School Learning,*** Benjamin Bloom. New York: McGraw Hill, 1976.

74. See "Teachers Coaching Teachers," Beverly Showers. In ***Educational Leadership.*** April 1985 (Vol. 42, #7). pp. 43-48; and "Implementing the Coaching of Teaching," Joanna Dee Servatius and Shereen E. Young. In ***Educational Leadership.*** April 1985 (Vol. 42, #7). pp. 50-53.
75. "A Systematic Approach to Improving Conference Skills," Richard Kindsvatter and William W. Wilen. In ***Educational Leadership.*** April 1981 (Vol. 38, #7). pp. 525-29.
76. "Learning Communities for Curriculum and Staff Development," Anne Wescott Dodd and Eileen Rosenbaum. In ***Phi Delta Kappan.*** January 1986 (Vol. 67, #5). pp. 380-84.
77. "The Madison Workshops—One Approach to Staff Development," Howard Henderson. In ***Phi Delta Kappan.*** January 1986 (Vol. 67, #5). pp. 384-85.
78. "A School University Partnership That Fosters Inquiry-oriented Staff Development," Forrest W. Parkay. In ***Phi Delta Kappan.*** January 1986 (Vol. 67, #5). pp. 386-89.
79. See ***Teacher Expectation and Student Achievement: Coordinator Manual,*** Sam Kerman and Mary Martin. Bloomington, Ind.: Phi Delta Kappan, 1980; "Teacher Expectation and Student Achievement," Sam Kerman. In ***Phi Delta Kappan.*** June 1979; and "Student Social Class and Teacher Expectations: the self-fulfilling prophesy in ghetto education," Ray C. Rist. In ***Harvard Educational Review.*** August 1970 (Vol. 40). pp. 411-51.
80. See "On Leadership and Student Achievement: a conversation with Richard Andrews," Ron Brandt. In ***Educational Leadership.*** September 1987 (Vol. 45, #1). pp. 9-15; "Clinical Supervision for Principals," Wilma F. Smith and L. Andrews. In ***Educational Leadership.*** September 1987 (Vol. 45, #1). pp. 34-37; "Assessing and Developing Principal Instructional Leadership," Philip Hallinger and Joseph F. Murphy. In ***Educational Leadership.*** September 1987 (Vol. 45, #1). pp. 54-61; and "Good Seeds Grow in Strong Cultures," Jon Saphier and Matthew King. In ***Educational Leadership.*** March 1985. pp. 67-73.
81. ***Cultural Literacy: what every American needs to know,*** E. D. Hirsch, Jr. Boston: Houghton-Mifflin, 1987. p. xiii.
82. ***The Closing of the American Mind: how higher education has failed democracy and impoverished the soul of today's students,*** Allan Bloom. New York: Simon and Schuster, 1987. pp. 338-39 ff.
83. ***Paideia Problems and Possibilities,*** Mortimer J. Adler. New York: MacMillan, 1983. p. 8 ff. See also ***The Paideia Proposal: an educational manifesto,*** Mortimer J. Adler. New York: MacMillan, 1983.
84. See ***When Teachers Face Themselves,*** Arthur Jersild. New York: Teachers College Press, 1955.
85. "The Reform of National Accreditation," Gollnick and Kunkel. pp. 310-14.
86. "Teacher Collaboration: new partnerships to attack old problems," Andrew C. Porter. In ***Phi Delta Kappan.*** October 1987 (Vol. 69, #2). p. 148. Porter cites as the source of the quote "Teachers as Full Partners in Research," Jack Gajewski. In ***IRT Communications Quarterly.*** Summer 1982. p. 2.
87. ***How Children Fail,*** John C. Holt. New York: Dell, 1970.
88. ***Eupsychian Management,*** Abraham Maslow. Homewood, Ill.: Irwin and Dorsey, 1965; and ***Motivation and Personality,*** Abraham Maslow. New York: Harper and Row, 1970.
89. "A Study of Perceived Need...," Lyman Porter. ***Journal of Applied Psychology.*** 1961

(Vol. 45). pp. 1-10.

90. ***The New School Executive: a theory of administration.*** Thomas Sergiovanni and Fred Carver. New York: Dodd, Mead, 1973. pp. 58-59 ff.
91. ***Work and the Nature of Man,*** Frederick Herzberg. Cleveland: World, 1966; and ***The Managerial Choice: to be efficient and to be human,*** Frederick Herzberg. Homewood, Ill.: Dow Jones-Irwin, 1976.
92. ***The Organizational Society,*** rev. ed., Robert Presthus. New York: St. Martin's Press, 1978.
93. ***Modern Organization,*** Victor Thompson. New York: Knopf, 1961.
94. See ***The Human Side of Enterprise,*** Douglas MacGregor. New York: McGraw Hill, 1960; ***Management and Organizational Development,*** Chris Argyris. New York: McGraw Hill, 1971; "The Likert School Profile," Rensis Likert. (Paper presented at the American Educational Research National Convention: February 27, 1973) reprinted in part in ***Organizational Behavior in Education,*** Owens. pp. 54-55; ***Work and Motivation,*** Victor H. Vroom. New York: Wiley, 1964; ***The Managerial Grid,*** Robert R. Blake and Jane Srygley Mouton. Austin: Scientific Methods, 1964; and ***Management of Organizational Behavior,*** 3rd ed. Paul Hersey and Kenneth H. Blanchard. Englewood Cliffs: Prentice-Hall, 1977. pp. 161-67.
95. See, for example, the following: ***A Theory of Effective Leadership.*** Fred Fiedler. New York: McGraw Hill, 1967; ***Managerial Effectiveness.*** William J. Reddin. New York: McGraw Hill, 1970; and ***Leadership and Decision Making,*** Victor H. Vroom and Philip Yettin. Pittsburgh: University of Pittsburgh Press, 1973.
96. ***Organizational Behavior in Education,*** Owens. p. 139.
97. ***Professional Supervision for Professional Teachers,*** Thomas Sergiovanni, ed. Alexandria, Va.: ASCD, 1975; and ***Developmental Supervision,*** Carl Glickman, Alexandria, Va.: ASCD, 1975.
98. "ED Gets an Evangelist of the Right." In ***The American School Board Journal.*** May 1981 (Vol. 168, #5). pp. 18-19.
99. "The New Private Schools and Their Historic Purpose," Patricia M. Lines. In ***Phi Delta Kappan.*** January 1986 (Vol. 67, #5). p 374. In her article Lines, a consultant with the U.S. Dept. of Education, gives an excellent outline of the role of religious private education in America from the days of ***The New England Primer*** and ***McGuffey Readers*** to the present. A similar outline may be found in "Religion and Education," Norma Hernandez and Jorge A. Descamps. In ***Encyclopedia of Educational Research,*** 5th ed. pp. 1601-13.
100. All of this data may be found in "Private School Enrollment and Tuition Trends," Mary Frase Williams. In ***The Condition of Education,*** 1986. pp. 186-207. Williams lists her sources in the bibliography on p. 207.
101. "Useful Facts and Figures about American Public Education," John D. Marrs. National School Board Association. 1986.
102. See "The World as Seen by Students in Accelerated Christian Educational Schools," Dan B. Fleming and Thomas C. Hunt. In ***Phi Delta Kappan.*** March 1987 (Vol. 68, #9). pp. 518-23. See also "The Changing Demography of Private Schools: trends and implications," Bruce Cooper. In ***Education and Urban Society.*** August 1984. p. 432.
103. "Public and Non-Public Schools: finding ways to work together," Phyllis L. Blaunstein. In ***Phi Delta Kappan.*** January 1986. (Vol. 67, #5). pp. 368-72.
104. "Supreme Court Strikes Down Louisiana Creationism Act," Thomas J. Flygare. In ***Phi Delta Kappan.*** September 1987 (Vol. 69, #1). pp. 77-79.
105. "Supreme Court Strikes Down Louisiana Creationism Act," Flygare. pp. 77-79.
106. "Supreme Court Strikes Down Louisiana Creationism Act," Flygare. pp. 77-79.
107. "The Significance of the Decision in 'Scopes II'," Edward B. Jenkinson. In ***Phi Delta***

Kappan. February 1987 (Vol. 68, #6). pp. 445-51.

108. "The Significance of the Decision in 'Scopes II'," Jenkinson. p. 446.
109. "The Significance of the Decision in 'Scopes II'," Jenkinson. pp. 445-51.
110. "The Significance of the Decision in 'Scopes II'," Jenkinson. p. 448.
111. "The Significance of the Decision in 'Scopes II'," Jenkinson. p. 448.
112. "The Significance of the Decision in 'Scopes II'," Jenkinson. p. 449.
113. "The Significance of the Decision in 'Scopes II'," Jenkinson. pp. 448-49.
114. "Wrong in Every Respect," David Remes. In ***Education Week.*** December 3, 1986. p. 24.
115. ***Education Week.*** November 5, 1986. p. 19.
116. "Textbook Controversies: a 'disaster for public schools?'," Charles L. Glenn. In ***Phi Delta Kappan.*** February 1987 (Vol. 68, #6). pp. 451-55.
117. See ***Censorship: evidence of bias in current textbooks,*** Paul Vitz. Ann Arbor, Mich.: Servant Books, 1986.
118. "Creationists Have a Day in Court—and Lose." In ***The American School Board Journal.*** March 1982 (Vol. 169, #3). pp. 16, 18, and 22.
119. "Creationists Limit Dogmatic Darwinism." In ***The American School Board Journal.*** May 1981 (Vol. 168, #5). pp. 17-18.
120. See ***Religious Schooling in America,*** James C. Carper and Thomas C. Hunt, eds. Birmingham, Ala.: Religious Education Press, 1984. pp. 10 and 14; and "The World as Seen by Students in Accelerated Christian Education Schools," Dan B. Fleming and Thomas C. Hunt. In ***Phi Delta Kappan.*** March 1987 (Vol. 68, #9). pp. 518-23.
121. "The World as Seen by Students in Accelerated Christian Education Schools," Fleming and Hunt. pp. 520-21.
122. "The World as Seen by Students...," Fleming and Hunt. p. 522.
123. "ACE Responds," Ronald E. Johnson. In ***Phi Delta Kappan.*** March 1987 (Vol. 68, #9). pp. 520-21.
124. "Public and Non-public Schools: finding ways to work together," Blaunstein. p. 369.
125. See "Public and Non-public Schools...," Blaunstein. pp. 368-72.
126. "Equity Issues in Education," Patricia B. Campbell and Susan Klein. In ***Encyclopedia of Educational Research,*** 5th ed. p. 582.
127. "Equity Issues in Education," Campbell and Klein. p. 582.
128. ***The Persistent Problems of Education,*** Paul Woodring. Bloomington, Ind.: Phi Delta Kappa Educational Foundation, 1983. p. 74.
129. "Equity Issues in Education," Campbell and Klein. p. 582.
130. ***Persistent Problems of Education,*** Woodring. p. 73.
131. ***Persistent Problems of Education,*** Woodring. p. 73.
132. ***Persistent Problems of Education,*** Woodring. p. 73. See also ***Changing Population Patterns,*** John G. Keane. Washington, D.C.: U.S. Bureau of the Census, 1987. Keane, the Director of the U.S. Census Bureau, states that the estimated 1986 U.S. population was 239.4 million people and stood at about 237 million in 1984. (The actual 1980 census put it at 226.5 million.) In 1984 the black population was estimated at 28.6 million; the Hispanic, Asian, and remaining population groups at 9.4 million. Keane also notes that the birthrate of whites is declining while among Hispanics and blacks it is increasing. As a result the 84% white figure is apt to be somewhat lower in reality.
133. ***Persistent Problems of Education,*** Woodring. p. 73. In his discussion, Woodring quotes the U.S. Census as placing the U.S. black population at 11%, the U.S. Asian population at 1.5%, and the U.S. Hispanic population at 6.4%.
134. ***Persistent Problems of Education,*** Woodring. pp. 72-76.
135. ***Persistent Problems of Education,*** Woodring. p. 74.
136. ***Persistent Problems of Education,*** Woodring. pp. 74-75.

137. "Equal Opportunity and Federal Policy," Clarence Thomas. In ***Education Week.*** June 16, 1982. p. 24.
138. "Public Choice, Yes; Vouchers, No!" Mary Anne Raywid. In ***Phi Delta Kappan.*** June 1987 (Vol. 68, #10). pp. 763-64. See also ***Shades of Brown: new perspectives on school desegregation,*** Derrick Bell, ed. New York: Teachers College Press, 1980.
139. ***The Troubled Crusade,*** Ravitch. pp. 180-81.
140. ***Marva Collins' Way,*** Marva Collins and Civia Tamarkin. Los Angeles: Jeremy P. Tarcher, Inc., 1982. pp. 184-86.
141. "L.A. Decision: is busing dead?" In ***The American School Board Journal.*** May 1981 (Vol. 168, #5). p. 14. Five of the six Los Angeles School Board members opposed busing and applauded the ruling, although ACLU and NAACP lawyers planned appeals to the U.S. Supreme Court.
142. "L.A. Decision: is busing dead?" p. 16.
143. See "The 19th Annual Gallup Poll of the Public's Attitude toward the Public Schools." In ***Phi Delta Kappan.*** September 1987 (Vol. 69, #1). pp. 17-30; and "The 18th Annual Gallup Poll of the Public's Attitude toward the Public Schools." In ***Phi Delta Kappan.*** September 1986 (Vol. 68, #1). pp. 43-59.
144. "Supreme Court Confused by Reverse Discrimination," Thomas J. Flygare. In ***Phi Delta Kappan.*** September 1986 (Vol. 68, #1). pp. 77-78.
145. "Supreme Court Confused by Reverse Discrimination," Flygare. p. 77.
146. "Supreme Court Confused by Reverse Discrimination," Flygare. p. 78.
147. See "Watching a Changing Court: will the center hold." David G. Savage. In ***Phi Delta Kappan.*** October 1987 (Vol. 69, #2). pp. 135-37.
148. "Court Ducks RIF and Race Issue." In ***The American School Board Journal.*** December 1982 (Vol. 169, #12). p. 6. See also "A Break for White Males?" In ***The American School Board Journal.*** May 1981 (Vol. 168, #5). pp. 16-17.
149. See ***The Social Context of Instruction: group organization and group processes,*** Maureen Hallinan et al., eds. New York: Academic Press, 1984; ***An Examination of Literature...,*** Helene Hartman. Master thesis: C.W. Post Center of Long Island University, 1970; "Ability Grouping," Marsha Ream. In ***Research Summary.*** Vol. 1968-S3. Washington, D.C.: National Education Association, 1968; ***Class Organization for Instruction,*** J. Wayne Wrightstone. In "What Research Says to the Teacher." #13. Publication of the NEA first printed in 1957 and updated in a fifth printing in 1969; and ***Grouping in Education,*** Alfred Yates, ed. New York: Wiley, 1966.
150. See ***A Place Called School,*** John I. Goodlad. New York: McGraw Hill, 1984. pp. 156-57. Goodlad discusses the subject throughout his text. See index references under "tracking."
151. See "Results and Future Prospects of State Efforts To Increase Choice among Schools," Joe Nathan. In ***Phi Delta Kappan.*** June 1987 (Vol. 68, #10). pp. 746-52.
152. See "Central Park East: an alternative story," Deborah Meier. In ***Phi Delta Kappan.*** June 1987 (Vol. 68, #10). pp. 753-57; and "Inside a School of Choice," Robert L. Fizzell. In ***Phi Delta Kappan.*** June 1987 (Vol. 68, #10). pp. 758-60.
153. "Choice: the parents' perspective," Van D. Mueller. In ***Phi Delta Kappan.*** June 1987 (Vol. 68, #10). pp. 761-62.
154. "Public Choice, Yes; Vouchers, No!" Raywid, pp. 762-69. Raywid sees schools of choice as much better than the proposals for voucher systems which simply pay parents a certain dollar amount per child, then let them select any school, public or private. She cites the work of Frances Fowler who studied voucher systems in France. Fowler found that wealthy kids ended up going to private schools, while poorer kids could only afford the public ones. With alternative schools, choices might exist for poorer students as well. See "The French Experience with Public Aid to Private Schools,"

Frances C. Fowler. In ***Phi Delta Kappan.*** January 1987 (Vol. 68, #5). p. 358.

155. "The Female Educator at Midlife," Mary Lynn Crow. In ***Phi Delta Kappan.*** December 1985 (Vol. 67, #4). pp. 281-84; and "Women Administrators: profiles of success," Lillian C. Woo. In ***Phi Delta Kappan.*** December 1985 (Vol. 67, #4). pp. 285-88.
156. "Helping Women Prepare for Principalships," Christa Metzger. In ***Phi Delta Kappan.*** December 1985 (Vol. 67, #4). p. 292. See also ***Recent Trends in the Representation of Women and Minorities in School Administration and Problems in Documentation,*** Effie Jones and Xenia Montenago. Arlington, Va.: Office of Minority Affairs, AASA: July 1982. A 1979 NEA study found 67% of the teaching force to be women with only 14% holding principalships. Men were found to hold 80% of elementary, 97% of junior high, and 99% of senior high principalships. The 1982-83 rate for Canada was similar with women holding only 18% of the principalships. See "Women in the Principal's Chair in Canada," Karin L. Porat. In ***Phi Delta Kappan.*** December 1985 (Vol. 67, #4). pp. 297-301; and "Introduction: barriers to equity—women, educational leadership and social change," Sari Knopp Biklin. In ***Women and Educational Leadership,*** Sari Knopp Biklin and Marilyn B. Brannigan. Lexington, Mass.: D.C. Heath, 1980. p. 13.
157. "Women in the Principal's Chair in Canada," Porat. pp. 297-301.
158. "Conflict and the Female Principal," Lynn H. Erikson. In ***Phi Delta Kappan.*** December 1985 (Vol. 67, #4). pp. 288-91.
159. "Helping Women Prepare for Principalships," Christa Metzger. In ***Phi Delta Kappan.*** December 1985 (Vol. 67, #4). pp. 292-96.
160. ***Marva Collins' Way,*** Collins and Tamarkin. pp. 184-86.
161. "Why Chapter 1 Hasn't Made Much Difference," David W. Savage. In ***Phi Delta Kappan.*** April 1987 (Vol. 68, #8). pp. 581-84.
162. "Black Teachers: a drastically scarce resource," Patricia Albjerg Graham. In ***Phi Delta Kappan.*** April 1987 (Vol. 68, #8). pp. 598-605.

Chapter Five

Inside the School —
Inside the Classroom

Chapter Five

Inside the School — Inside the Classroom

FINALLY, WHEN ALL is said and done, education takes place within the school itself, in the classrooms and corridors, the playing fields and locker rooms. It is to these venues we turn in this last chapter, and specifically to the following topics: student behavior and the attitudes which shape it; grouping and grading; and curriculum.

These are complex and controversial topics. They involve things like selling cocaine in the bathroom, teaching or not teaching current events in the classroom, tracking or not tracking in the high school. They are topics which are highly interrelated and often emotionally charged. In discussing them, I promise not to sit on the educational fences so often occupied by people who write or speak about our schools. I also promise to try to substantiate my positions with research and an explanation of my thought processes. If that leads me into a philosophical tributary here and there, I beg your indulgence, but I think you will find the excursions useful.

Student behavior and the attitudes which shape it

At the beginning of this book I was insistent on pointing out that the child we are teaching today is radically different from the child who inhabited the schools of America during the first half of this century. It is now time to document that further, but even more, to assess why some of the most negative differences have arisen and to offer some ideas about what we can *really* do (please note the emphasis) to improve things.

David Clark of the University of Virginia tells us that "high school seniors in the U.S. do not express alarm over the schools they attend or the teachers with whom they work. By and large, they like school, give their schools high ratings, and view their teachers as both knowledgeable and competent."[1]

Unfortunately, the opinions of these seniors are not shared by many, many prominent educators, and indeed one of the things I believe has contributed to our present condition has been an over-reliance on the views of the children whose behavior is, in the aggregate, alarming, instead of on the views of the professionals in the field. Listen to what a few of them have to say about students and schools today.

From William Bennett, former U.S. Secretary of Education, we hear the following:

> Improvements in important test scores are at a "dead stall"...We're paying top dollar to educate our children, but we're sure not getting top return.[2]

From Mary McClellan of Indiana University we hear that "running in the halls, chewing gum, cutting in line and talking in class were the major problems for educational administrators in the 1940's. A list compiled by administrators today would include more alarming problems such as drug abuse, child abuse, and adolescent pregnancy."[3]

Thomas Lasley of the University of Dayton tells us that to many modern anthropologists "what students are learning in U.S. schools is a propensity to engage in self-centered and often hostile behavior,"[4] and no less than Perry London of the Graduate School of Education at Harvard University has this to say:

> For a variety of reasons, schools must lead the battle against the worst psycho-social epidemics that have ever plagued the children of our society.[5]

To what exactly are these educators referring? They are speaking of a tidal wave of social malaise so broad as to encompass almost every behavioral abnormality we can document, and to understand the passion behind their words, we will need to investigate the landscape of childhood more fully. We will do so in two phases: a look at what is actually going on with our kids, and a look at some of the causes of and factors contributing to today's youth-behavior. It is in this second phase that we will also view some suggestions aimed at turning the behavioral tide of our children.

What is going on? In assessing the way in which youngsters act today, we will start with a laundry list of items and then probe each in modest detail. The list includes: (a) a lack of academic achievement, (b) emotional problems relating to divorce, child abuse, and childhood suicide, (c) crime and the breakdown of discipline, (d) alcoholism (e) drug abuse, and (f) teenage pregnancy.

(a) Lack of academic achievement. It might seem that one could reasonably chart the academic progress of children by comparing the grades of one generation with the grades of another. Unfortunately, that is not so because over the years the criteria for giving grades have changed. As we shall discover later in this chapter, "grade inflation" has made it difficult if not impossible to assess current student achievement, especially as it might be compared to the achievement of students twenty, thirty, or forty years ago. However, we can look at norm-referenced, standardized tests such as national reading tests, Scholastic Aptitude Test (SAT) scores, American College Testing (ACT) program scores, and Graduate Record Exam (GRE) results to get some idea of what is going on. We can also look at surveys of student knowledge done by reputable institutions such as the National Foundation for the Humanities and at the school retention statistics compiled by the agencies of our government. Let us turn to some of this data.

The U.S. Department of Education provides us with a twenty-five year overview of SAT scores which shows that from a high of 980 in 1963 (478 verbal and 502 math), American children sank to a low of 890 in 1981 (424 verbal and 466 math), then rose slightly to 906 in 1985 (431 verbal and 475 math). We have already discussed these figures in a previous chapter. What is important here is that since 1985, despite record high spending amounting to $169.7 billion dollars for the 1987-88 school year, SAT scores have remained at the 906 mark.[6] Moreover, between 1986 and 1987, ACT scores have decreased slightly (from 18.8 in 1986 to 18.7 in 1987) as has the percentage of high school graduates (down from 71.7% to 71.5%).[7]

It is, in addition, something of a myth in the assessment of student achievement that a majority of our high school students goes on to college. Actually, less than one-third of our high school graduates attend a four-year college, as the following table from the U.S. Department of Education illustrates:

Patterns of Post-High School Activity
(Class of 1980)[8]

What students were doing	1 year after HS (% of Class of '80)		4 years after HS (% of Class of '80)	
In a 4-yr. college/not working	16.9	32.3	11.9	29.9
In a 4-yr. college/working	15.4		18.0	
In a 2-yr. college/not working	6.0	16.8	1.7	7.5
In a 2-yr. college/working	10.8		5.8	
In a vocational school/not working	1.8	3.8	0.6	1.7
In a vocational school/working	2.0		1.1	
Involved in other study	3.1		1.1	
Working full time/not in school	24.5	35.5	39.4	47.7
Working part time/not in school	11.0		8.3	
Other (unemployed; homemaker; military; looking for work; not in labor force due to prison, disability, etc.)	8.7		12.3	

It is especially important to the future of American education to note that the lack of four-year college students is exacerbating a dwindling supply of teachers. Compare the chart above with the one below in this regard.

New Teachers: Projected Demand and Supply
(1986 Projection)[9]

Year	Demand (medium range projection)	Supply projections: Low	Medium	High
1990	118,000 new teachers	102,000	139,000	181,000
1993	211,000 new teachers	95,000	133,000	190,000

Finally, it is important to remember that the average SAT scores of teachers remaining in education is 922, only 16 points above the current national high school average. Indeed, the Graduate Record Exam scores required for most entrants by the graduate schools offering advanced training to our teachers have dropped sharply since 1964. GRE's are given in three parts: a general quantitative test, a general verbal test, and a test in the subject area in which the student will specialize. The following table of GRE performance illustrates the sad reality of student achievement decline as it continues from high school to college and from college to graduate school.

GRE Performance 1964-1985 — assembled by category[10]

Much Better	Moderately Better	Same	Moderately Worse	Much Worse
Math	Physics	Gen. quant.	Psychology	Gen. verbal
		Biology	Education	Literature
		Economics	Music	History
		Engineering	Geology	Sociology
		Chemistry		Pol. Science

According to this data, in 14 of 16 areas, performance was the same or worse. In 9 of 16 areas (56%), it was worse—in many cases, including general verbal skills, much worse. It cannot be emphasized too strongly that it is the English, History, and Education major with much less command of verbal skills and in much less possession of the skills of his/her subject specialty who is now teaching and for the foreseeable future will be teaching our children. The legacy of poor student performance is a cyclical one. The mediocre high school graduate of yesterday has become the mediocre teacher of today, and the failures of today's high school generation will be visited upon us until the end of this century at least. If we don't see a significant rise in standards, the sad spiral of student achievement will persist well into the next century.

I wish I could tell you that these statistics are just numbers, but in the day-to-day push-pull of education, they become people. In my own personal observations, both as a clinician traveling the country and as a supervisor and teacher within my own state, I am appalled at what I see. In the area of the fine arts and English with which I am most conversant, I consider a school lucky if half its staff is competent. I know English teachers who cannot spell, music teachers who cannot read a score or play a piano, drama teachers who sicken the art of theatre, history teachers who don't know when the Thirty Years War was fought—or even more, why it is important to today's world. No, these are not just numbers. They represent people who shortchange children and a nation—*your* children, *your* nation.

But if test scores such as the ones above are not your cup of tea, let us turn to other indicators of student achievement. Here is what the U.S. Department of Education says about reading levels among our students:

> While the overwhelming majority of young adults adequately performs tasks at the lower levels [of the reading scale], sizable numbers appear unable to do well on tasks of even moderate complexity. Only a small percentage is estimated to perform at levels typified by the more challenging tasks.[11]

And reports on the acquisition of general knowledge by our students are equally alarming. According to the National Assessment of Educational Progress in Princeton, New Jersey, most U.S. eleventh graders are woefully ignorant of simple, critical data. For example, while 95% know that Edison invented the light bulb, only 30% know when Andrew Jackson was President. Barely 25% know when Lincoln was President; fewer than 25% knew the novels of Thomas Hardy; only 20% had read an Ibsen play; and well over two-thirds had never read Dickens' *A Tale of Two Cities* or Hemingway's *The Old Man and the Sea.*[12]

(b) Severe emotional disorder. "Our society has largely abandoned the norms that prevailed until the end of World War II," writes Harvard's Perry London.

> The era of holocaust, of nuclear weaponry, and of ubiquitous television has also brought ideological ambiguity and social disorganization—and offers fewer social resources for combatting them than we have ever known...This puts a new burden on the schools, which cannot be wholly borne by ordinary classrooms and curricula...The schools must become more important agents of character development, whose responsibility goes beyond such matters as dress, grooming, and manners. Their new role must include training for civility and civic virtue, as well as a measure of damage control for personal maladjustment.[13]

We will return to London's call for new curricula and "damage control" later in this chapter. For now it is important that we understand the statistical reality behind his words.

Consider just what has happened and will continue to happen to the American family. Divorce rates have doubled since 1960 and now affect one million children a year. Unmarried, cohabitating couples and single-parent families with children under fifteen years of age have increased dramatically in the last decade. Between 40% and 50% of all children born in the 1970's will live in a single-parent home for an average of six years before becoming independent. Currently, 40% of black children and 20% of all American children do live in single-parent homes. In 1984, more than 1.5 million children under the age of eighteen were living with *neither* parent. Economic need and changes in women's work patterns created over 8 million latchkey children by the mid-1980's.[14]

These are devastating figures by any reckoning, but, even more, they prognosticate an incalculable damage because ours is still a society whose laws and mores are structured around the sanctity of the family unit. It is impossible to underestimate the degree to which learning declines are created and fostered by declines in the stability of the American family. For most children, it is hard enough under normal circumstances to cope successfully with the demands of growing up and going to school. For children who come to the educational well already starved for emotion and bereft of psychological stability, it is a nearly impossible task.

Many of our adolescent young have told us in hideously graphic terms that indeed death is a preferable course of action than facing life in the world we have given them. Childhood suicide rates have risen 300% in the last quarter century (1962-1987). They now number 6,000 per year with about 500,000 unsuccessful attempts annually—and the experts feel that the true figures are even higher because many drug overdoses and deaths due to lethal automobile accidents involving intoxicated drivers cannot legally be classified as suicides.[15] Even without the real statistics, suicide is now the third most common cause of death for people between the ages of fifteen and twenty-four. The grizzly reality is that most suicides have a history of family breakdown, usually a history involving drugs, alcohol, continuous conflict, depression, and delinquency. Most of our childhood suicide attempts are female (by a ratio of 4:1) whose most prevalent method of attempt is drugs. Most of our "successful" childhood suicides are boys (by a ratio of 3:1), 67% of whom choose guns as the means of ending their lives. You have but to know one of these children to be shaken from the complacency of thinking that the current generation is like any other.

Finally, the severe emotional volatility of today's classroom population can be charted in statistics less final than suicide. Uncounted thousands—we are just now beginning to sift through the numerical reality—are abused physically, abused sexually, or ravaged by eating disorders ranging from obesity on the one end to anorexia on the other. 500,000 American children run away from home each year to be the street people, prostitutes, drug dealers, and unclaimed corpses of our land.[16]

(c) Crime and the breakdown of discipline. There are very few observers of the American educational scene who do not see in far too many schools serious, often criminal, breakdowns of student behavior. Even the high school seniors of David Clark's 1987 study who in most respects liked their schools cited crime and the lack of discipline as public education's number one problem.[17] In this instance, their perceptions and the perceptions of professional educators are in accord. Where once, as Robert Hampel notes, "discipline, propriety and control were the order of the day,"[18] students in the post-1945 era, particularly the post-1960 years, were allowed much wider behavioral latitudes. Sparked by philosophies such as those of A.S. Neill which state that because children learn when they want to rather than when they are told to, many schools turned to a student-regulated behavioral code which radically changed the environmental tone of education.

I do not mean to imply here that the "citadel high school" of the 1940's produced educational excellence while students in Neill's Summerhill school produced nothing. The philosophy of self-regulation which Neill and many of his bent espouse is a good deal more complex than just "doing one's own thing." In fact, misinterpretations of Neill led to a whole series of debates in which the roots and responsibilities of student behavior were thoroughly aired.[19] Nor do I want us to return to the often cruel strictness of the pre-1945 era. What I actually advocate will be the subject of a discussion some pages hence. I am at this juncture just making the point that school behavioral standards were allowed by the schools themselves to change from an environment where, for example, smoking was, in Hampel's words, "unthinkable,"[20] to one in which boards of education designated smoking areas as a student right. I am also saying that at the time of this writing, the end of the decade of the 1980's, many educators have concluded that student behavior has become so disruptive as to preclude educational excellence; that, as Thomas McDaniel writes, "discipline must improve if U.S. education is ever to rise above mediocrity."[21]

The reasons for McDaniel's statement become fairly obvious when one looks at the kind of thing that has become a regular occurrence in today's schools. Drug selling, theft, violence, and other law violations go on with alarming frequency, particularly in urban schools and schools with large populations. 35% of all junior and senior high schools, for example, report that students have been caught dealing drugs in school. 82% report thefts of items over $10 in value. 72% report student behavior which in other ways violates not merely school etiquette but statutory law (assault, rape, etc.). Principals report that the lack of an alternative environment for chronic misbehaviors constitutes a severe problem and presents a "serious limitation to the school's ability to maintain order."[22]

Study after study substantiates the principal's view that academic excellence is doomed if the environment of the school is not controlled. Willis Furtwengler's list of criteria for effective schools, for example, includes the following six items:

1. Frequency and seriousness of disciplinary problems
2. Scores on standardized tests
3. Overall school climate
4. Degree of student/staff involvement
5. Fiscal support
6. Quality of administrative leadership[23]

Lieberman and Miller cite a raft of research supporting what they list as five criteria for an effective school:

1. A sense of order
2. High staff expectations for student achievement
3. Strong leadership from the principal
4. Schoolwide control of decisions
5. Clear goals collectively agreed upon[24]

Even the federal government places the tone of the learning environment high on the five items found most often in academically successful schools:

1. Strong principal leadership
2. A safe, orderly environment
3. High teacher morale
4. Collegiality and cooperation among staff
5. Teacher control of classroom and school policy[25]

In fact, it is interesting to note the U.S. Department of Education's comparison of these five items between public schools (where behavioral problems are high and academic achievement is low) and Catholic schools (where behavior is more controlled and achievement somewhat higher).

Comparison of Effectiveness Criteria: public vs. Catholic schools[26]

Criteria	Catholic Schools % of positive rating	Public Schools % of positive rating
1. Principal leadership	59.1	49.8
2. Safe, orderly environment	72.9	39.4
3. High teacher morale	84.8	74.1
4. Staff cooperation	67.9	52.4
5. Teacher control	81.1	65.9

Note that the most significant discrepancy between the two systems occurs in the area of "a safe, orderly environment."

(d) Student alcoholism. Drinking and the associated vehicular slaughter through alcohol-related accidents have become epidemic among American school children. Despite organizations such as Mothers Against Drunk Driving (MADD) and Students Against Drunk Driving (SADD), the problem of adolescent and pre-adolescent alcohol consumption remains serious and ubiquitous. Nor is the problem one merely isolated to the 1980's. London reports that from the 1950's onward surveys of American children from twelve years old to twelfth graders have reported alcohol use in at least 25% of the population. A 1983 study indicated that 30% of the students in grades 10-12 are drunk six or more times a year. A 1981 study suggested that there are about 3 million problem drinkers (alcoholics or "borderline" alcoholics) in the 14-17 age group. A 1985 study done by the National Institute on Drug Abuse which included both tobacco and alcohol consumption in the data showed that between 1975 and 1985 adolescent alcohol use rose from 90% to 92% of high school seniors, an incredible statistic by any reckoning.[27]

(e) Student drug use. Alcohol and tobacco are but two items in the staggering array of substances abused by today's children. The list below, compiled by the 1985 National Institute of Drug Abuse, is somewhat more complete. The percentages of student use given are not for the faint of heart.

Percentages of High School Seniors
Reporting Drug Use[28]

Drug	% of Class of 1975	% of Class of 1985
Marijuana/Hashish	47	54
Inhalants (general)	NA	18
Amyl and Butyl Nitrates	NA	8
Hallucinogens (general)	NA	12
LSD	11	8
PCP	NA	5
Cocaine	9	17
Heroin	2	1
Other Opiates	9	10
Stimulants	NA	26
Sedatives (general)	18	12
Barbiturates	17	9
Methaqualone	8	7
Tranquilizers	17	12
Alcohol	90	92
Tobacco	74	69

The significant rise of cocaine and marijuana use in the last decade to epidemic proportions is particularly noteworthy since major efforts on the federal, state, and local levels have been undertaken during this time frame to reduce student drug involvement. In terms of comparing today's children with children in the pre-1945 and immediate post-war years, for most of the drugs listed above there are no figures available simply because the problem in earlier times had just not articulated itself to the point where statistics were felt necessary. That alone is a comparison of frightening proportions.

(f) Student pregnancy. The change in adolescent behavior from that of 1945 to that of the 1980's is documented nowhere more dramatically than in the area of adolescent sexual behavior and particularly in the realm of adolescent pregnancy. In 1947 over 57% of the pregnancies of women in the 15-19 year-old category were post-marital conceptions. By 1982 the figures had exactly reversed themselves; 57% of the pregnancies were out-of-wedlock. Compare this to the 25-29 year-old category where the figures remain virtually the same from 1947 to 1982 (i.e., 91-93% of pregnancies are post-marital in both eras). The conclusion is that teens are engaging in adult sexual behavior with far more frequency, at far earlier ages, and with a precipitous disregard for the consequences.

In 1960, girls under 16 bore 25,000 babies. By 1977, it was 42,000 with over 250,000 babies born to women under 20 years of age. Since 1978, 10% of *all* teenage girls become pregnant *annually*.[29] Mary McClellan tells us that 40% of the female high school dropout problem is due to pregnancy and that the cost to society for keeping a 15-year-old mother and child is $18,130 annually. She goes on to quote a 1986 Louis Harris poll which found that the greater the sexual activity of the child, the lower the child's academic achievement.[30]

Academic slippage is but one of many results of the sexual explosion of our young. Another, even more critical, is the replacement of "home values" for "street values." In 1960, teens stated that their parents were their chief source of information about sex. In 1980, the chief source was "peer information."[31] Can it be very surprising, then, that one-fifth of all babies born in cities larger than 100,000 are born to teenage mothers, or that there are now 1 million teen pregnancies a year (of which 400,000 are aborted, 470,000 are carried to term, and 13,000 end in miscarriage).[32]

U.S. girls under 15 are fifteen times more likely to give birth than their peers in any other Western nation, and over 50% of American public school administrators believe the problem to be so severe that schools should not only require sex counselling but should also dispense birth control devices.[33] U.S. teen pregnancy, in fact, is twice that of England, France, and Canada; three times that of Sweden; and seven times that of the Netherlands. Four of every ten U.S. women become pregnant before the age of twenty with adolescent childbirth costing the nation over $16 billion a year from 1985 on—and it might be wise to note that $16 billion was the entire 1986 federal allotment for education. Just to finish off the picture, of the 1 million teenage births each year, 80% are reported as "unintended;" and it is of interest to note that rates of sexual activity have increased much faster among whites than minorities so that "the increase in births to unmarried teens is entirely attributable to whites."[34]

Contributing factors of youth behavior and recommended courses of action. Our children behave as they do because they reflect the social, economic, physical, and psychological contexts in which they live. If we wish to understand and change their behavior, we must therefore be willing to analyze and, if need be, modify the world in which we ask them to grow. In the pages below we will do that by focusing on five areas:

(a) Conflicts between biological and social evolution
(b) Failures of the present generation
(c) Poverty and racism
(d) The general tone of social policy
(e) The general tone of school policy

(a) Conflicts between biological and social evolution. For all intents and purposes, the babies being born today are not biologically radically different from babies which were born one thousand, five thousand, even ten thousand years ago. Better nutrition and health care have made us somewhat bigger and stronger; surely our life expectancy has increased; and as we shall discover we reach sexual maturity a bit faster. But in most fundamental respects we are far more like our ancestors than different from them. That is true of biology. It is not true of society. In our social evolution, we would be unrecognizable to a cliff dweller, a cave dweller, or a nomadic plainsman of ten thousand years ago. Our cities, our transportation, our schools, our every social manner would be as foreign to him as a society from outer space might seem to us.

Why do I mention this? What has it to do with our schools? I bring it to your attention to make the point that today's young people are caught in a monumental conflict between what nature imposes upon them on the one hand and what society imposes on the other. Specifically, their biology makes them capable of adult behavior both sexually and psychologically from the age of about thirteen onward. Socially speaking, however, they are minors until age eighteen. In some cases, they do not have the full rights of peerage until age twenty-one. For those who go to college and graduate school, true independence may not arrive until the mid-twenties. The years between the onset of biological maturity and both legal and financial independence are doomed by the circumstances of modern life to create tremendous stresses within our children—stresses in which the mandates of nature tug them sometimes not so gently into adulthood, while the demands of school and the legal constraints of society keep them in the status of dependents.

This conflict did not exist ten or twenty thousand years ago when the average lifespan was not seventy but thirty. For a culture whose oldest people rarely saw a fourth decade, the onset of puberty at thirteen or fourteen meant that teenagers had to become parents. If they waited until their twenties or thirties to bear children, they would die before those children could fend for themselves. Such delays in reproduction would have meant the extinction of the species—the parents dead by the natural process of events, their children dead by neglect. In primeval times, then, biology and society were in a synchronization which promoted survival.

Over the centuries, the biology remained more or less constant while the society became incomprehensibly more complex, pushing as it did so the age of independence further and further from the onset of physical maturation. As the gap between the two widened, children found themselves in greater and greater degrees of tension and conflict. Rebellions over the restrictions imposed upon them have in part led to the sexual excesses, substance abuses, and behavioral breakdowns we have witnessed in the last fifty years.

There is, in this regard, a fascination and very important article by Chamberlain and Girona of Bowling Green University which indicates that modern physiology is exacerbating the push-pull between biology and society. "In the period from 1870 to 1930," they write, "the mean age of the onset of menstruation fell from 16.5 years of age to 14.5, a decrease of two years over a sixty-year span. In the last twenty years, however, it has dropped the same amount, from 13.5 years in 1950 to a predicted mean for 1970 of 11.5."[35] Better health care in the twentieth century has thus not only increased the life span of the American child but has also led to an earlier age of sexual maturity. There can be little doubt that this has only made the gap between physical maturation and social maturation wider and thus made growing up more difficult.

There is a second factor which in modern America has exacerbated the conflicts between biological and sociological maturity, and it is the denial or rushing of childhood itself. The work of Postman, Suransky, and Elkind seems to demonstrate fairly conclusively that in the post-World War II era, many of the innocent and carefree qualities of childhood have been seriously eroded.[36] We ask our children to develop academic precocity at younger and younger ages; we often push them to accept responsibilities far beyond their capability; we even at times encourage them to graduate high school early, as if their well-being was tied to attending college before their peers. For many, such things rob children of the spontaneity and unfettered play upon which the emotional stability of childhood often rests. To quote Elkind, "The real purpose of education—prompting curiosity, creativity, and the ability to combine the skills of thought—is taking a back seat to doing well on highly specific achievement tests."[37]

To rob children of childhood in a society in which there are legal, moral, and psychological constraints on expressions of adult behavior only adds insult to injury where the conflict between biological and social development is concerned. It says to the child, "Eschew the abandonment of your early years in pursuit of more adult aims, but do not expect to be given the rights of an adult in exchange for your compliance." Such child-rearing policies only make the stresses of being young greater because they rob youngsters (whose path to adulthood is already blocked by sociological sanction) of an escape to the safety of childhood. The boy and girl in high school, then, whose bodies and spirits are quite capable of sexual intercourse, for example, must not only obey the strictures of home and society to avoid physical consummation, but must also not exhibit the immaturity of childhood innocence. They are trapped in a paradox whose dimensions all too often lead to the behavior described earlier in this chapter.

What do we do about this dilemma? There is not much we can do. The dilemma is the price we exact upon ourselves for progress—medical progress, economic progress, social progress. The same teenager who fights with Mom and Dad over Saturday's curfew also covets the VCR he got for Christmas. That VCR would not have been possible in the forest primeval. It took years of schooling to produce, and in order to eliminate the tension between biological and social mandates, we would also have to eliminate the VCR and restructure the society which produced it. Perhaps the best thing to do with the conflict between biology and society is simply to recognize it and to be sympathetic to the children who must endure it. I have found in my own dealings with students that the most strict behavioral standards become more palatable when I discuss the biological/sociological paradox which makes them necessary. Simply acknowledging the problem and allowing it to be treated seriously and openly seems to alleviate its sharpness.

(b) Failures of the parent generation. As most behavior is learned, the role models we set before our children perforce contribute to the behavior which our children adopt. Not strictly of its own accord, but in concert with all the factors we are investigating here, it is fair to say that to one extent or another children do things because they are emulating the behavior of their parents, matinee idols, sports heroes or political leaders.

The parents of the 1980's who cut their teeth on the values of the 1960's have presented a significantly altered home environment to today's child. A divorce rate of 49%, the decision to bear children out of wedlock or to raise them in single-parent families, and an economy which forces both mother and father to work have left millions of our children with less supervision and less emotional stability than most previous generations. Add to this the fact that post-1960 values led many parents to use and abuse drugs, and it is not difficult to see why today's students experience so many problems.

The reality is that the American family has been changed, and it is a reality with which we had better come to grips. Professors Heath and McLaughlin of Stanford University are careful to point out that in 1986 only 7% of American families fell into the mold we define as "traditional," that is, a family in which the father works, the mother keeps house, and the children are well-fed and adequately clothed. Indeed, because the American family has been so radically transformed, Heath and McLaughlin caution against relying too heavily on parent-involvement programs to improve student performance in school. They find many of today's educational reform initiatives inadequate to meet the child resource policies demanded by the sociological changes occurring in family life. They write that the current "parents as partners" craze "will, we fear, be no more successful in equipping the nation's children for the future than were those that came before."[38]

Whereas the push-pull between biology and society is a conflict for which there are no ready remedies, there are indeed things we can do to address the problems of a failed parent generation. They fall into two areas: providing services for our current crop of "victims," and providing proper education so that the next generation is better prepared for the serious business of child-rearing.

Family counselling; individual psychological counselling; drug and alcohol abuse intervention programs; and an immediate, dramatic increase in student support services are a must for America. If you can make your voice heard on these scores, do it, and don't be sidetracked by the nay-sayers who tell you that there is no money in your community budget. That is simply not an acceptable excuse any longer. The money is there. Our GNP was $4 trillion, remember, and billions upon billions of it went for defense cost overruns, welfare cheats, cocaine, and other absolutely non-productive expenditures. (We've already analyzed the data.) We can, if we have the will, restructure our tax codes and our spending priorities to provide what we need. There really are no acceptable alternatives.

Whatever programs we can institute to help the "damage control" of the present, however, our real hope is to prevent the recurrence of a failed parent generation in the future. That will necessitate policies to foster attitudes both social and personal which are different from present attitudes.

From a personal point of view, it is time to ask our children to stop thinking of themselves so much and to consider the repercussions of their actions on others—particularly on offspring. For example, for every pregnant mother who gives up tobacco and drink, there is one less unhealthy fetus and perhaps one less troubled student down the road. For every father who gives up smoking a joint in favor of eating a carrot, there is one more positive role model for a future pupil. But even more, our next crop of parents must learn to prepare financially for their children. We are not going to serve our progeny well if we have them when we cannot afford them. The selfish mother and father who crave a child only to turn it over to a baby sitter in order to go out and make a buck (which probably isn't even big enough to pay the child's pediatrician bills, let alone provide for its college education) are only creating yet another twenty years of latchkey neglect. The teenager who hasn't got sense enough to stay away from intercourse or sense enough to use birth control if sex is a permanent part of the social landscape is only condemning America to twenty more years of needless social welfare.

From a social point of view, we have got to start counselling tomorrow's parents today. We have to adopt policies which prevent latchkey neglect and unwanted adolescent pregnancy. That will entail curricular programs to introduce youngsters to facts about sex and family planning long before they are captured by the precocity of contemporary student behavior. We will look at such curricula later in this chapter. On another social front, we will need to provide the day-care centers and early childhood nurseries which will allow mothers who must work the ability to leave their children in a safe, nurturing environment. How can we expect to get women off the welfare roles if we do not free them from their children long enough to learn skills or hold down jobs? To do this we are going to have to provide schools and industry with the capital to build and staff centers for early childhood care. And again, saying there is no money for such things not only obfuscates the problem, it also promotes a lie. We have the money in our societal coffers. We but need the will to use it for these purposes.

Finally, we ought to ask more of our non-parental role models. Every athlete who takes drugs or who puts a higher salary ahead of the welfare of the team, every political figure who sells favors to a special interest group, every matinee idol who tries to steal a headline by flaunting a low neckline or an illicit romance diminishes the entire social fabric from which young children develop their value system. When we let the million dollar ballplayer become a prima donna or allow the corrupt politician to get off with a slap on the wrist or support the artistic products of show business personalities who trade on prurience or impropriety for a living, we only insure that our children will for yet another generation absorb mores which lead to aberrant behavior. Think about that when you buy your next baseball ticket or elect your next judge or see your next movie.

(c) Poverty and racism. Harold Hodgkinson, Senior Fellow for the American Council on Education, tells us some very important things about the present and future population of America. First, it is aging rapidly. People over 65 now number

24 million. The fastest growing age category is the over-85 population. In 1983, for the first time in America's history, there were more people over age 65 than teenagers. The repercussions of such trends are enormous. To name just one, the resources needed for social programs such as education, social security, and help for the poor will become sorely taxed. As Hodgkinson points out, we have already gone from 17 workers for each retiree to 3.4 workers, and as our post-1945 baby-boomers reach retirement age around the year 2000, the ratio will decline even further.[39]

But there is much more to the demographic picture than age. Not only is America getting older, it is also becoming less white. It takes each woman having 2.1 babies to keep the population stable (2 babies to replace parents and .1 to account for infant mortality). Today Mexican-American women are having 2.9 babies; blacks, 2.4; Puerto Ricans, 2.1; and whites, only 1.7. 73% of the increase in children between the ages of 1 and 6 are occurring in only five states—Texas, California, Florida, North Carolina, and Arizona—all states with large minority populations.[40] The U.S. Department of Education adds to this picture. High school completion rates when broken down by race show that currently, and for the past ten years, minorities have done very much worse than whites. The Department's figures are distilled below:

High School Completion by Race: 1974-1985[41]
(Age group = 18-19 year-olds. Figures are % of age group.)

Year	White	Black	Hispanic	Total Population
1974	76.2	55.8	48.9	73.4
1980	76.1	59.3	46.1	73.7
1985	76.7	62.7	49.8	74.6

These statistics are corroborated by Hodgkinson who gives us the ten best and ten worst states in terms of high school retention. His tables are given below, and in viewing them it is important to realize that minorities—those who have traditionally been the victims of poverty and racism in far greater proportion than whites—are much higher percentages of the population in the states with the worst retention figures.[42]

High School Retention Rates
Top Ten

	State	Percent
1.	Minnesota	86.0
2.	North Dakota	84.9
3.	Iowa	84.8
4.	South Dakota	82.8
5.	Wisconsin	82.3
6.	Nebraska	81.3
7.	Montana	80.9
8.	Kansas	80.5
9.	Utah	80.2
10.	Wyoming	80.0

Worst Ten

	State	Percent
41.	California	68.0
42.	Kentucky	67.3
43.	Alabama	67.1
44.	North Carolina	67.1
45.	Tennessee	66.7
46.	New York	65.9
47.	Georgia	64.3
48.	Florida	63.7
49.	Louisiana	63.4
50.	Mississippi	61.8

Efforts to deal with the poverty and racism behind the data for minority student outcomes have largely been unsuccessful. That is because giving a special educational program to a black or Hispanic child may for the moment impact favorably on the child, but it in no way tackles the economic and social disorders which lie behind the surface. It is a band-aid on a cancer, and we are only kidding ourselves by continuing to hope it will cure our pedagogical or sociological diseases. Indeed, if one wishes to take a really cynical view, the band-aids are applied by very clever people who seek to give the illusion of dealing with the problems of poverty and racism, but who are really using the band-aids to grow rich on the one hand and *keep* minorities in servitude on the other. For example, it can be eloquently argued that busing to achieve racial balance, while giving the surface appearance of dealing with America's racism, did little to improve race relations or minority educational achievement. What it did do was make the bus and oil companies a little richer and delay the onset of really meaningful educational action.

What might be argued in the case of busing is, in fact, argued in the case of the Title I/Chapter 1 programs aimed at improving the education of minorities and breaking the cycle of poverty and racism which trap them. The argument is made by, among others, Robert Slavin of Johns Hopkins University. Slavin reports that in 1987 3.9 billion dollars were spent on such programs and that most of them "are simply not adequate for the job they're supposed to do."[43] The problem is not the amount being spent but rather the programs themselves. The research done by Slavin at Johns Hopkins indicates that student gains from present programs don't last; that some of the programs, like those which involve classroom pullouts, are actually counterproductive; and that the most effective programs were ones which tended *not* to follow Chapter 1 guidelines or even use 100% of Chapter 1 funding. Again, the programs are at best misguided attempts to deal with the problem. At worst they are clever ways to siphon billions of dollars into the hands of people whose chief motivations may be far from ending the poverty and racism which plague America's minorities and lie behind so much of their aberrant student behavior.

Alright then. If not Chapter 1, if not affirmative action, if not open enrollment, if not forced busing, then what? What can we *really* do to attack America's poverty and the racism which perpetuates it, especially in minority populations? Here are a few suggestions.

(1) Workfare. Maintaining a person capable of work on the welfare roles is the cruelest hoax we can play. While it provides an income, it also insures that the recipient will never become independent, self-productive, or wealthier than a subsistence-class citizen. Therefore, in order to collect welfare, able-bodied recipients should be required to attend programs which assess their abilities and train them in marketable skills.

(2) Child-care centers. To implement a workfare program, society will have to insure that welfare recipients with dependent children have places to leave those children during job training classes and then during the hours when actual employment will occur. Child-care centers run out of schools, businesses, hospitals, churches, or private agencies are thus a necessity for present American culture. It would also be of enormous benefit if such centers began the day with a parent-counselling session, a session in which the self-esteem of welfare mothers might be raised so that they see themselves as more than brood sows whose sole function in life is to be impregnated for the purpose of bringing more babies into poverty. The encouragement of contraception, of family planning, of avoiding promiscuity, and of positive self-development cannot be ignored if we wish to change the human psychology which lies beneath the surface of poverty. The poor who breed children for whom they cannot provide must begin to take responsibility for perpetuating their own misery and the misery of successive generations. To do this they need the kind of education and birth control devices an enlightened child-care center could provide.

(3) Meaningful work. Training for jobs is, of course, absolutely meaningless without the jobs themselves. To eliminate welfare poverty, then, America must be willing to provide employment to unemployed, able-bodied people once they are trained. While the greatest source of employment is the private sector, the economic and psychological variables within the private sector to create jobs are so unpredictable as to be virtually unreliable in any *real* attempt to put people to work. The theory of President Reagan's economics that large monetary gains for corporations and wealthy individuals would fuel the creation of new jobs which would "trickle down" to the poor has been painfully disproven. A more realistic assessment of economic theory comes from psychologists such as Karen Horney who pointed out more than a half century ago that fiscal policy is driven more by factors like greed and the desire to acquire power. Given vastly larger profits, the tendency in the era of "Reaganomics" has been for the wealthy to pocket them rather than rechannel them for the eradication of poverty.[44] In any event, such profits were not, in fact, devoted toward the elimination of our lower-class poverty, and it is safe to assume that at this juncture in America's social development, private industry is going to need a push from the public sector.

Toward that end, there are dozens of meaningful public works projects which are crying to be done across the length and breadth of the nation. These are projects which—though their costs would be enormous—would, like the TVA program of F.D.R.'s years, pay the nation back many times over if successfully completed. Moreover, they are projects which would fuse the efforts of public and private sectors. And once again, please don't say the money for them is not there. It *is* there, and in this case would even include a good deal of welfare money which currently gives very little back by way of productivity or tax income. Here are but three of many projects which could employ America's underclasses for decades with work that would give the workers a real sense of pride in the strengthening of the nation. First, a national watershed and reservoir system might be built to channel flood run-off from chronic flood rivers to holding areas and pumping stations which could then send it to areas of drought. Think of how much misery that might save both flood and drought victims and how much it might mean to the stability of food prices. Second, we might refurbish our transport infrastructures so that our roads, tunnels, and bridges are once again safe and strong. Third, we could rebuild our ghettos with ghetto labor, either granting ghetto residents outright ownership of that which they renovated or making them cooperative owners with existing slumlords. We did as much or more for settlers by giving away land to encourage the building of our Western frontiers. Such projects could rebuild our urban frontiers and give to current slum dwellers a direct and personal stake in the reclamation of their neighborhoods.

(4) Tough anti-discrimination enforcement. Finally, to the extent discrimination is practiced in denying jobs and/or housing to qualified minorities, it is time American courts exacted tough penalties, penalties which would *mandate* significant financial restitution to the aggrieved *and* prison terms for the guilty. Far more than busing, true integration would be brought about if minorities who could afford decent housing were sure they could purchase it regardless of the racial characteristics of the community in which it existed. I remember as a youngster from Brooklyn worshipping the ground upon which Jackie Robinson walked. I also remember that when he tried to buy a house in the district in which I went to high school, the white residents of the road on which that house stood petitioned him to stay out. He bought instead in the next town over, and although I was a sorely disappointed kid, I cannot even imagine what Robinson and his family felt. But even worse, none of the residents who signed the petition ever paid a dollar's worth of damages or served so much as a minute's worth of jail time. That kind of nonsense has to be stopped if we want to *really* eliminate the racism which lies at the root of our troubled schools.

(d) The general tone of social policy. In a host of ways, the social policies of America and the laws which support them contribute to and even encourage our children toward anti-social behavior. In this section of our discussion we will look at four examples: (1) the concept of peerage in contemporary America, (2) the hidden hypocrisy of our national holidays, (3) our way of dealing with drug-and alcohol-related offenses, and (4) our way of dealing with youth vandalism.

(1) Peerage. By peerage we mean the right to equal treatment—equal treatment under the law and in the normal flow of daily events. Just what constitutes peerage in America today is difficult to say because the nation is a hodgepodge of contradictions. For example, on the one hand, we don't accord peerage to children designated as "minors." They can't drive or vote or hold office. The can't marry, sign contracts, drink alcohol or engage in a host of other activities we reserve (legally, psychologically, and morally) for "adults." On the other, we apply the rights of peerage in absolutely (and, to me, incomprehensibly) inconsistent ways. We say that one can vote at eighteen but not drink until twenty-one, and for neither do we establish any criteria other than age by which we might insure socially constructive rather than destructive behavior—though we do establish such criteria for driving a car. In the case of driving we have not only age requirements but physical eyesight requirements, written examination requirements, and driving test requirements. There are no similar requirements, however, for rights like voting, and indeed some laws (such as reading tests to insure voter competence) have been struck down as discriminatory and unconstitutional.

By making the application of peerage inconsistent, we weaken and cloud its meaning. By granting peerage to citizens on the basis of age alone, we have destroyed the notion that our young people owe anything to the American democracy. I cannot think of two more lunatic policies, and I am convinced that we will not find a way out of our present quagmire until we come to our senses on this issue.

Peerage in the American democracy should not be granted as a right by age. It should be a privilege which is earned, and the opportunity to earn it should be accorded each citizen in equal measure for as long as a citizen needs it. To understand what I mean, let me offer a definition of peerage and state what I believe should be required to obtain it.

Peerage in a true democracy should be the right to do whatever one wishes to do as long as his or her actions do not inhibit another citizen from enjoying the same right. In this regard several things should be understood. First, any "inhibiting consequence" must derive from an act itself, not an interpretation of the act by another person. For example, if a sculptor wishes to sculpt a statue of a nude figure, he or she would retain that right free from the restraint of a censor who might find the naked human form offensive. Moreover, a museum would retain the right to display the work since neither its creation nor display would *force* anyone to view it. Second, the standard of peerage would not extend to children, the infirm, or other citizens judged by the best legal, medical, and social evidence to be incapable of acting in their own self-interest or the interest of the society. (Just exactly when peerage would accrue to a citizen will be discussed below.) Finally, citizens acting in violation of the standard of peerage would be restrained from those actions and, to whatever extent the laws provide, would forfeit their right to participate further in the democracy.

The application of this standard of peerage to the various aspects of society is fraught with ramifications far too numerous for this text. How such a standard might apply to the doctrine of free speech, or euthanasia, or electoral campaign financing, or the right of a government to establish and maintain an army is a subject for a much larger treatise on the ethics of a democracy. While such a treatise may be part of a future text, this one must confine itself to the application of a peerage standard to education and the behavior of today's youth. Let us then return to that area and confront the question raised earlier, namely, "when shall a citizen be accorded the right of peerage?"

As I stated above, I do not believe that peerage is a condition which should be bestowed upon a citizen simply because he or she has reached an arbitrary (and, for America today) inconsistently applied age. I say this because age in and of itself—as in the case of a driver's license—is no accurate judge of personal competence. For exactly the same reason we require a certain amount of public education for our children (i.e., the well-being of the democracy), we should require *both* a fixed age (I suggest 16, 17, or 18) *and* graduation from high school for the privileges of peerage (exclusive of the right to work). This policy would insure the society not only that an individual has met a certain standard of physical maturity but also that he/she has met a standard of emotional, psychological, and intellectual maturity at least sufficient to complete a basic education.

If we *really* want our dropout problem, our truancy problem, our student achievement problem to turn around, we ought to say to our children, "Kids, unless you graduate high school, except for the right to work, you don't drink or drive or vote or marry or sign contracts or hold public office." I believe that a basic high school education is what we *owe* the democracy in exchange for its civil blessings.

Because I can hear some objections already howling across the corners of my desk as I write this, let me proceed by quickly noting some important additions to my comments. The first is that provisions for alternate educational programs be made for citizens who, because of economic hardship, or mental, emotional and physical handicaps, cannot fulfill normal requirements. The second is that citizens who are denied peerage (because due process has judged them according to the best available evidence incapable of acting in their own interest) be cared for by kin and/or state in a manner providing for comfort and dignity. The third is that in gray areas (such as the Tenth Amendment to the Constitution with its vague specification of powers, or the rural youngster whose economic survival depends upon driving a tractor before earning a high school diploma) judgments be weighted in favor of the individual's freedom to act rather than society's right to restrict that freedom.

Barring these addenda, however, what I recommend here would get a whole lot of people who otherwise pooh-pooh their responsibility toward learning to pay their dues to society for the privilege of being treated as adults. And if the present laws hold that a thing like insuring reading skills as a requirement to vote is unconstitutional, all I can say is that the laws are wrong. They can be wrong, you know. Remember that at one time our courts told us that Dred Scott was property and that alcohol was illegal. Putting it in the law statutes doesn't make it right. It is precisely because our statutes can be altered by amendment that we can rectify our errors. And as far as I am concerned it is a monumental error to say to a child that the rights of peerage are to be obtained by nothing more than the passage of eighteen or twenty-one years. In a democracy, where social survival is predicated upon the competence of the electorate, more must be required. For me, that "more" consists of mastering a high school education, and for that reason it is of paramount importance that we insure an equal, ever-present opportunity for every citizen to secure an education and that we set the curricular requirements for that education with the utmost care (a topic to which we shall return later in the chapter).

(2) The hypocrisy of national holidays. It may seem a trivial point beside issues such as peerage in a free society, but the celebration of many of our national holidays has become a hypocrisy which sets exactly the wrong social tone and encourages exactly the wrong social behavior. What do we do on Presidents' Day or the Fourth of July or Veterans' Day to honor the memory of the people who gave so much toward the survival of our land? We take off from school, take off from work, drink, party, blow up a few fireworks. Hardly a fitting tribute to the likes of

Lincoln or Washington or the thousands upon thousands of common folk by whose blood we forged the survival of the nation. I believe this hypocrisy should end. And, mind you, I'm all in favor of vacations and holidays. But let's call them "Fun Day" or "National Holiday #1," and not dishonor our past or mislead our future generations with the labels we use now. In fact, the social tone I would like to see would involve giving *more*, not less, on a day a national significance. Why not in memory of Lincoln *add* an hour of donated labor to every job? After all, Lincoln never cut his workday short for us. Why not in honor of Martin Luther King, Jr. lay an *additional* brick, plant an *additional* row, teach an *additional* class—not for the personal gain of it, but to make the nation stronger and to promote the feeling of national conscience he wished for us? Then, we might celebrate our holidays without hypocrisy, without dishonoring the accomplishments of our heroes by using them as an excuse to avoid work or cheapen the real meaning of social responsibility.

(3) Alcohol and drug policies. A third example of how we set the wrong social tone lies in the way we deal with our alcohol and drug abuse problems. While stopping the flow of drugs into our country or setting minimal age requirements for the consumption of alcohol are necessary, neither addresses the issue of demand. The plain fact is that millions of our citizens *want* substances they can abuse, and as long as there is a demand which can lead to a profit, there will be people who arrange for a supply. "Just saying no" to this situation is an assininely stupid approach to the problem. It insults the intelligence of anyone who knows anything about the psychology of addiction or the role which crime and political corruption play in that psychology. If we *really* wish to attack the problem, here are some things to try.

For chronic drug users: mandated treatment center programs which would include both medical care and psychological counselling. For drug dealers: mandated jail terms with no plea-bargaining and no possibility of parole. My recommendation is a twenty-year sentence. I would think that any sentence less than five years would be laughable. For a reduction in the frequency of crime, the power of the underworld, and the degree of political corruption: the dispensing of drugs through hospitals under medical supervision and governmental control. For those caught driving while intoxicated: one year in jail and a permanent loss of the right to drive in any state. For every citizen: a drug/alcohol test along with the other requirements for a driver's license. For anyone involved in an accident while under the influence of drugs or alcohol: a permanent loss of license and a mandated jail term whose length would depend on the degree of damage and injury. I would recommend a minimum of five years with no parole, twenty years for serious injury, and life imprisonment for permanent injury or death.

These measures would necessitate a large increase in spending for our legal system, from officers to judges, to courts, to prisons. They would also necessitate increases in medical, social, and educational programs. To which I reply, so be it. If we have one out of every five of our kids using cocaine today, we had better start spending the money because if we don't, by the middle of the next century there may be nothing significant left of our kinds.

Before leaving this topic, since it involves our penal system and penal values, it might be wise to address what ought to be done in all those new jails we build so that the children we may place within them do not come out worse than they were before.

Today our prisons often involve very little by way of rehabilitation and even less by way of having criminals restore to society some measure of what they have taken. Both factors represent yet another example of social failure for America. The first thing we ought to do to remedy the situation is to require that in exchange for their offenses criminals give a percentage of their earnings to their victims upon their release from prison. The second is that we separate hardened criminals from first offenders and expand the opportunity for all inmates to develop educationally. Finally, we ought to realize that criminals who commit either capital crimes or crimes involving deliberate bodily harm to others do not *ever* belong in society again.

I am not in favor of capital punishment for several reasons: it precludes the study of criminals, it precludes the possibility of individual redemption, it is often inequitably applied against the poor or less influential, and it allows no redress in the event of an error. I am therefore an advocate of life imprisonment with no parole for *all* criminals convicted of capital crimes or crimes involving the deliberate attempt to harm others. Parole is out of the question for me because our knowledge of criminal psychology and our current record of predicting the recurrence of criminal behavior is simply too poor to risk the well-being of innocent people. All this having been said, however, I must add that a life sentence in our present system is unproductive both to society and to the prisoner. It condemns most inmates to a life of loneliness or forced homosexuality, and in such circumstances no human being could retrieve much of his soul or return much to society. What I advocate, then, are penal colonies where eventually inmates might date and marry, though they would in such an event have to agree to sterilization so that innocent children would not suffer in a confined environment. In exchange for a more or less normal life, the inmate would have to agree to learn a skill which would lead to work that would benefit the community harmed by his or her criminal behavior. For example, the driver in a get-away car used to rob a bank in which a guard had been killed might be required in exchange for the privileges of a penal colony to learn how to repair and service all kinds of cars. Automobiles in need of repair by the government or schools or hospitals or the poor might then be shipped to the penal colony repair shop to be fixed and returned at no cost to the owner.

Whatever the ins and outs of an actual system might be, the point is that to set a meaningful social tone for our children, our laws ought to truly deal with alcohol and drug offenders, and our prisons ought to truly try to be both rehabilitative to the criminal and restitutive to the society.

(4) Youth vandalism and property crimes policies. I can recall seeing a Phil Donahue show recently in which the subject of "house trashing" was discussed. "House trashing" is a phenomenon which occurs when a teenage party—usually held while parents are away—becomes so rambunctious that substantial damage is done to the home in which the party is held. In interview after interview, parents and law officials bemoaned the fact that there was no way to prevent such occurrences. A similar hopelessness seems often to be evidenced in cases of vandalism involving graffiti or littering.

Again, allowing offenders to escape lightly in such situations non-plusses me. Besides the obvious answers of not giving parties, not leaving children alone, and providing for more police patrols in neighborhoods where such behavior is prevalent, is the meaningful treatment of the offender. What would I consider meaningful? The suspension of peerage privileges for a year accompanied by one year of mandated community weekend service. I would hope that a kid caught trashing a house would think twice about it if, instead of being able to drive around town with his or her buddies, the next fifty-two weekends were spent picking up trash from our roadways or scouring the sides of a graffitied subway train. And even if this approach were not wholly successful as a deterrent to other would-be vandals, not using it (or somethiing like it) gives a clear message to our young. It says that we accept vandalism as a way of life against which we can and will do nothing.

When such a tone is set in the general community we must expect that it will become a dominant force in our schools. And when we couple such a social tone with an equally ineffective school tone, we end up with a recipe for educational disaster.

(e) The general tone of school policy. We have already noted that an ordered, safe environment is essential for education to proceed effectively, and we have already seen that in far too many instances, such an environment is lacking in American public schools. It is now appropriate to ask what policies we are presently adopting which contribute to a poor school atmosphere and what we might do to turn things around. Below are a series of factors we can address in this regard. Let us consider each in turn.

(1) The treatment of aberrant behavior. There was a district where vandalism to the auditorium was an ongoing problem. Over a two or three year period, thousands of dollars of damage occurred in the form of broken seats, battered pianos, even a fire. Finally, because he had decided to patrol the area personally, the building's assistant principal caught two students in the act. Not only were they discovered vandalizing, but they were also caught defecating on the auditorium floor. Under sharp questioning, they revealed the long history of the vandalism and the names of all the students who had participated. Finally, the faculty thought, we'll get rid of these kids. What followed, however, was a perfunctory superintendent's hearing in which the students received a five-day suspension. No psychological testing was done, no damage was paid for, no alternate environment was provided for youngsters who clearly did not belong in a normal school.

There was another district where a girl was suspected of having smoked marijuana while on a class trip. Upon questioning—done with the knowledge of her mother—she admitted the wrong-doing. The mother, however, was a faculty member and one of the leaders of a militant district union. The daughter was a student with a fine high school record and an eye on some of the more prestigious colleges in the area. To shield the girl from any possible action, it was made clear both to the teacher in charge of the trip and to the building principal that, should disciplinary procedures be initiated, considerable pressure would be brought against them. The principal then immediately ordered that all written communiques concerning the incident be destroyed. All pending action was halted, and the memory of the incident was stricken from the school—with this exception: the students involved knew what had happened and remembered at least one way they might continue to use marijuana without fear of reprisal.

To the extent events such as those above continue—and from the statistics they seem all too frequent—it will be impossible to turn the tide of aberrant student behavior. In fact, behavior is apt to get worse because inaction on the part of schools is a clear signal to students that behavioral standards are unimportant and unenforced. Unless we make them important, we can expect to continue to see our school hallways littered with trash, our school windows broken, and our school children engaged in personally and socially destructive activities.

The inability of school officials to take meaningful action in the area of aberrant student behavior stems in part from a somewhat confusing and sometimes contradictory legal atmosphere. Before the nation's focus on civil rights in the post-1945 era, the doctrine of "in loco parentis" pretty much allowed schools to act literally "in place of the parents." School authority to regulate student behavior was very broadly defined and very seldom challenged. Since World War II, with the emergence of civil rights positions of greater and greater militancy, that has changed. Perry Zirkel, Professor of Education and Law at Lehigh University, and Henry Reichner, a lawyer practicing in Philadelphia, describe the transition in this way:

> Rather than reject the application of "in loco parentis"...courts have tended to limit the doctrine by allowing reasonable punishment in light of the totality of circumstances, including such factors as the nature of the infraction, the method of discipline, and the age of the student.[45]

The problem in recent years is that court challenges of school authority have left a patchwork quilt of guidelines so vague as to discourage many school officials from dealing with improper student behavior. How may a student dress? How may he or she wear their hair? Can a locker be searched for drugs? Can a student be searched? Is corporal punishment permitted, and if so, under what circumstances? Is it legal to require a student to study? The decisions in cases which raise such questions, like those in the affirmative action cases discussed earlier, are not always clear-cut. Consider some of the following examples.

The New York State Department of Substance Abuse has reported since 1984 that in New York about 13% of the students in school, or about 1 out of every 8 students, attends class under the influence of drugs or alcohol. Teachers are urged to report students who may be "stoned" in class so that testing and treatment can follow and potentially dangerous behavior can be avoided. However, U.S. Federal courts (and some state courts, such as those in New Jersey) have held that testing for drug use through urinalysis is a violation of the Fourteenth Amendment right of due process and the Fourth Amendment guarantee against unreasonable search and seizure. In cases such as Anable vs. Ford (Arkadelphia, Arkansas) and Odenheim vs. Carlstadt (East Rutherford, New Jersey), the courts have prohibited the very action which might verify the suspicions of a teacher.[46]

Just to make the "search and seizure" situation more confusing, there is the 1985 Supreme Court ruling in the case of New Jersey vs. T.L.O. in which the Court held that searches *were* constitutional if school officials had "reasonable suspicion" of illegal substances. Zirkel and Reichner explain the seeming contradiction of these decisions by stating that, while modern courts do not any longer grant unlimited "in loco parentis" powers to schools, they seem to allow such powers if it can be clearly shown that circumstances justify the use of the powers, either to maintain school order or to avoid potentially hazardous situations. They cite the 1977 Supreme Court case of Ingraham vs. Wright as a substantiation of their position. This was a case in which the issue was corporal punishment, and they quote the Court's ruling as follows:

> Although the early cases viewed the authority of the teacher as deriving from the parents, the concept of parental delegation has been replaced by the view—more consonant with compulsory education laws—that the state itself may impose such corporal punishment as is reasonably necessary "for the proper education of the child and for the maintenance of group discipline."[47]

To give a hypothetical illustration of how this modified use of powers might apply, a teacher today is not viewed as having the right to slap a student who might be swearing, but the teacher would have the right to use force against that student if he or she were deliberately blocking a stairwell during a fire drill. Here is another example. A school may not have the right to tell students how to dress, but if a boy in shop class with long hair was running the risk of catching it in a machine, the school could require him to either cut it or pin it in such a way that the danger was removed. Similarly, girls whose blouses or skirts might be too revealing could be compelled to wear more conservative attire if it were demonstrated that the more revealing clothes caused distractions in class which made teaching more difficult.

However one may react to the legal interpretation of events by Zirkel and Reichner, it is clear that school authority today is more circumscribed and is apt to be decided on case-by-case bases rather than sweeping principles. Such conditions make many educators fearful of pushing too hard in the area of student behavior, lest a legal reversal or a personal lawsuit ensue. On the other hand, Zirkel and Reichner point out that some recent decisions have held teachers liable in situations where their inaction resulted in negative consequences. So it seems that modern educators are caught on the horns of a dilemma. If they choose to exercise their authority, they run the risk of being taken to court for overstepping their bounds. If they choose not to act, they can be taken to court for not taking "proper care" of their students.[48]

Finally, the confusion becomes even greater when considering colleges and students over the age of eighteen. Here the "in loco parentis" doctrine has been sorely eroded, almost to the point where attempts at defining school behavioral standards have become nonexistent. William Kaplin writes:

> The emergence of the student veteran; the loosening of the "lock step" pattern of educational preparation which led students directly from high school to college to graduate work; and finally, the lowered age of minority—all combine to make the "in loco parentis" relationship between institution and student less and less tenable.[49]

In light of all this, the question still remains, "what do we do in the treatment of aberrant student behavior to improve our present condition?" I believe the first thing we should do is to allow schools to mandate the psychological testing of children whose behavior is clearly outside normal limits. If a parent would object to such a course of action, then I could easily countenance a due-process procedure where an impartial judge might render a final decision. In no way, however, should a parent have the final word. Parents are too partial, and many of them have a lot to hide.

If, after testing and diagnosis, a chronically aberrant pupil whose behavior has clearly been abnormal is judged to be incapable of functioning successfully in a regular school environment, we ought to be able to remand that pupil to an alternate environment. Again, we may wish to provide due-process protection against abuses in such cases, but clearly it should not be the right of any student to destroy the learning environment of a school—and the principals of America agree on this point. As we have already noted above, the lack of alternate environments for chronic misbehavers has been cited by principals as a major element in the inability to maintain order in our schools.[50]

The "alternate environment student" would be equally entitled to the rights of peerage after successfully completing an alternate program, and every effort and resource applied to help "regular school students" achieve this goal should also be applied to the "alternate school population." Such a system would put a stop to our meaningless, endless string of detentions and suspensions. Perhaps if students knew that after a certain number of detentions and/or suspensions, or after the commission of a serious infraction, they would forfeit their right to attend a regular school, there would be fewer instances of aberrant behavior. And we might even exact a penalty for chronic misbehavers who need to be removed to an alternate environment by delaying their peerage rights (particularly the right to drive) by a certain number of months or years—depending on the severity of their infractions. In this way, we might encourage students to be responsible for their own actions or at the very least force them to accept the consequences of them.

There is another thing we might try in dealing with improper student behavior, and it involves a technique which appears to be enjoying more and more success—peer pressure. Oddly enough, this suggestion comes from my own high school days where something similar was used to great effect. We might try saying to an entire school that any acts of vandalism or theft or student violence would be dealt with by cancelling all student activities. Faced with the loss of its football games, junior proms, school musicals, class trips, etc., the students might really begin to police their own domain. I'll tell you this, under such a policy, I'd hate to face the boys' football squad if, as a result of my smoking in the bathroom, Saturday's football game were cancelled.

Finally, I would restore the doctrine of having students work constructively for the school as a penalty for improper behavior. I see nothing wrong with asking a child to scrape gum from desks if he or she has been caught sticking gum on the furniture. As long as the restitutive labor is not harmful to the child, it would truly make him or her think twice before engaging in the casual (or not so casual) defacing of public property. Washing blackboards, sweeping halls, washing off graffiti, etc. can all become positive object lessons in the resurrection of a good school environment.

(2) The theory of educational enticement. Not long ago, I found myself attending a meeting with the guidance counselors and the director of curriculum in a district in which I had been asked to speak. The state education department had recently mandated one unit of fine arts to be added to high school graduation requirements, and as the state music chairperson, I was asked how the district might comply in the area of music. Fortunately, the state had suggested a curriculum, and

I proceeded to answer by reviewing the major items that the state wished covered, one of which was a unit on music history and great composers.

"Oh, we can't do that," one of the guidance counselors piped up. "Our students would never sit still through a Mozart symphony."

The hair on my neck began to bristle.

"Don't you think it's important for a high school senior to graduate with some knowledge of the history of the world's great culture?" I asked.

"Sure," the counselor replied. "But it's a matter of class control. We prefer to give our students material they like. They respond better and learn more."

"Do you adopt the same attitude for math?" I pressed. "If a kid isn't into logarithms or equilateral triangles, do you substitute figuring out baseball averages?"

There was no answer, of course, because the educational philosophy behind the policy was patently absurd. Class control should never be predicated on the nature of the curriculum. If a teacher has trouble with a class, what should be addressed are the teaching style, the manner in which the subject is presented, classroom atmosphere, etc. Yet, you would be amazed how often curricula are watered down either to create a non-challenging academic environment or to entice students to enroll in classes. Such policies are devastating to the academic tone of a school, yet they persist in school after school. In effect, they say to the kids, "We'll give you cotton candy if you agree to sign up for our courses and be good little boys and girls." Bribery in the world of educational standards is commonplace. Consider the philosophy espoused by Jere Brophy of Michigan State University. "Teachers must find ways to motivate their students voluntarily to try to do well what is required of them," Brophy writes. Liking a subject, seeing value in it, even expecting to do well, Brophy goes on, may not be sufficient motivation. What are needed, in addition, are extrinsic rewards—prizes, honor rolls, praise, privileges, competition victories, etc.[51]

It is not that I am against an extrinsic boost now and again, but I see a great danger in the reward theory because it has become a fetish with unduly accented importance. Listen to what Bruce Jackson has to say about the philosophy of easy courses and enticing curricula.

> Some students—including gifted youngsters—have their own interpretation of this philosophy. They reason that the reward for successfully completing hard work is just more and harder work. Why bother?...It is smart to be "dumb" where the payoffs are lower expectations, less pressure, and lots of individual help and attention...For many youngsters special programs function...as refuges from the more rigorous demands of the regular classroom...If Math Fundamentals yields five units of high school credit (and possibly an A or a B), why strive for a grade of C or D in Algebra?[52]

Jackson's solution to the problem, and I agree with him, is to eliminate unnecessarily easy courses (or to offer them for no credit), to insist on homework in every course, to insist on attendance requirements for every course, and to deglamorize easy courses by making them more demanding. The reason Jackson makes sense is that he restores the message of the work-ethic as well as the status of the teacher as an educator. For far too long, teachers have been relegated to the position of baby sitters and entertainers by sub-standard curricula. If custodial education is your cup of tea, why put your kids in a school? Put them in a playpen. And if their learning is dependent upon entertaining them, don't hire people with master's degrees. Hire Sammy Davis, Jr.

False praise, a reliance on extrinsic rewards, and offering "enticement curricula" are cruel hoaxes. They give students a false sense of themselves and prepare them poorly for the realities of the workplace. I've seen it hundreds of times. The lackluster English class which concentrates on watching video tapes is "really cool" for the student who has learned laziness as a way of life. It is cool, that is, until college applications come around and the kid is mowed down by candidates who have sweated out their basic courses at a high school with a rigorous curriculum.

It is time we stopped the charade and return to the educational ethic of the immigrants who forged this country. Education to them was a blessing, not a burden. They needed no enticements to learn the curricula. The "enticement" was an escape from poverty and a chance at the brass ring. Far too many of our kids have forgotten that ethic, and far too many educators have been willing partners in the process of amnesia.

(3) A lack of student accountability. In a variety of ways, most students today are allowed to develop habits of irresponsibility which render them less and less accountable for the academic commitments they make. Consider some of the following examples. If a student fails a course, many times the course can be made up in summer school. A student thus gets the luxury of attending eight weeks of classes where once eight months were required. I do not believe students should be given this "convenience." If a course is failed, it should be repeated the next year, and if that delays graduation and the concomitant rights of peerage, so be it. What we ought to be doing during the summer is offering remediation, enrichment, driver education, etc. And while we're on the subject, it is important to note that summer school is an American convenience not wholly duplicated in other nations. We offer summer school because our children attend regular school only 180 days a year. In most European countries attendance is required for 220 days. In Japan it is 240 days. Perhaps it might yield better results if America lengthened its school year instead of offering summer school. (Also, it might be wise to bear in mind that the teacher who complains of poor pay is drawing that pay for approximately two months—16%—less work than the average twelve-month employee. The teacher salaried at $25,000 is thus earning the equivalent of $29,000 in a "normal" job.)

Another way in which students are encouraged to be irresponsible is the lack of attendance standards applied to them. As long as a pupil receives passing grades, he or she is credited with the course regardless of the number of days absent. The precedent that policy sets for the American work force is disastrous, and we see its negative repercussions in American worker absenteeism and lack of productivity. The solution is to require 90% attendance for course credit in school regardless of grade point average. At 180 days of school, that is 18 allowable absences (or about one day every two weeks)—a liberal standard, indeed. And lest you think this too strict, allowances could be made for long-term illness in cases where a broken leg or hepatitis kept a child at home. In such instances, home tutoring might be provided with attendance credit given for every day of tutoring.

Yet a third way in which academic irresponsibility is encouraged is the manner in which students are permitted to drop courses at the secondary level. In far too many instances, they can drop at anytime. So if the academic pressure begins to get intense, the student simply runs away from it by opting out of the course. The remedy for such escapism is not hard to see. No student should be allowed to drop any class until a period of one or two months has passed. This would ensure a "fair trial" for the student. After that, there should be no more than a two-week "window" in which drops could be made. When that window passes, the student must keep the commitment for the duration of the course. Exceptions could, of course, be made for severe illness or severe emotional pressure, but these should be made only in consultation with teacher, parent, student, and administrator. Further, where practicable, late drops approved in such a manner should not automatically result in a study hall. As much as possible, failure to keep pace with a class should result in taking a less rigorous class rather than no class at all.

(4) Teacher fear. In the absence of meaningful student discipline and in the presence of militancy on the part of parents who can frequently become abusive, many teachers seek nothing so much as to rid themselves of troublesome children. Where in more benign times a teacher might not have hesitated to fail a poor student or even give a low grade, now many teachers take another tack. They pass the student on to become someone else's problem. They look the other way when they see a scuffle in the hallway; they acquiesce to the all-protective parent rather than stand up for principles or policies they once fought for. Fear of reprisal is a real thing in education. Many is the flat tire, broken window, or torn car antenna which owes its fate to a disgruntled student. I know a teacher whose dog was set on fire and another whose front door was blown up because students were retaliating for an entirely proper grade or disciplinary action. In my own career, I have seen my wife attacked with ice, my property vandalized, my license plates stolen simply for marking honestly or reporting school wrong-doing.

The intimidation and coercion of educators by delinquent students and rednecked parents go beyond destroying the tone of a school. It is despicable, often criminal, behavior which survives because of the cowardice of administrators and the communities in which they serve. The solution is simple to state, if not to do. Schools must stand tall for the enforcement of the law and the protection of property and people. If that means police patrols in halls or parking lots, if it means prosecution of juveniles, if it means legal action against parents—then that's what it means.

How a cowardly administrator or board of education member whose refusal to act has led to the present situation can live with themselves is beyond me. But I tell you, I know many of them who will read these words and not give a second thought to the evil they have promoted. Some of them won't even think they did anything wrong. Perhaps a law requiring them to be responsible for the consequences of their inaction might make it harder to be a coward than it is to be courageous. If a student commits a serious offense and is subsequently "let off" by a principal, a superintendent, or a board member, perhaps they ought to bear some responsibility for a future offense. Perhaps that might force a little honesty and courage into the system.

(5) Counterproductive bureaucracy and experimentation. For many educators, the incessant bureaucracy of American public education—often headed by board members and administrators who know next to nothing of classroom realities—presents an ongoing problem which erodes the academic tone of our schools. Jack Frymier writes that the misconceived curricular reforms and endless regulations imposed upon teachers by this bureaucracy "blunt" teacher enthusiasm and "stifle their creativity." His study indicates that schools achieve much better student outcomes where there is less increased centralization of authority, fewer court-ordered changes, and a decrease in unionization.[53] Like Marva Collins, Paul Copperman points to many of the imposed trends of the post-1960 era as the cause of today's problems. Bureaucrats who insisted on "free behavior" standards for educational institutions, Copperman writes, left "many of the students coming out of these schools...intellectually crippled for life." Similarly, curricular gimmicks such as the "new math" were adopted without evidence of worth from rigorous norm-referenced testing.[54]

The solution to such bureaucratization is two-fold. The first is that no administrator should ever be totally out of the classroom nor any board member elected without first completing a graduate degree in educational governance. (We have already discussed these issues.) The second is that sweeping bureaucratic decisions should not be undertaken unless there is at least serious consultation with and (hopefully) majority-vote agreement of the teachers who must implement the reforms.

(6) High-tech gimmicks and illusions of progress. The extrinsic rewards of which Brophy speaks are not limited to things like praise, privileges, and prizes in the modern educational world. They take a more technically-oriented (and to me a more insidious) form in the incessant promotion of gadgetry. It is not that the gadgets—the computers, calculators, word processors, televisions, synthesizers—are in and of themselves insidious. It is that they are touted as things which will improve student performance and remediate poor student skills. Nothing could be further from the truth. Improperly used, they delay the development of real skills by creating the illusion that the student is doing the work. They teach a reliance on external technology rather than internal competence, and when extolled by a "public relations philosophy" they do not liberate children. Rather, they turn children into more and more dependent people who cannot add unless there is a calculator, spell unless there is a word processor, think unless there is a computer.

The high-tech age has been upon our schools for at least the last fifteen years. Never have so many of our children been so "electronically literate." Yet our test scores do not rise, our worker productivity continues at a low ebb, and our geopolitical and economic competitiveness fails to improve. Could it be that our gadgetry is not the Messiah it was cracked up to be?

We have already seen that the more television a student views, the worse he or she performs. George Comstock comments that greater TV viewing is associated with not only lower academic achievement but also greater antisocial behavior, greater misbehavior, greater perceived parental neglect and rejection, greater fear of crime, and lower self-esteem. I am convinced that the over-reliance on external gadgets breeds a similar degree of dysfunction in other areas as well. Consider, by way of evidence, the following from L.R. Stewart. In an article in *The American School Board Journal*, he assures us that the ubiquitous microcomputer can improve outcomes in reading, history, math, social studies, geography, science, special education, English, creative writing, and music. Listen, for example, to what he says of the last two items on his list.

"Rough drafts of student writing composed on the computer can become finished works when students insert the text into computer generated outlines of their compositions," he writes, and then goes on to say that computers and synthesizers in the area of music "allow students to control the tone, pitch, tempo, and rhythm of up to sixteen instruments or voices. Students, consequently, can create entire musical compositions."[55]

I tell you as both a writer and composer that this is utter nonsense. The organization of good writing is not done by a machine but inside the mind of the writer. That is true for all kinds of writing, including academic writing, but it is even truer for creative writing. Things like imagery, characterization, thematic focus, scene architecture, and dozens of other items of literary craft cannot be legislated by a computer simply because they occur in an infinite variety which depends upon the subject matter and the creativity of an author. To think that a rough draft of anything can be turned into a "finished work" by a computer is an insult to every writer who has ever lived. More, it is a lie to the student, and in the process of being propagated, it is a sure means of seriously stifling the student's creativity.

In musical composition, Stewart's words are so false as to be laughable. No computer program can replace the rigors of counterpoint, harmony, form, and orchestration which lie at the root of all worthy composition from Machaut to Milton Babbitt. To think that a computer will create "entire compositions" is as preposterous as believing that operating one of those push-button keyboards which gives you canned rhythm and harmony is equal to playing the piano. Those machines are insults to the Horowitz's and Rubensteins and Cliburns of the real world of music, and using them only prevents the user from really mastering the art.

These gadgets allow for educational masturbation of the cheapest, most dishonest kind, but lest you think I would completely destroy the gadgets, think again. They can be extremely useful *after* one develops internalized skills. *After* the child has learned to spell and diagram sentences, to organize thoughts and outline papers, the word processor and computer can be an aid to more convenient writing. *After* the musician has mastered the rudiments of chord grammar, harmony, counterpoint, form, and orchestration, the synthesizer can be a powerful new instrument. *After* the artist has learned the basics of drawing, computer graphics can be a productive adjunct to brush and palette. *After* the student has learned to add and subtract, to think spatially in geometry, to reason symbolically in algebra, the calculator and computer can be put to use.

These tools must never be allowed to do our basic training or our thinking for us, yet in so much of today's education they are. And I see this trend as part of a larger one—a trend in which everything formerly done *by* people is now done *for* them. The television entertains us without our active participation where formerly the book or even the radio required us at least to imagine. The calculator figures for us; the computer organizes; the electric piano plays. And in the process, if we let it happen, we are continuously diminished. The cocaine gives us a high where once we might have gloried in an accomplishment of our own making. We seek self-worth in an "ethnic day parade," as if just being black or Jewish, Irish or Christian were enough to ennoble ourselves. It is not and never was. We must each *earn* the right to self-pride. It must come through our own labor and our own accomplishments. Once we consign that right to the word processor or the computer, they simply become our new cocaine.

The solution? Make passing the math test *without* a calculator the pre-requisite for using one. Make writing the paper *without* the word processor the requirement for owning one. Make harmonizing a chorale melody *without* the computer synthesizer the first step toward buying one. Do these things and we will see a restoration of self-reliance upon which we can build a *real* educational renaissance.

(7) Effective schools criteria. Finally, the general tone of a school is governed by the manner in which the effective schools criteria discussed earlier are addressed. To the extent they occur, the tone will be of a high quality. To the extent they are ignored, the tone will suffer. By way of a composite of the work of Furtwengler, Liberman, Miller, and the U.S. Department of Education, below are the eight criteria most associated with an effective school:

- Low frequency of disciplinary problems
- High staff expectation of students
- High quality of administrative leadership
- A safe, orderly environment
- Strong fiscal support
- Clear goals collectively arrived at
- High student/staff involvement
- High standardized test scores

Grouping and grading

There are few things which impact more on the academic life of a child than the groups into which he or she is placed or the grading procedures to which he or she is subjected. In the pages below we will examine these topics to see how they are addressed by educators today. Here and there suggestions will be made as to how seemingly irreconcilable points of view may be made compatible, but the real significance of the grouping and grading policies we encounter will occur as we apply them to curricula in the final section of this chapter. Let us begin with a discussion of grouping.

Grouping. If you were to plant a flower garden, you would never expect all your flowers to bloom on the same day or to exhibit the same color characteristics one after the other. Some may bloom early, some late. Some may have an intense, vivid hue. Some may be more pastel. Every seed is not equal to every other, and in the world of flower gardens we accept that. We may even be grateful for it as it can fill our garden with a rich variety.

Unfortunately, we do not always extend the same courtesy of thought to our children. They are not equal, child after child. Some bloom early, some late. Some shine brightly, some dully. We are not equal, person after person. We vary in ability, in mood, in character, and in the capacity to learn. Yet, because of the fiscal and logistical realities of modern public education, we ask our children to learn uniformly. With only small exceptions, we group them by age and when our teaching term is done, we ask them all to pass their final tests on the same day.

I am not going to advocate that we allow our children to start or finish school at any age; that we permit them to learn at any pace they choose in the manner of Neill's self-regulated Summerhill. From a purely practical point, that would be impossible given our total school population. It would require tens of thousands more schools, hundreds of thousands more teachers, and tens of billions more dollars—none of which we have or even project the prospect of having for the foreseeable future. And even if magically we did have the resources, it is not at all clear that self-regulated education would produce any better results.

Why then do I tell you about children and flowers? To show you that we face in modern public education something of an irreconcilable paradox. Finance and logistics force us to treat our children with a tremendous amount of uniformity, yet we know that they are not equal. Some are gifted, some are average, some are slow—and many exhibit varying characteristics according to the subject matter, the teacher, the grade level. It is, perhaps, foolish to hope that in a complex society such as ours we will ever fully come to grips with this paradox, but we can and do at least try to cope with it.

In the world of education, "coping" in this area falls into two broad camps. On the one hand, we can group children heterogeneously. That is, we can populate our classes so that they contain children of mixed abilities (bright, average, slow). On the other hand, we can group homogeneously so that all bright kinds are in one class, all average kids in another, all slow kids in yet another. The pros and cons of these two approaches have been the focus of a raging debate for nearly the entirety of this century. It is one of the most important debates in education, for how a child is grouped significantly affects his or her development not only through school but through life. Moreover, how America addresses the issue of ability grouping will have a significant bearing on her competitiveness with other developed nations, each of whom addresses the grouping issue in its own particular way (as we have already discussed in Chapter Two).

It is an unfair oversimplification to lump all pro-heterogeneous or pro-homogeneous educators together. Many excellent educators realize the complexity of the grouping problem and adopt policies designed to deal with a multiplicity of issues. To cite just a few questions which can be raised in this regard, one can ask if homogeneity can be applied at all grade levels. Should it be confined only to certain grades? Does a child gifted in math necessarily evidence superior skills in English? If not, how does one schedule such a child in elementary school? How would scheduling occur at the secondary level? Does remediation constitute a kind of "ability tracking?" If so, how does one reconcile a heterogeneous ideology with the need for remediation in "at risk" students who would drop out or fail out without it? These are just a few of the issues which attend this complex and controversial area.

To make some sense of it, let us view some of the more prominent arguments presented by proponents of each ideological camp and then turn our hand to suggestions which might reconcile the paradox we observe.

(a) The issues pro and con. James Conant, surely one of the best educational minds of the post-World War II era, wrote in his classic study of American teachers that some skills, because they manifest themselves at an early age, demand the special cultivation which homogeneous grouping can provide. "Music affords the best example," Conant explains. "Musical talent manifests itself at an early age, and unless it is developed during the school years, there is extremely little likelihood of a person's becoming an accomplished performer."[56]

Conant's words came at a time in the history of American education when homogeneity was fashionable. Sputnik had put tremendous pressures on American education, and while the philosophical thrust of the nation was still egalitarian, the mandate to catch up to Russia was clearly demanding the development of individual potential. President Kennedy's commission on national goals in education expressed it this way:

> Our devotion to equality does not ignore the fact that individuals differ greatly in their talents and motivations. It simply asserts that each should be enabled to develop to the full, in his own style and to his own limit. Each is worthy of respect as a human being. This means that there must be diverse programs within the educational system to take care of the diversity of individuals; and that each of these programs should be accorded respect and stature.[57]

The Federal Government, in fact, embarked upon a number of projects during the "Sputnik era" which were designed to foster the development of children along homogeneous lines. The then Department of Health, Education, and Welfare, for example, supported a conference of fifty universities aimed at stimulating honors programs for gifted students. Lanora Lewis, one of HEW's representatives to the conference, wrote as follows:

> The most talented students are capable of the best work. The sooner they are identified and provided with opportunity to make ample use of their talents as they mature, the more they will encompass and master in the years they spend in formal education. It is the aim of honors work to enable the best students to do the best of which they are capable.[58]

The government's view was shared by many members of the educational community at the time Lewis was writing. Dorothy Westby-Gibson, for example, argued in 1966 that students could be grouped by both ability and "teachability."[59] Carl Hansen expressed the view that a four-track high school (honors track, college track, general track, and basic track) was a workable, desirable reality.[60] Indeed, as far back as 1927, educators had argued for ability groups. Consider the following from Ryan and Crecelius:

> Ability grouping, in its simplest aspect, is a refinement of grading. The same principle and purpose which led to the grading of the public schools of this country now point to ability grouping as the next logical step.[61]

Today, with education once again in a state of publicly-viewed crisis, many educators are revoicing their desire to deal with students in some form of tracking procedure. Mitchell and Williams of Eastern Washington University, for example, have recently completed a worldwide study on ability grouping for the development of gifted and talented students. With some reservations about the egalitarian treatment of children (expressed, by the way, in communist as well as non-communist countries), they report most nations "are deeply aware of the fact that their own survival—and perhaps the survival of the planet—depends in large measure on the careful nurturing of their best young minds."[62]

America's response to the current wave of attention on gifted and talented education and the resultant homogeneity it requires has been fragmentary at best. Even in places where homogeneity is accepted, standards for selecting students and programs applied to those involved vary widely. Lauren Sosniak of the University of Illinois (Chicago) writes that many programs targeted for the gifted population are never even applied to the right group. PSAT classes for students with C's and D's are cited as a prime example. Sosniak concluded that in America today "considerable confusion exists regarding what kinds of experiences ought to be provided [gifted] students."[63] In a similar vein, Langenbach and Blitch at the University of Oklahoma find the "current definitions of giftedness are too narrow. Nearly every student exhibits some kind of gifted behavior...Overemphasizing the giftedness of a few creates an elitist group of students."[64] They recommend that educators use student performance in a variety of areas—not just a few test scores—to determine who is gifted and what programs are appropriate for each gifted child.

Actually, Langenbach and Blitch speak to a much wider issue, the issue of subject prejudice and how it affects grouping and curriculum. For example, many a "gifted program" limits itself to students who excel in the "basic four" areas of English, math, science, and social studies. But as Conant observed, giftedness may also manifest itself in music, in athletics, in mechanical skills, in culinary skills, etc. If we are to be concerned with homogeneity in a real and consistent manner, should we not also address programs designed for the "non-academically gifted" as well?

We shall return to this question—a most important one—later. For now, it behooves us to remember that even with all the educational support for homogeneity, there is the other side of the issue. There are many educators who vehemently oppose any kind of tracking. Thus, to more meaningfully articulate a policy on grouping, we need to view the philosophy of this opposing camp.

Consistently and for the last quarter century, no less than John Goodlad, one of the most respected names in modern education, has argued passionately against the homogeneous grouping of students. He sees it as a means of socioeconomically handicapping minorities which should ultimately be banned by law. Consider some of his comments on the subject. "Nearly all children can learn from quality literature," he writes.

> Nearly all can learn a second language, and nearly all can benefit from studying the important concepts of algebra. Some will learn more, some less. But tracking excludes many children from ever being in classes where these "high status" subjects are taught.[65]

"Tracking in secondary schools..." he adds, "is so embedded and has proven so intransigent that it is more likely to be settled by the courts than by persuasion."

> And since tracking appears to block the poor and disadvantaged from access to knowledge which might serve to advantage them, pressure to abolish it will undoubtedly find its way to the judicial branch of government. It is conceivable to envision a day when tracking will be prohibited as is now the case in Sweden.[66]

Goodlad is not a lone voice crying in the night. There are other prominent, respected educators who feel as he does. In their definitive study on ability grouping, Peterson, Wilkinson, and Hallinan conclude that homogeneity has several negative impacts, whatever positives it may have for high-track students. These negatives involve the low social status of students in lower tracks as well as deterrents to learning for less gifted pupils. Hallinan writes as follows:

> Studies of peer relations in tracked and ability grouped classes show marked differences in the social status of students at different ability levels. Since academic status is a component of social status, high-tracked or grouped students tend to be more popular with their schoolmates than their lower-tracked peers. At the same time, students in low tracks and ability groups are often labelled "slow learners" by teachers and class mates, which lowers their esteem in the eyes of their peers...Ability grouping may actually be detrimental to children in average-and lower-ability groups... There is a slight trend toward improving the achievement of high ability groups but that is offset by substantial losses by the average and low groups...Tracking and ability grouping depresses growth in academic achievement for students in low groups.[67]

Gerald Bracey, Director of Research and Evaluation for the schools of Cherry Creek in Colorado, is even more forceful than Hallinan in his criticisms of homogeneity. "Grouping classes by ability," he states, "has no positive effect on achievement." Citing the recent studies of Grant and Rothenberg, Bracey goes on to say that teachers appear to create better learning environments for brighter students and students in higher socioeconomic classes than for lower-achieving or lower socioeconomic groups. This tendency leads to what Stanovich calls the "Matthew effect," a condition in which "the rich get richer while the poor get poorer;" that is, a learning environment in which the brighter do better and the less able do worse. Bracey concludes that the research indicates the need for "serious rethinking of the use of ability grouping and a more vigorous search for viable alternatives..."[68]

What Bracey advocates is echoed by other nationally prominent scholars. For Mortimer Adler and the others of his Paideia Group, tracking is antithetical to the egalitarian education demanded by the ethics of a democracy.[69] For Ernest Boyer, "putting students into boxes can no longer be defended. To call some students 'academic' and other 'nonacademic' has a powerful and, in some instances, devastating impact on how teachers think about the students and how the students think about themselves." The current three-track system—academic, vocational, and general," Boyer goes on, "should be abolished. It should be replaced by a single track program—one that provides a core education for all students..."[70]

The positions of Goodlad and Bracey, Adler, Hallinan, and Boyer are to some degree supported by the research on tracking. I say "to some degree" because the research varies somewhat from study to study. Thelen, for example, writing in 1967, viewed ability grouping research from 1931 to his day and reported that "in general, the findings are clear. Grouping either homogeneously or heterogeneously by ability produces almost the same result."[71] That conclusion is for the most part supported by Tewksbury, Brown, Morgenstern, Beggs, Goldberg, Passow, and Svensson—particularly for the elementary level student.[72] However, there are reputable studies by competent scholars which are at odds with Thelen's rather all-encompassing statement. In 1966, for example, Alfred Yates of the Department of Education at Oxford University conducted an international study of ability grouping for UNESCO's Institute for Education in Hamburg. His assessment was that the research was inconclusive, that more research was needed, and that grouping by ability "should be confined during primary and early secondary stages to sub-grouping within classes...and that any subsequent grouping...at later secondary stages...be constantly reviewed by systematic research."[73]

In 1966 Walter Borg conducted a series of studies while serving as Chairman for the Bureau of Educational Research at the College of Education of Utah State University. His conclusions for both elementary and junior high students were rather mixed. Ability grouping on the elementary level led to better achievement for superior students. Average students appeared to show no difference in achievement with either homogeneous or heterogeneous grouping. Slower students achieved more with regular, non-tracked grouping. On the junior high level both superior and average students did better with ability grouping while slower students continued to achieve more when heterogeneous grouping was used.[74]

Wrightstone reports that on the elementary level academic growth is slightly better with homogeneous grouping, though parents and teachers both observe better emotional and social development with heterogeneity. On the secondary level, however, parents, teachers, students, and administrators hold favorable attitudes toward homogeneity—even when criteria for selection to various tracks is inconsistent and student achievement not often better than with heterogeneous grouping.[75] Ream is in general agreement with Wrightstone[76] as is Copperman who favors heterogeneity on the elementary level and ability grouping on the secondary level.[77]

So there you have it. On the one hand, educators who are crying for ability grouping tell us that no less than the fate of our planet depends upon it. On the other hand, we hear claims that ability grouping is only marginally beneficial for gifted students and unduly stigmatizes average and below-average students, a disproportionate percentage of whom are minority pupils who have been disadvantaged by poor socioeconomic backgrounds and a lack of facilities. And each camp points to research which seems at best inconclusive. What do we do in the face of this conflicting evidence?

(b) Reconciliations of the paradox. The first thing we must do is adopt a philosophical position. Do we want some kind of homogeneity or not? If the answer is no, then we wash our hands of the whole affair and group children randomly. If the answer is yes, then we must seek those modes of homogeneity (or tracking or ability grouping) which maximize the benefits and minimize the drawbacks. Taking a philosophical stand one way or the other ought not to be an unreasoned procedure. The fate of too many children and, indeed, the future of our country cannot be allowed to rest on a merely arbitrary position. Let us then make an observation before we take our stand. It is a simple observation born out by testing, experience, and common sense alike. People *are* different in ability.

People *are* different in ability, and we must acknowledge that fact. Some of us will run a four-minute mile, others will be lucky to reach a finish line walking, and millions will lie somewhere in between. Some of us will play the piano like Rubenstein, others will putter in the Sunday parlor, and millions will never do either. Some of us will be Jonah Salks; some great carpenters; some custodians; some senators. We cannot play "The Emperor's New Clothes" with our society or like ostriches bury our heads in the sand to deny the reality of difference. We *are* different in ability, in capability, in the desire to achieve, in the backgrounds which help or hurt our achievement, in the mental and physical and spiritual resources which lie at the core of achievement. We *are* different.

Beyond this observation, however, is a second—well, not so much an observation as a conviction. There is, or at least *ought* to be, dignity in our differences. And finally, there is the hope that inside *every* child is the capacity to do *something* well.

My plea for American education is that we recognize and service the differences between students, that we do so by giving *equal dignity* to *all* subjects, and that we seek to unlock the full potential of each child so that he or she finds the joy of doing something (perhaps many things) well. It is against this philosophy that I take my stand on grouping, and it is that homogeneity is necessary. It is necessary not just to challenge the gifted, but also to remediate the weak and to stimulate the students in between. The trick is to establish programs of homogeneity which pay attention to and deal effectively with the research showing that homogeneous grouping can have negative consequences. In doing this we must ask two questions: 1) where do we group, and 2) how do we group?

In at least one respect, Goodlad, Boyer, Hallinan, and Oakes are right. When tracking is applied at the elementary level, a gap is created between students—a gap which is destined to grow larger as the years pass. Like the arms of an angle which get wider apart the further one moves from the vertex, the disparity between the advanced tracks and the slower ones becomes greater with each passing year. By the time elementary students reach high school, whatever social and/or psychological stigmatization has occurred, slower track students will not have the academic preparation needed for many courses. Being deprived of these courses—or even of the chance of taking them—such students will find themselves behind in the race for college acceptances, for a good deal of vocational training, and thus for a fair share of America's socioeconomic brass ring. When one adds to this reality the great bulk of research indicating that tracking on the elementary level is not even significantly beneficial to the brightest students, it is not hard to conclude that in the regular classroom, homogeneity should be reserved for the high school years.

There is, however, the other side of the question as expressed by Conant. Some skills can't wait for high school. If we don't provide the musician and the athlete with homogeneous groupings which allow for the development of giftedness at an early age, it may be too late by the time high school rolls around. The Olympic gymnast must make a commitment well before high school if there are to be any gold medals won, and the kid who ends up with a music scholarship at Juilliard or Oberlin has been practicing and competing for it since grade school. Do we not owe something to these children? And if so, what justification do we have for witholding acceleration and/or enrichment from academically gifted children whether or not the gains are enormous or the needs immediate?

My conclusion is that we owe enrichment to the gifted and remediation to the slow in every discipline at the elementary level. Because tracking is a counterproductive means of achieving this end, however, my suggestion is that we accomplish our aims with alternate means. Specifically, I recommend cooperative grouping and non-class-time enrichment and remediation. Let us take a closer look at these concepts.

The technique of cooperative grouping grows out of the "control theory" of psychology articulated by William Glasser. Glasser, after much study, concluded that the greatest amount of student achievement and the fewest behavioral problems occur in school activities such as athletics, music performing groups, theatre, school newspapers, etc. because these activities fundamentally require students to work together toward a common goal, a goal which is seen as being both attainable and important. "Half of all students are not working," Glasser writes, "because they perceive that school will not satisfy their needs..."

> The next step is to ask ourselves, "Where in school do things work well now?" The band, the orchestra, the drama program, athletics, the school newspaper, and the yearbook. In each of these situations students are working together in some sort of group...This kind of endeavor has...been accurately labelled "cooperative grouping."[78]

The essence of cooperative grouping is the structuring of curricula so that within a heterogeneous classroom, tasks can be assigned according to the ability of the student in an overall plan in which each student contributes to an overall class goal. Roy Smith offers the example of an elementary or junior high class studying the vocabulary of the Middle Ages. A class assignment such as publishing a medieval newspaper might be given in which tasks can be differentiated so that brighter students have more challenging work (such as writing articles) while slow students have less challenging assignments (like looking up individual words). All students work together in small, closely-monitored groups to bring the various elements of the paper together, and finally the paper is published to the academic satisfaction of the entire class.[79]

A growing body of research evidence is mounting to suggest that such approaches on the elementary and junior high level "tend to promote more learning than do competitive or individualistic learning experiences."[80] They certainly address the question of having each student work to his/her potential in an environment which is essentially heterogeneous and thus one in which interaction is possible among all students with a minimum of stigmatization.

Actually, cooperative grouping and individualized enrichment are ideas which are not new to Glasser. In 1963 Marian Schiefele published a book in which gifted children—identified through a variety of means, including academic performance, physical skills, creative skills, behavioral traits, and standardized test scores—are serviced by individualized instruction and specialized grouping.[81] They are, however, ideas which are being rediscovered and ones whose time has, perhaps, at long last arrived.

Another idea to reconcile the ability grouping paradox on the elementary and junior high levels is the enrichment and remediation of students on non-class time; that is, before school, after school, and during the summer. There is no reason why students who are grouped heterogeneously in "normal" classrooms during the "regular" day cannot be accorded the benefits of homogeneity at other times. This can be accomplished at very little cost through the device of flexible hours for the teachers involved, thereby saving the burden of additional salary lines. It is also a scheme which can have extremely positive sociological benefits because it can constructively occupy latchkey children who might otherwise be left unattended. Programs involving homogeneity during the summer, moreover, can begin to address the issue of a longer school year for American pupils, thereby bringing them into educational alignment with their counterparts from other nations—counterparts with whom they must share an economically competitive world.

We will see later on how these concepts can fit into the curriculum and scheduling of a typical elementary and/or junior high day, and it may be wise to note that the techniques of cooperative grouping and summer enrichment/remediation can also be useful on the high school level. For now, however, it remains only to say that these concepts must be applied to *all* subject areas in order to meet the philosophical guideline discussed earlier. It is not only the mathematician of tomorrow but the musician as well, not only the physician but the athlete as well, who must derive dignity from the infusion of homogeneity into an essentially heterogeneous elementary experience. With this caveat, let us move on to concepts of grouping at the high school level.

Virtually all American high schools have a core curriculum for which all students, regardless of ability, are accountable. Beyond these subjects, there are advanced work and specialized courses which are designed to accommodate different student interests and different ability levels. Given this structure, it is relatively easy to postulate a high school scheme in which homogeneity is the grouping mode for the basic core, and self-selection or prerequisite selection is the mode for advanced and special courses. Let me elaborate.

English, math, science, social studies and (for most schools now) foreign languages are the subject areas which constitute the academic core of most American high schools. By the time a student reaches the ninth grade level, he or she has already established clear learning patterns and a clear record of academic performance from which placement in a track is not only possible but, for me, desirable. I say desirable because by the time a student has reached high school the necessity for either remediation, if needed, or enrichment, if appropriate, has become acute. The demands of college and work force do not allow the luxury of time. If high school freshmen have their eyes set on Harvard, they damn well better get an enriched education in grades 9-12 or they will not be competitive for acceptance. And if they have not mastered elementary and junior high skills by their ninth grade year, they damn well better catch up by their twelfth grade year or they will not be able to get their share of the socioeconomic pie when we pat them on the fanny and send them out from commencement exercises to face the real world. Thus, a three-stream approach for these basic academic areas is necessary: advanced stream, average stream, and remedial stream.

Having said this, however, there are other required courses where homogeneity is not only *not* necessary but where it may also be undesirable. In music performance or classroom music subjects, art, physical education, life skills, or civics classes, the story may be different. Let's take the civics class where topics involve the workings of a democracy. Here students (who must ultimately function as citizens in a heterogeneous society) need to hear the views of all segments of the population. In such a class, homogeneity is not only unnecessary, it is counterproductive to the aim of the course and the well-being of the society.

You may ask, at this point, if the music, art or phys. ed. student does not also deserve the benefits of enrichment and/or remediation. The answer is, of course, yes, for all the reasons discussed above, and there are both scheduling and grouping mechanisms to provide them. Enrichment in phys. ed. for gifted athletes is, in fact, the junior and senior varsity team program which exists in virtually all schools. For students who cannot engage in a normal gym class, there are homogeneous "alternate" phys. ed. classes or individualized assignments possible. Individualized work is especially appropriate in an art class in which children of widely different abilities can each explore personal potential in a heterogeneous setting. Music programs almost always have general groups in which students perform (band, orchestra, chorus) and select groups chosen by audition (choirs, wind ensembles, string quartets, jazz ensembles).

There are even inventive ways of combining the homogeneous/ heterogeneous modes to the benefit of all. Let me tell you of one. A kind of cooperative grouping called "ability grouping synthesis" allows one to construct a curriculum in such a way that a class may be temporarily divided into streams during a given unit to work in homogeneous settings. Then, after a few days, the class is remixed heterogeneously for full-group interaction. Earlier in this decade I was fortunate to receive several grants which allowed me to create synthesis models in both fine arts and English curricula. The models were evaluated in preliminary studies and our data yielded some very encouraging results. The groups exposed to synthesis had better academic achievement in the subjects in which synthesis took place, better overall academic achievement, fewer dropouts, and better school attendance than control groups. As I said, these were preliminary models and, while our data were accurate, the models were not as rigorously constructed as they might have been. When the testing funds ran out, the longitudinal model construction and evaluation we had planned became impossible. But the concept is still there, theoretically sound, somewhat successfully field-tested, waiting for more research.

To continue with homogeneity on the high school level, there is a kind of "natural selection" which occurs as most students begin to sort out their abilities and preferences. The student who enjoys and succeeds in math, for example, in most cases goes beyond the required algebra and geometry courses to trigonometry and calculus. Trigonometry and calculus thus become somewhat homogeneously populated. They are courses for which prerequisites are necessary and into which only the better math students venture, as a rule. The same is true for the music theory course. For these subjects, the intensity of the curricula, its advanced nature, and the presence of prerequisites in and of themselves create a homogeneous experience. It is thus imperative in America's comprehensive high schools that such courses continue to be offered in *all* curricular areas, and that guidance staffs, parents, teachers, administrators, and ultimately colleges afford an equal dignity to them. That is not now the case. The child gifted as an auto mechanic may not have the same higher educational opportunities as the one gifted in physics. And I can tell you from many years of painful observations that a gifted young musician will be turned from the field by a parent or guidance counselor whose own personal aspirations lean toward a career in business. We will return to the topic of "subject prejudice" later in this chapter. For now, it is only important to note the integral relationship between homogeneity, subject prejudice, and the ubiquitous phenomenon of seeing adults try to live the lives of children for them.

Before leaving the topic of grouping, there is another important and interrelated question to consider: how does grouping affect various diploma programs and how does it affect policies of "special education?" Beyond the division of students by academic ability (bright, normal, slow), there are further divisions wrought by necessity, some of which we have already touched upon. These are the "special programs" applied to handicapped children, immigrant children, and children who are chronic misbehavers. To the extent such children can be mainstreamed into regular elementary and junior high classes and into the academic tracks of a high school, they, of course, should be. However, either on a temporary basis or, if needed, on a permanent one, American schools must become capable of servicing them in alternate programs which perforce constitute a homogeneous grouping.

At times, this may be a sociologically enforced condition due to patterns of immigration. At times, it may be a governmental mandate, such as the federal laws governing the education of the handicapped. Whatever the causes, the aims of these programs must be two-fold: 1) to aid the student in a condition of immediate need, and 2) to move the student as expeditiously as possible back to the academic mainstream. Virginia Garton, Past-president of the Board of Education of Sheboygan, Wisconsin, describes in a heartwarming article how the Sheboygan schools were able to do this with ESL (English as a Second Language) programs for the Hmong people of Vietnam who entered their schools after the Vietnam War had created global refugee problems.[82]

It is important to note that special programs which persist through the twelfth grade year may require special diploma regulations. This becomes particularly critical when peerage rights or socioeconomic advancement depend on high school graduation. It may be that some handicapped children, for example, are *never* fully mainstreamed. It may be that children who are chronic misbehavers *never* fulfill the standards of a normal school because special standards are required in an alternate school. In such instances, alternate diplomas which require alternate standards should be provided by the system.

It is also important to note that special problems and special programs may not be academic in nature. For instance, a physical handicap such as blindness may in fact occur with a child on any academic ability level. It is only after the Braille or large-letter reader machines are made available to a blind student that we can unlock the door to learning so that an academic assessment can be made of the child. The same is true for an ESL program where language barriers mask ability or an alternate school program where emotional problems make true academic assessment impossible.

Finally, before we leave the topic of grouping it is appropriate to touch once more upon the economic ramifications of homogeneity. There is no getting around the fact that special programs for the gifted, the remedial, the handicapped, the disturbed, the linguistically illiterate are going to cost money—and lots of it. There is also no denying that often classes for these children are smaller than those for the average mainstream child (both because there are fewer "special" students and because large class sizes make working with them virtually impossible). Smaller classes translate to more teachers and more money. If you've read this far, you can already hear my answer: the money is there—we have no choice but to spend it. To this argument, however, let me add one more. *Not* spending the money on these kids during their school years costs us untold millions more in items such as lost productivity and criminal or anti-social behavior later. The untapped potential of a gifted scientist makes us that much less competitive as a nation. The unresolved conflicts of a troubled teenager makes us that much more likely to breed another robber or child-abuser or alcoholic or welfare client. The money spent here is vital as an investment in ourselves—incalculably more vital than the billions we now pour into cocaine, weaponry, needlessly flashy cars, or political corruption. Again the choice is ours.

Grading. In the years since World War II, the grades which are given in American public schools have undergone something of a metamorphosis. There are more kinds of grades than ever before; they stand for more things than ever before; and they have taken on an ever-increasing significance for the way in which we assess and group our children. In our brief view of grading we will begin by looking at the various purposes to which grades can be put.

Kurt Geisinger observes that grades may be informational, institutional, motivational, used for sorting and selecting, used for research purposes, and used as an introduction to the career evaluations we often experience after schooling is over.[83] Beyond these purposes, however, grades may refer to different things. A grade may judge a student relative to his or her peers, relative to self-potential, or relative to an objective standard. In the American public education system it is important to see the interrelationship between the purpose of a grade and the standard of grading applied to a given student in a given situation. Let us consider as an example a grade for a basketball unit in a high school phys. ed. class. Grading students in such a class relative to the standards of a National Basketball Association professional would be nonsensical for the average student. However, it might not be so nonsensical for a gifted athlete bucking for a big-time college scholarship. And if the class were an alternate experience for wheelchair-bound students, a grade relative to physically normal peers would be as meaningless as one relative to an NBA pro.

It is important for educators, students, and parents alike to be able to make grading judgments relative to the situation at hand. For most situations, school grades tend to reflect the performance of a student relative to peers of the same ability level. That is, in a heterogeneous class, the standard of measurement would be the mean of the total performance. In a homogeneous class it would be the mean of the particular track perhaps viewed in conjunction with the total student population. An advanced-track student taking a norm-referenced, standardized statewide test, for example, might be judged not only relative to the state average but relative to the rest of the advanced-track students. In any event, students ought to have the benefit of every purpose for which grades can be used. A creative writing student, for example, needs to know that his/her compositions can be evaluated in three ways: relative to how he/she has been doing, relative to how students on that level are generally expected to do, and relative to great writers such as Melville or Tolstoy or Emily Dickinson.

All too often we deny this kind of comprehensive evaluation to our students either because we have teachers who are not able and not willing to provide it or because we are so bogged down with peer-reference approaches that the rest of the evaluation escapes us. The ability to give truly comprehensive evaluations is made more difficult by the nature of the subject being graded. Some subjects demand certain modes of grading while other subjects demand other modes. This concept may become clearer if we look briefly at some commonly available grading modes.

The most frequently encountered public school grades are probably the numerical grades on the 0 - 100 scale where 65 is usually the lowest passing grade. Beyond this, however, there are alpha-grades (A, B, C, etc.) which can occur with or without pluses or minuses (B+, A-, etc.); simple pass-fail grades (sometimes with an "honors" level thrown in); subjective grades with terms like "excellent," "good," "fair-average-satisfactory," and "poor-unsatisfactory" (sometimes abbreviated "E," "G," "S," and "U"); and the 0-4 college index scale. The chart below gives a rough comparative analysis of the various systems.

Grading Systems Comparison

Numerical	Alpha	H-P-F	E-G-S-U	0-4 index
0 - 64	F	F	U	0
65 - 69	D	P	U/S	1.0
70 - 74	C-/C	P	S	1.5
75 - 79	C/C+	P	S	2.0
80 - 84	B-/B	P	S/G	2.5
85 - 89	B/B+	P	G	3.0
90 - 94	A-/A	H	E	3.5
95 -100	A/A+	H	E	4.0

The kind of grade one encounters is often geared to the subject or the educational environment. In an elementary school setting, for example, a grade for "social adjustment" would rarely if ever be given in numerical terms. Here the "E-G-S-U" approach would seem the most appropriate. A high school math course, however, can quite conveniently use the 0 - 100 numerical scale because of the very nature of the work. A creative writing course might fare better with the alpha-system only because a more subjective assessment on the teacher's part is called for.

It is easy to see that all this variety can create many problems for our schools. In a high school, for example, with its great diversity of courses, how does one achieve a unanimity of practice from teacher to teacher? And, in any setting, are students to be assessed relative to self, peer, or objective standard? In general we tend to use descriptive and alpha-grades in the pre-high school years and numerical grades in high school. Colleges generally use the 0-4 index. We also tend to let our grades stand for an evaluation relative to peers. I have no great objection to these practices as long as teachers are able to convert one system to another (e.g., change an "A" to a 95 or 96 if it is necessary to do so), and as long as teachers are willing to let students know how they are doing relative to self and to objective standards. Unfortunately, in these matters I have found my colleagues wanting more often than not.

But setting such deficiencies aside, there are four additional practices regarding grading in today's public schools which I find antithetical to good education. They are grades based upon "subject prejudice;" the phenomenon of "grade inflation;" the great differences between teachers, locales, and national standards; and the frequent lack of congruence between curricula and testing. We have already discussed some of these issues, but let us touch upon all of them briefly in the context of the present topic.

It is a sad but true reality that Americans do not accord equal dignity to all subject areas. Having spent the majority of my life teaching in the fine arts, I can say that with great personal sadness. If you happen to be a student whose interests or talents lie in the home ec. room, or the chorus room, or the metal shop, the subject prejudices of our schools make it a great deal more difficult for you to get quality instruction, equality of grading, or personal recognition. The only "non-academic" area in which this is not true is the area of athletics where recognition—indeed, adulation—on the school level mirrors that found in society on the professional level. We will deal with the intellectual folly of this phenomenon later in this chapter when we discuss the "back-to-basics" movement in American curriculum development. For now in our discussion of grading it is important to see how grades are often used to promote subject prejudice.

In far too many instances, it is required that "non-academic" courses give grades on the honors-pass-fail basis while "academic" courses give alpha or numerical grades. I remember once arguing the point with a board of education member and receiving the comment that it was "perfectly all right to have kids in chorus sound like barking dogs, as long as they can participate without worrying about their grade."

"What if the student involved intends to go into music professionally?" I asked. "Doesn't that student need a grade and a quality musical experience?"

The board member paused a moment before retrenching from her position as an educational Philistine. "Well, then, make it an option for them to have which ever they choose."

"Should we also make it an option in math and English?" I asked.

"Oh no. Of course not," she shot back.

"Why not?" I pressed.

"Because math and English are important," was the reply.

That such attitudes are on the face of it wrong seems axiomatic, yet many professionals plead guilty to academic subject prejudice. Listen to what Conant has to say on the issue.

> The American public and the professional educators...are still a bit uncertain as to why instruction should be provided in art, music, foreign language, and physical education...As I have talked to the teachers and professors active in the four areas I am here exploring, I have become impressed with an attitude something like an inferiority complex that seems to arise out of the lively competition for the...students' time and interest.[84]

Besides relegating non-academic subjects to different grading modes, many schools now embark upon the practice of "grade weighting." Here courses which determine a student's overall average are weighted as to degree of difficulty. Advanced-placement academics are generally weighted more than average-track or non-academic courses, even though A-P students have been judged capable of handling the work. Again, such practices bespeak an educational bigotry repugnant to the persona of the student and counterproductive to the occupational vitality of the nation. Having sat in A-P calculus courses, music theory courses, and courses in sculpture, I can tell you it was sculpture which gave me the most trouble. Degrees of difficulty are relative to the student, and processes which define difficulty by grade weighting are both arbitrary and insulting. Even more, as we shall see later, they are at the core of a philosophy which undermines the dignity of the child and robs the child of the freedom to define his or her special course of development.

We have already touched on the subject of grade inflation, that is, the artificial boosting of a grade for any of a variety of reasons. Under no circumstances can grade inflation be condoned, for it is the perpetration of a lie, and when grade inflation begins to infringe on the area of student retention, it becomes a truly harmful educational practice. Copperman expresses his concern about the negative effects of grade inflation in his work, *The Literacy Hoax*. He points out that by 1977 over 81% of American high school grades were A's or B's, a percentage far in excess of normal distribution curves. He cites, as a dramatic example of the misleading nature of such grades, the case of the valedictorian at Western High School's class of 1976. The grade inflation at Western (Washington, D.C.) had literally made this youngster an "A" student. The kid's scores on the norm-referenced nationwide SAT tests, by contrast, were a pitiful 280 on the math and 320 on the verbal portion. When the valedictorian applied for admission to prestigious George Washington University, he was summarily rejected by an admissions office which quickly saw through the dishonesty of the high school grades. Asked to comment on the incident, Dean Joseph Ruth of the University said, "My feeling is that a kid like this has been conned. He thinks he's a real scholar. His parents think he's a real scholar. He's been deluded into thinking he's gotten an education."[85]

While not taking as strong a stand on the ravages of grade inflation as Copperman, Geisinger also cites some serious problems resulting from the phenomenon. He lists the potential effects of grade inflation as "the declining incentive value of grades to encourage students to work, changes in students' self-assessment of their skills, the increased awarding of academic honors, and the increased difficulty graduate and professional schools encounter in making admissions decisions."[86] However you slice it, grade inflation erodes the standards of American educational judgment and renders American schools less and less capable of deciding who should pass and who should fail.

Not long ago I came upon an example of the problem with one of my own students, a student who had entered my theatre class with aspirations of becoming a writer. She was, at the time of the incident, in the final term of her senior year in high school. To prepare for an upcoming unit on writing dramatic scenes, she showed me a sample of her work for a recent assignment in her creative writing class. The assignment was to write a children's book geared to the level of a primary school student. She complied by writing and illustrating (beautifully, I might add) a story of a young girl taking her first violin lesson. While the story was adorable and the pictures as cute as could be, the writing was absolutely atrocious— particularly for a senior about to graduate and pursue a college major in the creative arts. The sentences were incorrectly punctuated. Many of them were grammatically flawed. Word order was badly handled. Even the spelling was terrible. The contraction "she'd" was written "shede," and the musical term for plucking a string, pizzicato, was spelled "pitsacato." However, the worst part of the paper was that the English teacher, generally regarded as one of the school's best, had made not a single correction, but rather had given the paper an A+.

I know as both an educator and a writer how horribly competitive this young girl's chosen career is, and I know that in very short order when she leaves high school she will have to face the reality of her deficiencies. I do not believe that she will be able to overcome them because for too many years her teachers passed her and passed her when they knew that her work was substandard. In the end, unknowing, like a goat stepping off a cliff, she will have her heart broken by the real world with which she will soon compete. I try to help her by gently making the corrections my colleagues refuse to make, but in my own heart I sense it is too late, and I weep for her and hope she will be strong enough to overcome the disappointments which lie so needlessly ahead.

To be absolutely fair about it, the views on retention (i.e., being "left back") are somewhat mixed within the educational community, and my own position is not as one-sided as the story above might have you believe. Let us look at some of the recent research in this area before articulating a final policy.

President Reagan's "Nation at Risk" report advocated stricter promotion policies for reasons very similar to the ones stated above. In this, the report echoed the sentiments of the American public, 72% of whom told the 18th Annual Gallup Poll on Education that tougher promotion standards were needed. Actually, according to Smith and Shepard, American school retention rates are comparatively high already. We retain 15-19% of our school population. Japan retains only about 1%.[87]

There is mounting evidence, however, that retention in the primary and junior high grades is counter-productive both educationally and financially. Research by Holmes, Matthews, Hammack, Borg, Larabee, and others reveals a host of negative repercussions from policies of early retention. Young children who repeat grades, for example, are usually emotionally worse off because they are out-of-place with physically and psychologically less mature classmates. Retention increases costs by as much as 8% over alternatives such as tutoring and summer study. Children who are left back are far more likely to drop out of school in later years. Because wealthy parents can afford early childhood education classes, special tutoring, and summer enrichment programs, retentions tend to be skewed more to socioeconomically disadvantaged children.[88] There is even evidence which suggests that the academic gains made by students who are left back are *less* than the gains made by students who are passed on with their own age group.[89]

Caught between the disadvantages of early retention and the hideous ramifications of passing students who don't deserve to pass, it would seem a middle ground policy might lead to the best results. Such a policy could allow an elementary or junior high student to be passed along *once* with subsequent tutoring, summer school, or remediation. Should a second sub-par year occur, the child could be placed in an alternate learning environment with others of similar dysfunction to embark upon alternate curricula which would lead to an alternate high school diploma.

For high school students who have clearly shown normal learning capabilities, this modified retention policy would not be necessary. Failing a course would simply mean repeating the course. Failing a series of courses would mean repeating them in the normal school environment, in summer school, in a fifth year of high school, or in an alternate high school—whichever would be most appropriate for the situation at hand. Under no circumstances, however, should a high school student be allowed to graduate with skills substandard for the program in which the student is enrolled.

Once we come to grips with our subject prejudice and retention problems, we will have to address the issue of grading discrepancies from teacher to teacher and locale to locale. Without some sort of standardization it is really impossible to assess the meaning of any given grade. For example, without knowing the teachers involved, how could we compare the A+ given by the creative writing teacher who inflates grades with an A+ or B+ or C+ from a creative writing teacher who is a rigorous, demanding marker? The answer is that we just can't, and that is why norm-referenced, standardized tests like Stanford Achievement Tests, California Tests of Basic Skills, Iowa Tests, Scholastic Aptitude Tests or New York State Regents Exams are necessary. Beyond these, however, within each district, each school, and each department, educators are going to have to come up with common standards and common grading procedures. All of which leads us to our last consideration in the area of grading, the concept of congruence.

The term congruence (or alignment, as some educators prefer to say) refers to the way in which tests and curricula accurately reflect each other. If our tests and thus our grades do not cover what our teachers cover in class, they become relatively meaningless evaluative tools. To say this in another way, we must be sure that we teach what we wish to test and test what we wish to teach. As fundamental as this sounds, for a good many years in the post-1945 era educators shunned such policies, claiming that they stifled teacher creativity by forcing teachers to "teach to the test," that is, to cover only the material they knew would be asked in test situations.

I never saw anything wrong with covering material in this way, and I still don't. I do not think that congruence need limit what a teacher does. It only sets a basic parameter which the teacher is perfectly free to augment. I rather feel that the teachers who complain about congruence are those who do not want to be held accountable for the performance of their students on standardized tests, and if that is true, it is a position which cannot be tolerated any longer if America is to address her educational problems in a serious way.

To effect any real congruence, we must start with a detailed, well-conceived curriculum, for it is only when we decide what information we wish to impart to our children that we can design tests and give grades which accurately reflect how our children have absorbed that information. Thus, we shall conclude our view of modern public education with a discussion of our various curricula.

Curriculum

After all is said and done, after the teacher has been trained, the student has been enrolled, and all the mechanisms of the educational system have been put into working order, we face our most important question: what do we teach? The answer to this question is neither obvious nor uniform. It depends upon our motives not only as an educational system but as a society, and it depends upon the variations of our educational environment. Do we teach values or data or both? Do we teach opposing views or just commonly held ones? Do we teach "basics" or an extended curriculum? Do we teach controversial topics or "safe" ones? Do we teach the same kinds of things to eight-year olds as we do to eighteen-year olds? Do we teach the same things to a child in New York City's Spanish Harlem as we do to a child living on a ranch in Havre, Montana? And if we do, *why* do we? And if we do not, *why* not?

To help us sort through these and other questions which arise in discussions of curriculum, we will divide our discussion into three major topics: (1) the general philosophical concepts which lie behind the formation of curricula, (2) an airing of some pressing curricular issues, and (3) a proposal of a sample K-12 curriculum in which specific courses and daily schedules will be presented for each of the traditional school levels (primary, junior high, and senior high).

General philosophical concepts of curriculum. Earlier in this text we talked about the Trobriand Islands and the differences in the feelings of "child ownership" between so-called primitive and so-called civilized societies. In American culture, adults often extend the doctrine of parental control from the legal, moral, and psychological to the curricular. We have already observed this phenomenon in our earlier discussion of Christian fundamentalism and the teaching of evolution. It is now time to articulate a philosophy of curriculum development and dissemination with this phenomenon in mind.

I cannot conceive of a policy more at odds with the ideals of democracy than one which establishes schools as places of indoctrination rather than information and training. It will be difficult if not impossible for America in particular and mankind in general to survive and progress if children are deliberately manipulated in school, deliberately withheld from a variety of knowledge, or deliberately shut away from ideas which may conflict with local or even national norms. The essence of a democracy is an electorate capable of thinking for itself, and that requires possession of information and ideas—*all* information and ideas, not just those which are espoused by a particular parent, a particular religious sect, or a particular political party.

I submit it is time we stopped equating the presentation of knowledge and ideas with the *acceptance* of them. It is important for American children to learn the tenets of Communism, for example, not because we want to turn them into little Marxists but because they will be incapable of dealing with Communism from a position of ignorance. How can we expect our kids to think for themselves about issues like "creationism vs. evolution" unless they know what creationism and evolution are?

For some people the philosophy of curricular openness will not be difficult to accept. For others, many of whom have a deep psychological need to avoid subjects painful to themselves, curricular openness is anathema, for it requires the ability to cope with the existence of divergent views. Let me give you two examples which are particularly controversial in the America of the late 1980's.

The spread of the disease we call AIDS through the homosexual community into the drug culture and finally the heterosexual community has sparked a lively debate in America on so-called "alternate life styles." In particular, the phenomenon of homosexuality has found two opposing camps. There are those who see it as an acceptable behavorial choice and those who see it as something of an aberrant deviation from the norm. As today's students come to grips not only with their own emerging sexual identities but with problems such as the AIDS epidemic, they are going to have to cope with conflicting theories of homosexuality. Is it, as many gay activists claim, an acceptable, even natural, mode of behavior, or is it as Freud claimed a state of arrested development which masks deeper neuroses and anxieties? Our citizens will need information on both sides to make the important legal, ethical, and medical decisions which await our democracy. Curricular openness would have the topic appropriately discussed so that those decisions can be intelligently made.

The free-market capitalism of our democracy has long practiced an economic policy which acts as an incentive for some types of behavior and a disincentive for other types of behavior. Traditionally, we encourage borrowing and the spending of money we don't have by allowing the interest we pay on borrowed money to be deducted from our taxable income. Conversely, with people who live within their means to the point where they can put money into the bank, we discourage savings by having the interest on savings added to their taxable income. Recently, the American economy has undergone a substantial change in that America is now a debtor nation forced more and more to seek investment capital from foreign countries such as Japan. Among the many ramifications of this position is the phenomenon that less and less of America is being owned by Americans and more by citizens from abroad. Curricular openness would not only allow this issue to be aired but would ask the students of today how they might wish to deal with the de-Americanization of the American economy in the future. If one day a student working in a job controlled by foreign investors is asked to accept a different pay scale or work ethic or corporate structure, he or she will need information to be able to cope with change. And if America wishes to avoid that day, students might have to consider a serious revision of current tax laws. What, for example, would happen if the incentive/disincentive formula were reversed—if savings interest were deducted from taxable income and interest on borrowings were added? However such an issue might be decided, no intelligent decision could be made if the issue were not aired in the first place.

It is with the doctrine of curricular openness that we shall proceed. In doing so, we will consider three facets of curriculum philosophy: (a) defining the purposes of a K-12 education in terms of general outcomes, (b) defining the tasks of education by level (K-graduate school), and (c) exploring the concept of functional relevance in subject matter.

(a) The purpose of a general K-12 education in the American democracy. If indoctrination is not to be the reason we send our children to school, then what should be? What is it we should seek to accomplish for students between kindergarten and high school graduation?

There are no shortages of curriculum philosophy in the American academic community. From the general theoretical works of scholars such as Jerome Bruner and B. Othanel Smith[90] to detailed courses of study as far back as Elmer Brown's curricula for the classical, normal, commercial, linguistic, and scientific high schools of 1907,[91] scholars have told us what they think we ought to be teaching. For a good many years, the curricular landscape of twentieth century America was dominated by the work of John Dewey in a movement which came to be known as "progressive education." Though the term is no longer used, having died with the passing of Dewey in the 1950's, much of Dewey's ideas still survive. Essentially, Dewey was after the education of the whole child, not just that part of the child which would absorb the "three R's" and some religious indoctrination. The man whose life led from the agriculturally-based America of the post-Civil War era to the incipient space technology of the post-World War II era brought American education into the modern age.

For Dewey, in both the classroom and the world of experience, a well-educated citizen meant one with not only academic insight but physical, psycho-social, vocational, and civic insights as well.[92] His was a philosophy which spawned the idea that good education in a free society owes a kind of development and dignity to every child. It was the idea, as Keller puts it, "that every human being has a talent...and that the distinction between 'creative' talents and the ordinary run-of-the mill talents is an unnecessary man-made distinction." To use Somerset Maugham's words, "There is no more merit in having read a thousand books than in having plowed a thousand fields...(or in) being able to find out what is wrong with a stalled motor car."[93]

Recently, scholars have given us curriculum mandates in all conceivable forms from the laundry list of cultural terms by E.D. Hirsch[94] to the course-by-course suggestions of Boyer and Goodlad.[95] Roberts and Cawelti have, in fact, published a kind of historical summary of curricular thought in the post-1945 era which includes the data of the Harvard Committee (1945), the Conant Report (1959), the Broudy subject clusters (1964), the Cawelti General Education Model (1982), and the College Board Competency and Content Statement (1983), as well as the work of Boyer and Goodlad.[96] All of these to one extent or another carry the stamp of John Dewey in that they see the purpose of modern public education as being multifaceted.

In 1955, President Eisenhower's White House Conference on Education articulated fourteen goals for American public schools, beginning with the mastery of fundamental skills in reading, writing, and mathematics and including items such as a knowledge of the U.S. heritage, aesthetic appreciation, physical health, and the development of effective work habits.[97] More recently, general curricular purposes have been articulated by Adler and Fantini. Adler states that the three fundamental objectives of a modern public education should be personal development, the development of citizenship, and vocational development. "To achieve these three objectives," he writes, "the character of basic schooling must be general and liberal." He goes on to say that:

> ...it should have a single required 12-year course of study for all, with no electives except one—an elective choice with regard to a second language, to be selected from such modern languages as French, German, Italian, Spanish, Russian, and Chinese...This...excludes what should be excluded—all forms of specialization, including particularized job training.[98]

Fantini's curricular goals are similar. His first is the mastery of basic skills: "not only the familiar three 'R's,' but also those skills that allow us both to adapt ourselves to our environment...and to adapt our environment to ourselves." His second is "the identification and cultivation of talent;" his third, learning to perform as "an economic and political participant" in society.[99]

Whether or not one agrees completely with any of these views we can draw upon them all to construct our own curricular mandate. In the paragraphs below, we shall do that, articulating the reason each curricular objective is important.

One can postulate five general goals for education in the American democracy:

(1) The development of the mind
(2) The development of the spirit
(3) The development of the body
(4) The development of individual talent
(5) The development of the citizen

Let us view each in turn.

(1) The development of the mind. It is, on the face of it, an absolute necessity for children to learn to use their minds, and no educator I have ever read has denied the primacy of this curricular goal. It is convenient to divide mental training into three areas: the mastery of the basic skills of reading, writing, and arithmetic figuring; the development of various thinking skills as described by Bloom and others; and the development of what I call "study skills" which have implications far beyond a child's school years.

To say that in any of these aspects American public education has done a laudable job would be to exaggerate the reality greatly. In the area of reading, for example, most current studies show that while "disadvantaged" students have made some progress in reading, they still read at much lower levels than "advantaged" students who themselves have made precious few gains since 1971.[100] Nor is the reading crisis new to the post-1970 era. One can point to the work of educators such as Ursula MacDougall as far back as 1952 to demonstrate substandard reading performances in past generations.[101]

In the area of the development of thinking skills, there has been a spate of work in the last few years to suggest that we have been ignoring what Bloom calls "higher order skills" (analyzing, judging, evaluating, creating, etc.) in favor of "lower order ones" (recognizing, imitating, etc.). Robert Marzano, for example, writes:

> In recent years many Americans have come to recognize that students in our schools do not think as skillfully and critically as we might wish...Such philosophers as Robert Ennis, Matthew Lipman, and Richard Paul hold that the development of rational thinkers should be the primary goal of education.[102]

Richard Paul, in fact, argues that thinking skills are fundamental to the ability of a democracy to sustain itself. He suggests (and he is not alone) that it is not simply the present curriculum but the poor quality of teachers and administrators which is responsible for the failure of American children to learn how to think.
Here are his own words:

> Unlike the case of computer skills or other technical skills, there is a natural disinclination for people to recognize the degree to which they themselves have not developed critical thinking skills. Educators tend to retreat to

> simplistic curriculum packages that do not lay an appropriate foundation for higher level...thinking skills.[103]

Correcting this deficiency in American education thus depends not only on our ability to see that thinking skills are important and to infuse them into our lesson plans subject-by-subject, but also on our ability to turn out the teachers and administrators willing and able to do so. As with so many of our educational problems, this one is tightly interwoven with the problem of teacher training, and we will have to attack them both simultaneously if we really wish to improve our schools. One way we can attack the curricular part of the problem is by teaching the skills necessary for academic study and success. Because these skills demand higher order mental processes, their inclusion in our curriculum would not only increase student outcomes but develop mental capacity as well. Here are just a few such study skills: note-taking, outlining, memorizing, essay-and paper-writing, test-taking, time-organizing. The techniques involved in these activities once learned become a foundation for life. Outlining, for example, teaches one to think structurally. Time-organizing not only benefits the student but years later the working parent. To the extent teachers include these skills within their subject curricula, they immeasurably service their students and the society. Intelligent districts might coordinate the study skills taught by an entire faculty so as to produce a unanimity of methods and expectations from the earliest grades to the latest.

(2) The development of the spirit. One has but to look at the ingestion of drugs and alcohol, the spread of school violence, the terrible death toll from auto accidents and suicides, and the hundreds of thousands of unwanted pregnancies amongst our school population to conclude that our children are in a state of spiritual crisis. At any time, their spiritual and emotional growth would be an important curricular goal. Today it is an imperative we had better not ignore. Our curriculum must reflect from the earliest grades onward a concern for the development of the souls of our children. Their spiritual and emotional growth can be fostered by courses in the arts, in philosophy, and in religion. Their psychological growth can be fostered by courses which address the self in relation to the self and to others. Later in this topic we will look at some specifics in this area—and they will be controversial to some. Before closing your mind to them, however, re-read some of the statistics on student behavior and ask yourself if silence in this curricular domain will address the problems meaningfully.

(3) The development of the body. It is not enough for us to dismiss the physical development of our children with a perfunctory round of exercises in gym class. We need to help them establish the habits and attitudes which will keep them healthy for a lifetime. This involves not only the exercise regimens appropriate for young, growing bodies but also the exposure to skills and knowledge which will serve them beyond their school years. Not that sports like baseball or football are to be belittled, but they do not service the forty-year-old long after gym classes are over. Walking skills, jogging skills, aerobic exercise skills, tennis, swimming, ping-pong, square dancing, etc. are far more appropriate activities for lifetime fitness. So are the attitudes which promote good personal hygiene. How our students eat, dress, groom themselves, brush their teeth, visit their doctors are all ingredients to be covered in this curriculum. Finally, it is here that we must from the earliest ages teach our children how to avoid drugs, alcohol, cigarettes, and the sexual excesses which may lead to unwanted pregnancy or venereal disease.

Again, these are controversial topics whose subject matter will have to be approached with great sensitivity. Ours is still a repressed society, and there will be many parents who will not want their children exposed to the knowledge in these subject areas. Perhaps we will have to make such courses voluntary, requiring the consent of parents. If we do so, we should take the opportunity to study what happens to the children exposed and not exposed to the knowledge. Longitudinal research in this area would enable us to know whether or not our education was truly effective. Certainly, we will need to train teachers especially carefully for this curriculum. They will have to be knowledgeable, sensitive to both child and community, and personally at ease with the topics they cover.

But cover those topics they should. That is the opinion of expert after expert. Susan Klein, Senior Research Associate for the U.S. Department of Education, for example, writes that most teachers on all grade levels shy away from topics which call for mention of genitalia, reproduction, sexual activity, menstruation, or even swearing. "If teachers remain silent, " she says, "they avoid controversy but teachable moments are lost. The children, of course, will continue to discuss virginity, or any other aspect of sexuality, without guidance from adults."[104] What Klein observes about sex education is echoed by others in the area of alcohol and drug abuse curricula. Both Lowell Horton of Northern Illinois University and William Hansen of the University of Southern California, for instance, stress that early intervention with counselling, peer support groups, and classes must replace educational silence if students are to have a better chance for a healthier life.[105] Some educators, such as Larry Cuban of Stanford University, are even beginning to doubt whether classroom teaching can meaningfully cope with sex, drug, and alcohol problems in our student population. Cuban suggests alternate approaches like state-funded family planning clinics and making parents financially responsible for babies born to children under eighteen.[106]

(4) The development of individual talent. America is a nation of strange prejudices where talent is concerned, and it expresses those prejudices both academically and economically. Doctors, lawyers, engineers, architects, etc. are vaunted professionals. As a rule they are highly paid and thus the courses designed to prepare students for these professions have a high degree of prestige. Parents want their kids to have them; guidance counsellors give them preferential treatment in the scheduling wars. Students with talents in these areas are pampered, catered to, and accommodated. On the other side of the coin, home economics, music, art, industrial arts, and business are not high prestige courses because as a rule the public does not perceive careers with large incomes stemming from them—people such as Julia Child, Leonard Bernstein, Marc Chagall, or Thomas Edison notwithstanding. And then there is the world of athletics in which only one in a hundred thousand makes big money but where (pardon the Freudian analysis) one can glorify sexual performance by substituting other feats of physical prowess. The young athlete, thus pampered and promoted, becomes the surrogate performer for all of us over-the-hill folk.

Parents, many of whom are living out their fantasies through their children, are famous for trying to wheedle high prestige courses for kids, and schools whose administrators and guidance staff are all too willing to play the game often become parental tools. "Smart" kids are dumped into high prestige courses while "slow" kids get music, art, metal shop, or home ec.

The whole sorry cycle is a travesty of reality, and the reality is that no generation ought to have the hubris to push its children anywhere because *nature* (or God or genetics) and *not* people is the creator of our abilities. We are only the facilitators. In any given generation we will spawn so many doctors, poets, scientists, musicians, mechanics, etc., and no amount of effort on our part will change that. We may push the talented pianist into a career in surgery or the talented chef into a career in law, but we cannot obfuscate the talent. In the end we are stuck with an unhappy doctor and a frustrated lawyer.

I once heard a famous Hollywood star asked if she wanted her daughter to go into show business. "I don't care what my daughter does," she responded, "as long as she looks forward to Monday." There was more wisdom in that line than in all the curricular platitudes I've heard in twenty years of teaching.

What we ought to be doing if we want whole and happy children and a whole, happy society is finding out where the talent lies in each child and providing a means of developing it without prejudice so that every child has dignity and a place in the world. To do this we must have a multiplicity of subject exposure for a child's self-exploration, and a multiplicity of courses for self-development. And in this process, Mortimer Adler notwithstanding, we should try to prepare our students to market their talents in careers which afford both personal and economic satisfaction. If our schools met this curricular goal with any kind of frequency, we would cut our dropout rate enormously because school would become a place for meaningful personal development. The excitement of the classroom would quickly outpace the artificial "high" of the marijuana joint, and we would rapidly change the course of our direction. To do this, though, we need to come to grips with two difficult things: first, we must accept that *all* talent has dignity and deserves nurturing, and second, we must ask our parents to accept what their children are, regardless of what they wish them to be. When this happens, we will begin to experience changes not only in our course offerings but in our colleges as well, for it will be sociologically prestigious for a college to give a degree in automotive mechanics and perhaps that will begin to equalize the pay differential between the mechanic and the lawyer. Later in this chapter we will explore the subject areas and courses which can help make the development and marketing of an individual talent a more realizable curricular goal.

(5) The development of the citizen. Alex Molnar of the University of Wisconsin tells us that Americans are participating less and less in the election process and that they are receiving information much of which "is either incomplete or so devoid of content that it is useless as a basis for making informed political judgments." He goes on to say that:

> This problem has been amplified by the increasing concentration of the ownership of the mass media into fewer and fewer hands and the growing

> tendency of the federal government to withhold information from the public in the name of "national security."[107]

That Americans choose not to participate in their participatory democracy nonplusses me. What a waste of the thousands upon thousands of brave souls who died in battle and wilderness to forge this nation. But more than waste, non-participation is a danger, for as citizens are less active they are more susceptible to being controlled and manipulated by government, media, or private industry. In time the cancer of non-participation can eradicate a democracy and leave its people at the economic or ideological or governmental mercy of a tyrant. To avoid such a catastrophe, our public school curricula must develop citizens with a keen view of their world and their nation. Our students must be able not only to see themselves with respect to the rest of mankind but also to muster the sense of civic responsibility to work for the preservation of the democracy and through it the preservation of mankind.

It is interesting to read the likes of Charles Beard, John Norton, and George Counts who wrote of American education at a time when America was poised on the brink of World War II. Beard pleaded for a school system "committed to the maintenance and improvement of American society;" Norton demanded that our classrooms develop a "broad social intelligence;" and Counts was eloquent on the need for citizenship training. He wrote:

> If democracy is to save itself, it must do far more than appropriate billions of dollars for military defense..In the last analysis...it is a question of the education of free men, broadly and fundamentally considered...The American public school through its life and program should proceed deliberately to foster and strengthen all those physical, intellectual, and moral traits which are the substance of democracy.[108]

These words, no doubt fired by the anxiety of a world war, are as true if not truer today for a globe whose miscalculations could bring planetary annihilation. There are really no options besides serious citizenship training, not only through classes which promote it, but, as California Congressman John Vasconcellos puts it, through "the practical experiences of being a citizen."[109] Again, later, we will discuss specific courses designed to accomplish this vital curricular goal.

(b) The task of education by grade level. Before going on to speak of current curricular problems and suggestions for a K-12 curriculum, it would be wise to have some idea of how the educational goals articulated above can be dealt with on each level of the educational ladder. What is it we should expect of our primary schools? Just what is important in a junior high setting? In answering questions such as these, for each level of school (primary, junior high, high school, college, and graduate school), we will view in general terms the psycho-social and academic tasks which should be accomplished.

The pressing psycho-social tasks of primary (i.e. elementary, K-6) school are two in number: beginning the development of successful interpersonal relationships and beginning the development of internal control mechanisms. By the time a child leaves the sixth grade, we expect him or her to have formed stable, normal peer relations and a positive working relationship with adults. We also expect that the self-centered outbursts and tantrums one experiences with a two-year-old, for example, have been modified by the capacity for self-control. Academically, we expect that by the completion of grade school children can read, write, and calculate in a manner appropriate to their age via the guidelines established for each subject area. Addition, subtraction, multiplication, division, rudimentary fractions, reading more than simple three-or four-word sentences, writing grammatically correct structures and paragraphs are all examples of skills we expect to be mastered by the onset of the middle school or junior high years. We also expect that at this level children can begin to use higher order thinking skills which call for comparing, evaluating, and even synthesizing data.

Before leaving the primary level, it is worth noting that accomplishing these early psycho-social and academic tasks can be greatly aided by two important modifications of many current school systems: smaller primary class sizes and the availability of pre-school and kindergarten programs. Mueller and his associates at the University of Indiana report that class size reductions to eighteen pupils resulted in "significant increases in students' reading and mathematics achievement and in their attitudes toward self and school."[110] Similar gains have been noted, particularly with "at risk" students, in programs which have supplied early academic and social intervention before first grade.[111] Though the cost of these programs is high, they are infinitely less expensive than the cost of coping with the anti-social behavior of many dropouts later. In addition, early childhood education programs meaningfully address the working parent/latchkey child syndrome by affording professional nurturing from the age of three onward. Thus, it is possible that the freeing of welfare recipients to join the tax-paying work force through early childhood programs might embrace much of the cost involved.

The psycho-social tasks of middle school or junior high school center decidedly on the emerging sexuality of students. These are the years of physical blossoming, and they should be marked by as smooth a transition through puberty as possible. Courses of study which enable children to understand and become at ease with their sexuality are a must, but even more important are successful relationships with peers and positive relationships with adults who are both nurturing and steadfast in the guidance they provide. Positive adult role models at this stage are particularly important in helping youngsters develop constructive as opposed to destructive values. An important adjunct to the sexual development of children here—and really an outgrowth of it—is the child's developing sense of democratic systems and his or her participation in them. The mechanisms of student government and class-oriented decisions (under the guidance of adults) is extremely useful at this age in the development of the fully mature citizen.

From an academic view, the middle school/junior high years are characterized by three distinct tasks: first, the solidification and polishing of basic reading, writing, and figuring skills; second, the development of higher order thinking skills such as synthetic reasoning, evaluative reasoning, and critical reasoning; and third, the broadening of exposure to various branches of study in an effort to find individual talents and interests. The most fruitful middle school/junior high school curricula are the ones which meaningfully address these areas. Above all, this age must mark the end of undifferentiated curricula and of passing students along who have not fully mastered the basic skills, for it is on the high school level that tracking as we have discussed it becomes an increasing imperative.

The psycho-social tasks of high school are in essence a continuation and refinement of what was begun on the middle school level. The child's sexual and social identity continues its transition to adulthood so that by the end of the high school years, the individual should have a relatively full sense of who he or she is and how he or she fits into society. At this age the sexual and social play of earlier years reaches mature expression. Dating is expected and important. Social acceptance is a paramount concern. Weaning from the authority of home is more dramatic. Psychological independence and the concomitant social, sexual, and economic ramifications of it become pressing personal tasks. Again, courses on this level must aid the transition to adult years constructively and gracefully. Similarly, activities (such as student governments) must bring the child closer and closer to full democratic peerage, for soon the child will attain legal peerage and must become accountable and responsible as a citizen.

Academically, high school years should accomplish three things: mastery of basic learning and thinking skills; mastery of a core curriculum which is aimed at the development of a well-rounded human being; and a continuing exposure to areas of learning in which the student may wish to participate for maximum personal and vocational fulfillment. It is thus in high school that curricula should be rigorous in their demands, mandatory in terms of an academic core, and expansive in an offering of electives.

It is on the college level that the transition from childhood to adulthood should be completed in every psycho-social area except the economic one. Being reliant on home—now both geographically as well as psychologically further removed—becomes (save the area of finances) less and less imperative. The student, by graduation, should be an adult with a firm emotional foundation and a developed sense of sexual and social identity with which he or she is prepared to live probably for the remainder of his or her years. Academically, college has two vital goals: the mastery of a core curriculum designed to allow full expression as an individual and functioning citizen, and the mastery of a course of study which directly prepares the student for vocational fulfillment or entry to a graduate school for further training.

Finally, by the post-graduate level (if there is one), the student should be a fully-developed psycho-social being. Marriage, parenthood, being able to live as a fully independent person are all expected choices of behavior. Academically, the post-graduate level is a time of intense specialization and preparation for careers which are usually at the pinnacle of the various professions.

In viewing the tasks of education at each level from primary to graduate school, it is important to remember that every child develops in a unique way. Thus, some may reach independence, vocational fulfillment, or psycho-social maturity either faster or slower than others. The various systems of education we offer must be intelligent and flexible enough to handle not only the great numerical mainstream but the exceptions as well.

(c) The concept of functional relevance. We shall conclude our general philosophical view of curriculum with a look at the concept of functional relevance, a concept which in effect says that if you cannot tell a student why it is important to learn a given thing, you really don't have the educationally moral right to teach it.

If we can harken back to William Glasser for a moment, we will remember his discovery that students learn best when they perceive that they can master the information at hand and that the information has some usefulness to them. Nothing is more absurd than saying to a child, "learn this because your grandfather did," or "do it because I tell you."

First of all, any teacher who does not know why his subject is relevant and who cannot articulate that relevance has failed to absorb what I consider to be a basic pedagogical principle. But beyond this, if we cannot justify what we teach to our students, ours is really not the process of enlightening them. It is merely the process of brainwashing them—and that is anathema to not only their development but also the very survival of a democracy in which free thought is paramount.

The doctrine of functional relevance is best applied when teachers can show not just how and why their subjects are related to the present lives of their students but also how they are interwoven with other subjects in a world which is not unidimensional but multidimensional.

There is a wonderful Zen Buddist saying about education which goes like this: before study, a tree is a tree; during study, it is less than a tree; but after study, it is more than a tree. By this it is meant that when you view something without a total understanding of it, you see it only in relation to itself. When you study it, by necessity, you dissect it into its constituent elements and for the moment it may lose its wholeness and identity. But when your study is over, you understand it not only in relation to itself but in context with the larger world. You look at the tree not naively as you once did but with a comprehension of what lies beneath the bark, inside the leaf. And that knowledge allows you to judge the tree not just in the light of a given day but as it may be in a storm or a drought or transplanted far from where you view it now.

So it can be with all subjects when teachers know how to relate them to the multidimensional world which touches their students. Let me give you an example of this concept as it was taught to me by a wonderful high school history teacher.

"What treaty ended the Thirty Years War?" he asked. "And when was it signed?"

Silence from the class, until an angry voice called out, "Why should we care, anyway?"

Now challenged to justify his subject—indeed his need to teach it and thus in large measure his reason for being—the teacher swung into action. His manner was without rancor. His humor was rough, and the students knew he was on their side.

"Because, you blockheads, the Thirty Years War devastated Central Europe and kept it from unifying as a nation. From 1648 until well after 1850, it struggled for its identity against the other centralized powers of Europe...And because its people never forgot how they had suffered at the hands of these powers...And because when they finally gained their own country, Germany, they tried to catch up with those powers by pursuing colonialistic policies which eventually sparked World War I...And because, upon their defeat in World War I, they suffered additional reprisals which made them susceptible to the propaganda and madness of Adolph Hitler which led them and our world in a second war...And because the second war, in which your own families may have suffered, led Russia to fear the reunification of Germany so much that she built a wall across Berlin and a gulf between Eastern and Western Europe...And because if you are ever asked to die in a war over that gulf, you ought to know where it really started and how a better understanding of the Treaty of Westphalia in 1648 might have prevented it."

I am paraphrasing from memory, of course, and I'm not at all sure that every great historian would agree with him, but the very fact that he could tell me what relationship the Treaty of Westphalia had to me not only made the treaty important, it showed me the dimensionality of all learning. Here is the concept in John Dewey's words:

> In a situation where the skills or arts and the subject matter of knowledge have become interwoven and interdependent, adherence to the policy forming the studies of secondary and collegiate instruction on the basis of many isolated and independent subjects is bound to result in precisely the kind of confusion we have at present.[112]

Dewey wrote those words in 1931. They are as true today, and in the articulation of our subject areas and courses below we will heed them by explaining the functional relevance of what it is we wish to teach.

Airing some pressing curricular issues. Before presenting a specific K-12 curriculum, it is appropriate here to discuss a few of the more general curriculum-related issues which have surfaced recently. Airing them now will save us the problem of dealing with them later and will allow the curriculum presented below to be viewed in a more understandable context.

(a) **Untested educational fadism.** We have already seen that many Chapter 1 programs for disadvantaged children are a waste of money.[113] Chapter 1, however, is not the only area in which fads have been foisted upon our schools at tremendous monetary and human costs before being sufficiently tested. The whole area of computers is a perfect example. After billions of dollars of CAI (computer assisted instruction), our children are no better off now than they were twenty-five years ago in terms of the mastery of basic skills. In fact, they may even be worse off because CAI has deprived them of intrinsic accomplishment. Take a sloppy mind and give it a computer and you have only allowed it to automate its sloppiness. But beyond this, we have failed to see that gadgets such as computers have serious flaws which often render them hazards rather than helps.

In my own work, I oversee a budget of nearly three-quarters of a million dollars. It has about 150 separate line item codes. I have learned over the years to keep my accounts by hand because "downtime" and delays virtually prohibit my computer records from being up to date or accurate. In my case, computerization actually costs my secretary and myself dozens of hours a month in the reconciliation of sluggish computer account statements with current hand-kept records. I am amused to see that Wall Street has encountered similar problems in the administration of arbitrage trading.

Not that I am against computers. You will see that right enough in the specific curricula below. But like the wasteful Chapter 1 programs, CAI programs should be tested before being applied to the curriculum, for there are many things which might inhibit their success. Gerald Bracey, for example, points to the work of Richard Diem at the University of Texas who notes that many teachers are not conversant with computer skills before CAI programs are applied. Thus, CAI programs often show no higher levels of student achievement than conventional programs.[114] Julie Vargas of the University of West Virginia adds that CAI designs often do not synchronize with the principles of good instruction. In fact she writes that because of the embarrassment connected with the hype and waste of computers in education, "a conspiracy of silence has extended to computer-assisted instruction." She goes on:

> Many technological innovations have been touted as aids to teaching and learning. Early in this century, Thomas Edison, excited by his invention of motion pictures, promised a great revolution in education...Many years later, similar claims were made for...television...Today, many educators predict that the computer will revolutionize education...They will do so, however, only if CAI programs adopt those features shown to be necessary for learning.[115]

Larry Cuban of Stanford University goes even further. He states that all reforms—electronic, curricular, behavioral, etc.—are doomed to fail if they cannot account for and mesh with the structures of our schools which remain persistent components of the educational process. He writes that large graded schools, self-contained classrooms, fifty-minute periods, etc. became the "organizational DNA" which forced teachers to adopt strategies such as the lecture method, large group instruction, reliance on textbooks and chalkboards, seatwork assignments, texts and quizzes, etc. Reforms which come down the pike riding the crest of any given educational fad rarely take ingrained structures into account. They are movements which shoot from the hip rather than changes which are well thought-out. "Until state policy-makers and national cheerleaders for change understand clearly the consequences for teachers of the reforms they propose, those reforms are likely to prove counterproductive for students, and for the teaching profession,"[116] says Cuban.

The moral is not to engage in wholesale reform until the reform has been properly tested. One does not in a science lab tout a hypothesis as a demonstrated reality until the tests are run. So, too, should it be with educational hypotheses—including the many I have proposed myself within these pages. Maybe tenure review will be a disaster. Perhaps degrees in educational governance for board of education members are unworkable. We will not know until we test the ideas, and until they are tested they should not be instituted ubiquitously.

(b) The "back-to-basics" movement. I hope that by this point I have given you enough information for you to conclude that the "back-to-basics" movement is on the face of it ridiculous. That our students should be competent in basic reading, writing, and thinking skills is axiomatic. Only an idiot would argue the point. But that a child's education should consist solely of "the basics" is a folly that only an idiot would support. What is a "basic?" Music was a "basic" for Andre Watts. Basketball was a "basic" for Julius Irving. Art was a "basic" for Pablo Picasso. Shop classes were "basic" for Henry Ford. Need I go on? We owe *all* children in a free democracy an education which allows them to pursue the talents and interests which will make them constructive, complete, contributing citizens. Any position to the contrary is the perpetuation of an evil which will only destroy the individual in the short run and the society in the long run. Whatever the costs (and, remember, we *have* the money), the pursuit of individual excellence requires more that the definition of a curriculum as English, math, science, and social studies.

(c) The "no-pass/no-play" mentality. Recently, in an effort to shore-up sagging academic performance, schools have adopted academic criteria for participation in certain extracurricular areas (mostly athletics and music). I find this policy terribly demeaning to those activities and terribly counterproductive to keeping kids involved and in school. They are nonsensical remedies which can be exposed as such by merely reversing the argument. If we would not let an athlete play because his or her math grade was an "F," would we also be willing to keep a gifted math student out of calculus if he or she failed gym class? The "penalty" for failing English ought to be repeating the course, not being denied the opportunity to develop in another area. And if the athlete should have to repeat a full year, the loss of playing eligibility, loss of time, and loss of potential athletic scholarships are serious enough consequences.

The "no-pass/no-play" philosophy stems from subject prejudice of the worst kind. Athletic ability is a God-given talent like any other, and any kid with it ought to be able to express it like any other. The same is true for musical ability. The fiasco which occurs on the college level over this issue is unbelievable. A student should be allowed to *major* in athletics, and no university should be permitted to draw an athlete to its campus unless it offers the student a realistic chance of graduating with a useful degree and vocational skill.[117]

(d) School calendars. It is time America considered a school calendar longer than 180 days. Other nations do it, and the low level of American educational performance certainly calls for it. It is also time we started to construct our existing calendars with a bit more intelligence. Opening school on Monday only to close it Tuesday for elections merely encourages kids (and parents) to stay home Monday and make a four-day weekend out of it. Mid-week vacations should either be eliminated or made part of "extended weekend" recesses where the extra intervening days are taken from the large Christmas and Easter vacation blocs.

On a similar note, allowing students to go through the summer with no work is a ridiculous waste of time—even if we do not extend the school year. Why not reading lists, book reports, special projects, etc. which would constitute the opening grades and units of the next year's classes?

Finally, the idea of allowing students to graduate high school early should be reserved for very special cases (such as abnormally advanced students or hardship cases involving finances, family crises, etc.). We have already noted that our children are growing up much too fast. For far too many, leaving school early merely rushes them into environments for which they are psychologically, socially, and intellectually unprepared. I do not rule out the practice, but it should be used with great caution.[118]

With all this in mind, let us proceed to our last topic, the proposal of a K-12 curriculum.

A proposed K-12 curriculum. Alex Molnar, Professor of Education at the University of Wisconsin, notes with some sadness that American curriculum planning has, on the whole, been inadequate. Before we begin to unfold our plan, it might be wise to read what he has to say.

> The period between the mid-1960's and the early-1970's was one of widespread experimentation...By 1972 the emphasis had begun to shift away from experimentation to evaluation of existing curriculum designs...It was widely accepted that research findings demonstrated that no single curriculum format had proven itself...Some curriculum scholars began to argue that curriculum designs based only on individual psychology, a theory of knowledge, or an analysis of society were inadequate. These scholars believe that curriculum design should be based on an understanding of (1) the relationship among these variables and (2) the relationship between school success and success in life.[119]

While I do not entirely agree with Molnar that the current scene lacks any widely accepted thought,[120] his words caution us to unfold our curricular thought against the background of broader educational goals. As we have already articulated those goals, we can now outline the various subject areas which can meet them in a scheme that takes into account the different psycho-social and academic tasks of the three school levels of our system (primary, junior high, and high school). The flow chart below provides a comprehensive visualization of our proposal which may make the proposal itself easier to follow.

Curricular Goals

1. Development of the mind
2. Development of the spirit
3. Development of the body
4. Development of individual talent
5. Development of the citizen

Subject Area Through Which Goals Are Met

1. English: reading, writing, study skills, literature
2. Social Studies: history, civics, current events, economics, geography, sociology, psychology
3. Math: arithmetic, statistics, algebra, geometry, trigonometry, calculus
4. Science: general science, earth science, biology, chemistry, physics
5. Foreign Language: Latin, French, German, Spanish, Italian, Russian, Chinese
6. Physical Education: life activities, team sports, fitness exercises
7. Art: drawing, painting, sculpture, ceramics, design, photography, art history, art appreciation
8. Music: band, orchestra, chorus, music history, music appreciation, music theory, musical theatre
9. Library/Business: research, typing, computers, word-processing, stenography, accounting, marketing
10. Technology: life mechanical skills involving electronics, plumbing, autos, other machines
11. Home/Health: sewing, cooking, nutrition, personal hygiene, substance abuse prevention, sex education, consumer education (involving banking, executing contracts, intelligent shopping), planning for major events like marriage, birth, death, setting up a home

Primary	**Junior High/Middle School**	**High School**
K-6	7-8	9-12
or	or	or
K-5	6-8	10-12

We will proceed in detailing our K-12 curriculum by first discussing briefly each of the eleven subject areas in the flow chart above and then outlining a daily model for a primary, junior high, and high school which incorporates those areas.

(a) K-12 curriculum subject areas. The five goals of American public education described above can be met through courses given in the eleven subject areas listed. As we shall see in the daily models which follow, each area is taught at each academic level through materials geared to the abilities and needs of the children on that level.

(1) English. It is in this subject area that reading and writing skills are to be developed. In addition it is here that the study skills of note-taking, outlining, test-taking, time-organizing, and paper-writing should be learned. Finally, it is here that students should receive exposure to the great literature of the world through stories, essays, novels, poetry, and dramas. It would seem that these things, particularly the skills needed for reading and writing, would be axiomatic but they are not. Consider the following from Charles Suhor, the Deputy Director of the National Council of Teachers of English.

> The content of the K-12 English curriculums should not include extensive study of grammatical forms, traditional or otherwise. The study of grammar is at best a liberal arts pursuit, not unlike the study of musical forms. As such, it merits comparatively low priority in elementary and secondary programs. The main language goals of pre-college English are fundamentally the process goals of improving speaking, listening, reading, and writing.[121]

I find Suhor's statement incredible. How, if not with grammar as a basic tool, does one improve speaking and writing skills? And how wrong to compare grammar to musical forms. Musical forms are analogous to literary forms not to grammatical structures. The sonata-allegro form is like the three-act drama, a mazurka is like a sonnet. In fact, the basic structures of music (intervals, scales, chords) are even labeled as "grammar" in some theoretical systems. One speaks of "chord grammar" in the system of triadic tonality, for example. Perhaps it is because of attitudes such as Suhor's that students raised on his curricula cannot write or speak correctly. In any event, in my English curriculum, grammar would be taught and reinforced at all grade levels, and mechanisms to do it (like sentence diagramming), which used to be a part of the curriculum but were removed in the name of "reform," would be reinstituted.

(2) Social Studies. It is here that the student should gain a knowledge not only of society but also of those skills which prepare him or her for "a lifetime of holding the office of citizen," as Bragaw and Hartoonian put it.[122] As a rule, primary grades ought to focus on the knowledge of self, family, and state, while secondary studies concentrate on American history and world history (increasingly divided in recent years into European history and so-called Third World studies). Additionally, on the middle school and high school levels, historical courses should be augmented by ones aimed at training the citizen to be an intelligent voter. These would include civics, geography, economics, current events, etc. Such classes need to be accompanied by student governments and civics projects so that the reality of democracy does not remain only on the printed page but becomes a living, breathing part of student life. Finally, for advanced secondary study, the social studies area can offer courses in sociology and psychology.

The importance of an open social studies curriculum to a free democracy cannot be underestimated. Here is where comparative religious beliefs and value systems can be discussed; here is where the tolerance for diversity can be fostered; here is where racism can really be fought and issues such as creationism vs. evolution really aired. It is here above all else where the nation vests its future.

(3) Mathematics. Professors Campbell and Fey of the University of Maryland have recently articulated the need for school math curricula to teach both computational skills and higher order thinking skills through the use of operations exercises and problem-solving. They go on to state how each of the various grade levels can accomplish this. Grades K-6 should concentrate on the traditional arithmetic operations with the additional topics of whole numbers, decimals, and fractions. Grades 7-8 should refine these skills and add problems involving studies of measurement and interest formulas. Secondary math should "offer students an array of curricular choices designed to match their achievement, ability, and interests."[123] Suggested is a two-strand system in which "general" stream students apply K-8 skills to consumer, career, and vocational fields and "college-bound" students study the traditional algebra, geometry, trigonometry, pre-calculus, and calculus regimen.

Campbell and Fey also speak about the failure of the so-called "new math" to improve student outcomes. They do not, however, blame this "discouraging experience with reform," as they put it, entirely on the curriculum. Poor teacher preparation was, they claim, a significant factor in the failure of the program, and that part of the program which sought to explain the underlying concepts of mathematical operations ought to be preserved in new curricula.[124]

The development of operation skills for consumer, career, and vocational needs; the availability of advanced secondary courses for college preparation; and the use of problem-solving techniques to teach higher order thinking skills on all grade levels make the Campbell/Fey plan an excellent one. It addresses the critical curricular goals of mental and vocational development at the same time that it allows mathematically talented students to press ahead and all students to apply math to their lives as citizens and consumers. Teachers involved in such a curriculum would not have much difficulty explaining to their students why they ought to be doing that homework assignment, and because the curriculum is both useful and able to be mastered by a cross-section of pupils, it has an excellent chance of success.

(4) Science. There is no other subject area in which modern curriculum has been as dynamic as the area of science. Scientific discovery has proceeded so rapidly and scientific change has been so universally applied that a periodic restructuring of the science curriculum has become an evermore important task. Ahlgren and Rutherford suggest that the K-12 science curriculum contain a common core from which students can branch out depending on interest and ability. They stress the teaching of concepts (such as the concept of evolution from atom to DNA to present life to future life) in an array of topics which covers the broad spectrum of sciences from practical science to biology, chemistry, physics, geology, astronomy, etc. What is perhaps even more important in this age where science often merges with issues of morality, they suggest a "frequent curricular crossover" between science and the humanities.[125] In this way, not only the issue of biological engineering can be studied, but its implications to the lives of citizens can be aired and discussed. What are the pros and cons of surrogate motherhood, nuclear power plants, space defense technology, medical advances? For the training of the citizen to decide such issues, our science classes need not only the disciplines of the laboratory but also the curricular space to put the concepts of the lab into a social context.

The writing of Rutherford and Ahlgren, however, raises an even larger issue, the usurpation of functional data by what I call "false rigor." The adherence to high curricular standards is something everyone wants, but often—usually in poor educators—high standards are equated with the ingestion and regurgitation of great quantities of facts. Often this kind of education is counterproductive to sound curricular goals, not only because the average student doesn't need all those facts to absorb the subject successfully, but also because the very processes of ingestion and regurgitation rob the curriculum of the time to relate subject area knowledge to the real world. For the student who is not headed toward a career in science, it is far less important to be able to name all the bones of the body than it is to discuss how good medical care can be made available to everyone in the democracy. The curriculum which sacrifices the latter for the former is not meeting the needs of its constituents. As Walker writes:

> A knowledge of science and technology does not necessarily prepare one to adapt to or direct social change. For that, we clearly need ways to deal in a more integrated fashion with the personal and social issues created by change. Substantial sectors of the public have consistently resisted efforts by public schools to address such personal and social-emotional issues, claiming that they should be handled by the family or church, but not by a secular, government-sponsored, tax-supported system of public schools. If the adjustments required grow more frequent and serious, some means must be found to help individuals adapt. The school will doubtlessly have some role to play in this process.[126]

(5) Foreign Language. How often have you heard students moan about having to take a foreign language? In the curriculum I propose below, it is required, and to answer all those moans, here are the words of linguist Myriam Met.

> Nationally there has been a growing recognition that American monolingualism is an unfortunate but real contributor to the lack of American competitiveness in world markets...In diplomacy, we are hindered by an inability to communicate openly and directly with those with whom we share critical interests...Within the United States...ethnic and linguistic diversity among our population will continue to increase for decades to come...Second-language proficiency may well be a social and occupational survival skill in many American communities...[127]

Met's argument is directed at the study of modern foreign languages which are globally usable (French, Spanish, Russian, etc.). I would extend the need for language to Latin as well, for learning Latin as a grammatic base aids the mastery of not only modern languages but English also. If not complete Latin studies of the

Gallic Wars, Cicero, and Horace, then at least a year of basic Latin grammar and vocabulary on the secondary school level should be reinstated.

Finally, Met notes that many language-teaching fads (such as the audio-linguistic method or ALM—nicknamed "planned parrothood" by many teachers) did not do the job which vocabulary memorization and drill had formerly done. She recommends linguistic immersion at the primary level with writing, grammar, and vocabulary extension reserved for middle school and secondary years, and the models below reflect her views.

(6) Physical Education. We have already talked about the physical education curriculum as one having the dual tasks of developing fitness for the child and regimens for a lifetime. Linda Bain of the University of Houston describes how these goals can be approached at each school level. Elementary school classes should build self-control, involvement, and basic motor skills, she writes. On the middle school level, classes should help students define personal goals, extend skills related to both fitness and motor function, and develop a sense of responsibility to self and others through team play. On the high school level, the themes of fitness, lifetime regimens, personal goals and team responsibility should be extended with the hope that they will continue after school years are over.[128] I find this type of curriculum to be ideally aligned with the general goals articulated above.

(7) and (8) Art and Music. Although they are separate subject areas, art and music are so closely related in terms of curricular function that it is appropriate to consider them together. Actually, the drama component of the English curriculum and any dance component of a physical education curriculum could also fit into a general discussion of fine arts education, so let us bear them in mind as well in the paragraphs below.

Fine arts courses address three of our five critical curricular needs directly. They develop the spirit by allowing students to express and understand emotions in constructive ways; they develop the mind by fostering higher order thinking skills such as creativity and critical judgment; and they address the development of individual talent by offering an incredibly wide—and little understood—range of career options. In yet another way, they also have a powerful effect on the development of the citizen through activities (like chorus, band, orchestra, drama, dance, and musical theatre) which force students to work together for a common goal (remember Glasser and the theory of cooperative grouping).

It is an unfortunate reality that the fine arts have received such short shrift in American public education, and in the history of education itself, it is one of the great ironies. For century after century, the leading universities of Europe based their curricula on the "trivium" and quadrivium," groupings of liberal arts courses which were considered the foundation of learning. The trivium consisted of grammar, rhetoric, and logic; the quadrivium of arithmetic, geometry, astronomy, and music. It was no accident that music was accorded this honor, for it is—to those who know it—at once a science and an art, a confluence of technical, social, literary, and spiritual ingredients. Sadly, not many policymakers in modern education know it, and as a result, music and art curricula are incredibly poorly treated.

Year after year, for example, high school guidance counselors (notorious for their ignorance, obstinacy, and subject prejudice) talk talented kids out of fine arts courses and go overboard to populate them with the dregs of the school. For a while I began to think that the prerequisite for being assigned to my music theory class (a rigorous, college-level course in choral harmonization and species counterpoint) was an I.Q. under 100, a hatred of geometry, the wearing of at least three earrings, and hair down to the pelvis.

Actually, for those of us in the arts, we are aware of the tremendous intelligence and sensitivity required for proficiency. We are also aware of how many careers the arts encompass (from music therapy to computer-design technology). Finally, we are aware of how the arts can do that most precious of all things, integrate learning. Consider in this last case, for example, what a child gets from performing in, say, FIDDLER ON THE ROOF: an exposure to music, poetry, the literature of Sholom Aleichem, set construction, scenic design, the technology of lights and sound, singing, dancing, instrumental performance, an appreciation of ethnicity, and an understanding of early twentieth century immigration patterns and the forces in European history which created them.

In the curriculum I propose below, I do not intend that the under-representation of fine arts education should continue, and for those of you who have taken the values decline and spiritual degeneration of today's youth seriously, I urge you to include the fine arts in the lives of your children.

Paul Lehman of the University of Michigan writes that at the elementary level, fine arts training should allow for an appreciation of the basic structures of the art and the ability to express oneself through these structures. In music this would include concepts such as notation, rhythm, harmony, melody, and musical performance of a vocal or instrumental kind. In art it would include things like line, color, value, shape, texture, and space as they are expressed through working with various media (paint, clay, collage, etc.). On the middle and secondary levels, Lehman postulates a refining of skills and a deepening understanding of the subject area through its works and its history. It is here that students will divide themselves between the "audience" and the "artists" of tomorrow. For those who opt for the former, courses in history and appreciation will suffice. For those who opt for the latter, history and appreciation are merely the precursors of more detailed study. In art such study will include things like drawing, painting, ceramics, photography, design, etc. In music it may include subjects such as harmony, counterpoint, musical theatre, and private vocal or instrumental lessons.[129]

(9) Library and business skills. It is in this subject area that students will learn how to become more independent in obtaining and manipulating data. The key word here is "independent." Independence (of mind, spirit, economic wherewithal, etc.) is the goal of all childhood development. Good schooling has as its primary aim nothing so much as its own obsolescence. Like a good doctor who wishes to see less of his patients because doing so means they are healthier, a good teacher works mostly for his not being needed. In successful education, the student *becomes* the teacher, just as in successful growth the child eventually becomes the adult.

In this subject area, pupils should learn to research, to find for themselves, whatever data is desired. Here, too, they should learn the technological skills needed to process that data. Computer skills, typing, word processing should all be taught.

Starting with basic and simple introductions on the elementary level, the curriculum should continue with research and keyboard training on more complex levels in the junior high years. On the high school level, elective courses should be available (traditionally through business departments or library media centers) for advanced training. The training here often integrates with other disciplines (computers and math, for example), but it most frequently centers on "business skills" through courses in office-related keyboarding, accounting, management, marketing, typing, or stenography. Not all students would specialize by taking these classes, but all should have, by the time they leave high school, a basic knowledge of research skills, typing and word processing skills, and computer keyboard skills.

Finally, it must be remembered in teaching this curriculum that the librarian, computer, typewriter, and word processor are not to replace the intrinsic thinking skills of the individual. They are to be considered (pardon the fine arts analogy) a real piano which makes music only when the pianist is a functioning being, not a "player" piano whose activation requires only the flipping of an "on-off button" and whose sounds are made by a mechanical piano roll.

(10) Technology. Formerly known to many in the post-1945 era as "industrial arts," this subject area has grown to be one of vital importance, especially for the everyday functioning of an independent citizen. "As citizens," James Benson writes, "we must make community decisions: we must plan the future of our cities, decide when to build schools and how to dispose of waste. As consumers we must know how to maintain our cars and homes; we must decide when to purchase services and when to do it ourselves."[130] To meet these demands our children must have a grasp of both the workings of technology and the management of it for personal and social uses. What do you do when the toilet doesn't work? How do you know when the $200 bill for a new auto air filter is legitimate or a rip-off? What constitutes an intelligent vote in a town which wants safe waste disposal? How does one "face a machine" without either terror or ignorance when mowing a lawn, using a blender, or cutting up logs for a winter fireplace? These questions are dealt with in a technology curriculum which on the elementary level begins with an awareness of tools and machines, and which on the middle school level expands that awareness not only in terms of being able to use more and more sophisticated equipment but also in seeing the general applications of technology to society. Finally, the high school curriculum should offer advanced courses for those students whose talents and interests will make them the carpenters and plumbers, engineers and architects, electricians, technicians, and mechanics of tomorrow.

(11) Home and health. What kind of education is it that fills a kid's head with the quadratic formula and never teaches him how to open up a checking account? Life skills (or "survival training" as one of my students calls it) are as needed for our children as "book training." Yet we pay almost no attention to it, and it costs us dearly. Look at how poorly we marry, how traumatically we deal with death, how ignorantly we shop, how blindly we initiate major projects such as renting an apartment or building a house, how stupidly we pollute ourselves with drugs and drink, how mindlessly we kill ourselves with poor nutrition, how self-destructively we engage in sex. It is here in this subject area which we have in the past called "home economics" that we can address these issues.

Again, home economics has never been a prestige subject. Like music and art it has been the victim of American academic prejudice for decades. The college-bound child is not shunted into home ec. by guidance staffs, nor is the parent hoping for his or her kid to become a doctor or lawyer happy about seeing home ec. on next year's class schedule. To which I reply that preparation for life belongs on everyone's schedule at every grade level, especially in a culture where moral degeneration, substance abuse, and family disintegration are as rampant as they are in ours. As Joanna Smith of the Indiana Department of Education writes:

> Home economics is the only curriculum area that focuses on the family and prepares students for family and home living. The field of home economics includes content areas such as consumer education and resource management; housing, furnishings, equipment, interior design and care; individual and family development; nutrition and food; and textiles and clothing.[131]

To this list, Richard Schlaadt of the University of Oregon adds topics such as accident prevention, community health (waste disposal, care of streets, etc.), environmental health, "family life" education (including sex education, family planning, and dealing with crises such as child abuse, rape, death, etc.), disease prevention, substance abuse intervention, etc.[132]

As we have mentioned above, the teachers who teach these topics must be especially well-trained. They must have a clear knowledge and control of their own attitudes and a great sensitivity to the delicacy of the topics and the reactions of their students. It may not be that American parents are ready for such courses in the public schools even though their children are suffering enormously due to the lack of them. Perhaps we will have to begin "preparation for life" classes by having parents sign consent forms for their children's participation. If that is what it takes, then that is where we should start. Sometimes—many times—education involves more than teaching the child. It involves teaching the home and community. Given the statistics of aberrant behavior we have already noted, what choice do we have?

In dispensing the home/health curriculum throughout the K-12 spectrum, it will be important to include all topics at every grade level. Sex is a reality to children long before puberty, as are child abuse, stress management, and substance abuse. Topics such as cooking, sewing, and shopping are as appropriate to a sixth-grader as to a twelfth-grader. So are topics like coping with death, birth, and marriage. It is not the topic itself which is the issue in disseminating the information of this curriculum but rather the appropriateness of the presentation to the grade level at hand. For example, dealing with birth for a second-grader will not require the details of family planning or anatomy one might present to a high school senior. Birth to a child is a phenomenon as yet far removed from personal reproduction. It will involve answering questions such as "where did I come from?" or "how is Mommy going to bring home a sister from the hospital?" in terms which a young mind can grasp. The questions on birth for the sexually active teenager will be quite different. They are apt to focus on things like contraception, pregnancy planning, or even the details of delivery.

It will be up to state and local curriculum experts to plan this subject area with the intelligence and sensitivity to service K-12 populations with material appropriate to child and community. But service them we must if we are to have healthy citizens.

(b) Curriculum models for primary and secondary levels. Now that we have viewed each subject area to see its contents and justify its relation to our basic curricular goals, we can unfold paradigms for each of the three common grade levels (elementary, junior high, and senior high). In doing this, let us remember that paradigms are models in the abstract. The details of class time, school calendar, scheduling, etc. which *real* schools experience are the reality to which models must bend when they are applied to actual situations. For our purposes here, let us assume that elementary means K-6; junior high, 7-8; and high school, 9-12. These are the most frequently-encountered American school structures. Finally, we shall proceed by setting out the model and then providing a brief comment to explain and amplify it.

A Model Elementary School Schedule

Period 0	7:15-8:00	Optional. Latchkey supervision (aide).
Period 1	8:00-8:45	English (common branch teacher).
Period 2	8:45-9:30	Social Studies (common branch teacher).
Period 3	9:30-10:15	Math (common branch teacher).
Period 4	10:15-11:00	Science (common branch teacher, specialist or team).
Period 5	11:00-11:40	Lunch.
Period 6	11:40-12:20	Supervised play (recess).
Period 7	12:20-1:00	Assigned activity or music group rehearsals.
Period 8	1:00-1:45	Art/Music. Daily alternation (specialist).
Period 9	1:45-2:30	Library-Business/Language. Daily alternation (specialist).
Period 10	2:30-3:15	Physical Education/Home-Health. Daily alternation (specialist).
Period 11	3:15-4:00	Optional. Remediation and enrichment (regular staff).

As we discussed earlier, this model rejects the idea of tracking in favor of the remediation/enrichment period. It should be noted that this period should also include opportunities for gifted athletes, musicians, and artists as well as gifted scholars. It could be scheduled in such a way that multiply-gifted or multiply-remediated children could be serviced. For example, a "select" music ensemble might meet on Mondays; a "select" art class on Tuesdays; a "select" soccer team on Wednesdays; etc. Finally, the remediation-enrichment period could be coordinated with a "latchkey play" program for kids whose working parents are not able to provide home supervision.

Instrumental music lessons in this paradigm would be on a thirty-minute rotational pull-out basis. The thirty-minute bloc could be designed to overlap periods so that a student would never miss the entirety of a given subject area.

The science offering might require an alternate teaching station, and if a specialist were used, a variable schedule, so that the specialist could service each common branch classroom teacher. This would be needed in any event for the music, art, and physical education offerings. Thus, Miss Jones's second grade class might begin period one with science while Mr. Smith's class would have music during the first period.

It should also be understood that the forty-five-minute instructional blocs contain the time between subject areas, the time needed to go to an alternate teaching station, and any break time for things like group games, milk and cookies, etc. Thus, the instructional time for a subject area would be more like thirty to forty minutes rather than the forty-five minutes a first reading might indicate.

Finally, for the model above, functionally handicapped students and ESL students would be mainstreamed wherever possible with separate facilities, schedules, and curricular demands provided where mainstreaming was inappropriate.

A Model Junior High School Schedule

Homeroom	8:00-8:15	
Period 1	8:15-9:00	English.
Period 2	9:00-9:45	Math.
Period 3	9:45-10:30	Social Studies.
Period 4	10:30-11:15	Science (lab in class on class time).
Period 5	11:15-12:30	Lunch/Music performing groups (45-min. rehearsal).
Period 6	12:30-1:15	Foreign Language (students select from available choices).
Period 7	1:15-2:00	Music/Art/Technology/Home-Health (10 weeks of each).
Period 8	2:00-2:45	Physical Education/Library-Business (A/B day alternation).
Period 9	2:45-3:30	Optional. Enrichment/Remediation.

Again, this model rejects classroom tracking. Instead it offers the enrichment/remediation period. Further homogeneity would occur as a result of extracurricular activities such as sports teams, dramas, and select musical groups which would meet after school. Other homogeneous grouping could easily occur with the establishment of student clubs (such as art club, science club, etc.) which would also meet at 3:30 p.m. An after-school club schedule allowing for a student to enjoy more than one area of talent would be fairly easy to work out.

Instrumental lessons would be on a rotation, pull-out basis (period 1 in one week, period 2 the next, period 3 the next, etc.). Students would be responsible for work missed during the day of the lesson, but makeup lesson times would also be provided by appointment with the music teacher for times when lessons fell on days in which tests or pressing reviews kept a child in regular class.

Each teacher in this model would be a specialist and students would pass from class to class as in a high school regimen. The forty-five-minute time blocs include three minutes for passing time so that forty-two minutes would be the actual instructional period. To maximize in-class time by minimizing locker visits, it would probably be wise to limit locker visitations to before school, lunchtime, and after school. Thus, with the exception of an emergency, a student would gather all morning material from a locker before homeroom, all afternoon material during lunch, and all homework material after school.

The schedule above should work for fall sports in areas where it gets dark by 5:00 p.m. (bearing in mind that an athlete would not be going to ninth period). For travel to away games, athletes could have an early dismissal in which, like the music lesson pull-out kids, they would be responsible for any missed work.

Finally, as in the elementary grades, mainstreaming would be provided for "functionally handicapped" or ESL students wherever possible. Otherwise, alternate facilities and regimens would be provided. It is important to note, however, that at the eighth grade level, the policy of passing a substandard student on to the next grade would stop. Eighth grade failures would have to master the curriculum either by repeating a year or by going to summer school. In that way, with the exception of high school transfer students who were sub-par, the high school population would be starting the ninth grade year with fundamental skills and academic performance on a ninth grade level.

A Model High School Schedule — Four Years

Grade 9
(minimum of 7 credits required)

Homeroom	8:00-8:15	
Period 1	8:15-9:00	English 9. American literature.
Period 2	9:00-9:45	Social Studies 9. American history.
Period 3	9:45-10:30	Science 9. Concepts and contemporary issues I.
Period 4	10:30-11:15	Math 9. Algebra 9 or General Math 9.
Period 5	11:15-12:30	Lunch/Music performing groups (45-min. rehearsal).
Period 6	12:30-1:15	Language 9 (from choices available including Latin).
Period 7	1:15-2:00	Physical Education/Technology 9 (A/B day alternation).
Period 8	2:00-2:45	Music/Art (appreciation courses) (A/B day or semester alternation).
Period 9	2:45-3:30	Study hall or elective.

Grade 10
(minimum of 6 credits required)

Homeroom	8:00-8:15	
Period 1	8:15-9:00	English 10. World literature.
Period 2	9:00-9:45	Social Studies 10. World history (Europe and "Third World").
Period 3	9:45-10:30	Science 10. Concepts and contemporary issues II.
Period 4	10:30-11:15	Math 10. Geometry or General Math 10.
Period 5	11:15-12:30	Lunch/Music performing groups (45-min. rehearsal).
Period 6	12:30-1:15	Language 10 (continuation of choices).
Period 7	1:15-2:00	Physical Education/Technology 10 (A/B day alternation).
Period 8	2:00-2:45	Study hall or elective.
Period 9	2:45-3:30	Study hall or elective.

Grade 11
(minimum of 6 credits required)

Homeroom	8:00-8:15	
Period 1	8:15-9:00	English 11. Advanced literature, writing skills, civics reading (papers, journals, etc).
Period 2	9:00-9:45	Social Studies 11. Geography and economics.
Period 3	9:45-10:30	Civics 11. Current events.
Period 4	10:30-11:15	Physical Education/Home and Health 11.
Period 5	11:15-12:30	Lunch/Music performing groups (45-min. rehearsal).
Period 6	12:30-1:15	Required elective.
Period 7	1:15-2:00	Required elective.
Period 8	2:00-2:45	Study hall or elective.
Period 9	2:45-3:30	Study hall or elective.

Grade 12
(minimum of 5 credits required)

Homeroom	8:00-8:15	
Period 1	8:15-9:00	English 12. Advanced literature, writing skills, technical reading (contracts, etc.).
Period 2	9:00-9:45	Social Studies 12. Sociology and psychology.
Period 3	9:45-10:30	Civics 12. Current events and a community project.
Period 4	10:30-11:15	Physical Education/Home and Health 12.
Period 5	11:15-12:30	Lunch/Music performing groups (45-min. rehearsal).
Period 6	12:30-1:15	Required elective.
Period 7	1:15-2:00	Study hall or elective.
Period 8	2:00-2:45	Study hall or elective.
Period 9	2:45-3:30	Study hall or elective.

Sample High School Electives for Student Specialization

Music
Theory I/II
History
Musical Theatre
Composition
Select ensembles (after school)

Physical Education
Dance
School Teams (after school)
Gymnastics

Language
Levels III, IV, V
in selections available

Home and Health
(Shakespeare, etc.)
Advanced Cooking
Advanced Sewing

Science
Chemistry (with lab)
Physics (with lab)
Advanced Biology (with lab)

Mathematics
Trigonometry
Calculus
Statistics
Computer/math skills

Art
Photography
Drawing I/II
Painting I/II
Design
Ceramics
Sculpture

Business
Secretarial Skills
Accounting
Management
Equipment Use

English and Drama
Stagecraft
Acting
Creative Writing
Specialized Literature

Performance Groups
(after school)

Technology
Auto Shop
Electronics
Wood Shop
Metal Shop
Drafting

Social Studies
Law
Government
Comparative Religions

The high school model above has several items of importance attendant to it. They are listed numerically below.

(1) Tracking would occur in three streams (remedial, normal, and enriched). It would occur only in the English, math, social studies, science, and language curricula, *not* in the required music, art, physical education, technology, home and health, or civics curricula. Additional tracking by self-selection would occur as each student took his or her electives and as upperclassmen took courses for which there were prerequisites. Finally, the try-outs for school teams and auditions for select

performing ensembles in music and drama would create additional homogeneous groupings.

(2) Because of the tremendous variety of offerings, a comprehensive high school curriculum such as this would be well-advised to adopt a fixed schedule from year to year. There are apt to be many "singleton courses" (courses with only one class section available) in this scheme, and to avoid scheduling conflicts, a fixed schedule would allow students and guidance counselors to plan several years ahead. For example, if Spanish IV and Creative Writing were each offered only once and both were scheduled for fourth period, students would know that in year X they could take Creative Writing and then take Spanish IV in year Y.

(3) The schedule leaves eleven openings for electives so that students would have the opportunity both to explore new areas and specialize in those which might lead to career choices or college majors.

(4) Science labs for advanced courses would not be on class time but would require a second, adjacent period.

(5) Pull-out lessons for both vocal and instrumental performers would occur on a rotational basis with makeup times available and students responsible for work covered in their absence. Similarly, athletes dismissed early for away-game travel would be responsible for work missed.

(6) The schedule demands twenty-four credits for graduation and twenty-one required courses. This design would help to assure a more comprehensive public school training and at the same time discourage the trend toward early graduation. However, it should be noted that the required course load diminishes in the eleventh and twelfth grades so that early graduation is possible. The diminished load also makes it possible for students who have to work to schedule all their classes early in the day so that an early dismissal will allow them to get to their jobs.

(7) The required community project of the twelfth grade year (an idea first stated definitively by Boyer in his work on the American high school) could take many forms and, in fact, might be fulfilled in any of the four years. Giving blood, cleaning school or town areas, senior citizen or latchkey child volunteer work, marching band participation for football games and local parades, civic or benefit concerts, cooperative programs with local businesses or government agencies are all examples of how this requirement might be met. The number of hours or degree of involvement needed to satisfy the requirement could fairly easily be determined by the school. The important thing is that the concept be preserved and the requirement satisfied by the end of twelfth grade.

(8) The degree of specialization possible in this paradigm means that, in areas where separate magnet high schools (whole schools devoted to one specialization such as New York City's Bronx High School of Science) are neither possible nor desirable, "schools within schools" can meet the needs of highly directed students. For example, a gifted musician with an eye on a Juilliard School of Music audition might, in the scheme above, easily schedule four years of a performing group, Music Theory I, Music Theory II, and Composition. With participation in select after-school groups, private lessons, and home practice, such a student would be very marketable in the highly competitive world of the college music major. The student's high school music regimen would thus constitute a kind of "school within" the general academic environment.

(9) The seventy-five minute lunch bloc could easily be arranged to handle a school which would not have the ability to feed all its students in one period. By having an "A-lunch" and a "B-lunch" segment, the feeding burden would be halved. "A-lunch" kids, for example, would eat from 11:15 - 11:45 and have the 11:45 - 12:30 time for study, socialization, emergency meetings, etc. "B-lunch" kids (containing all the music performing students) would rehearse from 11:15 - 12:00 and eat from 12:00 -12:30. Similarly, faculty could be given A or B schedules during which they could eat and hold conference hours for students with special problems, independent projects, or other needs. Again, the times indicated here include passing time between classes, and the same locker visitation procedures described in the junior high regimen would apply.

(10) As noted in the sampling of elective course offerings above, select music and drama groups, athletic teams, and school clubs would meet after 3:30 p.m.

(11) For schools in geographical regions which make fall sports or agricultural commitments difficult with the times indicated here, there are many remedies for problems which might arise. The entire schedule could be moved back to begin at 7:15 or 7:30 a.m. Games might be scheduled for Saturdays. Fields could be lit for night games. Again, it should be understood that these schedules are paradigms for which many individual district adjustments might be made.

(12) The schedule itself does not say it but summer assignments for the next year's courses and summer school for last year's failures should be considered as important components.

(13) To whatever extent possible, functionally handicapped or ESL students should be mainstreamed into regular classes. Where this is not possible, the school must provide a "fourth track" which may need to articulate alternate curricula with alternate graduation requirements.

(14) Finally, for severely handicapped students or students with severe behavioral problems, alternate schools must be provided. These may adopt curricula of a very different nature from the model above and have very different graduation standards. However, for the effective treatment of the "special" child and the preservation of a workable educational environment for the "normal" child, alternate high schools are really a "must."

References for Chapter Five

1. "High School Seniors React to Their Teachers and Their Schools," David L. Clark. In ***Phi Delta Kappan,*** March 1987 (Vol. 68, #7). pp. 503-04. A surprising 23% of high school seniors even report that they would like to become teachers.
2. ***State Education Statistics Supplement: student performance and resource inputs, 1986 and 1987*** (wallchart, commentary, and press release). Washington, D.C.: U.S. Department of Education, February 1988. pp. 1 and 2 of commentary and press release.
3. "Teenage Pregnancy," Mary McClellan. In ***Phi Delta Kappan,*** June 1987 (Vol. 68, #10), p. 790.
4. "Teaching Selflessness in a Selfish Society," Thomas J. Lasley. In ***Phi Delta Kappan,*** May 1987 (Vol. 68, #9). p. 674. Lasley cites anthropologist Ashley Montague as his source in the book ***Learning Nonaggression*** (New York: Oxford Univ. Press, 1978, pp. 3-9).
5. "Character Education and Clinical Intervention: a paradigm shift for U.S. schools," Perry London. In ***Phi Delta Kappan,*** May 1987 (Vol. 68, #9). pp. 667-68.
6. See ***The Condition of Education,*** 1986 ed. p. 36; and the ***State Education Statistics Supplement,*** February 1988, cited earlier.
7. ***State Education Statistics Supplement,*** February 1988. Wallchart and press release figures. It is interesting to note that these declines were accompanied by an annual increase of teacher wages from $25,201 in 1986 to $26,551 in 1987. It is also worthwhile noting that the high school completion rate for 18-19 year-olds is 74.6%, indicating that some of the high school dropouts in the 71.5% figure are returning to school to get equivalency diplomas before age twenty. It is also important to realize that schools, especially high schools, are dealing with more students than ever before. In 1900 only 11% of students 14-17 years old were in school. By 1940 that figure had risen to 73%. Today it is nearly 100% of whom 72% graduate. Our 28% dropout rate is thus, from the broad historical perspective, less alarming than a more narrow view might produce. See ***The Condition of Education,*** 1986 ed., p. 42; and "Inside the Citadel in 1940," Robert L. Hampel. In ***Phi Delta Kappan.*** June 1986 (Vol. 67, #10). pp. 703-07.
8. ***The Condition of Education,*** 1986 ed., pp. 44-45.
9. ***The Condition of Education,*** 1986 ed., pp. 64-65.
10. ***The Condition of Education,*** 1986 ed., pp. 102-03.
11. ***The Condition of Education,*** 1986 ed., pp. 46-47. The quote is accompanied by explanatory statistics. "Basic" reading skills (a score of 200 on the reading scale) are defined by tasks such as filling out a job application or changing money. 98.6% of our students are literate at this level. "Adept" skills (score of 300) are defined by tasks such as reading a newspaper or a bus schedule. Here only 54.4% are literate. "Advanced" reading skills (score of 350), such as understanding a technical journal, are possessed by only 20.9%.
12. ***The Nation's Report Card: literature and U.S. history,*** Arthur N. Applebee, et al. Princeton, N.J.: National Assessment for Educational Progress/Educational Testing Service, 1987. p. 8 ff.
13. "Character Education and Clinical Intervention," London. p. 670.
14. See "Character Education and Clinical Intervention," London. p. 668; and the following: "Interparental Conflict and the Children of Discord and Divorce," Robert E. Emery. In ***Psychological Bulletin.*** Vol. 92, 1982. pp. 310-30; and "Divorce: a

child's perspective," E. Mavis Heatherington. In ***American Psychologist.*** Vol. 34, 1979. pp. 851-58.

15. See the ***New York State Governor's Youth Suicide Prevention Council Interim Report,*** December 1985; "Character Education and Clinical Intervention," London. p. 669; and "Suicide Among the Young," Deborah Burnett Strother. In ***Phi Delta Kappan.*** June 1986 (Vol. 67, #10). pp. 756-59.
16. "Character Education and Clinical Intervention," London. p. 669. London reports that as of 1987 there have been more than one million cases of child abuse reported annually. That is double the 1978 rate.
17. "High School Seniors React to Their Teachers and Their Schools," Clark. p. 508. 43.5% of the seniors listed this as the most serious problem. The next most serious problem was substance abuse (mentioned by 37.2%). Only 12.8% of the seniors interviewed thought that curriculum and instruction were the most serious problem.
18. "Inside the Citadel in 1940," Hampel. pp. 703-04.
19. See ***Summerhill: a radical approach to childrearing,*** A.S. Neill. New York: Hart, 1960; ***Freedom—Not License!,*** A.S. Neill. New York: Hart, 1966; and ***Summerhill: for and against,*** Harold Hart, ed. New York: Hart, 1970.
20. "Inside the Citadel in 1940," Hampel. p. 703.
21. "A Primer on Classroom Discipline: principles old and new," Thomas McDaniel. In ***Phi Delta Kappan.*** September 1986 (Vol. 68, #1). p. 63.
22. ***The Condition of Education,*** 1986 ed., pp. 78-79.
23. "Implementing Strategies for a School Effectiveness Program," Willis J. Furtwengler. In ***Phi Delta Kappan.*** December 1985 (Vol. 67, #4). pp. 262-65.
24. ***Teachers, Their World, and Their Work,*** Ann Lieberman and Lynne Miller. Alexandria, Va: ASCD, 1984. p. 89.
25. ***The Condition of Education,*** 1986 ed., p. 82.
26. ***The Condition of Education,*** 1986 ed., pp. 82-83.
27. See the following: "Character Education and Clinical Intervention," London. p. 669; ***What, When, and How To Talk to Children about Alcohol and Other Drugs: a guide for parents,*** Gail G. Millgram. Center City, Minn.: Hazelden, 1983; "Health Hazards Associated with Alcohol Consumption," M.J.Eckardt, et al. In ***Journal of the American Medical Association.*** Vol. 246, 1981. pp. 648-66; "Schoolchildren and Drugs: the fancy that has not passed," Richard A. Hawley. In ***Phi Delta Kappan.*** May 1987 (Vol. 68, #9). pp. K1-K8 (special section).
28. "Schoolchildren and Drugs: the fancy that has not passed," Hawley. p. K3.
29. "Character Education and Clinical Intervention," London. pp. 668-69.
30. "Teenage Pregnancy," Mary McClellan. Interviewing children 12-17 years of age, Harris found 37% of the students getting C-F grades had regular sex while the same was true for only 25% of B students and 21% of A students.
31. "Teenage Pregnancy," McClellan. p. 790.
32. "Teen Pregnancy: it's time for the schools to tackle the problem," James Buie. In ***Phi Delta Kappan.*** June 1987 (Vol. 68, #10). pp. 737-39.
33. "Teen Pregnancy: it's time for the schools to tackle the problem," Buie. p. 738.
34. "Teen Pregnancy: an issue for schools," Asta M. Kenney. In ***Phi Delta Kappan.*** June 1987 (Vol. 67, #10). pp. 728-36. The quote occurs on p. 730 and Kenney cites as her source the ***National Center for Health Statistics Report.*** July 18, 1986 (Vol. 35, #4).
35. "Our Children are Changing," Leslie J. Chamberlain and Riccardo Girona. In ***Curriculum Planning: a new approach.*** Boston: Allyn and Bacon, 1983. p. 129. The authors cite as their source "Illegitimacy in the United States," Cuthright Phillips. In ***Demographic and Social Aspects,*** Vol. 1, C.F. Wertoff and R. Parke, Jrs., eds. Washington, D.C.: 1969.

36. See ***The Disappearance of Childhood*** by Neal Postman; ***The Erosion of Childhood*** by Valerie Suransky; and ***The Hurried Child*** by David Elkind. Reviews and synopses can be found in "Histrionics and Help for Childhood," Thomas Shannon, Jr. In ***American School Board Journal.*** December 1982 (Vol. 169, #12). pp. 18-19.
37. "Histrionics and Help for Childhood," Shannon. p. 19.
38. "A Child Resource Policy: moving beyond dependence on school and family," Shirley Brice Heath and Milbrey Wallin McLaughlin. In ***Phi Delta Kappan.*** April 1987 (Vol. 68, #8). p. 577.
39. "The Right Schools for the Right Kids," Harold Hodgkinson. In ***Educational Leadership.*** February 1988 (Vol. 45, #5). pp. 10-15.
40. "The Right Schools for the Right Kids," Hodgkinson. pp. 10-15.
41. ***The Condition of Education,*** 1986 ed., p. 42.
42. "The Right Schools for the Right Kids," Hodgkinson. p. 12.
43. "Making Chapter 1 Make a Difference," Robert E. Slavin. In ***Phi Delta Kappan.*** October 1987 (Vol. 69, #2). p. 110.
44. See ***The Neurotic Personality of Our Times,*** Karen Horney. New York: Norton, 1937. pp. 162 ff.
45. "Is 'In Loco Parentis' Dead?," Perry A. Zirkel and Henry E. Reichner. In ***Phi Delta Kappan.*** February 1987 (Vol. 68, #6). p. 467.
46. See "In the Classroom Stoned," Jessica Shannon. In ***Phi Delta Kappan.*** September 1986 (Vol. 68, #1). pp. 60-62.
47. "Is 'In Loco Parentis' Dead?," Zirkel and Reichner. p. 468.
48. "Is 'In Loco Parentis' Dead?," Zirkel and Reichner. p. 469.
49. ***The Law of Higher Education,*** William A. Kaplin. San Francisco: Jossey-Bass, 1985. p. 6.
50. ***The Condition of Education,*** 1986 ed., pp. 78-79.
51. "Synthesis of Research on Strategies for Motivating Students to Learn," Jere Brophy. In ***Educational Leadership.*** October 1987 (Vol. 45, #2). pp. 40-48.
52. "Lowered Expectations: how schools reward incompetence," Bruce Jackson. In ***Phi Delta Kappan.*** December 1985 (Vol. 67, #4). pp. 304-05.
53. "Bureaucracy and the Neutering of Teachers," Jack Frymier. In ***Phi Delta Kappan.*** September 1987 (Vol. 69, #1). pp. 9-14.
54. ***The Literacy Hoax,*** Copperman. pp. 66-72.
55. See "Mass Media," George Comstock. In ***Encyclopedia of Educational Research.*** New York: The Free Press, 1982. pp. 1149-57; and "Here's What Classroom Computers Can Do." In ***The American School Board Journal,*** March 1982 (Vol. 169, #3).
56. ***The Education of American Teachers,*** James B. Conant. New York: McGraw Hill, 1963. p. 183.
57. ***The Non-graded High School,*** Frank B. Brown. Englewood Cliffs, N.J.: Prentice-Hall, 1963. p. 35. An overview of the changing tides of thought on ability grouping is provided in: ***Classroom Grouping for Teachability,*** Herbert A. Thelen. New York: John Wiley, 1967. pp. 1-44.
58. ***Talent and Tomorrow's Teachers: the honors approach,*** Lanora G. Lewis, ed. Washington, D.C.: U.S. Dept. of Health, Education, and Welfare, 1963. p. 5. The government also put out publications to encourage underachievers to excel. See ***Guidance for the Underachiever with Superior Ability,*** Leonard M. Miller, ed. Washington, D.C.: U.S. Dept. of Health, Education, and Welfare, 1961.
59. ***Grouping Students for Improved Education,*** Dorothy Westby-Gibson. Englewood Cliffs, N.J.: Prentice-Hall, 1966.

60. ***The Four-Track Curriculum in Today's High Schools,*** Carl E. Hansen. Englewood Cliffs, N.J.: Prentice Hall, 1964.
61. ***Ability Grouping in the Junior High School,*** Heber Hinds Ryan and Philipine Crecelius, New York: Harcourt, 1927. pp. 1-2.
62. "Education of the Gifted and Talented in the World Community," Bruce M.Mitchell and William G. Williams. In ***Phi Delta Kappan.*** March 1987 (Vol. 68, #7). p. 534. The report indicates that in comparison to nations such as Russia (and even less developed Asian countries such as Taiwan, South Korea, and the Phillipines), U.S. programs were found to "lack central direction."
63. "Gifted Education Boondoggles: a few bad apples or a rotten bushel?," Lauren A. Sosniak. In ***Phi Delta Kappan.*** March 1987 (Vol. 68, #7). p. 537.
64. "Use Performance, Not Just Test Scores, To Select Kids for Gifted Programs," Michael Langenbach and Judith Young Blitch. In ***The American School Board Journal.*** November 1982 (Vol. 169, #11). p. 50.
65. "We Must Offer Equal Access to Knowledge," John I. Goodlad and Jeannie Oakes. In ***Educational Leadership.*** February 1988 (Vol. 45, #5). p. 18.
66. ***A Place Called School: prospects for the future,*** John I. Goodlad. New York: McGraw Hill, 1984. p. 297. See also ***School, Curriculum, and the Individual,*** John I. Goodlad. Waltham, Mass.: Blaisdell, 1966; ***The Non-graded Elementary School,*** John I. Goodlad and Robert H. Anderson. New York: Harcourt, 1959; and "The Great American Schooling Experiment," John I. Goodlad. In ***Phi Delta Kappan.*** December 1985 (Vol. 67, #4). pp. 266-71.
67. ***The Social Context of Instruction,*** Penelope L. Peterson, Louise Cherry Wilkinson, and Maureen Hallinan. Orlando, Fla.: Academic Press, 1984. p. 232.
68. "The Social Impact of Ability Grouping," Gerald W. Bracey. In ***Phi Delta Kappan.*** May 1987 (Vol. 68, #9). pp. 701-02.
69. See "The Paideia Proposal: rediscovering the essence of education," Mortimer Adler. In ***The American School Board Journal.*** July 1982. pp. 17-20. Adler states that egalitarianism "means a one-track system of schooling...giving all the young the same kind of schooling, whether or not they are college bound." (p. 17). See also ***Paideia Problems and Possibilities,*** Mortimer Adler. New York: MacMillan, 1983.
70. ***High School: a report on secondary education in America,*** Ernest L. Boyer (for the Carnegie Foundation for the Advancement of Teaching). New York: Harper and Row, 1983. p. 126 ff.
71. ***Classroom Grouping for Teachability,*** Thelen. p. 29.
72. See the following: ***Non-grading in the Elementary School,*** John L. Tewksbury. Columbus, Ohio: Merrill, 1967; ***The Non-graded High School,*** Frank B. Brown. Englewood Cliffs, N.J.: Prentice Hall, 1963; ***Grouping in Elementary School,*** Anne Morgenstern, ed. New York: Pitman, 1966; ***Non-graded Schools in Action,*** David W. Beggs and Edward G. Buffie. Bloomington, Indiana: University of Indiana Press, 1967; ***The Effects of Ability Grouping,*** Miriam Goldberg and Harry A. Passow. New York: Teachers College Press, 1966; ***Ability Grouping and Scholastic Achievement,*** Nils-Eric Swensson. Stockholm: Almquist and Wiksell, 1962; "Eliminating Tracking Successfully," Phil Swartzbaugh. In ***Educational Leadership.*** February 1988 (Vol. 45, #5). p. 20; and "Ability Grouping and Student Achievement in Elementary Schools," Gerald W. Bracey. In ***Phi Delta Kappan.*** September 1986 (Vol. 68, #1). pp. 76-77.
73. ***Grouping in Education,*** Alfred Yates. New York: Wiley, 1966. p. 134.
74. ***Ability Grouping in the Public Schools,*** Walter R. Borg. Madison, Wisc.: Dembar Educational Research Services, 1966. pp. 88 ff.

75. ***Class Organization for Instruction,*** J. Wayne Wrightstone. In ***What Research Says to the Teacher #3,*** 5th printing. Washington, D.C.: NEA, 1969.
76. "Ability Grouping," Marsha A. Ream. In ***Research Summary,*** 1968-S3. Washington, D.C.: NEA, 1968.
77. ***The Literacy Hoax,*** Copperman, pp. 85-88.
78. "The Key to Improving Schools: a conversation with William Glasser," Pauline B. Gough. In ***Phi Delta Kappan.*** May 1987 (Vol. 68, #9). pp. 656-59.
79. "A Teacher's View on Cooperative Learning," Roy Smith. In ***Phi Delta Kappan.*** May 1987 (Vol. 68, #9). pp. 663-66.
80. "Student-Student Interaction: ignored but powerful," Roger T. Johnson and David W. Johnson. In ***Journal of Teacher Education,*** July-August 1985. p. 23. See also "Adapting Instruction to Individual Needs: an eclectic approach," Deborah Burnett Strother. In ***Phi Delta Kappan.*** December 1985 (Vol. 67, #4). pp. 308-11.
81. ***The Gifted Child in the Regular Classroom,*** Marian Schiefele. New York: Bureau of Publications, Teachers College, Columbia University, 1963.
82. "How the Coming of the Hmong Transformed the Schools on Main Street," Virginia Garton. In ***The American School Board Journal,*** November 1982 (Vol. 169, #11). pp. 47-48.
83. "Marking Systems," Kurt F. Geisinger. In ***Encyclopedia of Educational Research.*** New York: The Free Press, 1982. pp. 1139-48.
84. ***The Education of American Teachers,*** Conant. pp. 180-81.
85. ***The Literacy Hoax,*** Copperman. p. 105.
86. "Marking Systems," Geisinger. pp. 1139-48. See also: "Academic Interest Rates and Grade Inflation," J.F. Davidson. In ***Educational Record.*** 1975, Vol. 56. pp. 122-25; and "Grade Inflation: neither freedom nor discipline," A. Etzione. In ***Human Behavior.*** 1975 (Vol. 4, #10). pp. 11-12.
87. "What Doesn't Work: explaining policies of retention in the early grades," Mary Lee Smith and Louie A. Shepard. In ***Phi Delta Kappan.*** October 1987 (Vol. 69, #2). p. 130.
88. See "The Effects of Nonpromotion on Elementary and Junior High School Pupils," C. Thomas Holmes and Kenneth M. Matthews. In ***Review of Educational Research.*** 1984. Vol. 54. pp. 225-36; "Large School System Dropout Reports: an analysis of definitions, proceedings, and findings," Floyd M. Hammack. In ***School Dropouts: patterns and policies,*** Gary Natriello, ed. New York: Teachers College Press, 1986; "Ability Grouping in Public Schools," Walter Borg. In ***Journal of Experimental Education.*** 1965. Vol31. pp. 1-97; and "Setting the Standard: alternative patterns for student promotion," David Larabee. In ***Harvard Educational Review.*** 1984. Vol. 54. pp. 69 ff.
89. "What Doesn't Work: explaining policies of retention in the early grades," Smith and Shepard. pp. 129-34.
90. See ***The Process of Education,*** Jerome Bruner. New York: Vintage, 1960; and ***Fundamentals of Curriculum Development,*** B. Othanel Smith. Yonkers, N.Y.: World, 1957.
91. ***The Making of Our Middle Schools,*** Elmer E. Brown. New York: Longmans, Green and Co., 1907. The term "middle school" at that time was akin to "high school" today. Brown's work described New York City's five-track "magnet" approach to high school curricula in a discussion of the 5,109 public and 2,100 private high schools existing at the turn of the century.
92. See ***The Transformation of the School,*** Lawrence A. Cremin. New York: Knopf, 1961. This book traces the history of "progressive education" from 1876 to 1957.

93. ***The Comprehensive High School,*** Franklin J. Keller. New York: Harper and Row, 1955. pp. 2-3.

94. See ***Cultural Literacy: what every American needs to know,*** E.D. Hirsch, Jr. Boston: Houghton-Mifflin, 1987. The list appears alphabetized on pp. 152-215. It contains over 3,600 items from Achilles to DNA to Ghandi to "The Road Not Taken" to Yom Kippur and Emile Zola.

95. See ***High School: a recent report on secondary education in America,*** Ernest L. Boyer (for the Carnegie Foundation for the Advancement of Teaching). New York: Harper and Row, 1983. p. 115 states a core curriculum; and ***A Place Called School: prospects for the future,*** John I. Goodlad. New York: McGraw Hill, 1984. pp. 286-90 suggest a curricular balance by percentage of courses in given areas.

96. ***Redefining General Education in the American High School,*** Arthur D. Roberts and Gordon Cawelti. Alexandria, Va.: ASCD, 1984. pp. 5-7.

97. ***The Persistent Problems of Education,*** Paul Woodring. Bloomington, Ind.: Phi Delta Kappa Educational Foundation, 1983. pp. 14-15.

98. "The Paideia Proposal: rediscovering the essence of education," Mortimer Adler. In ***The American School Board Journal.*** July 1982. p. 18. See also ***Paideia Problems and Possibilities,*** Mortimer J. Adler. New York: MacMillan, 1983. On p. 34 programs for enrichment and remediation are discussed.

99. "The Right to Quality Education," Mario Fantini. In ***Curriculum Planning: a new approach,*** 4th ed. Glen Hass, ed. Boston: Allyn and Bacon, 1983. pp. 13-18.

100. See "The National Assessments in Reading: are we misreading the finds?," John B. Carroll. In ***Phi Delta Kappan.*** February 1987 (Vol. 68, #6). pp. 424-30; and "Reading Styles Research: 'what works' isn't always phonics," Marie Carbo. In ***Phi Delta Kappan.*** February 1987 (Vol. 68, #6). pp. 431-35. Carbo suggests a multiplicity of approaches to deal with different students in different situations. She goes on to say that to some extent America's "appallingly poor reading" (p. 431) is caused by U.S. publishers whose book hypes "are dictating to a great extent how reading is taught" (p. 434). She suggests an eclectic approach to solve the problem.

101. See ***If Your Child Has Reading Difficulties,*** Ursula Cooke MacDougall. New York: The Dalton School, 1952.

102. ***Dimensions of Thinking: a framework for curriculum and instruction,*** Robert J. Marzana, et al. Alexandria, Va.: ASCD, 1988. pp. 1-2. See also "Creativity by Design," D.N. Perkins. In ***Educational Leadership.*** September 1984 (Vol. 42, #1). pp. 18-25; and "The Cultivation of Reasoning through Philosophy," Matthew Lipman. In ***Educational Leadership.*** September 1984 (Vol. 42, #1). pp. 51-56.

103. "Critical Thinking: fundamental to education in a free society," Paul W. Richard. In ***Educational Leadership.*** September 1984 (Vol. 42, #1). p. 6. See also "Teaching Critical Thinking: eight easy ways to fail before you begin," Robert J. Sternberg. In ***Phi Delta Kappan.*** February 1987 (Vol. 68, #7). pp. 456-59; "Teaching for Thinking: Louis E. Raths revisited," Selma Wasserman. In ***Phi Delta Kappan.*** February 1987 (Vol. 68, #7). pp. 460-66; "On Teaching Thinking Skills: a conversation with B. Othanel Smith," Ron Brandt. In ***Educational Leadership.*** October 1987 (Vol. 45, #2). pp. 35-39; ***The Art of Teaching,*** Gilbert Highet. New York: Knopf, 1963. pp. 174-263 (in which Highet discusses the techniques of great teachers. Particularly relevant is his discussion of Dewey, p. 238 ff.)

104. "Sex Education and Gender Equity," Susan Shurberg Klein. In ***Educational Leadership.*** March 1988 (Vol. 45, #6). p. 69.

105. See "The Education of Most Worth: preventing drugs and alcohol abuse," Lowell Horton. In ***Educational Leadership.*** March 1988 (Vol. 45, #6). pp. 4-8; and "Effective School-based Approaches to Drug Abuse Prevention," William B. Hansen.

In ***Educational Leadership.*** March 1988 (Vol. 45, #6). pp. 9-12.

106. "Sex and School Reform," Larry Cuban. In ***Phi Delta Kappan.*** December 1986 (Vol. 68, #4). pp. 319-21.

107. "The Issue at Hand: a republic—if we can keep it," Alex Molnar. In ***Educational Leadership.*** October 1987 (Vol. 45, #2). p. 69.

108. ***The Unique Function of Education in American Democracy.*** Charles A. Beard. Washington, D.C.: NEA, 1937. p. 85; ***Education and Economic Well-being in American Democracy,*** John K. Norton. Washington, D.C.: NEA, 1937. p. 34; ***The Education of Free Men in American Democracy,*** George S. Counts. Washington, D.C.: NEA, 1941. pp. 49-50.

109. "Education in the Experience of Being Citizens," John Vasconcellos and Brian M. Murphy. In ***Educational Leadership.*** October 1987 (Vol. 45, #2). p. 71.

110. "Effects of Reduced Class Size in Primary Classes," Daniel Mueller, et al. In ***Educational Leadership.*** February 1988 (Vol. 45, #5). pp. 48-50. The program was begun in 1984 by the state of Indiana at a cost of $100 million.

111. See "Policy Options of Preschool Programs," Lawrence J. Schweinhart, et al. In ***Phi Delta Kappan.*** March 1987 (Vol. 68, #7). pp. 524-29; and "Kindergarten in America: five major trends," Sandra Longfellow Robinson. In ***Phi Delta Kappan.*** March 1987 (Vol. 68, #7). pp. 529-30. Robinson reports a growing trend toward pre-primary education. In 1974, for example, only 23 states offered ubiquitous kindergarten programs. By 1986 it was 46 states. Today only Mississippi, New Hampshire, Oregon and Vermont provide kindergarten for less than 90% of their eligible populations.

112. ***Curriculum Development,*** Hollis L. Caswell and Doak S. Campbell. New York: American Book Co., 1935. pp. 276-77. From ***The Way Out of Educational Confusion,*** John Dewey. Boston: Harvard University Press, 1931. pp. 17-18.

113. "Making Chapter 1 Make a Difference," Slavin. pp. 110-19.

114. "High Road, Low Road, End of the Road for CAI and Programming?," Gerald W. Bracey. In ***Phi Delta Kappan.*** March 1987 (Vol. 68, #7). pp. 546-47.

115. "Instructional Design Flaws in Computer-Assisted Instruction," Julie S. Vargas. In ***Phi Delta Kappan.*** June 1986 (Vol. 67, #10). pp. 738 ff.

116. "Persistent Instruction: another look at constancy in the classroom," Larry Cuban. In ***Phi Delta Kappan.*** September 1986 (Vol. 68, #1). p. 11.

117. See "Is 'No Pass, No Play' No Good?," In ***Music Educators Journal,*** January 1988 (Vol. 73, #5). pp. 38-41 contain a cross-section of views on the subject.

118. See "Rethinking the School Calendar," Charles Ballinger. In ***Educational Leadership.*** February 1988 (Vol. 45, #5). pp. 57-61.

119. "Schools and Their Curriculum: a continuing controversy," Alex Molnar. In ***Current Thought on Curriculum: 1985: ASCD yearbook.*** Alexandria, Va.: ASCD 1985. pp. 19-20.

120. See ***Educational Programs That Work,*** ed. 16 (1986). Longmont, Colorado: Sopris West, Inc., 1986. Publication of the U.S. Dept. of Education's National Diffusion Network; and ***High School: a report on secondary education in America,*** Ernest L. Boyer. New York: Harper and Row, 1983. pp. 117 ff. Both documents articulate a proposed high school curriculum in depth.

121. "Content and Process in the English Curriculum," Charles Suhor. In ***Content of the Curriculum: 1988 ASCD yearbook.*** Alexandria, Va.: ASCD, 1988. p. 50.

122. "Social Studies: the study of people in society," Donald H. Bragaw and H. Michael Hartoonian. In ***Content of the Curriculum, ASCD 1988 yearbook.*** p. 10.

123. "New Goals for School Mathematics," Patricia F. Campbell and James T. Fey. In ***Content of Curriculum,*** ASCD, 1988. p. 63.

124. "New Goals for School Mathematics," Campbell and Fey. pp. 56 ff.

125. "Rethinking the Science Curriculum," F. James Rutherford and Andrew Ahlgren. In ***Content of the Curriculum,*** ASCD, 1988. p. 84.
126. "Curriculum and Technology," Decker F. Walker. In ***Current Thought on Curriculum.*** Alexandria, Va.: ASCD, 1985. p. 96.
127. "Tomorrow's Emphasis in Foreign Language: proficiency," Myriam Met. In ***Content of the Curriculum,*** ASCD, 1988. pp. 93-94.
128. "Curriculum for Critical Reflection in Physical Education," Linda L. Bain. In ***Content of the Curriculum,*** ASCD, 1988. pp. 133-48.
129. See "What Students Should Learn in the Arts," Paul R. Lehman. In ***Content of the Curriculum,*** ASCD, 1988. pp. 109-32.
130. "The Transition from Industrial Arts to Technology Education," James M. Benson. In ***Content of the Curriculum,*** ASCD, 1988. p. 168.
131. "Reconceptualizing the Home Economics Curriculum," Joanna B. Smith. In ***Content of the Curriculum,*** ASCD, 1988. p. 181.
132. "School Health Education," Richard G. Schlaadt. In ***Content of the Curriculum,*** ASCD, 1988. pp. 149-66.

Afterword

WHAT WE DO about the decline of American public education will hinge upon two things: our ability to perceive that seemingly separate educational issues are dynamically interrelated and our commitment to attack a multiplicity of problems simultaneously.

The interrelationship of issues can be seen in many of the things we have viewed in this text. One cannot divorce creationism in the curriculum, for example, from the issue of local control. One cannot talk of dropout prevention without speaking of the subject prejudices which lower the esteem of children. One cannot meaningfully understand poor school attendance rates unless one understands the issues of poverty and racism which may underlie them.

Understanding the complexity of the issues, however, will not be enough. America is going to have to make up its collective mind to attack its education problems in real terms. To do that, Americans are going to have to stop playing public relations games with all their useless rhetoric and substitute instead a well-funded, programmatic reform on many fronts.

Unions must allow the removal of dead wood. Colleges must train and encourage teaching excellence by first admitting that their current policies and professors have in the main been a failure. Government is going to have to provide both funding and leadership in amounts which will make present efforts (especially federal efforts) look puny. Students are going to have to accept a measure of discipline and an upgrading of work ethics. Society as a whole is going to have to reaffirm a more positive set of values by refusing to tolerate aberrant behavior in the way it has. Teachers and administrators are going to have to do a lot of soul-searching to admit their weaknesses and restructure their curricula. Parents are going to have to snap out of their lethargy and re-establish a reverence for learning and a supportive partnership with their children's schools. And boards of education are going to have to train themselves for their jobs and stop seeing education as their personal plaything.

But above all else, these things are going to have to happen simultaneously. It will do no good to improve a curriculum if our children remain stoned in the classroom. It will do no good to cure an addict if, once cured, he or she will face a teacher who is poorly trained. It will do no good to resurrect the training of America's teachers if local boards of education tie their hands with insane policies. It will do no good to have meaningfully enlightened boards if the governments and tax structures of the nation do not give them the wherewithal to run effective schools. No one answer is going to be an answer at all. America will either fight on many fronts simultaneously or she will lose the battle.

I am not hopeful that America is going to do this. I rather think our leaders too cowardly and our people too lazy. However, I am convinced that there is no alternative but to try. If we do not try, we shall surely lose our society—perhaps even our world. If we do try, at least there is a chance we can succeed. It is against those odds that I have written this text and ask you to consider its ideas. The ideas may not work upon trial, but the present reality is surely not working. I offer them because there is nothing for it but to offer them.

It may be that unions are not ready for tenure review, boards of education not ready to go to school, presidents not ready to speak the truth, parents not ready to stop acting like children. Perhaps there are no answers and ours is a species doomed to decay and crisis. But if that is true, if there is anything left when the crises have passed, we will eventually need new ideas to build upon the ashes. It is my hope that, like Conway's Valley of the Blue Moon, we may find one or two of them here.

Bibliography

1. "Able Students Going into Teaching" in ***Phi Delta Kappan,*** Vol. 68, #8 (April 1987).
2. Adler, Mortimer J. ***Paideia Problems and Possibilities*** (New York: MacMillan, 1983).
3. __________. ***The Paideia Proposal: an educational manifesto.*** (New York: MacMillan, 1982).
4. __________. "The Paideia Proposal: rediscovering the essence of education" in ***American School Board Journal*** (July 1982).
5. Albjerg, Patricia. "Black Teachers: a drastically scarce resource" in ***Phi Delta Kappan,*** Vol. 68, #8 (April 1987).
6. Almond, Gabriel, et al., eds. ***Progress and Its Discontents*** (Berkeley: Univ. of California Press, 1982).
7. Ambach, Gordon M. "State and Local Action for Education in New York," in ***Phi Delta Kappan*** (November 1984.)
8. "The Anatomy of Success in the Superintendency" in ***Phi Delta Kappan,*** Vol. 62, #1 (September 1980).
9. Anderson, Beverly and Pipho, Chris. "State Mandated Testing and the Fate of Local Control" in ***Phi Delta Kappan*** (November 1984).
10. Anderson, Bill H. and Snyder, Karolyn J. "Leadership Training for the School Board Member: one approach" in ***Education***, Vol. 100, #3 (Spring 1980).
11. Andrews, Frank M., ed. ***Research on the Quality of Life*** (Ann Arbor: Institute for Social Research, Univ. of Michigan, 1986).
12. Angell, George W., ed. ***Faculty and Teacher Bargaining: the impact of unions on education*** (Lexington, Mass.: Lexington Books, 1981).
13. Apple, Michael W. "Making Knowledge Legitimate: power, profit, and the textbook" in ***Current Thought on Curriculum*** (Alexandria, Va.: ASCD, 1985).
14. Applebee, Arthur N. et al. ***The Nation's Report Card: literature and U.S. history*** (Princeton, N.J.: Educational Testing Service, 1987).
15. Argyris, Chris. ***Management and Organizational Development*** (New York: McGraw Hill, 1971).
16. Armbruster, Bonnie B. et al. "Readability Formulas May Be Dangerous to Your Textbooks" in ***Educational Leadership,*** Vol. 42, #7 (April 1985).
17. Atkinson, Carroll and Maleska, Eugene T. ***The Story of Education*** (Philadelphia: Chilton, 1962).
18. Bain, Linda L. "Curriculum for Critical Reflection in Physical Education" in ***Content of the Curriculum*** (Alexandria, Va.: ASCD, 1988).
19. Ballinger, Charles. "Rethinking the School Calendar" in ***Educational Leadership,*** Vol. 45, #5 (February 1988).
20. Beard, Charles A. ***The Unique Function of Education in American Democracy*** (Washington, D.C.: Educational Policies Commission, NEA/AASA, 1937).
21. Beggs, David W. and Buffie, Edward G. ***Non-graded Schools in Action*** (Bloomington, Ind.: Indiana Univ. Press, 1967).
22. Bell, Derrick, ed. ***Shades of Brown: new perspectives on school desegregation*** (New York: Teachers College Press, 1980).
23. Bennett, William J., ed. "Statement and Fourth Annual Wall Chart of State Education Statistics" (Washington, D.C.: U.S. Department of Education, 1987).

24. Bensen, M. James. "The Transition from Industrial Arts to Technology Education" in ***Content of the Curriculum*** (Alexandria, Va.: ASCD, 1988).
25. Berne, Eric. ***Games People Play: the psychology of human relationships*** (New York: Grove Press, 1964).
26. Blake, Robert R. and Mouton, Jane S. ***The Managerial Grid*** (Austin: Scientific Methods, 1964).
27. Blaunstein, Phyllis L. "Public and Non-public Schools: finding ways to work together" in ***Phi Delta Kappan,*** Vol. 67, #5 (January 1986).
28. Bloom, Allan. ***The Closing of the American Mind*** (New York: Simon and Schuster, 1987).
29. Bloom, Benjamin. ***Human Characteristics and School Learning*** (New York: McGraw Hill, 1976).
30. ___________. ***Taxonomy of Educational Objectives*** (New York: McKay, 1956.)
31. Bogie, Cheryl E. and Bogie, Donald W. "Teachers' Preference toward Alternate Systems of Salary Increment" in ***Education,*** Vol. 99, #2 (Winter 1978).
32. Borg, Walter R. ***Ability Grouping in the Public Schools*** (Madison, Wisc.: Dembar Educational Research Services, 1966).
33. Bowman, Thomas et al. ***Finding Your Best Place To Live in America*** (New York: Red Lion, 1981).
34. Boyer, Ernest L. ***High School: a report on secondary education in America*** (New York: Harper and Row, 1983).
35. Bracey, Gerald W. "High Road, Low Road, End of the Road for CAI and Programming" in ***Phi Delta Kappan,*** Vol. 68, #7 (March 1987).
36. ___________. "The Social Impact of Ability Grouping" in ***Phi Delta Kappan,*** Vol. 68, #9 (May 1987).
37. Bragaw, Donald H. and Hartoonian, H. Michael. "Social Studies: the study of people in society" in ***Content of the Curriculum*** (Alexandria, Va.: ASCD, 1988).
38. Brandt, Ronald S. "On Leadership and Student Achievement: a conversation with Richard Andrews" in ***Educational Leadership,*** Vol. 45, #1 (September 1987).
39. ___________. "On Teaching and Supervision: a conversation with Madeline Hunter" in ***Educational Leadership*** (February 1985).
40. ___________. "On Teaching Thinking Skills: a conversation with B. Othanel Smith" in ***Educational Leadership,*** Vol. 45, #2 (October 1987).
41. ___________, ed. ***Content of the Curriculum*** (Alexandria, Va.: ASCD, 1988).
42. Braun, Robert J. ***Teachers and Power: the story of the American Federation of Teachers*** (New York: Simon and Schuster, 1972).
43. "A Break for White Males?" in ***American School Board Journal,*** Vol. 168, #5 (May 1981).
44. Brenner, Charles. ***An Elementary Textbook of Psychoanalysis*** (Garden City, N.Y.: Doubleday 1955).
45. Breslin, Robert G. and Klagholz, Leo F. "Paying Faculty Members What They Are Worth" in ***Educational Record,*** Vol. 61 (Winter 1980).
46. Brinks, Jane T. "Is There Merit in Merit Increases?" in ***Personnel Administrator,*** Vol. 25, #5 (May 1980).
47. Brogden, J.D. ***Developing Communications Skills in Non-committed Learners*** (West Nyack, N.Y.: Parker, 1970).
48. Bronowski, Jacob. ***The Ascent of Man*** (Boston: Little, Brown and Co., 1973).
49. Brophy, Jere. "Synthesis of Research on Strategies for Motivating Students To Learn" in ***Educational Leadership,*** Vol. 45, #2 (October 1987).
50. Brower, R. ***Television and the Public*** (New York: Holt, Rinehart, and Winston, 1973).

51. Brown, Elmer Ellsworth. ***The Making of Our Middle Schools*** (New York: Longmans, Green, and Co., 1902).

52. Brown, Frank B. ***The Non-graded High School*** (Englewood Cliffs, N.J.: Prentice-Hall, 1963).

53. Brown, Rexford. "Who Is Accountable for 'Thoughtfulness'?" in ***Phi Delta Kappan,*** Vol. 69, #1 (September 1987).

54. Brubacher, John S. ***A History of the Problems of Education*** (New York: McGraw Hill, 1966).

55. Bruner, Jerome S. ***The Process of Education*** (New York: Vintage, 1960.)

56. Bucci, Jerry Michael. ***Love, Marriage, and Family Themes in the Popular Song: a comparison of the years 1940 and 1965.*** (Ed. D. dissertation, Teachers College of Columbia Univ., 1968.)

57. Buchler, Justus, chairman. ***Introduction to Contemporary Civilization in the West,*** 3rd ed. (New York: Columbia Univ. Press, 1960).

58. Buie, James. "Teen Pregnancy: it's time for the schools to tackle the problem" in Phi ***Delta Kappan,*** Vol. 68, #10 (June 1987).

59. Burdin, Joel L. "Teacher Certification" in ***Encyclopedia of Educational Research,*** 5th ed. (New York: The Free Press, 1982).

60. Burke, Brian T. "Merit Pay for Teachers: Round Valley may have the answer" in ***Phi Delta Kappan,*** Vol. 64, #4 (December 1982).

61. Butts, R. Freeman and Cremin, Lawrence A. ***A History of Education in American Culture*** (New York: Holt, 1953).

62. Campbell, Patricia B. and Klein, Susan. "Equity Issues in Education" in ***Encyclopedia of Educational Research*** (New York: The Free Press, 1982).

63. Campbell, Patricia F. and Fey, James T. "New Goals for School Mathematics" in ***Content of the Curriculum*** (Alexandria, Va.: ASCD, 1988).

64. Carbo, Marie. "Reading Styles Research: what works isn't always phonics" in ***Phi Delta Kappan,*** Vol. 68, #6 (February 1987).

65. Carnoy, Martin. "Economics and Education" in ***Encyclopedia for Educational Research,*** 5th ed. (New York: The Free Press, 1982).

66. Carol, Lila N. et al. ***School Boards: strengthening grassroots leadership*** (Washington, D.C.: Institute for Educational Leadership, 1986).

67. Carroll, John B. "The National Assessments in Reading: are we misreading the findings?" in ***Phi Delta Kappan,*** Vol. 68, #6 (February 1987).

68. Casey, William F. "Would Bear Bryant Teach in Public School: the need for teacher incentives" in ***Phi Delta Kappan,*** Vol. 60, #7 (March 1979).

69. Caswell, Hollis L. and Campbell, Doak S. ***Curriculum Development*** (New York: American Book Co., 1935).

70. Catterall, J. "Tuition Tax Credits for Schools" in ***IFG Policy Perspectives*** (Stanford: Stanford Univ. Institute for Research on Educational Finance and Governance, 1981).

71. ___________ and Thresher, T. ***Proposition 13: the campaign, the vote, the after-effects*** (Stanford: Stanford Univ. Institute for Research on Educational Finance and Governance, 1979).

72. Cawelti, Gordon. "Guess What? Big City Superintendents Say Their School Boards Are Splendid" in ***American School Board Journal*** (March 1982).

73. Chamberlain, Leslie J. and Girona, Ricardo. "Our Children Are Changing" in ***Curriculum Planning: a new approach*** (Boston: Allyn and Bacon, 1983).

74. Chambers, J. ***Educational Cost Differentials and Allocation of State Aid for Elementary/Secondary Education: report #79-B4.*** (Stanford: Stanford Univ. Institute for Research on Educational Finance and Governance, March 1979).

75. Church, Robert L. *Education in the United States: an interpretive history* (New York: The Free Press, 1976).
76. Cistone, P.J. and Iannaccone, L. "Educational Governance: contradictions and tendencies" in *Education and Urban Society,* Vol. 12 (1980).
77. Clark, David L. "High School Seniors React to Their Teachers and Their Schools" in *Phi Delta Kappan,* Vol. 68, #7 (March 1987).
78. Cogan, Morris. *Clinical Supervision* (Boston, Houghton-Mifflin, 1978).
79. Cohan, Irving M. *An Investigation of Procedures* (Masters Thesis: Graduate School of Education, Long Island Univ., Merriweather Campus, 1967).
80. Cohen, Michael. "State Boards in an Era of Reform" in *Phi Delta Kappan,* Vol. 69, #1 (September 1987).
81. Collins, Marva and Tamarkin, Civia. *Marva Collins' Way* (Los Angeles, Jeremy P. Tarcher, Inc., 1982).
82. Conant, James B. *The Education of American Teachers* (New York: McGraw-Hill, 1963).
83. Copperman, Paul. *The Literacy Hoax: the decline of reading, writing, and learning in the public schools and what we can do about it* (New York: Morrow, 1978).
84. Costa, Arthur L. and Garmston, Robert. "Supervision for Intelligent Teaching" in *Educational Leadership* (February 1985).
85. Counts, George S. *The Education of Free Men in American Democracy* (Washington, D.C.: Educational Policies Commission, NEA/AASA, 1941).
86. "Court Ducks RIF and Race Issue" in *American School Board Journal,* Vol. 169, #2 (December 1982).
87. Cramer, J.F. and Browne, G.S. *Contemporary Education: a comparative study of national systems,* 2nd ed. (New York: Harcourt, 1965).
88. "Creationists Have a Day in Court — and Lose" in *American School Board Journal,* Vol. 169, #3 (March 1982).
89. "Creationists Limit Dogmatic Darwinism" in *American School Board Journal,* Vol. 168, #5 (May 1981).
90. Cremin, Lawrence A. *The Transformation of the School* (New York: Knopf, 1961).
91. Cuban, Larry. "Persistent Instruction: another look at constancy in the classroom" in *Phi Delta Kappan,* Vol. 68, #1 (September 1986).
92. __________. "School Reform by Remote Control in California" in *Phi Delta Kappan* (November 1984).
93. __________. "Sex and School Reform" in *Phi Delta Kappan,* Vol. 68, #4 (December 1986).
94. Cunningham, Luvern L. and Hentges, Joseph. *The American School Superintendency, 1982: a full report* (Arlington, Va.: American Association of School Administrators, 1982).
95. *Current Thought on Curriculum* (Alexandria, Va.: ASCD, 1985).
96. Curtis, Jerry and Neill, Shirley B. *Staff Dismissal: problems and solutions* (Arlington, Va.: American Association of School Administrators, 1978).
97. Curtis, Lynn A., ed. *American Violence and Public Policy* (New Haven: Yale Univ. Press, 1985).
98. Danzberger, Jacqueline P. "School Boards: the forgotten players on the education team" in *Phi Delta Kappan,* Vol. 69, #1 (September, 1987).
99. Dennis, Lawrence J. "Why Not Merit Pay?" in *Contemporary Education,* Vol. 56, #6 (Fall 1982).
100. Dewey, John. *Experience and Nature* (New York: Dover, 1958).
101. Dickstein, Morris. *Gates of Eden: American culture in the sixties* (New York: Basic Books, 1977).

102. ***Differentiated Staffing.*** Report of the Central New York Office for Educational Planning and the Nassau Regional Office for Educational Planning (BOCES), 1971.

103. Dodd, Anne Wescott and Rosenbaum, Eileen. "Learning Communities for Curriculum and Staff Development" in ***Phi Delta Kappan,*** Vol. 67, #5 (January 1986.)

104. Doherty, Robert E. "Does Teacher Bargaining Effect Student Achievement?" in ***Faculty and Teacher Bargaining: the impact of unions on education*** (Lexington, Mass.: Lexington Books 1981).

105. Dolan, Edward F., Jr. ***International Drug Traffic*** (New York: Franklin Watts, 1985).

106. Donley, Marshall O. ***Power to the Teacher: how America's educators became militant*** (Bloomington, Ind.: Indiana Univ. Press, 1976).

107. Doremus, Richard R. "What Ever Happened to Kalamazoo's Merit Pay Plan?" in ***Phi Delta Kappan,*** Vol. 63, #6 (February 1982).

108. Doyle, Andrew. "Local Control of Schools — a Myth." Special Bulletin of the Missouri School Boards Association (January 28, 1976).

109. Doyle, Dennis and Finn, Chester. "Does More State Aid for Education Make Local School Districts Obsolete?" in ***Basic Education*** (June 1984).

110. Drucker, Peter F. ***Concept of the Corporation*** (New York: John Day, 1946).

111. "ED Gets an Evangelist of the Right" in ***American School Board Journal,*** Vol. 168, #5 (May 1981).

112. "Educational Administration and Organization: a 40-year perspective" in ***Educational Researcher,*** Vol. 11, #2 (February 1982).

113. ***Educational Programs That Work,*** 12th ed. National Diffusion Network (Longmont, Colorado: Sporis West, Inc., 1986).

114. Edwards, Sara A. and Barnes, Susan. "A Research-Based Staff Development Model That Works" in ***Educational Leadership,*** Vol. 42, #7 (April 1985).

115. Elsberg, Ted. "Schools Need Tenured Leaders" in ***The New York Times*** (November 13, 1982).

116. Elvin, Lionel, ed. ***The Educational Systems in the European Community*** (Berks, England: NFER-Nelson Publishing Co., 1981).

117. Engelmann, Siegfried. ***Your Child Can Succeed*** (New York: Simon and Schuster, 1975).

118. Engleman, Finis E. "Point of View: whither governance of public education?" in ***School Administrator*** (October 1977).

119. Eymonerie, Maryse. "Salary Scales: pros and cons" in ***Academe Bulletin of the AAUP,*** Vol. 66, #2 (March 1960).

120. Fantini, Mario. "The Right to Quality Education" in ***Curriculum Planning: a new approach*** (Boston: Allyn and Bacon, 1983).

121. ___________. ***What's Best for the Children?: resolving the power struggle between parents and teachers*** (Garden City: Anchor/Doubleday, 1975).

122. Feinberg, Gerald and Shapiro, Robert. ***Life beyond Earth*** (New York: Morrow, 1980).

123. Ficklen, Ellen. "Personal Financial Disclosure: is it your civic duty or indecent exposure?" in ***American School Board Journal*** (February 1985).

124. Fiedler, Fred. ***A Theory of Leadership Effectiveness*** (New York: McGraw Hill, 1970).

125. Finn, Chester, Jr., chief of research. "What's Happening in Teacher Testing." Federal report on teacher competency tests. (Washington, D.C.: Office of Educational Research and Improvement, U.S. Department of Education, 1987).

126. Fischer, Louis. "Academic Freedom and Tenure" in ***Encyclopedia of Educational Research,*** 5th ed. (New York: The Free Press, 1982).

127. Fitzpatrick, B. ***Women's Inferior Education*** (New York: Praeger, 1976).

128. Fizzell, Robert L. "Inside a School of Choice" in ***Phi Delta Kappan,*** Vol. 68, #10 (June 1987).

129. Fleming, Dan B. and Hunt, Thomas C. "The World As Seen by Students in Accelerated Christian Schools" in ***Phi Delta Kappan,*** Vol. 68, #7 (March 1987).

130. Flexner, E. ***Century of Struggle*** (New York: Atheneum, 1974).

131. Flygare, Thomas J. "Some Thoughts on the Tennessee Textbook Case" in ***Phi Delta Kappan,*** Vol. 68, #6 (February 1987).

132. ___________. "Supreme Court Confused by Reverse Discrimination" in ***Phi Delta Kappan,*** Vol. 68, #1 (September 1986).

133. ___________. "Supreme Court Strikes Down Louisiana Creationism Act" in ***Phi Delta Kappan,*** Vol. 69, #1 (September 1987).

134. Fort, Joel. ***The Addicted Society*** (New York: Grove Press, 1981).

135. Fowler, Frances C. "The French Experience with Public Aid to Private Schools" in ***Phi Delta Kappan,*** Vol. 68, #5 (January 1987).

136. Frank, Andre Gunder. ***Crisis in the World Economy*** (New York: Holmes and Meier, 1980).

137. Frazier, N. and Sadker, M.P. ***Sexism in School and Society*** (New York: Harper and Row, 1973).

138. Freud, Sigmund. ***Civilization and Its Discontents*** (London: The Hogarth Press, 1930).

139. ___________. ***An Outline of Psychoanalysis,*** trans. James Strachey (New York: Norton, 1949).

140. ___________. ***Sexuality and the Psychology of Love*** (New York: Collier, 1963).

141. Friewald, J. Leo. "Tenure — Another Sacred Cow about To Bite the Dust" in ***Phi Delta Kappan,*** Vol. 61, #1 (September 1979).

142. Frymier, Jack. "Bureaucracy and the Neutering of Teachers" in ***Phi Delta Kappan,*** Vol. 69, #1 (September 1987.)

143. Fuchs, Victor R. ***How We Live*** (Cambridge, Mass.: Harvard Univ. Press, 1983).

144. Furtwengler, Willis J. "Implementing Strategies for a School Effectiveness Program" in ***Phi Delta Kappan,*** Vol. 67, #4 (December 1985).

145. Galbraith, John Kenneth. ***The Affluent Society,*** 4th ed. (Boston: Houghton Mifflin, 1984).

146. Gallup, Alec M. "The 18th Annual Gallup Poll of the Public's Attitude toward Public Education" in ***Phi Delta Kappan,*** Vol. 68, #1 (September 1986).

147. ___________ and Clark, David L. "The 19th Annual Gallup Poll of the Public's Attitude toward Public Education" in ***Phi Delta Kappan,*** Vol. 69, #1 (September 1987).

148. Gallup, George H., dir. ***The Gallup Poll: public opinion 1972-1977.*** (Wilmington, Delaware: Scholarly Resources, Inc., 1978).

149. Garton, Virginia. "How the Coming of the Hmong Transformed the Schools on Main Street" in ***American School Board Journal,*** Vol. 169, #11 (November 1982).

150. Geiger, Philip E. and Toscano, Gerald. "If You Follow These Proven Guidelines, Merit Pay for Administrators Can Succeed" in ***American School Board Journal,*** Vol. 167, #1 (January 1980).

151. Gideonse, Hendrick D. "The Necessary Revolution in Teacher Education" in ***Phi Delta Kappan,*** Vol. 64, #1 (September 1982).

152. Gimlin, Hoyt, ed. ***America's Economy: problems and prospects*** (Washington, D.C.: Congressional Quarterly, 1983)

153. ___________, ed. ***World Economy: changes and challenges*** (Washington, D.C.: Congressional Quarterly, Inc., 1983).

154. Glenn, Charles R. "Textbook Controversies: a disaster for public schools?" in ***Phi Delta Kappan,*** Vol. 68, #6 (February 1987).

155. Glickman, Carl D. ***Developmental Supervision*** (Alexandria, Va.: ASCD, 1981).

156. Goldberg, Miriam and Passow, Harry A. ***The Effects of Ability Grouping*** (New York: Teachers College Press, 1966).

157. Goldhammer, R. ***Clinical Supervision*** (New York: Holt, Rinehart and Winston, 1969).

158. Gollnick, Donna M. and Kunkel, Richard C. "The Reform of National Accreditation" in ***Phi Delta Kappan,*** Vol. 68, #4 (December 1986).

159. Good, Harry G. ***A History of American Education*** (New York: MacMillan, 1962).

160. __________ and Teller, James D. ***A History of Western Education*** (New York: MacMillan, 1969).

161. Goodlad, John I. ***The Dynamics of Educational Change*** (New York: McGraw Hill, 1975).

162. __________. "The Great American Schooling Experiment" in ***Phi Delta Kappan,*** Vol. 67, #4 (December 1985).

163. __________. "Let's Get On with the Reconstruction" in ***Phi Delta Kappan,*** Vol. 64, #1 (September 1982).

164. __________. ***A Place Called School: prospects for the future*** (New York: McGraw Hill, 1984).

165. __________. ***School Curriculum and the Individual*** (Waltham, Mass.: Blaisdell, 1966).

166. __________ and Anderson, Robert H. ***The Non-graded Elementary School*** (New York: Harcourt, 1959).

167. __________ and Oakes, Jeannie. "We Must Offer Equal Access to Knowledge" in ***Educational Leadership,*** Vol. 45, #5 (February 1988).

168. Gorton, Richard A. ***School Administration and Supervision*** (Dubuque, Iowa: Wm. C. Brown, 1972).

169. Gosling, H.W. ***Teacher Evaluation: an examination of formal expectations and actual content*** (Doctoral dissertation: Indiana Univ., 1978). UM#79-06002

170. Gough, Pauline B. "The Key to Improving Schools: an interview with William Glasser" in ***Phi Delta Kappan,*** Vol. 68, #9 (May 1987).

171. Guskey, Thomas R. "Staff Development and Teacher Change" in ***Educational Leadership,*** Vol. 42, #7 (April 1985).

172. Gutherie, James W. and Skene, Paula H. "Education Power Shift-II: local control gives way" in ***Compact*** (March/April 1974).

173. Guthrie-Morse, Barbara et al. "Assessing the Impact of Faculty Unions: the financial implications of collective bargaining" in ***Journal of Higher Education,*** Vol. 52, #3 (May 1980).

174. Hacker, Andrew, ed. ***A Statistical Portrait of the American People*** (New York: Viking, 1983).

175. Hall, G.E. ***A National Agenda for Research and Development in Teacher Education, 1979-1984*** (Austin, Texas: Univ. of Texas Research and Development Center for Teacher Education, 1979).

176. Hallinger, Philip and Murphy, Joseph F. "Assessing and Developing Principal Instructional Leadership" in ***Educational Leadership,*** Vol. 45, #1 (September 1987).

177. Halsey, A.H. ***Trends in British Society since 1900: a guide to the changing social structure of Britain*** (London: MacMillan, 1972).

178. Hampel, Robert L. "Inside the Citadel in 1940" in ***Phi Delta Kappan,*** Vol. 67, #10 (June 1986).

179. Hansen, Carl F. ***The Four-track Curriculum in Today's High School*** (Englewood Cliffs, N.J.: Prentice-Hall, 1964).

180. Hansen, William B. "Effective School-based Approaches to Drug Abuse Prevention" in ***Educational Leadership,*** Vol. 45, #6 (March 1988).
181. Harris, Jonathan. ***Super Mafia*** (New York: Julian Messner, 1984).
182. Hart, Harold, ed. ***Summerhill: for and against*** (New York: Hart, 1970).
183. Hartman, Helene. ***An Examination of Literature*** (Masters thesis, C.W. Post Center of Long Island Univ., 1970).
184. Hass, Glen, ed. ***Curriculum Planning: a new approach,*** 4th ed. (Boston: Allyn and Bacon, 1983).
185. Hawley, Richard A. "Schoolchildren and Drugs: the fancy that has not passed" in ***Phi Delta Kappan,*** Vol. 68, #9 (May 1987).
186. Hawley, Willis D. "Toward a Comprehensive Strategy for Addressing the Teacher Shortage" in ***Phi Delta Kappan,*** Vol. 67, #10 (June 1986).
187. Heath, Shirley Brice and McLaughlin, Milbrey Wallin. "A Child Resource Policy: moving beyond dependence on school and family" in ***Phi Delta Kappan,*** Vol. 68, #7 (April 1987).
188. Heilbroner, Robert L. ***The Worldly Philosophers*** (New York: Clarion, 1967).
189. Henderson, Howard. "The Madison Workshops — One Approach to Staff Development" in ***Phi Delta Kappan,*** Vol. 67, #5 (January 1986).
190. Hernandez, Norma and Descamps, Jorge A. "Religion and Education" in ***Encyclopedia of Educational Research,*** 5th ed. (New York: The Free Press, 1982).
191. Hersey, Paul and Blanchard, Kenneth H. ***Management of Organizational Behavior: utilizing human resources,*** 3rd ed. (Englewood Cliffs, N.J.: Prentice-Hall, 1977).
192. Herzberg, Frederick. ***The Managerial Choice: to be efficient and to be human*** (Homewood, Ill.: Dow Jones-Irwin, 1976).
193. ___________. ***Work and the Nature of Man*** (Cleveland: World, 1966).
194. Highet, Gilbert. ***The Art of Teaching*** (New York: Knopf, 1950).
195. Hill, Winfred F. ***Learning: a survey of psychological interpretations*** (San Francisco: Chandler, 1963).
196. Hirsch, E.D., Jr. ***Cultural Literacy: what every American needs to know*** (Boston: Houghton Mifflin, 1987).
197. Hodgkinson, Harold L. "Reform? Higher Education? Don't be Absurd!" in ***Phi Delta Kappan,*** Vol. 68, #4 (December 1986).
198. ___________. "The Right School for the Right Kids" in ***Educational Leadership,*** Vol. 45, #5 (February 1988).
199. Hoffman, Mark S., ed. ***The World Almanac,*** 1987 (New York: Pharos Books/Scripps Howard, 1987).
200. Holmes, C. Thomas and Matthews, Kenneth M. "The Effects of Non-promotion on Elementary and Junior High School Pupils" in ***Review of Educational Research,*** Vol. 54 (1984).
201. "Holmes Group Recommends Major Changes in Teacher Training" in ***Phi Delta Kappan,*** Vol. 67, #10 (June 1986).
202. Holt, John C. ***How Children Fail*** (New York: Dell, 1970).
203. Hopkins, Harry. ***The New Look: a social history of the forties and fifties in Britain.*** (Boston: Houghton-Mifflin, 1964).
204. Horney, Karen. ***The Neurotic Personality of Our Time.*** (New York: Norton, 1937).
205. Horton, Lowell. "The Education of Most Worth: preventing drug and alcohol abuse" in ***Educational Leadership,*** Vol. 45, #6 (March 1988).
206. Houstan, W. Robert and Newman, Katherine K. "Teacher Education Programs" in ***Encyclopedia of Educational Research,*** 5th ed. (New York: The Free Press, 1982).
207. "'Humanistic' Education is a Failure" in ***American School Board Journal,*** Vol. 168, #5 (May 1981).

208. Hunter, Madeline. "Let's Eliminate the Preobservation Conference" in ***Educational Leadership*** (March 1986).
209. __________. "Madeline Hunter Replies: develop collaboration; build trust" in ***Educational Leadership*** (March 1986).
210. __________. ***Mastery Teaching*** (El Segundo, Calif.: TIP Publications, 1982).
211. __________. ***Rx for Improved Instruction*** (El Segundo, Calif.: TIP Publications, 1976).
212. __________. "What's Wrong with Madeline Hunter" in ***Educational Leadership*** (February 1985).
213. Hurn, Christopher J. and Burn, Barbara B. ***Analytic Comparison of Educational Systems: overview of purposes, policies, structures, and outcome.*** (Washington, D.C.: National Committee on Excellence in Education, 1982).
214. Hurt, Henry. ***Reasonable Doubt*** (New York: Holt, Rinehart, and Winston, 1985).
215. Hurwitz, Mark W. "What Works Best: an elected or an appointed school board" in ***American School Board Journal*** (July 1972).
216. Iannaccone, Laurence. "Superintendents Make a Difference" in ***The School Administrator,*** Vol. 38, #8 (September 1981).
217. __________ and Lutz, F.W. ***Politics, Power, and Policy*** (Columbus: Merrill, 1970).
218. Iffert, Robert E. ***Retention and Withdrawal of College Students*** (Washington, D.C.: U.S. Department of Health, Education, and Welfare—Bulletin 1958 #1, 1958).
219. Ignas, Raymond and Corsini, Raymond J. ***Comparative Educational Systems*** (Itasca, Ill.: F.E. Peacock, 1981).
220. Imig, David G. "The Greater Challenge" in ***Phi Delta Kappan,*** Vol. 68, #1 (September 1986).
221. "Is 'No Pass, No Play' No Good?" in ***Music Educators Journal,*** Vol. 73, #5 (January 1988).
222. Jackson, Bruce. "Lowered Expectations: how schools reward incompetence" in ***Phi Delta Kappan,*** Vol. 67, #4 (December 1985).
223. Jacoby, Susan. ***Inside Soviet Schools*** (New York: Hill and Wang, 1974).
224. Jarolimek, John. ***The Schools in Contemporary Society: an analysis of social currents, issues, and forces*** (New York: MacMillan, 1981).
225. Jenkins, Evan. "Education Power Shift — I: the states have come a long way" in ***Compact*** (March/April, 1974).
226. Jenkinson, Edward B. "The Significance of the Decision in Scopes II" in ***Phi Delta Kappan,*** Vol. 68, #6 (February 1987).
227. Jennings, John F. "The Sputnik of the Eighties" in ***Phi Delta Kappan,*** Vol. 69, #2 (October 1987).
228. Jersild, Arthur T. ***When Teachers Face Themselves*** (New York: Teachers College Press, 1953).
229. Johnson, Carroll F. "How To Hire the Right Superintendent" in ***American School Board Journal,*** Vol. 169, #12 (December 1982).
230. Johnson, Roger T. and Johnson, David W. "Student-Student Interaction: powerful but ignored" in ***Journal of Teacher Education*** (July/August 1985).
231. Johnson, Ronald E. "ACE Responds" in ***Phi Delta Kappan,*** Vol. 68, #7 (March 1987).
232. Johnson, Susan Moore. ***Teacher Unions in Schools*** (Philadelphia: Temple Univ. Press, 1984).
233. Joki, Russell A. "Make Teacher Competency Your Policy" in ***American School Board Journal,*** Vol. 169, #11 (November 1982).
234. Kaplin, William. ***The Law of Higher Education*** (San Francisco: Jossey-Bass, 1985).
235. Keller, Franklin Jefferson. ***The Comprehensive High School*** (New York: Harper, 1955).

236. Kenney, Asta M. "Teen Pregnancy: an issue for schools" in ***Phi Delta Kappan,*** Vol. 69, #1 (September 1987).

237. Keppel, Francis. "A Field Guide to the Land of Teachers" in ***Phi Delta Kappan,*** Vol. 68, #1 (September 1986).

238. Kerchner, Charles T. and Mitchell, Douglas E. ***The Dynamics of Public School Bargaining and Its Impact on Governance, Administration, and Teaching*** (Washington, D.C.: National Institute of Education, 1981).

239. Kerman, Sam. "Teacher Expectation and Student Achievement" in ***Phi Delta Kappan*** (June 1979).

240. __________ and Martin, Mary. ***Teacher Expectation and Student Achievement: coordinator manual*** (Bloomington, Ind.: Phi Delta Kappa, 1980).

241. Killian, Michael G. "Local Control — the Vanishing Myth in Texas" in ***Phi Delta Kappan*** (November 1984).

242. Kindsvatter, Richard and Wilen, William W. "A Systematic Approach to Improving Conference Skills" in ***Educational Leadership,*** Vol. 38, #7 (April 1981).

243. King, Edmund J. ***Other Schools and Ours*** (Guilford, England: Billing and Sons, Ltd., 1979).

244. Kipp, D.F. "But These Board Members Drive Superintendents Crazy" in ***American School Board Journal,*** Vol. 169, #3 (March 1982).

245. Kirst, Michael W. "The Changing Balance in State and Local Power to Control Education" in ***Phi Delta Kappan*** (November 1984).

246. __________. "Sustaining the Momentum of State Education Reform: the link between assessment and financial support" in ***Phi Delta Kappan,*** Vol. 67, #5 (January 1986).

247. Klein, Susan Shurberg. "Sex Education and Gender Equity" in ***Educational Leadership,*** Vol. 45, #6 (March 1988).

248. Koehler, Michael D. "Schools with Lowerarchies: are they possible?" in ***Clearing House,*** Vol. 52, #9 (May 1979).

249. Komoski, P. Kenneth. "Instructional Materials Will Not Improve Until We Change the System" in ***Educational Leadership,*** Vol. 42, #7 (April 1985).

250. Kutkat, J.H. "Clash: superintendents oppose boards" in ***American School Board Journal,*** Vol. 168, #5 (May 1981).

251. "L.A. Decision: is busing dead?" in ***American School Board Journal,*** Vol. 168, #5 (May 1981).

252. Lambert, Linda. "Who Is Right—Madeline Hunter or Art Costa?" in ***Educational Leadership*** (February 1985).

253. Langenbach, Michael and Blitch, Judith Young. "Use Performance, Not Just Tests, To Select Kids for Gifted Programs" in ***American School Board Journal,*** Vol. 169, #11 (November 1982).

254. Lasley, Thomas J. "Teaching Selflessness in a Selfish Society" in ***Phi Delta Kappan,*** Vol. 68, #9 (May 1987).

255. LeCroy, Hoyt F. "The Ph.D. in Public Schools: how should graduate programs adopt?" in ***Music Educators Journal,*** Vol. 73, #5 (January 1988).

256. Lee, Patrick C. and Gropper, Nancy. "A Cultural Analysis of Sex Role in the School" in ***Journal of Teacher Education,*** Vol. 26, #4 (Winter 1975).

257. Lehman, Paul R. "What Students Should Learn in the Arts" in ***Content of the Curriculum*** (Alexandria, Va.: ASCD, 1988).

258. Letteri, Charles A. "Cognitive Profile: basic determinant of academic achievement" in ***Journal of Educational Research,*** Vol. 73, #4 (March/April 1980).

259. Lewis, Lanora G. ***Talent and Tomorrow's Teachers: the honors approach*** (Washington, D.C.: U.S. Department of Health, Education, and Welfare, 1963).

260. Lidz, Theodore. ***The Person: his development through the life cycle*** (New York: Basic Books, 1968).
261. Lieberman, Ann and Miller, Lynne. ***Teachers, Their World, and Their Work: implications for school improvement.*** (Alexandria, Va.: ASCD, 1984).
262. Lieberman, Myron. "Teachers Bargaining: an autopsy" in ***Phi Delta Kappan,*** Vol. 63, #4 (December 1981).
263. Lines, Patricia M. "The New Private Schools and Their Historical Purpose" in ***Phi Delta Kappan,*** Vol. 67, #5 (January 1986).
264. Lipman, Matthew. "The Cultivation of Reasoning Through Philosophy" in ***Educational Leadership,*** Vol. 42, #1 (September 1984).
265. London, Perry. "Character Education and Clinical Intervention: a paradigm shift for U.S. Schools" in ***Phi Delta Kappan,*** Vol. 68, #9 (May 1987).
266. Long, Robert Emmet, ed. "Drugs and the American Society" in ***The Reference Shelf,*** Vol. 57, #6 (New York: N.W. Wilson, 1986).
267. Lordon, John. "In Defense of the Preobservation Conference" in ***Educational Leadership*** (March 1986).
268. Lorraine, John. ***Global Signposts to the 21st Century*** (Seattle: Univ. of Washington Press, 1979).
269. Love, Byron. "On Local Control: who is in charge? Part III" in ***Michigan School Board Journal*** (April 1982).
270. ___________ and Kearney, C. Philip. "On Local Control: who is in charge? Part I" in ***Michigan School Board Journal*** (February 1982).
271. Lutz, F.W. and Iannaccone L., eds. ***Public Participation in Local School Districts*** (Lexington, Mass.: Heath, 1978).
272. MacDougall, Ursula Cooke. ***If Your Child Has Reading Difficulties*** (New York: The Dalton School, 1952).
273. Madaus, George F. and Pullin, Diana. "Teacher Certification Tests: do they really measure what we need to know?" in ***Phi Delta Kappan,*** Vol. 69, #1 (September 1987).
274. Malinowski, Bronislaw. ***Sex and Repression in Savage Society*** (New York: Humanities Press, 1953) (Reprinted from 1927 edition).
275. Mann, Dale. "Business Involvement and Public School Improvement, Part I" in ***Phi Delta Kappan,*** Vol. 69, #2 (October 1987).
276. Manwaring, Loretta. "On Local Control: who is in charge? Part II" in ***Michigan School Board Journal*** (March 1982).
277. Markham, Walter G. "A New Twist for Superintendent Selection" in ***American School Board Journal,*** Vol. 167, #9 (September 1982).
278. Marzano, Robert J. et. al. ***Dimensions of Thinking: a framework for curriculum and instruction*** (Alexandria, Va.: ASCD, 1968).
279. Maslow, Abraham. ***Eupsychian Management*** (Homewood, Ill.: Irwin and Dorsey, 1965).
280. ___________. ***Motivation and Personality,*** 2nd ed. (New York: Harper and Row, 1970).
281. Matthews, George T., chairman. ***Man in Contemporary Society: a source book*** (New York: Columbia Univ. Press, 1955).
282. McCarthy, Bernice. "What Format Training Teaches Us about Staff Development" in ***Educational Leadership,*** Vol. 42, #7 (April 1985).
283. McClellan, Mary C. "Teen Pregnancy" in ***Phi Delta Kappan,*** Vol. 68, #10 (June 1987).
284. McDaniel, Thomas R. "A Primer on Classroom Discipline: principles old and new" in ***Phi Delta Kappan,*** Vol. 68, #1 (September 1986).

285. McDonnell, Lorraine and Pascal, Anthony. ***Organized Teachers in American Schools*** (Santa Monica, Calif.: Rand Corp., 1979).

286. McGonagill, Grady. "Board/Staff Partnership: the key to the effectiveness of state and local boards" in ***Phi Delta Kappan,*** Vol. 69, #1 (September 1987).

287. McGreal, Thomas L. ***Successful Teacher Evaluation*** (Alexandria, Va.: ASCD, 1983).

288. McGregor, Douglass. ***The Human Side of Enterprise*** (New York: McGraw Hill, 1960).

289. McLaughlin, Milbrey Wallin and Shields, Patrick M. "Involving Low-Income Parents in the Schools: a role for policy" in ***Phi Delta Kappan,*** Vol. 69, #2 (October 1987).

290. Medley, Donald M. and Coker, Homer. "How Valid Are Principals' Judgments of Teacher Effectiveness" in ***Phi Delta Kappan,*** Vol. 69, #2 (October 1987).

291. Mehlinger, Howard D. "A Risky Venture" in ***Phi Delta Kappan,*** Vol. 68, #1 (September 1986).

292. Meier, Deborah. "Central Park East: an alternative story" in ***Phi Delta Kappan,*** Vol. 68, #10 (June 1987).

293. Meloy, Judy. "Of Hopes and Expectations" in ***Phi Delta Kappan,*** Vol. 67, #5 (January 1986).

294. Menendez, Shirley, ed. ***Educational Programs That Work,*** 12th ed. (Longmont, Colo.: Sopris West, 1986).

295. Mesarovic, Mihajlo and Pestel, Eduard. ***Mankind at the Turning Point*** (New York: Dutton, 1974).

296. Met, Myriam. "Tomorrow's Emphasis in Foreign Language: proficiency" in ***Content of the Curriculum*** (Alexandria, Va.: ASCD, 1988).

297. Meyer, Edwin J. "A Radical Proposal for Teacher Preparation" in ***Phi Delta Kappan,*** Vol. 67, #10 (June 1986).

298. Miller, Leonard M., ed. ***Guidance for the Underachiever with Superior Ability*** (Washington, D.C.: U.S. Department of Health, Education, and Welfare—Bulletin 1961 #25, 1961).

299. Miller, Leslie and Say, Elaine. "This Bold Incentive Pay Plan Pits Capitalism against Teacher Shortages" in ***American School Board Journal*** (September 1982).

300. Mills, James. ***The Underground Empire: where crime and governments embrace*** (Garden City, N.Y.: Doubleday, 1986).

301. Mitchell, Bruce M. and Williams, William G. "Education of the Gifted and Talented in the World Community" in ***Phi Delta Kappan,*** Vol. 68, #7 (March 1987).

302. Mitchell, D.E. "Measurement and Methodological Issues Related to Research on Incumbent Defeat and Superintendent Turnover" in ***Public Participation in Local School Districts*** (Lexington, Mass.: Heath, 1978).

303. Mitzel, Harold E., ed. ***Encyclopedia of Educational Research,*** 5th ed. (New York: The Free Press, 1982).

304. Molnar, Alex. "The Issue at Hand: a republic if we can keep it" in ***Educational Leadership,*** Vol. 45, #2 (October 1987).

305. ____________. "Schools and Their Curriculum: a continuing controversy" in ***Current Thought on Curriculum*** (Alexandria, Va.: ASCD, 1985).

306. Morganstern, Anne, ed. ***Grouping in the Elementary School*** (New York: Pitman, 1966).

307. Mueller, Daniel J. et al. "Effects of Reduced Class Size in Primary Classes" in ***Educational Leadership,*** Vol. 45, #5 (February 1988).

308. Mueller, Van D. "Choice: the parents' perspective" in ***Phi Delta Kappan,*** Vol. 68, #10 (June 1987).

309. Murray, Frank B. "Goals for the Reform of Teacher Education: an executive summary of the Holmes Group Report" in ***Phi Delta Kappan,*** Vol. 68, #1 (September 1986).

310. Muther, Connie. "What Do We Teach and When Do We Teach It?" in ***Educational Leadership,*** Vol. 45, #1 (September 1987).

311. __________. "What Every Textbook Evaluator Should Know" in ***Educational Leadership,*** Vol. 42, #7 (April 1985).

312. Myrdal, Gunnar. ***An American Dilemma: the Negro problem and modern democracy*** (New York: Harper and Brothers, 1944).

313. Nathan, Joe. "Results and Future Prospects of State Efforts to Increase Choice Among Schools" in ***Phi Delta Kappan,*** Vol. 68, #10 (June 1987).

314. Natriello, Gary, ed. ***School Dropouts: patterns and policies*** (New York: Teachers College Press, 1986).

315. Neill, A.S. ***Freedom—Not License!*** (New York: Hart, 1966).

316. __________. ***Summerhill: a radical approach to childrearing*** (New York: Hart, 1960).

317. Nevins, Allan and Commager, Henry Steele. ***A Short History of the United States*** (New York: Knopf, 1966).

318. Nicely, Robert F., Jr. "Higher-Order Thinking Skills in Mathematics Textbooks" in ***Educational Leadership,*** Vol. 42, #7 (April 1985).

319. Norton, John K. ***Education and Economic Well-Being in American Democracy*** (Washington, D.C.: Educational Policies Commission, NEA/AASA, 1940).

320. Nussel, Edward. "What the Holmes Group Report Doesn't Say" in ***Phi Delta Kappan,*** Vol. 68, #1 (September 1986).

321. Oakes, Jeannie. "Keeping Track, Part I: the policy and practice of curriculum inequality" in ***Phi Delta Kappan,*** Vol. 68, #1 (September 1986).

322. Odden, Allen. "Sources of Funding for Educational Reform" in ***Phi Delta Kappan,*** Vol. 67, #5 (January 1986).

323. Olivero, James L. and Buffie, G., eds. ***Educational Manpower*** (Bloomington, Ind.: Indiana Univ. Press, 1970).

324. Olson, Lunn. "An Overview of the Holmes Group" in ***Phi Delta Kappan,*** Vol. 68, #8 (April 1987).

325. ***On Further Investigation: report of the advisory panel on the Scholastic Aptitude Test score decline*** (New York: College Entrance Examination Board, 1977).

326. Osborn, Jean H. et al. "The Case for Improving Textbooks" in ***Educational Leadership,*** Vol. 42, #7 (April 1985).

327. Owens, Robert G. ***Organizational Behavior in Education,*** 2nd ed. (Englewood Cliffs, N.J.: Prentice-Hall, 1981).

328. Palmer, R.R. and Colton, Joel. ***A History of the Modern World,*** rev. ed. (New York: Knopf, 1960).

329. Parent, Joan M. "Roles and Responsibilities of Local School Districts" in ***American Education*** (March 1984).

330. Parkay, Forrest, W. "A School/University Partnership That Fosters Inquiry-oriented Staff Development" in ***Phi Delta Kappan,*** Vol. 67, #5 (January 1986).

331. Paul, Richard W. "Critical Thinking: fundamental to education for a free society" in ***Educational Leadership,*** Vol. 42, #1 (September 1984).

332. Pavan, Barbara N. "A Thank You and Some Questions for Madeline Hunter" in ***Educational Leadership*** (March 1986).

333. Perkins, D.N. "Creativity by Design" in ***Educational Leadership,*** Vol. 42, #1 (September 1984).

334. Perry, Charles, R. and Wildman, W.A. ***The Impact of Negotiations in Public Education: the evidence from the schools*** (Worthington, Ohio: Jones Pub. Co., 1970).

335. Peterson, Penelope L. et al. ***The Social Context of Education: group organization and group processes*** (Orlando, Fla.: Academic Press, 1984).

336. Pigford, Aretha Butler. "Teaching Evaluation: more than a game that principals play" in ***Phi Delta Kappan,*** Vol. 69, #2 (October 1987).

337. Pipho, Chris. "The Economy and Education" in ***Phi Delta Kappan,*** Vol. 68, #4 (December 1986).

338. ___________. "Rural Education" in ***Phi Delta Kappan,*** Vol. 69, #1 (September 1987).

339. ___________. "States Move Reform Closer to Reality" in ***Phi Delta Kappan,*** Vol. 68, #4 (December 1986).

340. ___________. "States on the Lookout for New Money" in ***Phi Delta Kappan,*** Vol. 68, #8 (April 1987).

341. Pitner, Nancy J. and Ogawa, Rodney T. "Organizational Leadership: the case of the school superintendent" in ***Educational Administration Quarterly,*** Vol.17, #2 (Spring 1981).

342. Plisko, Valena White, ed. ***The Condition of Education,*** 1984 ed. (Washington, D.C.: National Center for Educational Statistics).

343. Popham, W. James and Kirby, W.N. "Recertification Tests for Teachers: a defensible safeguard for society" in ***Phi Delta Kappan,*** Vol. 69, #1 (September 1987).

344. Porter, Andrew C. "Teacher Collaboration: new partnerships to attack old problems" in ***Phi Delta Kappan,*** Vol. 69, #2 (October 1987).

345. Porter, Lyman W. "A Study of Perceived Need" in ***Journal of Applied Psychology,*** Vol. 45 (1961).

346. Porter, Steven. ***Rhythm and Harmony in the Music of the Beatles*** (Ph.D. dissertation, City Univ. of New York, 1979). UM 7913156.

347. Powell, Arthur G. "Being Unspecial in the Shopping Mall High School" in ***Phi Delta Kappan,*** Vol. 67, #4 (December 1985).

348. Presthus, Robert. ***The Organizational Society,*** rev. ed. (New York: St. Martin's Press, 1978).

349. Price, Curtis. "Black Progress toward Educational Equity" in ***Educational Leadership,*** Vol. 38, #4 (January 1981).

350. Protheroe, Nancy, coordinator. ***An Overview of the NSBA/AASA Survey of School Board/Superintendent Relations*** (Arlington, Va.: Educational Research Service, 1986).

351. Putka, Gary. "Teachers Get More Pay and Power in the Wake of Reform Movements" in ***The Wall Street Journal*** (Sept. 21, 1987).

352. Rand, M. John and English, Fenwick. "Towards a Differentiated Teaching Staff" in ***Phi Delta Kappan,*** Vol. 49, #5 (January 1968).

353. Raths, James. "Evaluation of Teachers" in ***Encyclopedia of Educational Research,*** 5th ed. (New York: The Free Press, 1982).

354. Ravitch, Diane. ***The Troubled Crusade: American education 1945-1980.*** (New York: Basic Books, 1983).

355. Raywid, Mary Anne. "Public Choice, Yes; Voucher, No!" in ***Phi Delta Kappan,*** Vol. 68, #10 (June 1987).

356. Ream, Marsha A. "Ability Grouping" in ***Research Summary,*** Vol. #1968-S3 (Washington, D.C.: NEA, 1968).

357. Reddin, William J. ***Managerial Effectiveness*** (New York: McGraw Hill, 1970).

358. Reuben, David. ***Everything You Always Wanted To Know about Sex But Were Afraid To Ask*** (New York: McKay, 1969).

359. Riddle, Wayne. ***Public Secondary Education Systems in England, France, Japan, the Soviet Union, the United States, and West Germany: a comparative study.*** (Washington, D.C.: Congressional Research Service of the Library of Congress-Public Welfare Division, 1984).

360. Rist, Ray C. "Student Social Class and Teacher Expectations: the self-fulfilling prophecy in ghetto education" in ***Harvard Educational Review,*** Vol. 40 (August 1970).

361. Roberts, Arthur D. and Cawelti, Gordon. ***Redefining General Education in the American High School*** (Alexandria, Va.: ASCD, 1984).

362. Robinson, Sandra Longfellow. "Kindergarten in America: five major trends" in ***Phi Delta Kappan,*** Vol. 68, #7 (March 1987).

363. Rohlen, Thomas P. ***Japan's High Schools*** (Berkeley, Calif.: Univ. of California Press, 1983).

364. Rosenbaum, J. ***Making Inequality: the hidden curriculum of high school tracking*** (New York: Wiley, 1976).

365. Rosenthal, Alan. ***Pedagogues and Power: teacher groups in school politics*** (Syracuse, N.Y.: Syracuse Univ. Press, 1969).

366. Rostow, W.W. ***The Stages of Economic Growth*** (Cambridge, Mass.: Cambridge Univ. Press, 1960).

367. Roth, Robert A. "Emergency Certificates, Misassignment of Teachers, and Other 'Dirty Little Secrets'" in ***Phi Delta Kappan,*** Vol. 67, #10 (June 1986).

368. Rowe, Mary Budd. "Wait Time: slowing down may be a way of speeding up" in ***American Education*** (Spring 1987).

369. Ruch, Floyd L. ***Psychology and Life,*** 6th ed. (Chicago: Scott, Foresman, 1963).

370. Rutherford, F. James and Ahlgren, Andrew. "Rethinking the Science Curriculum" in ***Content of the Curriculum*** (Alexandria, Va.: ASCD, 1988).

371. Ruttan, Larry G. "Administrator Merit Pay—Theory into Practice" in ***Thrust for Educational Leadership,*** Vol. 8, #5 (May 1979).

372. Ryan, Heber Hinds and Crecelius, Philipine. ***Ability Grouping in the Junior High School*** (New York: Harcourt, 1927).

373. Sagan, Carl. ***The Cosmic Connection*** (Garden City, N.Y.: Anchor, 1980).

374. Salmon, Paul. "Who Runs Our Schools? A Definitive Answer is Impossible" in ***American School Board Journal,*** Vol. 169, #11 (November 1982).

375. Salvatore, Richard L. "Tenure Laws: another look" in ***Illinois Schools Journal,*** Vol. 58, #4 (Winter 1978-79).

376. Saphier, John and King, Matthew. "Good Seeds Grow in Strong Cultures" in ***Educational Leadership*** (March 1985).

377. Savage, David G. "Watching a Changing Court: will the center hold?" in ***Phi Delta Kappan,*** Vol. 69, #2 (October 1987).

378. ___________. "Why Chapter 1 Hasn't Made Much Difference" in ***Phi Delta Kappan,*** Vol. 68, #8 (April 1987).

379. Schaefer, William and Read, Bruce. "Use This Plan To Evaluate and Pay Administrators" in ***Executive Educator,*** Vol. 4, #7 (July 1982).

380. Scheifele, Marian. ***The Gifted Child in the Regular Classroom*** (New York: Bureau of Publications, Teachers College, Columbia Univ. 1953.)

381. Schlaadt, Richard G. "School Health Education" in ***Content of the Curriculum*** (Alexandria, Va.: ASCD, 1988).

382. Schrag, Francis. "It's Time for Merit Pay" in ***Learning,*** Vol. 11, #8 (March 1983).

383. Schuster, Jack H. "The Faculty Dilemma: a short course" in ***Phi Delta Kappan,*** Vol. 68, #4 (December 1986).

384. Schweinhart, Lawrence J. et al. "Policy Options for Pre-school Programs" in ***Phi Delta Kappan,*** Vol 68, #7 (March 1987).

385. Sergiovanni, Thomas J. "Leadership Behavior and Organizational Behavior" in ***Notre Dame Journal of Education,*** Vol. 4, #1 (Spring 1973).

386. ___________. ***Professional Supervision for Professional Teachers*** (Alexandria, Va.: ASCD, 1975).

387. ___________ and Carver, Fred D. ***The New School Executive: a theory of administration*** (New York: Dodd, Mead, 1973).

388. Servan-Schreiber, J.-J. ***The American Challenge*** (New York: Atheneum, 1968).

389. Servatius, Joanne Lee and Young, Shareen E. "Implementing the Coaching of Teaching" in ***Educational Leadership,*** Vol. 42, #7 (April 1985).

390. "Seventeen Percent of Teachers Flunk Exam" (Associated Press article) in ***Kennebec Journal*** (Augusta, Me.: August 27, 1987).

391. Shane, Harold G. "The Silicon Age and Education" in ***Phi Delta Kappan,*** Vol. 63, #5 (January 1985).

392. Shanker, Albert. "After Twenty Years, Lieberman's Vision Is Failing" in ***Phi Delta Kappan,*** Vol. 63, #4 (December 1981).

393. ____________. "Schools Pressed To Play It Safe: board oversight heavy-handed" in ***The New York Times*** (July 7, 1986).

394. Shannon, Jessica. "In the Classroom Stoned" in ***Phi Delta Kappan,*** Vol. 68, #1 (September 1986).

395. Shannon, Thomas A., Jr. "Histrionics and Help for Childhood" in ***American School Board Journal,*** Vol. 169, #12 (December 1982).

396. ____________. "Key to Educational Excellence Is the Local Community" in ***School Board News*** (October 19, 1983).

397. Showers, Beverly. "Teachers Coaching Teachers" in ***Educational Leadership,*** Vol. 42, #7 (April 1985).

398. Shulman, Lee S. "Assessment for Teaching: an initiative for the profession" in ***Phi Delta Kappan,*** Vol. 69, #1 (September, 1987).

399. Slavin, Robert E. "Cooperative Learning and the Cooperative School" in ***Educational Leadership,*** Vol. 45, #3 (November 1987).

400. ____________. "Making Chapter 1 Make a Difference" in ***Phi Delta Kappan,*** Vol. 69, #2 (October 1987).

401. Smith, Joanna B. "Reconceptualizing the Home Economics Curriculum" in ***Content of the Curriculum*** (Alexandria, Va.: ASCD, 1988).

402. Smith, Mary Lee and Shepard, Lorrie A. "What Doesn't Work: explaining policies of retention in early grades" in ***Phi Delta Kappan,*** Vol 69, #2 (October 1987).

403. Smith, Roy A. "A Teacher's View on Cooperative Learning" in ***Phi Delta Kappan,*** Vol 68, #9 (May 1987).

404. Smith, Wilma F. and Andrews, L. "Clinical Supervision for Principals" in ***Educational Leadership,*** Vol. 45, #1 (September 1987).

405. Smith, Winfield R. "Who Runs Our Schools? Superintendents—But That Must Change" in ***American School Board Journal,*** Vol. 169, #11 (November 1982).

406. Snyder, Karolyn J. "Clinical Supervision in the 1980's" in ***Educational Leadership,*** Vol. 38, #7 (April 1981).

407. Sosniak, Lauren A. "Gifted Education Boondoggles: a few bad apples or a rotten bushel?" in ***Phi Delta Kappan,*** Vol. 68, #7 (March 1987).

408. Spillane, Robert. "Some Unfortunate Assumptions" in ***Phi Delta Kappan,*** Vol. 64, #1 (September 1982).

409. ***Statistical Abstract of the United States, 1984,*** 104th ed. (Washington, D.C.: U.S. Department of Commerce, Bureau of the Census, 1984).

410. Stearns, M.S. and Cooperstein, R.A. "Equity in Educating the Handicapped" in ***Educational Leadership,*** Vol. 38, #4 (January, 1981).

411. Stern, Joyce D. and Williams, Mary Frase, eds. ***The Condition of Education: a statistical report,*** 1986 ed. (Washington, D.C.: Center for Educational Statistics, Office of Educational Research and Improvement, 1986).

412. Sternberg, Robert J. "Teaching Critical Thinking: eight easy ways to fail before you begin" in ***Phi Delta Kappan,*** Vol. 68, #6 (February 1987).

413. Stewart, L.R. "Here's What Classroom Computers Can Do" in ***American School Board Journal,*** Vol. 169, #3 (March 1982).

414. Stoddard, Robert. "This Board Hired a Superintendent Who Requested a Merit Pay Plan for Himself" in ***American School Board Journal,*** Vol. 166, #1 (January 1979).

415. Stow, Shirley and Sweeney, Jim. "Developing a Teacher Performance Evaluation System" in ***Educational Leadership,*** Vol. 38, #7 (April 1981).

416. Strother, Deborah Burnett. "Adapting Instruction to Individual Needs" in ***Phi Delta Kappan,*** Vol. 67, #4 (December 1985).

417. ___________. "Suicide among the Young" in ***Phi Delta Kappan,*** Vol. 67, #10 (June 1986).

418. Suhor, Charles. "Content and Process in the English Curriculum" in ***Content of the Curriculum*** (Alexandria, Va: ASCD, 1988).

419. Sullivan, Cheryl Granade. ***Clinical Supervision: a state of the art review*** (Alexandria, Va.: ASCD 1980).

420. Supranovich, Beth Bond. "Differentiated Staffing Revisited" in ***Phi Delta Kappan,*** Vol. 64, #1 (September 1982).

421. Svensson, Nils-Eric. ***Ability Grouping and Scholastic Achievement*** (Stockholm: Almquist and Wiksell, 1962).

422. Swartzbaugh, Phil. "Eliminating Tracking Successfully" in ***Educational Leadership,*** Vol. 45, #5 (February 1988).

423. Sylvester, Robert. "Research on Memory: major discoveries, major educational challenges" in ***Educational Leadership,*** Vol. 42, #7 (April 1985).

424. Tenner, Edward. "The Ph.D. outside Academe: some appalling facts" in ***Chronicle of Higher Education*** (February 1985).

425. Tewksbury, John L. ***Non-grading in the Elementary School*** (Columbus, Ohio: Merrill, 1967).

426. Thelen, Herbert A. ***Classroom Grouping for Teachability*** (New York: Wiley, 1967).

427. "This Revised Teacher Test Merits Attention" in ***American School Board Journal,*** Vol. 169, #11 (November 1982).

428. Thomas, Clarence. "Equal Opportunity and Federal Policy" in ***Education Week*** (June 16, 1982).

429. Thomas, William V. ***America in the 1980's*** (Washington, D.C.: Congressional Quarterly, 1980).

430. Thompson, Victor. ***Modern Organization*** (New York: Knopf, 1961).

431. Timpane, M., ed. ***The Federal Interest in Financing Schooling*** (Cambridge, Mass.: Ballinger, 1978).

432. Toffler, Alvin. ***Future Shock*** (New York: Random House, 1970).

433. Trump, J. Lloyd. ***A School for Everyone*** (Reston, Va.: National Association of Secondary School Principals, 1977).

434. Tucker, Marc and Mandel, David. "The Carnegie Report—a Call for Redesigning the Schools" in ***Phi Delta Kappan,*** Vol. 68, #1 (September 1986).

435. Tufts, Jean et al. ***Raising Public Awareness of Local Citizen Control of Education: NSBA 1980-81 task force report*** (Washington, D.C.: National School Board Association, 1981).

436. Ulich, Robert. ***The History of Educational Thought*** (New York: American Book Co., 1950).

437. Van Cott, Alan. ***A Study Concerning Educator Preference*** (Masters thesis, C.W. Post Center of Long Island Univ., 1974).

438. Vargas, Julie S. "Instructional Design Flaws in Computer-Assisted Instruction" in ***Phi Delta Kappan,*** Vol. 67, #10 (June 1986).

439. Vasconcellos, John and Murphy, Brian M. "Education in the Experience of Being Citizens" in ***Educational Leadership,*** Vol. 45, #2 (October 1987).

440. "The View from the Top—What's Beleaguering Superintendents These Days?" in ***Catalyst for Change,*** Vol. 10, #1 (Fall 1980).

441. Vitz, Paul. ***Censorship: evidence of bias in current texts*** (Ann Arbor, Mich.: Servant Books, 1986).

442. Vroom, Victor H. ***Work and Motivation*** (New York: Wiley, 1964).

443. __________ and Yettin, Philip W. ***Leadership and Decisionmaking*** (Pittsburgh: Univ. of Pittsburgh Press, 1973).

444. Walberg, Herbert J. et al. "Homework's Powerful Effects on Learning" in ***Educational Leadership,*** Vol. 42, #7 (April 1985).

445. Walker, Decker F. "Curriculum and Technology" in ***Current Thought on Curriculum*** (Alexandria, Va.: ASCD, 1985).

446. Wasserman, Selma. "Teaching for Thinking: Louis E. Raths Revisited" in ***Phi Delta Kappan,*** Vol. 68, #6 (February 1987).

447. Watts, Doyle. "Four Educators Comment on the Redesign of NCATE" in ***Phi Delta Kappan,*** Vol. 68, #4 (December 1986).

448. Watts, Gary D. "And Let the Air Out of the Volleyballs" in ***Phi Delta Kappan,*** Vol. 67, #10 (June 1986).

449. Webster, Bethuel M., chairman. ***The Facts about Drug Use.*** The Drug Abuse Council (New York: The Free Press, 1980).

450. Weinberg, M.A. ***A Chance to Learn: a history of race and education in the United States*** (Cambridge, Eng.: Cambridge Univ. Press, 1979).

451. Westby-Gibson, Dorothy. ***Grouping Students for Improved Education*** (Englewood Cliffs, N.J.: Prentice-Hall, 1966).

452. White, Phyllis L. "Evaluating Elementary Principals" in ***Phi Delta Kappan,*** Vol 69, #2 (October 1987).

453. Wiley, D. and Harnischfeger, A. ***Achievement Test Score Decline: do we need to worry*** (Chicago: Cemrel, Inc., 1975).

454. Wiley, Dinah. ***State Boards of Education: quality leadership*** (Alexandria, Va.: National Association of State Boards of Education, 1983).

455. Williams, Dennis A., et al. "Teachers Are in Trouble" in ***Newsweek*** (April 27, 1981).

456. Wilson, James Q. and Herrnstein, Richard J. ***Crime and Human Nature*** (New York: Simon and Schuster, 1985).

457. Wirt, F.M. "Political Turbulence and Administrative Authority in the Schools" in ***The New Urban Politics*** (Cambridge, Mass.: Ballinger, 1976).

458. Wirtenberg, J. et al. "Sex Equity in American Education" in ***Educational Leadership,*** Vol. 38, #4 (January 1981).

459. Wisniewski, Richard. "The Ideal Professor of Education" in ***Phi Delta Kappan,*** Vol. 68, #4 (December 1986).

460. Woellner, E. ***Requirements for Certification,*** 44th ed. (Chicago: Univ. of Chicago Press, 1979).

461. Woodring, Paul. ***The Persistent Problems of Education*** (Bloomington, Ind.: Phi Delta Kappa Educational Foundation, 1983).

462. __________. "Too Bright To Be a Teacher?" in ***Phi Delta Kappan,*** Vol. 68, #8 (April 1987).

463. Worner, Roger B. ***Student Diagnosis, Placement and Prescription*** (Bloomington, Ind.: Indiana Univ. Press, 1977).

464. Wrightstone, J. Wayne. "Class Organization for Instruction" in ***What Research Says to the Teacher #3*** (Washington, D.C.: NEA, 1957 - updated 1969).

465. Yates, Alfred, ed. ***Grouping in Education*** (New York: Wiley, 1966).

466. Zajda, Joseph I. ***Education in the U.S.S.R.*** (Oxford, England: Pergammon Press, 1980).

467. Zeigler, L.H. and Jennings, M.K. ***Governing American Schools*** (North Scituate, Mass.: Duxbury, 1974).

468. Zirkel, Perry A. and Reichner, Henry F. "Is 'In Loco Parentis' Dead?" in ***Phi Delta Kappan,*** Vol. 68, #6 (February 1987).

Index of Subjects